CW01367483

Governors, Politics and the Colonial Office

Royal Asiatic Society Hong Kong Studies Series

Royal Asiatic Society Hong Kong Studies Series is designed to make widely available important contributions on the local history, culture and society of Hong Kong and the surrounding region. Generous support from the Sir Lindsay and Lady May Ride Memorial Fund makes it possible to publish a series of high-quality works that will be of lasting appeal and value to all, both scholars and informed general readers, who share a deeper interest in and enthusiasm for the area.

Other titles in RAS Hong Kong Studies Series:

Reluctant Heroes: Rickshaw Pullers in Hong Kong and Canton 1874–1954
Fung Chi Ming

For Gods, Ghosts and Ancestors: The Chinese Tradition of Paper Offerings
Janet Lee Scott

Hong Kong Internment 1942–1945: Life in the Japanese Civilian Camp at Stanley
Geoffrey Charles Emerson

The Six-Day War of 1899: Hong Kong in the Age of Imperialism
Patrick H. Hase

Watching Over Hong Kong: Private Policing 1841–1941
Sheilah E. Hamilton

The Dragon and the Crown: Hong Kong Memoirs
Stanley S.K. Kwan with Nicole Kwan

Public Success, Private Sorrow: The Life and Times of Charles Henry Brewitt-Taylor (1857–1938), China Customs Commissioner and Pioneer Translator
Isidore Cyril Cannon

East River Column: Hong Kong Guerrillas in the Second World War and After
Chan Sui-jeung

Resist to the End: Hong Kong, 1941–1945
Charles Barman, edited by Ray Barman

Southern District Officer Reports: Islands and Villages in Rural Hong Kong, 1910–60
Edited by John Strickland

Cantonese Society in Hong Kong and Singapore: Gender, Religion, Medicine and Money. Essays by Marjorie Topley
Edited and introduced by Jean DeBernardi

Early China Coast Meteorology: The Role of Hong Kong
P. Kevin MacKeown

Forgotten Souls: A Social History of the Hong Kong Cemetery
Patricia Lim

Ancestral Images: A Hong Kong Collection
Hugh Baker

Escape from Hong Kong: Admiral Chan Chak's Christmas Day Dash, 1941
Tim Luard

Governors, Politics and the Colonial Office

Public Policy in Hong Kong, 1918–58

Gavin Ure

香港大學出版社
HONG KONG UNIVERSITY PRESS

Hong Kong University Press
14/F Hing Wai Centre
7 Tin Wan Praya Road
Aberdeen
Hong Kong
www.hkupress.org

© Hong Kong University Press 2012

ISBN 978-988-8083-94-7 *(Hardback)*

All rights reserved. No portion of this publication may be reproduced or transmitted in any form or by any means, electronic or mechanical, including photocopy, recording, or any information storage or retrieval system, without permission in writing from the publisher.

British Library Cataloguing-in-Publication Data
A catalogue record for this book is available from the British Library.

10 9 8 7 6 5 4 3 2 1

Printed and bound by Caritas Printing Training Centre, Hong Kong, China

Contents

Foreword		vii
Acknowledgments		ix
Chapter 1	Introduction	1
Chapter 2	Governors, Cadets, Unofficials and the Colonial Office	13
Chapter 3	The Origins of Policy, 1917–30	27
Chapter 4	Britain's Influence over Hong Kong's Policy, 1929–41	45
Chapter 5	Autonomy and the Threat to Sovereignty	67
Chapter 6	Income Tax and Treasury Control	87
Chapter 7	Constitutional Reform and Its Demise	111
Chapter 8	Post-war Housing Policy and the British Government	135
Chapter 9	Squatter Resettlement	163
Chapter 10	Financial Autonomy	191
Chapter 11	Conclusions	217
Notes		229
Bibliography		279
Index		287

Foreword

The sixteenth book in the Royal Asiatic Society's Hong Kong Study Series traces the development of political and constitutional conventions, rules that augment or diminish the power of various offices and actors, against a wider backdrop, including the evolution of Hong Kong society and the ebb and flow of power between: the Colonial Office; the Governor, "the man on the spot"; Hong Kong's Civil Service; and various Hong Kong actors, official and unofficial, expatriate and Chinese.

In this fascinating book, Gavin Ure fleshes out the impact of political figures and how their actions, and inactions, various imperial or Hong Kong political and administrative affairs. The tendrils of Hong Kong's budding autonomy from the United Kingdom are identified and followed with attention paid to the various actors, including observing which actors fade in importance and which ones seize more of the stage.

Rather than strictly being a historical narrative, as earlier books in the Royal Asiatic Society's Hong Kong Study Series have been, this book discusses the growth of a political state, bureaucratic autonomy, viewed through the political theory of the American political scientist Daniel Carpenter, the Freed Professor of Government at Harvard.

Governors, Politics, and the Colonial Office is not a break from a tradition, it is a natural extension for the Sir Lindsay and Lady Ride Memorial Fund, which we will follow up in addition to continuing our original format of more narrative-driven books exploring the history, culture and society of Hong Kong and neighbouring regions.

The Royal Asiatic Society's Hong Kong Studies Series was made possible by a generous founding donation of the Trustees of the Clague Trust Fund and an approximately matching donation from the Royal Asiatic Society, Hong Kong Branch in honour of our first Vice President, Sir Lindsay Ride, and his wife, Lady Ride, and generous donations from other donors.

The Sir Lindsay and Lady Ride Memorial Fund is always interested in both relevant proposals and manuscripts as well as donations and bequests to help us continue supporting books which might not otherwise have been published about Hong Kong and her region.

Christopher L.B. Young
President
Royal Asiatic Society, Hong Kong Branch
April 2012

Acknowledgments

I would like to acknowledge the help and assistance I have received from a wide range of people and institutions.

I would firstly like to thank the staff of the Hong Kong Public Records Office at Kwun Tong, especially Mr Bernard Hui and his colleagues, for their unfailing helpfulness and assistance. I would also like to thank the staff at the National Archives at Kew, London and the staff of the Rhodes House Library, Oxford for their permission to access the various personal papers housed there. I have also received unfailing help from the staff of the Hong Kong Special Collection at the University of Hong Kong whose collection of material on Hong Kong has proved invaluable. My thanks too, to Dr Norman Miners for his invaluable assistance in making transcripts of interviews of former Hong Kong government officials available to me and to Professor Steve Tsang for doing the same. I am grateful to the Director of Lands of the Hong Kong Special Administrative Region Government, Mr Patrick Lau, for his kind permission to views files in the possession of his department. I also wish to thank Mr Peter Yeung of the Hong Kong Resource Centre, Toronto, for his assistance, and the staff of the library at the University of Toronto; the Master of Massey College for kindly admitting me as a Visiting Scholar during my stay in Toronto; and the libraries of the School of African and Oriental Studies, the London School of Economics and the University of Edinburgh. I wish to express my grateful thanks to Professor Bernard Luk for his encouragement to teach a course on the history of Hong Kong at the University of Toronto and to the Department of History for allowing me to do so.

I would like to thank Professor Ian Scott, for his supervision during the preparation of my thesis and for his patient guidance throughout my research and writing. I also wish to thank Professor James Lee for his constant support. I also wish to thank Mr Stuart Leckie and Mr Michael Leung for their kind assistance. I also wish to thank friends and colleagues for their continual support during my research and writing, in particular Dr Christopher Munn, Mr Robin McLeish, Mr Kenneth Ness, Mr Alastair Singleton, Mr Alistair Dickson, Dr Peter C. C. Chau, Mr Arthur Kwok, Dr David Clayton and the late Mr C. Stewart Ross.

A very special mention must be made of my wife, Rosanna, without whose patient support and encouragement this book would never have been written.

1
Introduction

Who made policy in the British Crown Colony of Hong Kong? Was it Hong Kong's Governor and his senior civil servants? Or was it the British government through the Secretary of State for the Colonies (hereinafter the "Secretary of State") and Colonial Office officials? How much influence did leading locally domiciled Chinese, Portuguese and Indian and British expatriate businessmen and professionals wield? This book explores the different political factors and forces that lay behind some of the major policy issues which arose in the forty years between 1918 and 1958. It considers the extent to which the Hong Kong government formulated and implemented its own policies rather than those preferred by others.

In December 1984, the Sino-British Joint Declaration stated that the post-1997 Hong Kong Special Administrative Region would "enjoy a high degree of autonomy". This was later enshrined in Hong Kong's Basic Law of the Hong Kong Special Administrative Region of the People's Republic of China.[1] It was the first *de jure* recognition of the autonomy and was a formal recognition of Hong Kong's ability to forge its own policies in many areas. If autonomy, however, had never been formally granted by Britain, how had it come to exist? And, in the absence of any formal definition, what did autonomy mean?

The government of the British Crown Colony of Hong Kong was established through two constitutional documents, the Letters Patent and Royal Instructions. Issued by the British government in the name of the Crown,[2] they remained in force throughout Hong Kong's existence as a British Colony, subject to periodic updating. The Letters Patent allowed for the appointment of a Governor by the Crown as its representative in Hong Kong. He was assisted by civil servants, also known as officials, the most senior of whom were formally appointed by Britain. The Governor governed Hong Kong by powers granted under these two documents. These enabled him to establish a Legislative Council to make and enforce laws "for the Peace, Order and good Government" of Hong Kong and set out procedural rules on its operation. However, many powers were reserved to the British Crown. Laws enacted had to be referred to London for the Secretary of State to review and certify that they would not be disallowed. The British Parliament or the Privy Council could also enact legislation which would override locally enacted laws. The Governor was also constrained by Colonial Regulations made by the Secretary of State. Although they reinforced his position as "the single and supreme authority responsible to, and representative of, His Majesty,"[3] they also required him to seek the Secretary of State's approval of the annual estimates of revenue and expenditure, supplementary expenditure and the appointment, promotion and posting of his senior officials.

In practice, the British government's ability to exercise control over the Hong Kong government was more nuanced than these formal instruments of power might have suggested. The British government was largely dependent upon information provided by the Governor for its knowledge of what was happening in Hong Kong.[4] Opportunities for manipulation existed through skilful presentation of information or through obfuscation or delay. In respect of approval of the estimates, there was usually little the British government could do. If the estimates were not approved in time, Hong Kong would have been left without a budget.[5] Underperforming personnel was another problem periodically brought to the British government's attention.

With the long distances separating it from most of its colonies, Britain could never have contemplated governing them directly. Instead it did so largely through the Crown Colony system of government under which it exercised firm sovereignty. In a Crown Colony that meant "little more than the body of Colonial Service officers who represented the sovereignty of the Monarch."[6] Britain had to rely upon their expertise for the effective government of its colonies. This was helped by leaders and officials in both British and colonial governments coming from similar social backgrounds and sharing common values. There was an intuitive dependence on the soundness of their judgement and a belief that a Governor's decisions would be made in Britain's best interests. This led to a firm reliance upon what was commonly known as the "man on the spot."[7]

Hong Kong's Governor was also constrained by local political considerations. He had to rule with the advice of his Executive Council and enact laws with the advice of the Legislative Council.[8] The majority of the members of these two bodies consisted of senior civil servants and prominent and influential unofficial members drawn from Hong Kong's business and professional communities, both expatriate British and locally domiciled. Already respected leaders in their own communities, unofficials held their positions on these councils largely as a result of the Governor's patronage. An exception was made for the General Chamber of Commerce and the Justices of the Peace who, by convention, elected their own representatives who the Governor then nominated as unofficial members. Despite commanding an official majority on the Legislative Council, a Governor was expected to give due weight to unofficials members' views and not to govern with use of the official majority regardless.[9]

Hong Kong's government was legitimately and constitutionally accountable to the British Crown through a Cabinet minister. With the sovereign power's emphasis on oversight, with its controls over personnel and finance, it was not a power relationship from which the growth of a high degree of autonomy could have been expected. The Hong Kong government of the 1970s, however, has been described as exercising "a high degree of relative autonomy both within the territory and from the British government."[10] It was also thought to have exercised "a degree of freedom ... without precedent in British imperial history."[11] As the constitutional instruments under which it governed had not changed greatly over the years, either formally or in intent, how then had the Hong Kong government come to exercise such a high level of autonomy?

Basis of autonomy

There appears to be no widely accepted definition of autonomy.[12] Definitions posited have been developed to try and understand a particular relationship. Examples, in relation to local government, are that autonomy can be measured by the extent to which a local government is free from oversight by a higher tier of government, or is exempt from such oversight.[13] Another is that autonomy is "the freedom to exercise choice in local policy making and the capacity thereby to influence the well-being of local residents"[14] or that it is having "discretion in determining what they will do without undue constraint from higher levels of government, and ... the capacity to do so".[15] These are useful descriptive tools. The Hong Kong government of the period could, in some cases initiate policy and legislation and in others had limited or no capacity to do so. Nor was the well-being of local residents always a high priority. The Hong Kong government was also subject to Britain's oversight and constraint although, in practice, Britain often gave Hong Kong the benefit of the doubt.

Although these definitions help in understanding whether a polity may have exercised autonomy, they do not help explain how that autonomy might have arisen. The analogy between local government and the Hong Kong government is also not precise. Britain's central government had a very different relationship with its local government than it had with the Hong Kong government. In Britain, the central government governs the whole polity with local government having specific local functions. The government in Hong Kong was its sole government and the British government had no direct governance role. A more helpful analogy might, therefore, be to compare the relationship between the Hong Kong and British governments to that between a government and a body it creates, usually by statute, to undertake a specific function or range of functions. The duties and responsibilities of such bodies might have been narrowly defined, for example, to operate an airport, to manage an industrial estate or to build and operate a railway. Alternatively, they might have been more broadly defined as in the case of a colonial government, created by legal rather than statutory instrument, to govern a colony such as Hong Kong. Regardless of their nature, the tasks involved were complex. The subordinate body needed the authority, the organisational capacity and resources to analyse, plan and implement the policies and programmes arising from its functions. Some freedom of self-determination, however limited or otherwise that may have been, was therefore inherent in the creation of a subordinate body like the Hong Kong government.

Conversely, by establishing a colonial government in Hong Kong, the British government's ability to determine exactly how it governed was diminished. This was not, however, a complete abrogation of responsibility. The British government may have excised a degree of its authority and allocated it to Hong Kong but it still retained a general responsibility over how that authority was exercised. It also retained reserve powers over the Hong Kong government though these were, in reality, seldom used.[16] This constitutional accountability also meant the British government remained politically accountable for the Hong Kong government's actions although, in practice, it was seldom called upon to be so.

Once created, the subordinate body, in this case the Hong Kong government, had to contend with people and organisations which had an interest in or benefitted from its functions and responsibilities. These stakeholders consequently had an interest in seeking to influence what it did. They may have been closely involved with it through membership of its boards or councils. Taxpayers, who provided its resources, and those who sought its protection, also had an interest in how it operated. Thus different groups emerged with an interest in the Hong Kong government's policies and operations and in how it acquired and used its resources. The Hong Kong government's autonomy, therefore, also depended upon the extent to which it was able to formulate policies even when these differed from the preferences of such stakeholders. Conversely, a lack of autonomy could also have been due to the extent to which it was subject, or subjected itself to their direction.

Carpenter's theory of bureaucratic autonomy

The analysis in this book is informed by a theoretical framework of the nature and practice of bureaucratic autonomy advanced by Professor Daniel Carpenter.[17] In his work on bureaucratic autonomy, Carpenter examines the historical development of autonomy in the late nineteenth and early twentieth centuries among some US federal government agencies. He seeks to identify why some developed autonomy, as he defines it, and some did not. These organisations, such as the Post Office and the US Drug Administration, were able to decide their own policies, even when elected politicians in the US Congress either opposed them or would have preferred they had done otherwise. He examines factors he thinks contributed to these organisations' ability to develop their own policies even when they were constitutionally subordinate to the US Congress. He posits that autonomous organisations were those that had their own policies, the practical ability to formulate and implement them and a broad network of political support to make their implementation possible. These policies were different from those preferred by their ostensible masters. They also had to have the ability "to analyse, to create new programmes, to solve problems, to plan, to administer programmes with efficiency". The putatively autonomous organisations had also to be recognised as competent and capable of developing and implementing their own policies. There also had to be a widespread belief that only they could provide the services required or implement policies necessary to solve problems. For this to happen, the heads of such organisations needed to have built a coalition of support around their desired programmes.

Carpenter sees autonomy as something not granted but attained by a bureaucracy, largely through the efforts of its own leaders. He argues that bureaucratic autonomy can only exist when

> bureaucrats take action consistent with their own wishes, action to which politicians and organised interests defer even though they would prefer that other action (or no action at all) be taken.

An important element in this thesis is a necessary bias towards action. It is not enough for an organisation's leaders simply to engage in routine administration or to do only what is expected of them. If they only ever do what those to whom they are accountable would wish, they are not exercising autonomy. Nor is autonomy to be found

> in the ability of bureaus to take clandestine, undetected actions against the wishes of elected authorities ... only a weak autonomy is observed when agencies shirk while administering a law or policy that was of politician's design.

Autonomy develops, he argues, when an organisation's leaders take the initiative. They need a goal or objective for the organisation to achieve and a desire and ability to work to achieve it. This also requires the organisation to have the capacity to "forecast, plan, gather and analyse intricate statistical information and ... execute complex programs". This needs strong leadership by people Carpenter describe as "bureaucratic entrepreneurs." In US federal agencies, these were the innovative senior managers who developed new programmes and built political support for them. This, combined with the capacity and competence of the organisation's staff to plan, initiate and complete projects and maintain them over the longer term, marked out the autonomous organisation. The nature of the bureau was also important. It needed to have a sufficiently strong career structure to attract and retain staff of the right calibre recruited by senior staff in their own likeness. The success of those promoted to leadership roles depended not only on their own merits but also on the success of the organisation upon which their status depended.[18] It was this confluence of individual and organisational goals that motivated them.

Carpenter's framework and the Hong Kong government

There are both similarities and dissimilarities between Hong Kong's colonial government and the agencies Carpenter examines. The Hong Kong government was constitutionally accountable to the British Crown. It was a self-perpetuating bureaucracy whose members were recruited in the same image. It had to contend with stakeholders and political interests in Hong Kong in the shape of the leading Chinese and British elites. It had to manage the constitutional and political relationship with its sovereign master in London, usually through Colonial Office officials. They in turn were subject to control by ministers who were responsible to a cabinet which was answerable to a democratically elected parliament. Political pressure on a Minister in Britain was a factor which Hong Kong could not, in the long term, blithely ignore.

There are three principal differences in the examples in Carpenter's study and Hong Kong's colonial government. Firstly, the Hong Kong government, although non-sovereign, was the sole government in Hong Kong. It represented the sovereign government and had a duty to uphold that sovereignty. Almost anything Britain wanted done in Hong Kong was executed through the Hong Kong government: a partial exception was the armed services. The Hong Kong government was not, therefore, in the position of some United States federal government departments and agencies, which might have been competing with each other for authority or for resources. Public policy in Hong Kong could only be implemented by the Hong Kong government. This was to result in the Hong Kong government having to do things it either had not initiated or would rather not have had to do.

Secondly, Carpenter's criteria are drawn up in the context of "bureaucratic autonomy in democratic regimes". The apparent conundrum that he addresses is how government agencies made up of, and led by, unelected officials could formulate and secure authority for policy over the heads of elected officials and legislators. The Hong Kong government, in contrast, was a non-democratic minimalist regime governing a largely quiescent and undemanding local population. Links between politicians and Hong Kong's population ranged from minimal to non-existent. As argued above, however, it was still subject to some domestic political pressures although of a somewhat different nature from those in a country with a more representative government such as Britain. Lastly, Hong Kong was not a "modern state". Carpenter argues that

> nothing so distinguishes twentieth-century bureaucratic government from its predecessors as its ability to plan, to innovate, and to author policy.[19]

This was, he believes, an important contributory factor in the development of autonomy in the US agencies he examined. The Hong Kong government of this period was not a modern state by this standard. It lacked expertise in planning, innovation or ability to author policy. This sometimes had to be found elsewhere. It was at times forced by circumstances to attempt these things with varying degrees of success or failure.

Despite these differences, Carpenter's framework still leaves pertinent questions to be asked of the development of proposed new policies in Hong Kong. Whose policies were they? Were they the Hong Kong government's, the British government's or the unofficials'? Did the Hong Kong government have the capacity to formulate and implement new policies? If not, how were they formulated? What were the political factors behind new policies and from where did they emanate, Hong Kong or Britain? An important feature of Carpenter's framework, highlighted in earlier works by other scholars, is the proactive role of the bureaucratic entrepreneur. He was driven by a belief in an idea or a commitment to further a moral precept.[20] Such an outlook was seldom evident among Hong Kong's colonial officials of this period.[21] Much of their effort went into the maintenance of routine administration. The identification of bureaucratic entrepreneurs is therefore an important question examined in this book and the performance of the Governors of this period is examined with this question in mind.

The Hong Kong government and autonomy

The issue of autonomy has not been specifically addressed by most works on the Hong Kong government during the period under review. They have, however, recognised that there was more to the relationship between the Governor and London, and between the Governor and the unofficials, than a formal description of the constitutional relationship might have suggested. This was brought out by Mills, a visiting academic from the US, whose work was based on both documentary evidence and extensive interviews of people he met when he visited Hong Kong in the mid-1930s.[22] A record of who he met in Hong Kong is not readily available but his writings would tend to be corroborated by the work of another more general observer of the relationship between the Colonial Office, its colonies and their unofficials, Cosmo Parkinson. He spent thirty-six years in the Colonial Office and was Permanent Undersecretary from 1937 to 1942. His memoirs provide insight into how Colonial Office officials understood the workings of this tripartite relationship. It reflected the limits of both the Colonial Office to instruct Governors, and the need for Governors to be sensitive to the views of unofficials.[23]

In the early 1960s, G. B. Endacott wrote about the Hong Kong government in the years following the re-establishment of British administration in 1945 as if it was already acting with a degree of autonomy. He discussed the nature, work and scope of the Hong Kong government as if it was largely, though not entirely, an internally self-governing body. He made little reference to it having to seek authority for its actions from London. He did not appear to have believed that much policy, beyond proposed constitutional reform, originated from Britain. His general unstated thesis was that Hong Kong was the author of its own policies and, more pertinently, that it chose for itself how to operate its own government structure.[24]

Dr Norman Miners work, *Hong Kong Under Imperial Rule,* is perhaps recognised as the most definitive study to date on the workings of the Hong Kong government in the thirty years before 1941. This is a work of masterly description and provides the reader with a thorough understanding of the period. Steve Tsang, in *A Modern History of Hong*

Kong,[25] does not explicitly examine the question of the development of Hong Kong's autonomy. It is clear, however, from his arguments and from his presentation of Hong Kong's history in the period after the Second World War that he attributes the development of the Hong Kong government's policies and practices to its officials, particularly its Governors. He considers that their individual backgrounds and the different experiences they brought to bear were important factors influencing their policy choices. He presents Hong Kong's first post-Second World War Governor, Sir Mark Young as a forward-looking and progressive Governor to whom he attributes the institution of all reforms during his tenure. He thinks, too, that his successor, Sir Alexander Grantham, established himself as "one of the greatest Governors" and describes him as "progressive, dedicated to Hong Kong and willing to defend what he saw as the best interests of the colony". Tsang argues that Grantham's views of what was appropriate for Hong Kong differed from Young's because of his very different colonial experience. This, he believes, led him to oppose the constitutional reforms that Young had supported.

Scott implies that the Hong Kong government's relative autonomy in the 1970s "both within the territory and from the British government" arose as a result of a tacit compromise between the government and the population. This was that social services provided by government and continued economic growth gave the population hope that their standard of living would continue to rise. Another element was that government bolstered their position through the provision of improved social services and through incorporating elites at local district levels into the government apparatus and by

> a set of ideological propositions which proclaimed that government in Hong Kong was conducted only on the basis of "consultation and consent".

In practice it was government who interpreted what constituted consent, albeit on the basis of extensive formal and informal consultation.[26] The question of what prompted the provision of social services then arises and what role this capacity played in the development of the Hong Kong government's autonomy.

Goodstadt has specifically addressed the development of the Hong Kong government's autonomy.[27] He portrays this as a steady march towards autonomy from Britain conducted with almost ruthless efficiency. He considers that this was due, in part, to Colonial Office officials becoming increasingly distracted by the rapidly growing number of colonies seeking independence during the 1950s; to the dwindling expertise in colonial matters which resulted; and to the advantage then taken by Hong Kong officials to push for more informal devolution of power from Britain. He did not specifically define autonomy. Implicit is the concept of the Hong Kong government being able to decide for itself what it wanted to do, even when the British government, or its officials, would have preferred it had done otherwise. Again, implicit in his text is the political inability of British ministers and officials to impose their will and, conversely, the political ability of the Hong Kong government to impose theirs. The issues examined below seek to explore in greater depth why in some cases, the Hong Kong government was able to decide policies for itself and in others it was not.

Goodstadt marks out Grantham as a principal architect in the early development of the Hong Kong government's autonomy. It was Grantham who was "ruthless in managing his nominal masters in London". It was

> [h]is determination to expand Hong Kong's autonomy without too much regard for constitutional niceties [which] created a political and policy framework that was to dominate the political landscape until the arrival of Christopher Patten as Governor in 1992.[28]

This book will examine the extent to which Grantham was the mainstay of the early development of the Hong Kong government's autonomy. It will ask if the Colonial Office did display a falling away of interest in its charges and the extent to which Hong Kong government officials took up this slack. It will consider whether Grantham established anything as grand as a "political and policy framework" of such lasting eminence. It will argue that Grantham was not always the apparent author of policies that have been associated with him. A senior colleague remarked that Grantham's approach to issues was to side with the strongest side. The validity of this observation will be tested in this book which will, *ipso facto*, also test the validity of Goodstadt's and Tsang's views that he was a great Governor.

The forging of autonomy

This book will consider the ability, or otherwise, of the British Crown Colony government of Hong Kong to decide for itself how to govern Hong Kong. It will examine how the relationship between the Hong Kong and British governments and the unofficials worked in practice. It does not seek to examine the rights and wrongs of such a system: it seeks merely to examine and understand how it worked. A central theme is that the Hong Kong government's autonomy emerged as issues of contention which arose between it, the British government and the unofficials were mediated and resolved. Examining the factors that were behind the resolution of these issues help provide an understanding of how Hong Kong's autonomy developed. This book will examine how some such issues arose; what impact political and organisational structures had on how these issues were mediated and resolved; how important the leading personalities involved were; and what influence stakeholders had on the outcome. Events and issues examined are those which resulted in change, or where change was proposed, and which affected, or could have affected, the way in which the Hong Kong government operated or responded. It does not seek to provide a comprehensive history of such events; for that the reader must look elsewhere.

Firstly, Chapter 2 will examine the actors in this story. It will set out the roles of the Governor, his officials, the Secretaries of State and the Colonial Office officials. It will examine how they played their roles and the factors that impinged upon them. Chapters 3 to 10 will examine cases which arose between 1918 and 1958. Chapter 3 will examine issues which arose between 1918 and 1930. It will examine the belated introduction of factory legislation and legislation concerning the registration and eventual abolition of the system of *mui tsai*, a traditional Chinese form of female child servitude. It will examine the interplay of the Hong Kong government and the unofficials and the role of Colonial Office officials. It will consider the effect, detrimental to the development of autonomy, of ignoring the impact of British public opinion. It will also examine how residential rents came to be controlled in the face of both strong support for and objection to such action. Chapter 4 will examine how the Hong Kong government's lack of policy formulation capacity over such a fundamental issue as its currency resulted in it relying on expertise elsewhere in the form of the Chief Manager of The Hongkong and Shanghai Banking Corporation Limited (the "Hongkong and Shanghai Bank") and on experts in the British Treasury. It will consider, too, how recovery of a small degree of autonomy was achieved when some capacity was eventually created to implement the British government's desired policy over registration of *mui tsai*. The role of external influence was also visible in the part played by Hong Kong's first Financial Secretary, Sidney Caine, in the formulation and promotion of a policy to introduce income tax. In Chapter 5, it will be argued that autonomy increases when the exercise of sovereignty over the subordinate organisation is threatened. This will be studied against the backdrop of Britain's loss of Hong Kong to the force of Japanese arms and pressure from the United States and Chinese governments for its return to China after Japan's defeat. It will also be shown how, under such circumstances, the desire to ensure the recovery of sovereignty was greater than the British government's ability to change the way it exercised it.

The ability of a bureaucratic entrepreneur to define a distinctive policy, to develop the capacity to implement it and to build a coalition in support of it will be reviewed in Chapter 6 through the examination of the introduction of an unpopular income tax after 1946. The growing influence of stakeholders as a result of a financial dispute with the British government will also be examined. This theme will be analysed in more depth in Chapter 7 when unofficials took the lead in manoeuvring the British government into abandoning proposals over an issue as fundamental as constitutional reform. In Chapters 8 and 9 the implications of the Governor's failure in the role of bureaucratic entrepreneur will be examined through his inability to effectively address the problems of low-cost housing and squatter resettlement. How the resulting policy voids created by his inaction were filled from outside the bureaucracy will be explored. This will also show how autonomy was recovered through creation of capacity to address these policy areas effectively and how this eventually helped provide the platform for the emergence of the Hong Kong government's future high degree of autonomy. Chapter 10 will show that *de facto* financial autonomy was being exercised in the years before it was formally granted and how this vindicated the legitimising role of the unofficials in the Legislative Council.

This is a book about the role of the Hong Kong government, the Colonial Office and the unofficials in the formulation of public policy in Hong Kong. It is an examination of government processes in an era when the mass of the population was excluded from the formulation of public policy. It thus focuses to a large extent on official sources to understand what happened and why it happened. It does not seek to delve into the rights and wrongs of the policies concerned. The aim of this book is to attempt to understand how the Hong Kong government's autonomy began to emerge even when the British government did not explicitly grant any. It is not a story of a linear movement towards this state. Nor is it a story of the conception and execution of a plan to reach this goal. Rather, it is the story of the emergence of autonomy in spite of the Hong Kong government's initial inability to plan, in spite of its belief and claims that it had no capacity to either introduce new measures or implement them, and in spite of being pushed and prodded by external agents to do what it eventually did.

2
Governors, Cadets, Unofficials and the Colonial Office

Introduction

The Hong Kong government was a bureaucracy. Its members, Hong Kong's civil servants, formed part of a hierarchical organisation. Many of them made a full career in government service. They included professionals who worked in one department or a range of departments and generalists who were posted to different departments to administer and lead them. They were all answerable to the Governor who, in this period, had also previously worked in a colonial bureaucracy, either in Hong Kong or in another British colony. He was answerable to the Secretary of State for the Colonies, a politician in London and a Cabinet member. Answerable to him, and with whom the Governor had most dealings, were civil servants or officials who worked in the Colonial Office. Those at the senior level were also members of a bureaucracy, the Home Civil Service. Most spent their whole careers within the Colonial Office although some might have spent time in one or more colonies. They were mostly generalist administrators rather than professionals. They too formed their own hierarchy within which they could expect promotion. The story of the relationship between the Hong Kong and British governments could be characterised, therefore, as one between two separate interrelated government bureaucracies.

There were also external stakeholders. In Hong Kong these were the unofficial members of the Executive and Legislative Councils, known as the "unofficials". They were leading elements from the business and professional sectors of the expatriate British, local Chinese and other locally domiciled ethnic groups. Their cultural and ethnic differences were perhaps narrowed by their shared business and professional backgrounds. In Britain, the Secretary of State was also answerable to parliament though was seldom called upon to be so. Nevertheless, the prospect of having to defend a policy in Hong Kong that was patently indefensible in Britain could stimulate action.

The interaction of these different component parts had an important bearing on the power relationship between them. Governors were appointed by Britain, often with no prior experience of Hong Kong, to govern for a term of five years through senior civil servants who had spent a whole career there. Unofficials were leaders in their own communities, who may have been new to Governors but were well known to senior civil servants. Some Secretaries of State were influential and strong-willed such as Churchill, Passfield[1] and Lyttelton.[2] Some had a clear idea of what they wanted to achieve. MacDonald[3] was a strong pre-war proponent of colonial development and was instrumental in the passage of the Colonial Development and Welfare Act of 1940. Creech Jones[4] was rather idealistic and not always very effective. Some Colonial Office officials, through the force of personality and intellect exercised considerable influence on Hong Kong's policies, in particular Gerard Gent[5] and Sidney Caine.[6] Parliament could also be a conduit for the expression of British public opinion on Hong Kong's affairs. Its influence, as shall be seen, was more often indirect.

Hong Kong's population oscillated during this period. It rose from 600,000 in 1921 to 1.6 million in 1941 and back to 600,000 by 1945. By the end of 1946, it had recovered to 1.6 million and in 1956 had reached an estimated 2.5 million.[7] One crucial difference was that by 1956 most migrants from the Mainland had every intention of remaining in Hong Kong: previously many would have returned there when the economy or security had improved. Hong Kong's economy also went through many gyrations. In 1925–26, it suffered from a crippling boycott and later from the world-wide depression. Later in the 1930s, Hong Kong's currency was forced off the silver standard. Its economy then prospered on the back of the privations experienced in China through war with Japan. In 1937, Hong Kong had to contend with the impact of a massive influx of refugees from the Mainland and in 1941 it suffered the depredations of the invading Japanese and nearly four years of their military government. There was a rapid rehabilitation after the Japanese defeat followed by further influxes of refugees after the fall of the Kuomintang (KMT) and the establishment of a communist government. Other major changes occurred, not least the start of provision of publicly subsidised housing and the growth of manufacturing, already developed before 1941, which replaced trade with China as Hong Kong's economic mainstay.

This chapter will examine the background and interaction of the different players and the bodies to which they belonged. It will then briefly examine them in the context of Carpenter's theory of bureaucratic autonomy. It will compare the workings of these bureaucracies with the US Federal agencies that Carpenter analyses, identify similarities and differences and set out where Carpenter's theory could be helpful in identifying the emergence of the Hong Kong government's reluctant autonomy during this period. This will help inform the more detailed evaluation of how and why various policies were adopted in later chapters.

Governors

> In a crown colony the Governor is next to the Almighty. He is deferred to on all occasions. It is always "Yes, Your Excellency, Certainly, Your Excellency".[8]

This was the description given by Alexander Grantham,[9] one of Hong Kong's most prominent Governors. It might have been made only half in jest. A Governor was "the single and supreme authority responsible to, and representative of, His Majesty". This was outwardly most visible in the panoply of colonial power, the Governor's civil uniform worn on formal occasions and[10] the playing of the first six bars of the National Anthem when he appeared at public events. The Crown's status was reinforced by the award of imperial decorations and the deference customarily shown the Governor by Hong Kong's leading citizens. He was at the apex of social life in the British Crown Colony of Hong Kong.[11]

A Governor was appointed by the Crown.[12] This did not mean he was subordinate to the British sovereign personally but to the British monarch's government and to the sovereign in Parliament. The Governor of Hong Kong was appointed on the advice of the Secretary of State for the Colonies, a cabinet minister,[13] was accountable to him for his governance of Hong Kong, and could be removed by him.[14] This established one of two important principles of Crown Colony government, the subordination of the colonial to the imperial government. It was reinforced by the Governor's reliance on the Secretary of State for his approval of the Hong Kong government's financial estimates of revenue and expenditure, the appointment, promotion and posting of his senior and professional civil servants, and the need to seek an explicit statement from the Secretary of State that a law passed by Hong Kong's Legislative Council would not be disallowed. Nevertheless, subject to these reserved powers of the Secretary of State, a Governor had the power to nominate unofficial members of the Executive and Legislative Councils, to set the agenda for both these Councils and to agree to the introduction of Bills into the Legislative Council. A Governor, therefore, was in a very strong position to control what was, and what was not to be proposed as government policy.[15]

Hong Kong had nine Governors during the period under review. There were many similarities in their background. All except one had been career colonial civil servants. The exception was Reginald Stubbs[16] who had started as a clerk in the Colonial Office in 1900, but even he had served for seven years as Ceylon's Colonial Secretary before becoming Hong Kong's Governor in 1920. They had all been to public schools and most had been to Oxford or Cambridge universities except for Henry May[17] who went to Trinity College, Dublin and Robin Black[18] who went to Edinburgh University. They were all, except Northcote, Eastern Cadets, and had passed the same competitive examination to join the administrative service of Ceylon, Malaya or Hong Kong. Northcote had spent 30 years in Africa and came to Hong Kong from Guinea in South America. More exceptionally, three of this group—May, Cecil Clementi[19] and Grantham—had started as Hong Kong cadets and another—Black—had spent three years as Hong Kong's Colonial Secretary.[20]

This commonality of background, however, did not necessarily mean a common approach to issues or to relations with the Colonial Office and the unofficials. Each brought his own particular views and personality to the position. May was conservative and could be very sure of himself, even if it meant using the official majority in the Legislative Council to get his own way. Stubbs could be a little erratic but was financially astute. He also introduced a small, but important constitutional reform by granting the Finance Committee an unofficial majority. Clementi could also be very sure of his own mind, even if he upset the Secretary of State, and could be both innovative and conservative. He strenuously, and unsuccessfully, opposed the regulation of *mui tsai* but also appointed the first Chinese to the Executive Council. William Peel[21] was more accommodating and quietly got on with his work. Andrew Caldecott[22] won great respect locally, knew his own mind and was prepared to act upon it, even in the face of local opposition. Geoffry Northcote[23] and Mark Young[24] both had modernising tendencies, largely unfulfilled, whereas Grantham was conservative and slow to adopt new policies.

Some scholars have argued that the differences in their approach resulted from the different nature of their experience in the colonial service. The former Hong Kong cadets may have felt they had a surer idea of what was good for Hong Kong, even if their views had become somewhat dated by the time they became Governor. As important was the background of events that took place during their Governorship and the concomitant need to respond to them. Both Stubbs and Clementi had to contend with the 1925 strike and boycott. These originated from Canton and paralysed Hong Kong for some 15 months. Stubbs refused to deal with the strikers in Guangdong whereas Clementi had been willing to attempt to do so, although this did not help the end result. Northcote, despite his modernising tendencies, had to give priority to coping with a massive influx of refugees into Hong Kong escaping the advancing Japanese. Young ensured income taxes were introduced but did not have time to implement his proposed package of constitutional reforms. Grantham had to govern against a backdrop of major change in Chinese politics, vast waves of people from the Mainland this time moving into Hong Kong permanently and a large shift in the basis of Hong Kong's economy from trade entrepot to manufacturing.[25]

The Governor had the leading role within the colonial government, in substance as well as form. How a government responded to events, to pressures and demands from London, depended on him. The extent to which he wished to institute any new policy was also dependent upon him. No matter how pressing or cogent the advice he might receive from his senior officials, it was the Governor who decided how to respond. His influence was important and his role in shaping the autonomy of the Hong Kong government was a crucial one. He was in a position to act in the role of Carpenter's "bureaucratic entrepreneur". The extent to which each Governor was able and willing to do so is examined in this book.

Cadets

A Governor was provided with a civil service through whom he could govern. The most senior of these were the cadets. They were recruited in Britain as young university graduates and most of them spent their entire careers in Hong Kong.[26] They were not only at the apex of the government bureaucracy; in a Crown Colony like Hong Kong with no unofficial majority in the Legislative Council, they were the government.[27] The whole civil service was organised into a bureaucracy divided on a functional basis and tightly controlled from the centre by a secretariat.[28] It was through this bureaucracy, with its own hierarchy and rules, that the Governor administered Hong Kong.

The cadets owed their origin to Hong Kong's early days as a British colony. For almost the first twenty years, a gulf had existed between the British in the colonial administration and the majority Chinese population. This was mainly due to an absence of people on both sides of this divide with sufficient knowledge of each other's language and culture. There was also a dearth of competent personnel within government to ensure its efficiency and integrity. One of Hong Kong's early Governors, Sir Hercules Robinson,[29] successfully persuaded the Colonial Office to recruit young men through competitive public examination. They would initially be taught Chinese in order to act as interpreters, especially in the courts, and then later be posted to senior administrative positions within government. In practice, such was the shortage of talent, most cadets were posted as departmental heads on completion of their language training. The strength of the cadets was never very large. The first three arrived in Hong Kong in 1862. In 1920 there were 31 and this had increased to only 37 by 1941. From 1882, Hong Kong's cadets were part of the Eastern Cadetships and applicants for the civil services of Ceylon, Straits Settlements (Singapore, Malacca and Penang) and Malaya took a common entrance examination. In 1896, this was combined with the public examination for applicants to the Home and Indian Civil Services. In 1932, a unified Colonial Administrative Service was created and recruitment by competitive examination for the Eastern Cadetships was abolished. It was replaced by the system of interview and assessment used in selection of candidates for the rest of the colonial empire. The cadets had mostly been to one of the minor British public schools and gone on to Oxford or Cambridge Universities or one of the Scottish or Irish ones. They had many years experience running the Hong Kong government, wide knowledge of Hong Kong, its people and customs and an understanding of the local dialect, Cantonese.[30]

By the beginning of the twentieth century, a settled system of government had been established and the cadets had developed a reputation for efficient administration. In 1907, the Governor Sir Frederick Lugard[31] had found that the officials were

> certainly efficient; the place was small and administration was conducted according to a system which had been seventy years in the making.[32]

The cadets also constituted a cadre with a certain command of Chinese. This was obtained after two years of instruction in Cantonese upon first appointment, usually in Guangdong. A variable level of competence was achieved. Some, such as Cecil Clementi, James Stewart Lockhart,[33] and K. M. A. Barnett[34] achieved prominence as Chinese scholars. Others found that they were left with only a bare understanding of the language, insufficient to conduct no more than simple conversations. Outside of postings in the Registrar General's Office, later the Secretariat for Chinese Affairs, or the District Office in the New Territories, there was little call for the cadets to regularly use Chinese. Caine, seconded from the Colonial Office as Financial Secretary from 1937 to 1939, thought there was a limited need for the cadets to learn Chinese. He had found he could communicate in English with a wide range of leading Chinese people in Hong Kong.[35] Doubtless, there were also many with whom he could not.

Links between government and the Chinese community

In the 1890s, close institutional linkages were established between the cadets and the leading Chinese elites that were to last until after the Second World War. In 1891, Lockhart revamped existing leading Chinese organisations to bring them into a closer and more official relationship with government. He established the District Watch Committee as the most senior of these bodies. Established in 1867 by a group of Chinese merchants, it was a self-appointed committee which managed the watchmen it employed to protect its members' premises. Lockhart now gave the District Watch Committee a predominant role in the consultative system. Its position was established by statute enabling the Governor to appoint its members. Government also reformed the management structure of Tung Wah and Po Leung Kuk by empowering the Governor to appoint the members of their advisory committees.

Although the ostensible function of these committees was to oversee the administration and management of their organisations, their importance lay as much in their political role within the Hong Kong government structure, particularly up to 1941. They formed the upper end of a pyramid of committees and organisations, the senior of which, the District Watch Committee, was consulted on all major issues affecting the Chinese community.[36] Members of the District Watch Committee were, in most cases, drawn from serving or former directors of the Tung Wah or Po Leung Kuk. They, in turn, drew their directors from the Kaifongs and committees of other organisations as well as from the ranks of wealthy and successful businessmen. Members of the District Watch Committee, and members of the other committees, served for many years giving a great deal of continuity and stability and allowing the development of long-term relations with senior government officials. This gave formal recognition to established local Chinese community leaders and further consolidated and enhanced their leadership status within their own communities. It also provided the Hong Kong government with an institutionalised sounding board for its policies as they affected the Chinese community.[37]

Having established these committees, they had to be consulted. Shortly after Lockhart's reforms had been introduced, he reported that the District Watch Committee's

> advice on several important questions connected with the affairs of the Chinese community has been of great help to this department.

It was, however, a relationship that had to work both ways. Having created such a forum, views expressed could not have been simply disregarded when convenient to do so. It was recognised that benefits would need to pass in both directions. Each—the Registrar General and the Committee—would need to feel it gained from the special relationship.

Such was the importance of the District Watch Committee before 1941 that one contemporary observer reported described it as "the Chinese Executive Council". Not everyone accepted that the District Watch Committee represented the final say on local Chinese views. The Colonial Office was aware of its more conservative views and could discount them accordingly. Nor were Governors or cadets averse to soliciting its support or disapproval when it was to their advantage. By 1941, however, the District Watch Committee's influence was ebbing. It was revived in 1946 but did not achieve the same pre-eminence and was disbanded in 1949. Its prime function of security was now more effectively implemented by the police and its consultative role had been eclipsed by the Chinese community's direct voice on the Executive and Legislative Councils.[38]

Effectiveness of cadets

By the early twentieth century, the Hong Kong cadets had developed a certain smugness and complacency. Two observers wryly commented on their rather over-developed sense of self-worth. Lugard once referred to them as "the twice-born" and in 1910. Stubbs, on a mission from the Colonial Office to Hong Kong, claimed, in his own inimitable way, that they "were prepared to advance claims to act for the Almighty."[39] In 1930, Peel, concerned at the cadets' narrow outlook, commented that because of Hong Kong's small size,

> not only do they live for years in one another's pockets, but they never get a change from their environment ... this state of affairs leads to considerable "nerves" among a large number of the service ... It has made a very strong impression on me.

Although Sir Cecil Clementi and a Colonial Office official both agreed with Peel,[40] nothing was done about it. A local businessman thought that the cadets were hampered by their lack of knowledge of current developments in China. He also thought that they were "so strongly conservative, that it prevents them from moving with the times unless absolutely forced to do so". Caine considered that the Hong Kong cadets were essentially sound but became rather stale after spending their entire career in Hong Kong's rather stifling social atmosphere.[41] Although they administered government's routine business efficiently, few were capable of seeing beyond the demands of regular routine or capable of pioneering new policies in response to the challenges faced by Hong Kong's ever-changing society and economy. Their role was closely tied to what they probably felt Hong Kong people expected of their Government. This, in Grantham's eyes, was that

> provided ... Government maintains law and order, does not tax the people too much and that they can obtain justice in the courts, [Hong Kong people] are satisfied and well content to devote their time to making more money in one way or another.[42]

This was an outlook not dissimilar to that of the imperial Chinese mandarins. Although before 1941 many cadets spent their first two years in Canton learning Cantonese, it would appear they had most contact with their teachers rather than Chinese officialdom.[43] Perhaps the mandarin style was reinforced by the styles of communicating with the local population adopted by the Registrar General's Office. However, it was unlikely that the Hong Kong cadet system was consciously modelled on the Chinese imperial system. More likely their mores came from their middle-class Victorian upbringing reinforced by the sense of duty and responsibility inculcated in young men at British public school and university.[44] They may also have been influenced by the development of a British civil service ethos in the mid-nineteenth century. Perhaps they had also become so much part of a system which was

> totally absorbing the time of those concerned, who are therefore not inclined to any deep reflection on the ultimate consequences of what they are doing ... In time ... officials and public servants come to take the whole thing for granted—their own image of their official status, their own image of the public, their own concepts of service, of the imperial institute, of its polices, and of the entire doctrine of power supporting it all. They develop a habit of authority whose strength reflects the depth of deference paid to it.[45]

The cadets' intense conservatism might also have stemmed from their inability to see beyond the institutional structures established by Lockhart for governing Hong Kong's Chinese community. They tended to see what they had—the interlocking committee structure established by Lockhart—as the only solution to the problem of how to communicate effectively with the local Chinese population. It may have been fear that without the co-option of the leading Chinese merchants they would have been isolated and unable to establish any effective alternative links to the Chinese society they had to govern. This would then have left them helpless and, in their eyes, unable to govern Hong Kong, not a position that any "twice born" would have wanted to find himself in. In order not to threaten Lockhart's edifice, the cadets thus developed a reputation for being very conservative. Where new ideas were suggested they often originated from Governors or from senior Hong

Kong government people recruited from outside the cadet service. This conservative outlook lasted among some cadets until the 1960s when those recruited before 1941 eventually retired.[46]

It was very difficult to change the cadet system from within. The abolition of the Eastern Cadetships, for example, was only achieved after patient work and lobbying by Sir Ralph Furse,[47] the Colonial Office civil servant in charge of recruitment.[48] Cadets were, after all, appointed by the Secretary of State and their terms and conditions of service were protected by him. Changes to this system were difficult to make and certainly couldn't have been made on the basis that the calibre of staff recruited by the Secretary of State was somehow lacking. Hong Kong's cadets were also now, ostensibly, part of a unified Colonial Administrative Service with all the protections that this offered. Thus changes to Hong Kong's cadets could only come about slowly and with difficulty.

Colonial Office

Neither the Secretary of State nor the Colonial Office governed Britain's colonies; Governors did. The distances were too great and communications took too long for direct rule to have been a practical option. The Colonial Office's role was to supervise colonies, particularly their finances.[49] This stemmed from a Crown Colony's revenue being traditionally considered the hereditary revenue of the Crown. Any surplus not required was to be paid into the British Exchequer. In practice, there was very little, if any, surplus revenue from any colony for the British Treasury to purloin. A more pressing concern, however, was if a Crown Colony could not afford to pay its own way. Then the British government would have had no choice but to provide support from British public funds. This would have involved the British Treasury and resulted in even tighter financial control from London.[50]

The Colonial Office was staffed by members of the Home Civil Service. They would have taken the same entrance examination as the Eastern Cadets whom they supervised and would, therefore, have come from a similar background. Successful applicants joined as Assistant Principal and would most likely have been posted to one of the geographic divisions of the Colonial Office, supervising a particular group of colonies. Their role would have been to make initial comments on despatches received from colonies and pass them up to their seniors for their additional comment. They would tend to stay in the same department for many years and therefore built up a considerable knowledge about the colonies they supervised. However, they did not always impress those in the colonies whose work they supposedly supervised. One observer thought they were rather timid and had a tendency not to take decisions. Some, however, were impressive, particularly Gent and Caine. They were able to formulate their own ideas and, as shall be seen, push them through.[51] It would seem there were parallels with Hong Kong cadets. Many seemed to have been quickly absorbed into their respective bureaucratic cultures with only a few able to seek to change the parameters within which they worked.

Colonial Office officials did not act in their own name but in the name of the Secretary of State. Although he was a cabinet minister, a Secretary of State for the Colonies seldom enjoyed the same standing in Cabinet as his counterpart in the Treasury or the Foreign Office. Some were heavyweight politicians, such as Milner and Churchill. A few such as Oliver Lyttelton, whom Churchill appointed when he was Prime Minister, carried weight through their experience and force of personality. Others were considered to have had little political influence,[52] for example, George Hall[53] and James Griffiths.[54] Some had their own ideas they wished to push through, like Philip Cunliffe-Lister[55] in respect of trade and MacDonald in respect of Colonial Development and Welfare. Creech-Jones, a Secretary of State with high ideals for the colonies was, confided his Prime Minister, Atlee, "one of my mistakes". Many, like Passfield, probably found themselves in the position of having to

> authorise daily by initialling innumerable decisions one after another, on endless matters on which I can form only the roughest kind of judgement, on the advice of others.[56]

Secretaries of State were, however, politicians and not bureaucrats. They had to take account of political pressures that faced them, or may have faced them in parliament. These were rare in respect of Hong Kong but could have important consequences when they did arise. They could not be ignored. However, most matters concerning Hong Kong were dealt with by officials.

A Secretary of State was the Hong Kong Governor's constitutional link with Britain. Like all colonial governors, he owed his appointment to the Secretary of State. A Secretary of State, as a member of Cabinet, was answerable to the Prime Minister. He was also a member of one of the Houses of Parliament and had to be answerable to members, responding to whatever public political pressure might arise. A Governor could not hope to take a position which a Secretary of State would find politically untenable without expecting to be countermanded no matter how strongly he might feel supported by public opinion in Hong Kong. He could, however, strive to take and sustain a position counter to the views of Colonial Office officials if it was over a matter of little or no interest to a Minister and if his local position was strong enough. How such situations could arise will be examined in later chapters.

Unofficials

The unofficials provided a link between the Hong Kong government and the people it governed. They were not, nor claimed themselves to be, representative of Hong Kong's people but could be said to have been representative of the business and professional classes from which they came. The locally domiciled unofficial members, although also from the business and professional classes, might, on occasion speak up for the more disadvantaged in society. Regardless, they were an integral part of the political process and were thus an important factor in the power equation. It was not their constitutional position which made them important—the Hong Kong government could always use the official majority in the Legislative Council to ensure the passage of legislation although this seldom occurred—it was their influence over the shaping of government policy they were sometimes allowed to assume. This was in no small amount due to efforts made to reach a consensus before policies were formally submitted to the Legislative Council. It depended too on the extent to which a Governor would either allow unofficials' views to prevail or seek to influence or change them. Much depended on the issue at stake, the tenacity and character of individual unofficials and the Governor's attitude.

At the beginning of this period the Legislative Council had seven official and six unofficial members. The Governor presided with a seldom-used original vote and casting vote. One European unofficial was elected by the unofficial Justices of the Peace and another by the General Chamber of Commerce. They were then nominated by the Governor. Two European and two Chinese unofficials were also nominated by the Governor. In 1929 the Governor, Clementi, added a further two official and two unofficial members. Of the latter, one was Chinese and the other, for the first time, was Portuguese. All members came from a business or professional background; there were no representatives from a "grass roots" background. The Europeans were chosen either from among the top British merchant firms in Hong Kong, with Jardine Matheson and Co. predominating, or from among leading lawyers. The European members would have had multifarious links through their business connections, membership of the General Chamber of Commerce and of clubs like the Hong Kong Club and the Hong Kong Jockey Club. They would have had ample opportunity of knowing the British business community's prevailing views; indeed, in their senior business positions it would have been their business to have been so informed.

The locally domiciled unofficial members of the Legislative Council were in a not dissimilar position. They would have been fully aware of views affecting the local business community. They would also have had related ties of family, education, place of origin and involvement with community organisations such as the District Watch Committee, the Tung Wah Hospital and the Po Leung Kuk.[57] Their links with the local society would have been deeper than those of their British counterparts on the Legislative Council although they would have not gone much beyond the established local communities. They had far fewer, if any, links with newer immigrants. That is not to say that they spoke up for the underprivileged or understood them particularly well but it may have meant that they knew how a wider spectrum of people in Hong Kong thought. One member in particular, Sir Robert Kotewall, was well regarded as someone who could reflect local opinion vey accurately, an invaluable resource for government.[58]

The area where they were perhaps most influential was in the Finance Committee of the Legislative Council. In 1920, the Governor, Stubbs, had appointed all unofficial Legislative Council members as members of the Finance Committee. He restricted official membership to the Colonial Secretary, the Colonial Treasurer, later renamed the Financial Secretary, and the Director of Public Works. Government did not thereafter seek to use the official majority to overturn Finance Committee decisions. More often than not, government withdrew items that the unofficials opposed rather than risk defeat, sometimes resubmitting them suitably amended. This gave the unofficials considerable autonomy in appropriation matters such that, by 1947, a senior official could write,

> It has long been the custom in Hong Kong to abide by the decision of the Finance Committee with its unofficial majority, and not to use the official majority on Legislative Council to force through appropriation measures.[59]

Although appointed, the unofficials were not expected to do just as they were told or what might have been expected of them. Their views may sometimes have been unwelcome or disregarded, but they could not be ignored.

The China element

This book examines the constitutional sovereignty of Britain over its colony and how it operated in practice. It examines how, sometimes, the Hong Kong government got its way, sometimes the unofficials, and sometimes Britain. It is, in Carpenter's sense, a study of bureaucratic autonomy. The Chinese government was not part of this formal constitutional relationship: it was an external party to this tripartite relationship. What it did, or might do, had to be taken into account, but to be dealt with diplomatically or as an external threat. This posed its own difficulties especially during a period when the writ of China's central government did not cover the whole country. The Mainland government, however, did not seek to impose policies upon the Hong Kong government, except insofar as they would have directly benefitted China. It had no concern over, for example the provision of low-cost housing or Hong Kong's financial autonomy from Britain. China's involvement is therefore acknowledged where it arises in this book but the nature of the relationship is not examined in detail.

Britain's other colonies

Britain's other colonies had their own relationship with the British government and with their own local unofficials. Constitutionally, many went down the path of responsible government towards eventual independence, a destination not available to Hong Kong. Hong Kong was considered *sui generis:* very few other colonies were in quite the same position. To have examined the extent to which other colonies may have developed autonomy before independence in the manner this study has been conducted was beyond the scope of this work. Where feasible and relevant, reference is made to what happened in other colonies.

Summing up

It was within the bureaucratic framework described above that issues involving the Hong Kong government, the Colonial Office, Hong Kong's unofficials and, sometimes, members of the British Parliament were resolved. It will be argued in this book that the resolution of these issues was not dependent upon written and agreed procedures and protocols. Instead, new policies emerged from the practical realities of such relationships. As a contemporary commentator observed,

> the British Empire belongs to the realm of phantasmagoria rather than of sensory perceptions; outward forms have no necessary relation to actual realities.[60]

The studies in this book will help illustrate just what these realities were, how they were mediated and how they contributed to the development of autonomy.

3
The Origins of Policy, 1917–30

The 1920s saw increasing pressures for social change in Hong Kong. These pushed and nudged government towards increasing its reach by adopting new legislation. This was not change led or embraced wholeheartedly by a progressive government; rather, it was change taken hesitantly by a sometimes reluctant one. Tentative initial steps brought slow and, at times, unsteady change.

Change did not happen in isolation. Hong Kong's society and economy continued to grow and develop. Its population increased from 625,000 in 1921 to 850,000 in 1931.[1] This influx occurred against a backdrop of political instability and uncertainty in China after the 1911 revolution; the Japanese demands made on China; the growth of anti-imperialist sentiment in China; the rise of the Kuomintang (KMT) and the beginnings of the Chinese Communist Party (CCP). Large influxes of refugees from China were often the result and that put an enormous strain on Hong Kong's resources, not least on the availability and affordability of housing. This led to the imposition of rent controls and a commission of enquiry into housing which did not result in any concrete action.

Other external factors were the rise of Britain's obligations through membership of the League of Nations and the International Labour Organisation which exerted pressure to introduce social legislation. There was the growing influence of changing social expectations in Britain, for example, the protection of women and children, reflected in the election of two Labour governments and the involvement of what are now called non-government organizations (NGOs). Partly as a result of these changes, the Secretary of State and the Colonial Office now dispensed more advice and instruction to colonies on new areas of government activity.

By 1920, the structures established by Lockhart for maintaining contact with the local Chinese population through the elites had been in place for nearly thirty years. The senior cadets of this period had joined shortly after this system had been established, had grown up with it and had made it an integral part of the governmental system. It had not been designed, however, to cope with the pressures for social change that were developing from the 1920s. During this period, the Hong Kong government usually did not have its own distinct policies. It tended to react to pressures for change rather than initiate change. What influenced the Hong Kong government to change? If it did not instigate change, why did it take action? What was the Secretary of State's and the Colonial Office's role? What did the adoption of new policies say about the development of the Hong Kong government's autonomy? These questions will be examined through a review of the passage of legislation to regulate employment of children; why it imposed rent controls in the private housing market; and how and why legislation to control and regulate *mui tsai* was established but not brought into effect. It does not seek to generalise; not every case can be examined here—to do so would warrant a separate book. It does, however, seek to provide a detailed insight of what did happen in these cases and sets out a framework which can be used to examine other cases of this period.

Employment of children

Hong Kong's Sanitary Board was considered to be a rather dull, uninteresting and, by implication, a rather ineffective sort of sort of body.[2] In 1919 it was the vehicle through which pressure for legislation to regulate the employment of children in factories and workshops was brought to bear upon government in both Hong Kong and Britain. The Sanitary Board had been established in 1883 as a result of the Chadwick Report into Hong Kong's sanitary conditions. It initially had direct responsibility for the drafting of public health by-laws and for supervision of the Sanitary Department staff. In 1903, the Principal Medical Officer of Health became the Board's President, directly responsible to the Governor for the operation of the Sanitary Department. In 1908, after investigation into the department's workings, a cadet officer became President and Head of the Department. The Board then consisted of four official members and six unofficial members, four appointed by the Governor and two elected by those whose names appeared on the Jury List.[3] In 1919, the Colonial Veterinary Surgeon, Adam Gibson[4] was President of the Sanitary Board, a post he had held since May 1918. The full-time President and Head of the Sanitary Department, D. W. Tratman, a cadet officer, had also been appointed Superintendent of Imports and Exports and had left the Presidency of the Sanitary Board to his subordinate. This may have been because of a staff shortage when many expatriate civil servants had volunteered for military service overseas during the First World War.

Before 1921, Hong Kong had no factory legislation. Many young children accompanied their parents to the factories where they worked and where they were also employed. Older children often performed tasks best suited to children small enough to squeeze into constricted spaces such as boiler-chipping in the dockyards. Government, however, had not of its own volition taken the initiative to deal with this issue. It was left instead to members of the Sanitary Board to investigate and propose that government should legislate to limit the hours of work of children under 14 and prevent children under 13 being employed in certain hazardous industries.

One such member was Francis B. L. Bowley[5] who had been an unofficial member of the Sanitary Board since December 1915. He was a long-time resident and prominent local solicitor who had, at the turn of the century, served for several years as Crown Solicitor. He attended a meeting of the Church of England's Men's Society in December 1918 at which Miss Ada Pitts, a London Missionary Society missionary and another long-time Hong Kong resident,[6] spoke on child labour in Hong Kong. Bowley had already raised children's issues in Hong Kong in 1911 when he published a series of articles in the local press on Britain's Children's Act of 1908.[7] He was persuaded by Ada Pitts to raise this in the Sanitary Board.[8] He first did so in March 1919 when he asked the Acting Medical Officer of Health, Dr Alice Hickling, whether women and children should be protected in the workplace. Alice Hickling,[9] a medical missionary also of long-standing in Hong Kong, replied that an investigation was required. On 2 April, a sub-committee was appointed with Bowley as Chairman,[10] to enquire into "the limitation of the ages and hours for employment of children and the prevention of overcrowding in factories". They took evidence from the Sanitary Department's District Inspectors and formed their recommendations based on these findings. On 27 May 1919, their report was presented to a full meeting of the Board to which the members of the Sub-Committee, Dr Tso Seen-wan,[11] Chan Kai-ming,[12] and Dr Hickling, gave their unanimous support.

The report was short and to the point. With no compulsory universal education in Hong Kong, it was impractical to prohibit children of any age from employment. Children would have been left roaming the streets unsupervised and causing a nuisance. However, they recommended that section 16 of the Public Health and Buildings Ordinance be amended to permit the Board to make by-laws to prohibit the employment of children under the age of 14

> in any factory or workshop for more than 10 hours ... in any one day ... and prohibiting the employment of children under the age of 13 in any occupation likely to be injurious to his or her life, limb or health, regard having been had to his or her physical condition.

The report noted the Board was already empowered under the Public Health and Buildings Ordinance to regulate overcrowding in factories and workshops. The ordinance, however, provided no statutory definition of overcrowding. They recommended that the definition in the Factory and Workshop Act, 1901 in force in England and Wales be followed.

Bowley's arguments rested on two main points. His first was to refer to the peace negotiations underway in Versailles which, he argued, were not concerned with peace now but with establishing "those international arrangements which the Allies have devised for the prevention of wars in the future and for the betterment of mankind". These were the League of Nations and the International Labour Convention in both of which, he claimed, "the subject of the employment of women and children takes a very prominent position". He spelt out in detail the desired working conditions that should be met which, he argued, should apply to Hong Kong as part of the British Empire. The second was that regulation was necessary as manufacturing in Hong Kong had increased in recent years in the absence of any factory legislation. It also helped that many factories were not employing children for more than 10 hours a day or beyond 6pm so the proposed legislation would not unduly affect them. C. G. Alabaster[13] seconded Bowley's motion.

Gibson, supported by the Vice-President, William Chatham,[14] tried in vain to dilute Bowley's motion. He argued that sanitary inspectors would be unable to tell a child's age or to decide what an injurious occupation might be. He asked what children would do if not employed as there were no schools for them to attend. Bowley did not accept these arguments. He stated that the law could be framed in such a way to allow an inspector to declare that a child appeared to be below a certain age. Bowley, however, had carefully chosen his ground. His Sub-Committee, who had perhaps been chosen for their likely sympathies, supported him. Another Board member, Alabaster, also supported him. Only the President and Vice-President, Chatham, the Director of Public Works, were likely to oppose. The Secretary for Chinese Affairs (SCA), although a member of the Board, was not present. Dr F. M. G. Ozorio was sympathetic with only the views of Colonel G. B. Crisp, the army doctor, unknown.[15]

When considered by the Executive Council in June 1919, members asked Gibson for more information on hours worked by children, in which kind of factories, how many were employed and what wages they received. Details of his report, a month later, remain unknown. The Council considered that the matter "would more or less solve itself with the provision of an adequate number of schools" although there were no plans to bring this into effect. The Board's Vice-President, Chatham, also sat on the Executive Council and would have been unlikely to support measures he hadn't supported at the Sanitary Board meeting. Edwin Hallifax,[16] the SCA, a Sanitary Board member and a politically conservative officer, would also have likely supported the status quo.

Further agitation in Hong Kong for action on this issue probably resulted in the Executive Council agreeing in December 1919 to appoint a Commission to investigate the matter. In March 1920, however, when agitation had died down, and coinciding with Bowley's resignation from the Sanitary Board, the matter was allowed to rest. Further agitation arose in Hong Kong and in Britain. In May 1920, Dr Ozorio asked a question in the Sanitary Board and Bowley and Miss Pitts may have publicised the matter in Britain when they visited there in June 1929. In a question in the House of Commons in December 1920 an MP, Mr T. Cape, referred to a Sanitary Board proposal which had been rejected by the Legislative Council, though he probably meant the Executive Council. Colonial Office staff found the minutes of the Sanitary Board and Executive Council meetings concerned and replied to Mr Cape that they would ask the Governor to report what he had done in response to this proposal.[17] Bowley, now back in Hong Kong, raised the matter again with the Men's Society in February 1921. It was probably this agitation and the Colonial Office query which prompted the Executive Council on 24 March 1921 to appoint a Commission to enquire into the matter.[18]

Stubbs appointed a cadet officer, S. B. C. Ross,[19] Chairman with Dr Charles McKenny,[20] a government doctor, Ada Pitts, the Rev H. R. Wells,[21] Shouson Chow[22] and Li Ping as members. The inclusion of two missionaries would almost have guaranteed that some form of protection for women and children would be recommended. Missionaries, however, could have been expected, in the words of one scholar, to "work within limits" rather than, as a lay person might, "campaign without constraint".[23] Both Pitts and Wells had been in Hong Kong for many years and were well known and were probably likely to be relatively tactful in making their case to government. They would also have had credibility with other supporters of reform.

The Commission visited factories and took evidence from factory operators. It found that few children worked less than 70 hours per week. Conditions in glass factories were the worst. It concluded that although factory operators claimed the boys were apprentices, conditions were such that "it seemed unlikely that they would all live long enough or be healthy enough to take men's work". Children were sometimes employed either because of the particular work they could do or to occupy them while their mothers worked. Low wages, paid as piece rates, were thought to depress rates paid to adults. Factories had few amenities, not even washrooms or places to eat meals. Visits made found conditions, in some cases, to be worse than reported. Glass factories were particularly bad. Boiler-chipping by boys was particularly hazardous. In dockyards, the only reason boys were preferred was because they were cheaper; in Britain it was known that adults did this work and the Commission recommended this cease. It also found that many children had come from the Mainland for employment, introduced by a relative.

The Commission were "left in no doubt as to the necessity for legislation". They recommended that no child under 11 years old should be employed in factories or that any child under 13 should be employed as casual labour; that they should work no more than 54 hours per week, or more than five hours consecutively and should have one rest day in seven; that they should not be employed between 7 pm and 6 am; that they should be banned from working in dangerous trades. Inspectors "of good calibre" should be employed to enforce these regulations which were a good deal less than those in Europe. Although many children liked their work and the income they brought in was important to their families, the Commission tartly remarked that, "the question is essentially moral and not only economic. A child is not a correct judge of its own welfare". Members did disagree on compulsory education. The Rev Wells strongly supported its introduction but Li Ping and Shouson Chow thought that while desirable it would be expensive and would encourage migration of children from the Mainland to Hong Kong.

On 24 October 1921, the Commission submitted its report to the Governor who sent a copy to the Colonial Office. An official there wrote that "it is quite clear that conditions are deplorable and will have to be changed". There was also interest from other bodies, including from Dorothy, Viscountess Gladstone, who had written to the Colonial Office on behalf of the League of Nations Union. By this time, Stubbs was aware of the League of Nations Labour Conventions as in August 1921 he had been asked if Hong Kong would adopt five of them. Reference was made to this when legislation was introduced to the Legislative Council in September 1922. The Attorney General stated that it was government's intention to adopt

> as far as is possible, having regard to local conditions, the spirit of the provisions of the Draft Convention which was adopted at Washington on the 28th November 1919, by the International Labour Conference, which relates to the admission of children to industrial employment.

The Industrial Employment of Children Bill was introduced into the Legislative Council on 21 September 1922 and was passed unanimously at the following meeting on 28 September. The Officer Administering the Government (OAG),[24] Claud Severn,[25] spoke with some passion when he said that "it has always been a painful sight to see children carrying loads and to see very young children engaged for long hours in unsuitable industries". He also paid particular tribute to Ada Pitts and the Rev Wells.[26] Only Shouson Chow pointed out the hardships that may be caused poorer families by the loss of some income from their children.

There were three reasons why government so fully supported measures which three years previously they had deemed unnecessary. Firstly, working conditions of children were widely known to be deplorable although to what extent was perhaps not so widely known until the Commission reported. Secondly, questions were being raised in Britain about the issue and Hong Kong had no defensible cause for inaction. Thirdly, regulation of working conditions for children was now expected by the League of Nations. Again Hong Kong had no defence against inaction.

Rent controls

The successful imposition of rent controls in Hong Kong in 1921 showed that, on this occasion, the Hong Kong government had its own distinctive policy. Rent control helped to prevent both widespread exorbitant increases and the eviction of tenants perceived to be permanent Hong Kong residents. Government also had the capacity to implement such a policy, primarily through the services of the Secretary for Chinese Affairs where most disputes were first taken. Usually, only cases which involved a lot of money were taken to court.[27] Rent controls also had unusually wide political support within Hong Kong, from unofficial members of the Legislative Council and tenants protected by the legislation. Although Britain did not overtly support the legislation, neither did it oppose it.

The vast majority of the population earned little and could only afford to rent rooms or cubicles in Chinese tenement buildings. This housing was usually of poor quality and was overcrowded with poor ventilation and sanitation which could lead to the spread of disease. Others who rented better accommodation were expatriate businessmen, professionals and civil servants, and locally domiciled middle-class Chinese and others. This was especially true of the Portuguese community, many of whom were displaced by rich Chinese coming from Canton to seek refuge in Hong Kong.[28] Some also lived in accommodation provided by their employer. A small number of expatriate British businessmen and professionals owned their own property.

About 320 new houses had been built between 1911 and 1921. This had been insufficient to cope with the rise in Hong Kong's population from 456.739 in 1911 to 625,166 in 1921, a 37% rise in ten years.[29] This increase came mostly from growing immigration and would have been impossible for any house builder or investor to foresee. It was met instead by an increase in rents and, especially at the lower end of the market, in population density. Residential accommodation was also classified by race, reflecting the different perceived lifestyles the two communities tended to follow.

Domestic rents for the Chinese population had started to increase in 1918 and in 1919 for Europeans.[30] They had then been

> steadily and constantly rising for the last two or three years, and they have recently reached such a height as to impose a very serious burden on the tenants and to threaten to affect the prosperity of the Colony.[31]

The problem was also that existing tenants were being given notice to quit for tenants who could pay a higher rent. Many existing tenants were long-term Hong Kong residents and, perhaps for the first time, were described by government officials as "permanent residents". They were being replaced by people with no connection from outside Hong Kong and who officials referred to as "strangers". Some could afford to pay whatever rent was necessary to secure the accommodation they desired, often at the expense of the sitting tenant. The Hong Kong government laid claim to a duty to protect these sitting tenants when the Attorney General declared that "permanent residents have a greater claim to our consideration over 'strangers'."

In January 1920, Stubbs became concerned about the rapid increase in rents but was reluctant to interfere and impose controls. He believed government interference might affect the rate of house building. When the situation worsened the following month, Stubbs issued a warning in the Legislative Council that if he had

> given the impression that this Government will sit still with folded hands while the existing shortage of accommodation is exploited for private gain it is high time that that impression should be removed.[32]

He stated his intentions so clearly that he left himself with little room for manoeuvre.

In the middle of 1921 rents again started to rise rapidly although there was little clear understanding of why. The two main contributory causes were thought to be an influx of refugees escaping disorder across the border and "the failure on the part of property owners and others to keep pace with the normal development of the Colony".[33] One "subsidiary factor" was thought to be speculators who bought property, dispossessed sitting tenants, increased levels of partitioning and rented out smaller cubicles at higher rents.[34] Another was "the greed of certain landlords" which was aggravated by the recent prevalence of rent farming. A landlord would rent his property to a "farmer" who would then let it for whatever rent he could, either to sub-tenants or directly to tenants. In 1921, this had only recently become widespread among the larger and longer established landlords in Hong Kong who included large property owners such as Humphrey's Estate, Jardine Matheson & Co and the Land Investment Co. They had previously tried to let out their own properties but with little success.

Sir Paul Chater,[35] an unofficial Executive Council member since 1896 and one of Hong Kong's most successful land and property developer of his day, was adamantly opposed to rent controls. He thought it would destroy the confidence of Chinese investors in Hong Kong property and that matters should be left solely to the market. He hinted strongly that neither the Governor nor the senior cadets really understood the workings of the property market which he would be willing to tell them.[36] Despite the pride the cadets took in their links with the local Chinese population, their knowledge of local practices was perhaps less than they realised.

Stubbs and the other Executive Council members remained adamant that rent controls should be introduced. Stubbs was concerned about the rack renting being resorted to by landlords. He seemed quite genuinely outraged that a sitting tenant, unable to pay a higher rent, would be evicted to make way for someone who could. He seemed even more outraged that although eighteen months before he had warned landlords not to indulge in such behaviour they had ignored him. As he expressed it, "the landlords have chosen to defy the government and the public". Now, although he didn't wish to interfere in the workings of the market, he would set about controlling rents.

In the eighteen months since he had issued his warning, however, he had not prepared any detailed contingency plan. He suggested that maximum rents should be limited to 1914 or 1915 levels but, rather than introducing such a bill into the Legislative Council, he instead appointed a Committee consisting of the Attorney General and the Colonial Treasurer and three unofficials, Henry Pollock, H. W. Bird and Mr Lau Chu-pak[37]

> to consider and advise what steps should be taken to protect the tenants of domestic tenements from unreasonable increases in rental and from arbitrary termination of their tenancies.[38]

The Committee were given very little time to deliberate. It rejected Stubbs' proposal as impractical but whether they recommended the plan eventually adopted is unclear as they neither submitted a report nor reported back formally to the Legislative Council. Chater was dismissive of their efforts and thought that they had "not gone into the matter as thoroughly as they ought to". Nor did he think they had told the Governor of "the responsibility they will incur by passing of the Bill".[39] This was perhaps why they did not report back as they would have had a lot to answer for to their peers in business and the professions.

On 30 June, government tabled the Rents Bill for its first reading in the Legislative Council. It proposed the fixing of rents as from 31 December 1920 and, as long as tenants paid this rent, landlords were prevented from arbitrarily evicting them. New buildings were exempt from rent controls to encourage the development of new housing stock. The bill's second reading, committee stage and third reading all took place at the following Legislative Council meeting on 18 July 1921. There was an enormous amount of public interest as witnessed by the submission of several petitions with many hundreds of thousands of signatures in support of the proposed legislation and petitions from landlords against. Some were heard on the floor of the Legislative Council but arguments against the proposals were dismissed and the bill was passed unanimously. Rent control was not a new phenomenon in the British world. It had been imposed in Britain during the First World War and in Bombay and the Straits Settlements. The Hong Kong government was not, therefore, breaking entirely new ground.

The action of the landlords was seen as a challenge to government in two respects. One, at the risk of a little overstatement, was a challenge from some landlords to the government's authority. Stubbs was wont to see any opposition to his government in these terms. He had shown this trait in 1915 when he was Colonial Secretary of Ceylon. He had misread the motives behind communal riots which resulted in an overreaction by the colonial government and a large number of unnecessary deaths. Although the Colonial Office disapproved, he was not formally censured.[40] The other was a challenge to the wellbeing of people who were, perhaps for the first time, referred to as Hong Kong permanent residents. It was clear from discussion in the Legislative Council that the government and the legislature felt some responsibility towards protecting this group. The whole issue was so keenly felt by so many people from all of Hong Kong's different communities that it effectively united them as shown by the great popularity of rent controls. The Hong Kong government was seen to be acting in the interests of the people of Hong Kong.

Mui Tsai

The keeping of what, in Cantonese, was euphemistically known as *mui tsai*,[41] was a traditional Chinese custom which allowed the transfer of a daughter from one family to another. It was a socially acceptable way for a poor family to dispense with the responsibility, and cost, of a daughter's upbringing and transfer it to a family who could afford it. Upon maturity, a *mui tsai* would be married off, often as a secondary wife, and her adopted family would receive the dowry traditionally paid by the parents of the groom. Reformers in Britain equated *mui tsai*, the transfer of a girl for money and her inability to leave her employer, with slavery, an issue that aroused strong emotions.

Campaign for reform

The *mui tsai* system was first examined in Hong Kong in 1878 when an official investigation found that it was not a form of slavery. In 1917, the existence of *mui tsai* in Hong Kong came to the Secretary of State's attention with a claim from a visiting MP that it did amount to slavery.[42] The Governor, Sir Henry May, explained their position to the Colonial Office and said that without the *mui tsai* system, many infant girls would be left to die. The Colonial Office was reluctant to contradict the "man on the spot" but knew the system had to be made more publicly defensible. They suggested to May that *mui tsai* should be paid and be allowed to leave their employer if they wished. The OAG, Severn, replied, rather disingenuously, that they already received board and lodging, could leave their employers if they wished and that *mui tsai* were still common in China. The Colonial Office did not press the matter further "on the ground that interference with the system of adoption by purchase would probably do more harm than good".[43]

This view was to prove unsustainable. In August 1919, Clara, the wife of Royal Navy officer, Lieutenant-Commander Hugh Haslewood, was horrified "to find child slavery established and countenanced in a British colony". She wrote to Hong Kong's English-language press and cabled prominent philanthropists in Britain,[44] describing the system as "child slavery".[45] Stubbs, knew this was annoying local Chinese elites and arranged for Haslewood to be posted away from Hong Kong. The situation only worsened when on their return to Britain in December 1919, the Haslewoods set about mobilising influential public opinion. A question was asked in the House of Commons, Clara published letters in the press and lobbied societies likely to be interested. This included the influential Anti-Slavery and Aborigines Protection Society[46] who caused further questions to be raised in Parliament. By the end of 1920, the

Archbishops of Canterbury and York were writing letters to the Colonial Office on the subject.[47]

Although publicly the Colonial Office and the Secretary of State continued to defend the *mui tsai* system, privately officials tried to persuade Stubbs to introduce reforms. He would not accept a committee of enquiry from Britain, implying it would be composed of people "who would necessarily be ignorant of Chinese customs and modes of thought". Nor would he contemplate registration or inspection of *mui tsai* or prohibiting their transfer between employers. As if to vindicate him, local Chinese elites were indignant at being portrayed in Britain as "dealers in prostitutes and owners of slaves". In July 1921, a mass meeting was held to register their protest.[48] It was convened by two Chinese Legislative Councillors and was attended by 300 leading Chinese residents,[49] including three former District Watch Committee members, Shouson Chow, Ts'o Seen-wan and Chau Siu-kai,[50] two former Tung Wah Chairmen, and other directors or advisers to both the Tung Wah and the Po Leung Kuk.[51]

Feelings ran high.[52] The meeting refuted criticism that *mui tsai* were kept as slaves, for prostitution or for the sexual gratification of their masters or that their masters ill-treated them as they pleased. They stressed the benefits to the girls and resolved to form a "Society for the Protection of the *Mui Tsai*". Others, taking a more modern approach, supported the *mui tsai* system's abolition. They thought it "in the interest of humanity, the prestige of China and posterity, and also to keep pace with the advancement of civilisation" that the girls be emancipated. In September 1921 they established the "Anti-*Mui Tsai* Society" whose supporters came mostly from the churches, the YMCA and YWCA and the labour unions,[53] rather than the established Chinese elites.

Directions issued

In Britain, further pressure mounted on the Colonial Office and the Secretary of State. In February 1922, the Anti-Slavery Society and the Archbishops of Canterbury and York requested that Parliament hold an enquiry. On 19 February, Josiah Wedgwood[54] sent a personal note to Winston Churchill, the Secretary of State, arguing that "this *mui tsai* business is a small thing that you might put right with credit. It must go soon, and you should do it". Churchill rounded on his officials and told them he was no longer prepared to defend the system. In March, he declared to the House of Commons that his government would abolish the *mui tsai* system in Hong Kong within one year.[55] He told Stubbs to set up a commission to include local advocates for reform to investigate the *mui tsai* situation and make proposals for its abolition. He also instructed

Stubbs to "issue a proclamation immediately making it clear that the status of *mui tsai*, as understood in China, will not in future be recognised in Hong Kong". Stubbs, however, played this down and issued a much less strident proclamation. It was not disseminated widely and many *mui tsai* probably never knew about it.[56]

Stubbs set up a Commission as instructed with members from both the Society for the Protection of *Mui Tsai* and the Anti-*Mui Tsai* Society. It submitted its report on 29 May 1922 and proposed that all *mui tsai* be registered, that no new engagements or transfers be permitted, and that *mui tsai* under the age of twenty could be redeemed by their parents. All existing *mui tsai* should be obliged to continue in their present employment because, in an unfortunate choice of language, "the interests of the owner cannot be ignored". Stubbs realised their report would be unacceptable to Churchill and changed the recommendations. He instead proposed that all *mui tsai* over the age of eighteen be allowed to leave their employer when they wished; those under eighteen should be permitted to return to their parents, without payment, if they, or their parents, desired and *mui tsai* over the age of ten should receive a minimum wage.[57]

In September 1922, when a bill containing these measures was published in Hong Kong, Chinese members of the Legislative Council raised strong opposition to it. This was not based on any particular proposal but because the status of a *mui tsai* would change from being a family member to becoming an employee to the detriment of the girl.[58] Stubbs was disheartened at the possible opposition of all Chinese members to the bill. In a letter to his mentor at the Colonial Office, Sir Arthur Grindle,[59] he claimed that,

> This is the beginning of the end. I told you the other day that I believed we should hold Hong Kong for another fifty years. I put it now at twenty at the most ... we hold our position in Hong Kong because the Chinese are satisfied to be ruled by us so long as we do not make our yoke heavy and are willing to listen to their views and meet their wishes in matters which affect them nearly. They do not like us, but are passively loyal. If we interfere with their customs to an extent which they believe to be unreasonable, this passive acquiescence will be turned into more or less active opposition.

Stubbs feared that any reform would alienate the Chinese elites and thereby reduce Britain's ability to govern Hong Kong. He thought the Po Leung Kuk would cease to co-operate with government. This was related to the wider political role it and other Chinese societies played in providing official institutional linkages between the Hong Kong government and the Chinese community. If this disappeared, officials feared they would be unable to govern Hong Kong's large Chinese community.[60] Stubbs' unspoken but implied fear was that implementing controls over *mui tsai* would have destroyed Lockhart's carefully crafted system of links with the Chinese community. Without the co-operation of the Chinese elites, the Hong Kong government would have been isolated from the Chinese population. This, as he perceived it, would have made the governing of Hong Kong, a virtual impossibility. Despite his earlier feelings of contempt towards the Chinese elite over what he saw as their succumbing to intimidation during the seamen's strike, he now felt thoroughly intimidated by them. He thought they would now be able to summon up the courage to confront the government to which they owed that extra status they enjoyed in Hong Kong's Chinese society. The Hong Kong government had, as a result of the system it had created, allowed itself to be captured by the elite it had sought to co-opt.

Passage of legislation

When the Female Domestic Service Ordinance was debated in the Legislative Council in February 1923, Stubbs told members plainly that

> I have definite instructions from the British Government that the [*mui tsai*] system be abolished. On this there can be no compromise.[61]

The Chinese members of the Legislative Council chose not to oppose it.[62] Much of the new law repeated existing provisions but the new and most contentious issues were included in Part III of the Ordinance. This was to be brought into effect on a date to be decided by the Governor and was not introduced for six years. Stubbs claimed that the situation in 1923 was not conducive to introducing measures which lacked the support of the local Chinese. He was also concerned about reports that Sun Yat-sen in Canton was trying to create anti-British feelings. Churchill was no longer Secretary of State and his successor, the Duke of Devonshire, was not under the same political pressure to abolish the *mui tsai* system and did not interfere.

The result was a victory of form over substance, in Britain and Hong Kong. A government report produced one year later, based on information provided by the District Watch Committee, pronounced that no new *mui tsai* had been reported taken into employment.[63] For the next six years, no further questions were asked in Parliament on the matter. All the societies and individuals who had been so vociferous in their demands for the abolition of *mui tsai* now seemed satisfied with the new legislation.

Stubbs's government had exercised little autonomy over this issue. Until Churchill's declaration in March 1922, Stubbs' policy was no different from that of the local Chinese elites. After that it became the same as that of the British government. He seemed not to have any policy of his own. His initial refusal to contemplate reform reflected his view that no effective capacity could be created to regulate *mui tsai*. It was Stubbs' ineptness and lack of political or diplomatic skill that eventually caught him between two opposing factions. He tried to face down first one side and then the other, something only a Governor with greater political skills than Stubbs possessed could reasonably have attempted.

Campaign renewed

Reformers in Britain did not discover Stubbs' subterfuge until 1928. A letter from the Anti-Slavery and Aborigines Protection Society published in the *Manchester Guardian* claimed that the *mui tsai* system still existed in Hong Kong, that their numbers had increased, and that there had been reports of cruelty.[64] This message was widely disseminated in Britain and the Colonial Office asked the Governor to report. Clementi, like Stubbs, replied he was not prepared to implement legislation which he felt would prove ineffective.[65] This was most unhelpful as the Secretary of State needed to show his critics that the *mui tsai* system was being abolished. The Secretary of State told Clementi the decision to regulate *mui tsai* was British government policy; that the institution was indefensible in Parliament and must stand and that "what we are now concerned with is ensuring that the legal abolition is made as effective as possible in practice". Clementi still refused to implement Part III of the 1923 Ordinance until he was able to effectively enforce it. He considered this was "the more honest course; and I am entirely opposed to any schemes of legislative 'eyewash' ".[66]

By the time Clementi replied, a new Labour government was in power. The new Secretary of State, Sidney Webb, Lord Passfield was a renowned reformer and member of the Fabian Society. He simply directed Clementi to implement Part III of the 1923 Ordinance forthwith, and to make regulations for registration and inspection of *mui tsai* which would doubtless need the appointment of inspectors. Clementi introduced amending legislation into the Legislative Council but made it clear that he was acting under instructions.

Registration of *mui tsai* started in 1929. As progress was initially slow, with only eighteen registered in the first eighteen days, Clementi tried to persuade the Secretary of State to change his policy. He claimed the registration system was not working; that there was now a stigma attached to owning a *mui tsai;* and that they should instead become paid servants or, if too young, adopted daughters. The District Watch Committee, at "a stormy meeting" had expressed concern at the difficulties of implementing the scheme.[67] Colonial Office officials agreed with Clementi but the Labour Parliamentary Under-Secretary, the forthright Dr Drummond Shiels,[68] did not. He thought Clementi had tried to undermine the scheme and insisted every effort now be made to ensure compliance.[69] There was to be no change in policy.

Clementi's policy of not bringing *mui tsai* legislation into force failed because the Secretary of State simply instructed him to enforce it. Politically he could have done little else even if he had wanted to. Clementi believed he was acting in the best tradition of good government, an important ethos of British colonial administration.[70] This stance could persuade Colonial Office officials but not politicians. Clementi had disregarded the political situation in Britain. He had either been unaware of, or had wilfully ignored the political impact of British reformers and their supporters in Parliament upon an elected government. With a Labour government in power, the reformers themselves had taken office and had undermined Clementi's position. The age was now past when patronising but well-meant views like Clementi's could prevail. Public opinion could no longer be disregarded. Clementi's challenge to a Secretary of State's authority had unwittingly defined the limits of a colonial Governor's autonomy.

Conclusions

It is notable how little change was initiated by the Hong Kong Government. Regulation of working conditions for children in factories was initiated and promoted by a member of the Sanitary Board. It was given impetus through support from British Members of Parliament and Britain's membership of the International Labour Organisation. The warm official support the bill received during its passage through the Legislative Council sat uncomfortably with rejection of the need to do anything three years earlier. A similar process happened with *mui tsai* which came to prominence through pressures from Britain. Policy was not initiated by the Hong Kong government, which instead had policy imposed upon it.

The imposition of policies from outside was partly the result of the Hong Kong government's lack of policy formulation capacity. The provisions of legislation to protect children in factories were the product of a Commission, albeit one chaired by a cadet. It is unclear how much of the bill was drafted or proposed by government. A similar approach was taken in trying to formulate the details of a policy on rent control although it was less clear who actually did formulate them. It was, however, in the creation of capacity to implement these new policies where the groundwork of a future autonomy can be found. Once capacity to implement policies was created, it enabled government to become more knowledgeable about the issues being regulated. This was particularly the case with factory legislation and *mui tsai*. When the government had created the structure to implement new policies, and did it reasonably effectively, it had autonomy to exercise regulation which laid the foundation for doing more.

It is remarkable how beholden the Hong Kong government was to groups such as local Chinese elites in the case of employment of children and the regulation of *mui tsai*. It seemed a struggle to break away from the influence of such groups and have the confidence to take the lead and persuade others to support change. It may have been because the policies were not theirs that made government feel unable to persuade others to support them. This also showed the difficulties and limitations of the British colonial system. Britain could not easily impose its will upon an unwilling colony. It was not, as the Colonial Office was aware, a case of issuing instructions, although directives could be and were issued. Over contentious issues, they had to be backed up by firm political support in Britain. Without that, and in the absence of a Governor willing to take the initiative, opposition to change in Hong Kong could win the day. It took a great deal of effort and determination for a British government to ensure that its desired policy would be implemented. Once its policies were introduced, however, the British government then had to defer more to the colonial government on the extent and speed with which these could be enhanced or extended. How this developed in the following decade is examined in Chapter 4.

4
Britain's Influence over Hong Kong's Policy, 1929–41

Pressure for change accelerated towards the end of the 1930s. Change was still a slow and tentative process. Hong Kong's society and economy continued to grow and develop. Its population increased from 850,000 in 1931 to an estimated 1.64 million in 1941, boosted by the estimated 750,000 refugees who entered Hong Kong between 1937 and 1939 to escape the Japanese forces invading China.[1] Hong Kong had also been affected by the Depression of the 1930s and this caused budgetary concern in Hong Kong. The unofficials were so concerned about it that they pushed the government to set up a Retrenchment Commission to examine how government costs, mainly salaries, could be reduced. There were also external factors. The US government policy on the purchase of silver contributed to China's currency coming off the silver standard, a move quickly followed by Hong Kong. The Depression, and Britain abandoning the gold standard and adopting protectionist trade measures, led to a system of imperial tariff preferences which benefitted Hong Kong's manufacturers.

External pressures on Hong Kong to change continued during the 1930s and were to have a much bigger impact than in the previous decade. The lack of control over its currency was a major problem in the early part of the decade and was brought to a head by the impact of US silver policy on the Chinese currency and its effect on the Hong Kong dollar and Hong Kong's trade. The British government was at last able to insist that the Hong Kong government implement regulations for the registration of *mui tsai* which created the capacity to bring some kind of control to the system. Under the somewhat more insistent leadership of Governor Northcote and the Financial Secretary, Caine, measures to implement an income tax were taken. These latter two measures underlined the influence of the unofficials in policy making which was further underscored by their rejection of a government proposal to use public funds for the evacuation of non-Hong Kong domiciled British women and children, a measure foisted upon Hong Kong by the British government.

Currency

Before December 1935, the Hong Kong government had no mechanism with which to manage its currency. Its currency system was antiquated, even by the standards of the day. Legal tender consisted of large bulky silver dollars, about the size and weight of a British Crown coin and described by one British official as "inconveniently cumbrous." They were authorised under the Hong Kong (Coinage) Order, 1895, and consisted of the Mexican Silver Dollar, virtually obsolete by 1929, and the British Trade Dollar. Anyone could have the latter minted in Bombay if they provided the silver and paid for minting and transportation. The Hong Kong government provided subsidiary coinage.

From about 1890 silver dollars were replaced in circulation by banknotes. They were issued by The Hongkong and Shanghai Banking Corporation ("the Hongkong and Shanghai Bank"), the Chartered Bank and the Mercantile Bank and described by a British official as "unlimited customary tender". The note issues were limited by law or by charter. As at July 1929, the Hongkong Bank had issued $47.2m, the Chartered Bank $15.2m and the Mercantile Bank $1.7m.[2] As security, one-third of the Chartered and Mercantile banks note issue was covered by silver coin and the remainder by interest-bearing sterling securities. The Hongkong and Shanghai Bank note issue was covered 80–90% by silver coin or bullion and the remainder by interest-bearing securities. It alone could issue notes in excess of its authorised amount of $45m, subject to deposit of the equivalent in silver coin or bullion[3] and, until December 1929, on payment of a 1% tax. The note-issuing banks could issue notes to the maximum prescribed without reference to the Hong Kong government. Although banknotes were supposedly convertible, banks would not exchange them for silver dollars. They also discouraged customers from using silver dollars because they were costly to handle and store. Hong Kong dollar banknotes also circulated in Southern China where they were seen as a secure store of value. This circulation may have increased after 1911 as a result of debasement of Southern China's silver coinage and may have contributed towards a shortage of banknotes in Hong Kong.

These arrangements caused further complications. There had always been a premium on banknotes because silver dollars were costly for banks to handle and store. A premium of about 4%, which represented the cost of laying down silver dollars, was thought normal by the late 1920s. By July 1929, however, the premium had risen to 14%. The reasons for this were twofold. Firstly, because silver dollars no longer circulated, the value of the Hong Kong dollar was no longer linked to the price of silver bullion. Instead, it was linked to the supply of banknotes.

As their supply was limited, when demand for currency rose, so did the premium. Secondly, in 1929, demand did rise. Encouraged by the fall in the silver price, remittances home from the many Chinese working overseas had increased. These remittances were purchased in gold-based currencies but were paid out in the silver-based Hong Kong dollar.

This is where problems arose in Hong Kong. When the value of a commodity based currency rises above a certain point, imports of specie should increase which would allow additional notes to be issued. In Hong Kong, because notes had become the *de facto* legal tender and the currency had become divorced from silver, there was no increase in the supply of silver dollars. Banks were unwilling to import or mint them even when the silver price fell because there was no demand for them, and the costs and risk involved were high. When the demand for notes fell and the silver dollars were no longer required as backing, they had to be melted down at additional cost. There was thus no additional supply of notes and the note premium increased. This had serious implications for Hong Kong's trade with China. A higher note premium meant a higher exchange rate with the Shanghai dollar which made Hong Kong less competitive as a port and increased its costs to about 15% higher than Shanghai's.

In July 1929, when the premium reached 14%, Clementi felt he had to do, or be seen to be doing something. He was aware that "outside banking circles there was a dearth of expert authorities qualified to advise on matters of currency and exchange". Nevertheless, he instructed the Acting Colonial Treasurer, M. J. Breen,[4] to investigate. Breen found the problem "complex and obscure"[5] but also identified some of the complications outlined above. He thought a government note issue would not obviate these problems; that local banks could combine to resist the upward pressure on the exchange value of the dollar; that government could also remit the 1% tax on the Hongkong Bank's excess note issue; and that government should also accept top-class securities or commercial paper as security instead of insisting on silver coin. The Secretary of State might also be asked to provide technical help.

The note-issuing banks were quite adamant they had not caused the excessive note premium. This, they said, was the result of an excess of invisible exports over imports and not of any action by them. A sudden reduction in premium would be detrimental to trade and the only course was to wait until it fell of its own accord. They did not think an official enquiry or commission would help. The Colonial Treasurer warned a group of Chinese bankers that

> it was the definite policy of the Government and of the three banks of issue to grapple with the problem at the earliest moment and if necessary summon expert assistance in devising a permanent solution.[6]

It was the banks, not government, which were to influence events. This was especially so of Vandeleur Grayburn, the Hongkong Bank's Chief Manager. On 4 October 1929 the note premium had reached 20%. The banks, particularly the Hongkong Bank, started to buy sterling in a concerted effort to drive down the value of the Hong Kong dollar. They were spectacularly successful. Within days speculators had bought £2.5m and the note premium had halved. Later that month, there was a shortage of banknotes which was thought to have been caused when Grayburn stopped buying sterling. To address this, the other banks, meeting on 22 October as a Committee of the Associated Exchange Banks, agreed to reintroduce the silver dollar into circulation. They would pay out and accept silver dollars and the government also agreed to accept them in payment. This led to a greater shortage of notes as many people simply hoarded them after exchanging silver dollars for them.

To try and increase the note issue, banks minted and imported new silver dollars but still the note shortage persisted. The exchange banks wrote twice to government to implore them to remove the 1% tax on the Hongkong Bank's excess note issue. It did so on 9 December although it was not thought to have been the only cause of the Hongkong Bank's increase in note issue from HK$46m to HK$71m between 30 November 1929 and 28 February 1930. The Hongkong Bank still had to deposit silver dollars to cover the excess issue with all the costs this entailed and on which they received no return. This was probably due to a decision by Grayburn to increase the note issue at the Bank's expense. His earlier failure to increase the note issue when a shortage arose was to colour local opinion towards him and later to cast doubt upon whether one individual should have the power to manipulate Hong Kong's exchange value.

Hong Kong Currency Commission

When in the following March the premium started to rise again and inflationary pressures began to increase, the Hong Kong government felt it had to do something.[7] It appointed a Committee of Enquiry chaired by the Colonial Treasurer with local British and Chinese businessmen and bankers as members. They were to consider six questions: whether Hong Kong's present currency was best for its trade; to what extent the present currency system was unsatisfactory; how it could be remedied; whether the note premium was detrimental to Hong Kong's prosperity; was the link to silver advantageous to Hong Kong; and should the value of the Hong Kong dollar be stabilised, a euphemism for pegged to sterling.

Its report, published on 14 July 1930, was rather evasive. It found that a high note premium did depress Hong Kong's trade. The circulation of silver dollars was not the answer due to their inconvenience and cost. Bank settlements should be made in bar silver thus avoiding the costs of minting dollars. Only government should mint dollars which would avoid the accumulation of surplus stocks. Hong Kong's currency should remain on silver as long as China's did but should follow suit if China were to switch to the gold standard. Government taking over the note issue was not the answer. A treasury to store silver and staff to man it would be required and managing the exchange rate was thought best left to professional bankers. The government also had no-one capable of formulating or managing financial policy, a recurring theme during the next few years of deliberation in London. As long as China remained on the silver standard, support of the *status quo* seemed to have been the safest approach to take.

There was also an undercurrent of feeling against the influence of the note-issuing banks, especially the Hongkong Bank. The Hongkong Bank, with its unlimited note issue, was the only bank that could set the value of the Hong Kong dollar. This had reportedly caused some "enmity".[8] Kotewall, a Commission member, expressed similar concerns in a reservation to the report and claimed the public wanted government to be more involved in management of the currency. Many business people thought that control of the currency was too much in the power of the Chief Manager of the Hongkong Bank. Kotewall thought an Advisory Board could be established with "disinterested" parties as members to advise the government in times of emergency.[9]

Colonial Office Currency Committee

British government officials wanted to investigate further but had to admit they knew little of Hong Kong's situation. The Colonial Office set up its own Currency Committee, chaired by Sir John Campbell, their Economic and Financial Adviser, with members from the Treasury, Crown Agents and two banks. Campbell readily admitted the difficulty of the problem and realised someone would have to visit Hong Kong to investigate. Some members thought that Hong Kong would be prepared to implement whatever they recommended but the Colonial Office knew that the Secretary of State would have to persuade Hong Kong's commercial community and could not simply be expected "to induce them to do what he thought was right: some banks had done well out of the present system and might resent change".[10]

A three-man Commission spent five weeks in Hong Kong investigating and wrote a detailed and incisive report. The Commission pinpointed the power of the Hongkong Bank's Chief Manager to expand the note issue or not as a major failing. In 1929, it was his unwillingness to increase the note issue that had resulted in other banks importing up to 800 tons of "unnecessary coin". The Commission considered it was

> fundamentally wrong that the exchange value of a Colony's currency should depend on one person, and no less wrong that that person should be put in a position where he may constantly have to decide between the conflicting interests of the Colony and the bank.

The Commission recommended notes become unlimited legal tender; silver dollars become legal tender up to HK$10; notes should be convertible into silver bullion, not coins; silver should be stored by government; and a Currency Board should be established in London, with a Currency Officer in Hong Kong.[11] Anyone should be able to exchange silver bullion for notes which would provide an automatic corrective to the note supply. The Currency Committee accepted these recommendations, although the Treasury thought that as long as the Hongkong and Shanghai Bank increased the note supply when needed, the present system, although imperfect should continue.[12]

Hong Kong was not prepared to act upon these recommendations.[13] Local public opinion was still against change and, without the Secretary of State's political support, no matter how sound the Currency Committee's recommendations, there was no imperative for the Governor to act. Although the Currency Committee could do little but accept this it still disliked leaving Hongkong and Shanghai Bank's Chief Manager in virtual control of the note issue.[14] Peel had also passed Grayburn's comments on the proposed changes to the Colonial Office. The Commission members were particularly dismissive of his arguments against their proposals and thought he had overstated his position and misrepresented their report. Their views were passed to Peel who replied that there was still no local support for change and still proposed to take no action. In any case, nothing could happen until the end of 1935 when the Hongkong Bank's new storage facilities would be available.[15] The Currency Committee, somewhat reluctantly, accepted that matters wait until then.[16]

China comes off silver

The US Silver Purchase Act of June 1934 required the US Treasury to keep 25% of its reserves in silver. This pushed up silver prices and led to a massive export of silver from China. The Currency Committee was in a quandary amid the uncertainty of what China might do. It had previously concluded that Hong Kong should remain on the silver standard as long as China did but had no contingency plan if it did not. The Colonial Office admitted it did not know what to do, or if it should do anything at all. The Bank of England thought Hong Kong should remain linked to whatever currency system China had. Both they and the Crown Agents bemoaned the fact that Hong Kong had no mechanism, or personnel, to monitor and react to the changing situation.[17] Campbell thought the Committee should have a contingency plan in case China acted suddenly and there wasn't time to consider what Hong Kong should do next.

Matters became clearer when, on 15 October 1934, China imposed an export tax on silver. There were chaotic scenes in Hong Kong's local exchange market a few days later when the silver price in London fell. Peel's view, or rather Grayburn's upon whose advice he was reported to have acted, was that government "saw no reason to take any special steps" in regard to the "... action of China in regard to silver".[18] A few days later, the *South China Morning Post* commended the Hong Kong government's lack of panic and "hoped ... that the Hong Kong government's passivity conceals a plan that can be set moving quickly".[19]

There was no plan. Although the Colonial Office Currency Committee could now discuss Hong Kong's position in relation to action by China, it came to no firm conclusion. It recognised that as long as Hong Kong remained on silver, the value of its currency would be dictated by US silver policy. It considered that Hong Kong should not follow China blindly but also thought it should take no immediate action. The kernel of a plan started to develop when the Committee agreed to a suggestion from Norman Young of the Treasury that he draw up a contingency plan for Hong Kong. This later became the basis of the managed currency regime Hong Kong adopted some twelve months later.[20]

The Currency Committee were also frustrated by Hong Kong's inability to appreciate the harm being done by the rise in the value of its currency to its trade and economy.[21] The view in Hong Kong, however, was that China had only temporarily abandoned the silver standard and that it would revert when the situation improved. Although Peel was told that this was not a reason for inaction, he was not to be persuaded to act contrary to locally perceived wisdom.[22]

Hong Kong comes off silver

Matters settled until, in the middle of April 1935, a further increase in the silver price caused the value of the Hong Kong dollar to rise to 40% more than the Shanghai dollar which caused "growing anxiety"[23] in

Hong Kong. The US government had stated its intention to boost the silver price from US72 cents to US$1.29 per ounce and this had paralysed the local currency market. There was also an increased expectation that government would stabilise the Hong Kong dollar, either by coming off silver or banning its export.[24]

Neither Peel nor the Currency Committee knew what to do. Peel thought he might impose an export tax on silver, but seemed unsure. He was concerned that if the Hong Kong dollar was stabilised against sterling it would cause a large devaluation with attendant political risks. He made no firm recommendation and rather plaintively asked the Colonial Office what the Currency Committee had recommended.[25] The Currency Committee was unable to come to any firm view in this inconclusive environment. It agreed the future direction of the silver price was extremely uncertain and that an adviser should be sent out to Hong Kong soonest. It thought Hong Kong should impose a silver export tax as soon as the expert arrived, or before if circumstances warranted. No further action should then be taken until the effects of the silver tax were apparent and "the future of the Chinese currency was clearer". The Committee was also concerned that whatever happened, confidence in the banks should not be shaken.[26]

Peel left Hong Kong on retirement on 17 May and immediately the tenor of telegrams to London changed. Under his temporary successor, Thomas Southorn, they became crisper and more self-assured. His first one on currency started unequivocally with the words "essential factors of the situation are". These were firstly secrecy, for fear of flight from the currency; secondly, government must be prepared to act if necessary; thirdly, token coin must be available to replace silver coinage; and lastly, devaluation must include temporary stabilisation on sterling. He stated clearly that "unless the silver policy of the USA is radically modified I feel that Hong Kong must devalue" which he recognised would be unpopular. He would prefer to await the British Treasury representative, Norman Young's arrival before taking action although that might not prove possible. Telegrams were not normally drafted by Governors personally. This, however, was not a normal situation because of the need for secrecy. Telegrams on this subject were probably drafted by Peel and Southorn themselves and were thus more reflective of their own views and outlook than would normally be expected.

Young arrived in Hong Kong on 27 June and quickly sounded out local opinion. He thought it was not the right time to impose a silver tax. Since April the situation had now settled. Local opinion thought the fall in the silver price since May indicated a change in US silver policy and that Hong Kong had no need to act. The local business view was that Hong Kong should not act independently from China and that confidence in Hong Kong would be damaged if it was thought it went off the silver standard for some temporary gain. There was also a feeling that the worst was now over and that if Hong Kong devalued now there would be an outcry and demand for compensation. He also reported that the price of foodstuffs, especially rice, had fallen, as had rents, and that wages were falling.[27]

The Colonial Office and the Treasury did not think China would return to the silver standard soon and thought Hong Kong should impose a silver export tax. Southorn thought there was no need for a tax but the Colonial Office was again not prepared to insist action be taken in the absence of local support.[28] It also thought local opinion that the recent fall in the silver price betokened a change of heart in US policy was mistaken. Locally, although the banks were exporting large quantities of silver, this had not upset the silver market. This seemed to have settled in the knowledge that Sir Frederick Leith-Ross from the British Treasury and Britain's currency advisor on currency reform to the Chinese government was in China and Young, also from the British Treasury, was in Hong Kong.

Discussions between departments in London continued throughout the autumn in efforts to develop contingent action plans. It was felt that Hong Kong should come off the silver standard as soon as China formally did. There was debate about whether it should impose a silver tax before stabilising on sterling or whether it should immediately stabilise on sterling and, if so, at what exchange rate. This would have resulted in an immediate fall in the Hong Kong dollar's value which, although desired, it was thought better done in two stages, moving first of all to a managed currency to allow the value to adjust gradually. Hong Kong's silver would also have to be sold to provide backing for the managed currency. Leith-Ross thought the US might buy it at the same time as they took China's silver. The Secretary of State was not personally involved in these discussions and was happy to leave "the C(olonial) O(ffice) experts to do their best that they can for Hong Kong, as I am sure they will do."[29]

On Monday, 4 November 1935, the Chinese government announced that all silver was to be surrendered to the Central Reserve Bank in exchange for banknotes issued by them. Banknotes would then no longer be exchanged for silver but were to be convertible into other currencies. The Colonial Office authorised Hong Kong to impose a silver export tax if thought necessary. Southorn, in consultation with Grayburn, replied that he would prefer to wait until hearing whether the US would buy Hong Kong's silver. If they would, he would then prefer to stabilise immediately on sterling.[30] The Colonial Office, and to a somewhat lesser extent the Treasury, both favoured this but the Bank of England thought Hong Kong should come off silver but operate a managed currency before stabilising on sterling.[31]

By Wednesday, 6 November, the three leasing banks advised Southorn that an embargo on the export of silver should be made. They had already refused to exchange notes for silver except to *bone fide* customers. They wanted, however, to be able to meet forward contracts already made and be allowed to ship silver on Saturday before the embargo was enacted. Southorn recommended this as they had made these deals in good faith and he needed their co-operation on any new scheme. The Colonial Office concurred. Southorn did not want to switch to a managed currency before stabilising on sterling as the value of the Hong Kong dollar had dropped and there was less need to do so. It would also have been difficult to manage the currency if it was pegged to neither sterling nor the Chinese dollar. Southorn also preferred to await news on the sale of Hong Kong's silver to the US before changing.[32]

At noon on Saturday 9 November, the Hong Kong government announced an embargo on the export of silver. There had been much speculation that morning whether the government would stabilise on sterling but that didn't happen.[33] The issue of whether Hong Kong should switch straight to sterling or switch firstly to a managed currency was put before the Chancellor of the Exchequer. He wrote to the Secretary of State with what amounted to a direction that Hong Kong should not stabilise on sterling but should move to a managed currency.

There were wider political concerns. The US would not buy Hong Kong's silver until it knew what currency regime Hong Kong would adopt. If Hong Kong switched to sterling this would have been contrary to their interests and they might refuse to buy it. More importantly was the Japanese suspicion that China had left silver at Britain's behest and that it would later switch to sterling and join the sterling bloc. Neither the US nor France wanted China to switch to sterling. Hong Kong switching now might be thought a precursor to China doing so and might antagonise others. It was also thought that if Hong Kong switched to sterling before China did, if it ever did so, it might be taken as a lack of faith in China's ability to manage its own currency. The Chancellor requested, therefore, that Hong Kong be instructed to institute a managed currency.[34] The Secretary of State accepted the Chancellor's views and Southorn was told to introduce legislation to implement a managed currency. Importantly, he also instructed that it should be kept in step with the Shanghai dollar.[35]

This was a standard which, as Young commented "could not at the moment be expected to command confidence in the Colony" and the banks' co-operation would have been, in his view doubtful. The Hong Kong government, however, had one edge over the banks. The banks feared that the US would stop buying silver and wanted the Hong Kong government to sell their silver forward. Before it could do so, it had to take over the banks' silver. The banks therefore agreed to the proposed legislation under which the banks surrendered their silver in return for silver certificates which they could use as backing for the note-issue. The government would then sell the silver and use the proceeds to manage the currency. This was kept on par with the Shanghai dollar, which Shanghai kept on a par with sterling which helped maintain confidence in Hong Kong's new currency regime.[36]

The Currency Bill was introduced into the Legislative Council on 5 December without any prior notice and was passed in one sitting without debate. Under this law, banknotes became legal tender, the government took over all silver held against banknotes by the banks in exchange for notes of indebtedness and all other silver in Hong Kong had to be sold to government within one month. An Exchange Fund was established under the Colonial Treasurer, with Grayburn and Young as members, which had power to sell foreign exchange and silver. The Hong Kong dollar was now a managed currency.[37]

It was welcomed for bringing stability to what had become a very uncertain currency situation. The *South China Morning Post* said in an editorial that,

> The Government's measures have been received with encouraging satisfaction, and Government may rest assured that in the currency reform it (so far) enjoys the community's full confidence.[38]

These measures, as has been seen, were proposed but not authored by the Hong Kong government who had relied either upon experts in the British Treasury, or Grayburn, the Chief Manager of the Hongkong and Shanghai Bank in Hong Kong, for advice on currency policy. London had long recognised that the Hong Kong government did not even have "a competent officer charged with the duty of watching the (currency) situation".[39] In both London and Hong Kong, Grayburn's views on Hong Kong's currency had held sway. If, as Young reported, Grayburn had advised Peel in October 1934 that no action need be taken in respect of the currency, it was likely that he had also been advising Peel long before that. On that occasion, in the absence of any policy formulation capacity within his government, Peel had declined to accept London's legitimate concerns and recommendations and, in accepting his advice, had allowed Grayburn to set policy. The Hong Kong government had shown it had neither the capacity to formulate its own policy, let alone carry it out.

Southorn demonstrated that he was more his own master but was also at the mercy of events outside his control. He was also prevented from following his own preferred policy of switching to sterling although in practice that is what happened. This was because of the primacy of wider

British metropolitan policy preferences which overshadowed those of Hong Kong. These came, not from the Secretary of State but from his senior in Cabinet, the Chancellor of the Exchequer. It is notable that the Secretary of State was remarkably absent from this policy debate during the six and a half years of this saga. It was seen as a technical issue but, at this level, it was unable to trump the political concerns of the local business community in Hong Kong under a weak Governor. Nor were there any political concerns expressed in Britain at the weak state of Hong Kong's currency which might have added some political pressure from London. It was only from December 1935 that Hong Kong had a mechanism with which to manage the currency, a mechanism which was to last for another 38 years.

Mui tsai: Following instructions

Clementi left Hong Kong in February 1930 and was replaced by Sir William Peel. Before he left for Hong Kong, Peel was interviewed by Passfield and Shiels who

> made it very clear what the intention of His Majesty's Government was, and we impressed upon him the importance of carrying out the regulations in all thoroughness.[40]

Peel's quiet and steady implementation of these instructions changed the shape of the political forces involved. The Secretary of State now had an ally and not an obstacle in the Hong Kong government as Peel moved quickly to turn the local Chinese elites from opponents into ostensible supporters. Peel mobilised the District Watch Committee but to different ends. It now supported the regulations and asked that "owners of *mui tsai* ... carry out the requirements of the law without further delay".[41] By the end of the registration period, 4,368 *mui tsai* had been registered.[42] Shiels considered this "very satisfactory" but results might have been better but for Clementi's lack of enthusiasm in implementing the regulations. Not everyone was supportive. The Anti-*Mui Tsai* Society claimed there were 8,000 *mui tsai* in Hong Kong and that half had not been registered.[43] In Britain, the Anti-Slavery Society also thought that the number of *mui tsai* registered was too low.[44] Peel disputed these claims and said their figures were overstated.[45] This time, however, Hong Kong had a stalwart ally in Dr Shiels who defended both the registration process and the progress made by Hong Kong.[46]

The Colonial Office also came under pressure to register adopted daughters, a mechanism some thought was being used to disguise *mui tsai*. Peel, however, was this time able to successfully argue against the need for doing so. He now had authoritative sounding figures on numbers of *mui tsai* and he argued that, with inspectors in place, it would be difficult for owners to disguise them as "adopted daughters". The District Watch Committee and Dr S. W. Tso, a Legislative Council and District Watch Committee member, supported him on this. He did, however, say that he would register adopted daughters if there was evidence to show they were being used to evade the *mui tsai* legislation. Otherwise, because the District Watch Committee had been so supportive, he did not want to risk offending them unless it was "clearly necessary to prevent abuse".[47] The Colonial Office accepted Peel's view.

Loseby Committee

In 1934, the League of Nations' Permanent Advisory Committee of Experts on Slavery produced a report on *mui tsai* in Hong Kong and Malaya,[48] written by Sir George Maxwell, a former Colonial Secretary of Malaya. He sent a draft to the Colonial Office asking for Governors' comments. In response, Peel appointed a Committee in December 1934 to review and comment on Maxwell's report.[49] It was chaired by F. H. Loseby, a local lawyer and Executive Officer of the Kowloon Branch of the Hong Kong Society for the Protection of Children. Its members were J. M. Wong, a member of Stubbs' 1922 Commission and a member of the Anti-*Mui Tsai* Society; Miss D. Brazier in charge of Salvation Army social work in Hong Kong and Tang Shiu-kin,[50] a District Watch Committee member in his early thirties. They were also all on the Executive Council of the Hong Kong Society for the Protection of Children and J. M. Wong and Tang Shiu-kin had "frequently served on the committee of the Po Leung Kuk". Although its members were hardly unaware of the challenges facing disadvantaged children in Hong Kong, the Committee's report was disappointing. It lacked clarity and was poorly written. It urged that an enquiry be held into the sale and adoption of Chinese girls; stated that the law regulating *mui tsai* was imprecise; and that accurate figures could not be had, despite the figures the government had been reporting to London. Any additional funding, they felt "would be employed to better effect in welfare work among the poorer children" rather than enlarging the *mui tsai* inspectorate.[51] The report was much criticised when it was published in Britain.[52]

Woods Commission

In response, the Secretary of State quickly established his own Commission to examine the *mui tsai* issue in both Hong Kong and Malaya.[53] Caldecott, who had replaced Peel as Governor, welcomed this and reported that, since the passage of the 1923 Ordinance, the *mui tsai* system was now held in "popular contempt". He hoped, however, that the Commission "would set about their task in an understanding and sympathetic manner".[54] Not waiting for the Commission to report, he introduced a bill in May 1936 into the Legislative Council. This allowed the courts to impose custodial sentences for offences against *mui tsai* and brought Hong Kong into line with the Straits Settlements. It passed with official and British unofficial support[55] as, unlike his successor, Caldecott thought it unnecessary to try and win over the Chinese unofficials.

The Commission was chaired by Sir Wilfred Woods, a former Financial Secretary of Ceylon and respected former colonial civil servant. Its members were C. A. Willis, formerly of the Sudan Civil Service[56] and Miss Edith Picton-Turbervill,[57] a former Labour MP known for her militant feminism.[58] The Haslewoods were among the first to give evidence. They had never compromised in their campaign against the *mui tsai* system and had staunchly taken the British and Hong Kong governments to task. In their evidence before the Commission, however, they had to admit that excessive cruelty was uncommon and that "the moral dangers of the system … were debatable".[59] The Commission also took evidence from a deputation of societies led by the British Commonwealth League,[60] from Norman Smith,[61] Hong Kong's Colonial Secretary on leave in Britain, and from Sir George Maxwell. It then sailed for Hong Kong and Malaya and returned to Britain in August.

The Commission produced two reports. The Majority Report largely vindicated measures already in force. It pointed out that *mui tsai* was a system of domestic servitude and not vice; that in Hong Kong there had been "rapid progress towards abolition"; that "legislation had been enforced with a large measure of success"; and that registration had been largely complete. It recommended an increase in the Secretary for Chinese Affairs' powers to protect *mui tsai* and that girls' names be removed from the *mui tsai* register when they reached eighteen. It did not recommend registration of adopted daughters because this would be "administratively impracticable and politically objectionable".

The Minority Report, signed by Miss Picton-Turbervill but allegedly drafted by Maxwell,[62] disagreed that registration of *mui tsai* had been reasonably complete. Nor did it believe that "the methods recommended by the Majority Report will achieve the complete abolition of the *Mui Tsai* system". It claimed there was insufficient data to show that the adoption of girls was, in the majority of cases, for a legitimate reason. It recommended a simple system of registration for all adopted girls under 12 without differentiating whether or not they were *mui tsai*. It dismissed the Majority Report's recommendations as, at best, "useful administrative reforms".[63]

The Colonial Office knew of the Minority Report's political sensitivity and thought Miss Picton-Turbervill and Maxwell would gain considerable support in Parliament for its recommendations.[64] It was also supported by the Anti-Slavery Society and the Archbishops of Canterbury and York. Although the Secretary of State favoured early adoption of the Majority Report's recommendations, he told the Hong Kong and the Straits Settlements' Governors that the Minority Report "requires full and sympathetic examination" and enjoined them to consider it accordingly.[65] It was so sensitive that he warned them their comments were likely to be published.

Caldecott, who supported the Majority Report, unexpectedly departed Hong Kong in April 1937. It was left to his temporary successor, Colonial Secretary Norman Smith, to reply in detail. Smith, a long-serving cadet, told the Secretary of State that although he and his official and unofficial advisers supported the Majority Report, they were unanimous in their opposition to the Minority Report. He said he had the support of the District Watch Committee which he described as "the body which is most representative of enlightened Chinese opinion". He disparaged the Anti-*Mui Tsai* Society's views by saying that they could not "be held to outweigh the considered opinion of my principal European and Chinese advisors". The Colonial Office, however, gave very little weight to the District Watch Committee's opposition which it knew carried little or no weight in Britain.[66]

Northcote and reform

Hong Kong's next Governor, Sir Geoffrey Northcote, who arrived on 28 October 1937, quickly decided to go beyond the Majority Report's recommendations and proposed that girls be registered on their second transfer after adoption.[67] He persuaded others to support his cause, including Sir Shouson Chow and Norman Smith, but was initially unable to win over the Secretary of Chinese Affairs, R. A. C. North.[68] He thought this partial step could lay the groundwork for a more general notification of adoptions if that became necessary. The Colonial Office welcomed Northcote's proposals because they represented a major shift in official and unofficial thinking in Hong Kong and for a further extension of registration as became necessary. It also recognised the importance of not being too far ahead of local Chinese opinion and told Northcote that

> if useful results are to be obtained, it is essential that both official and unofficial opinion in Hong Kong should willingly co-operate in any reform, and it is most satisfactory that you have been able to carry important opinion with you in the plan you contemplate.[69]

The Colonial Office also thought Northcote's draft bills appeared to implement "the essential recommendations both of the Majority and Minority Reports of the *Mui Tsai* Commission". It felt that if the bills passed, "Sir Geoffrey Northcote will deserve much credit". Even Miss Picton-Turbervill was reportedly "expressing satisfaction with what the Hong Kong government is now proposing to do".[70]

The District Watch Committee was persuaded to support the wider registration of adopted daughters. Northcote generously accredited this to North's efforts, with the assistance of leading Chinese elites.[71] Perhaps as much was owed to Northcote's powers of persuasion and his willingness to use them. It was left to Legislative Council member M. K. Lo[72] to sum up the feeling of leading Chinese in Hong Kong. He felt that neither those in favour of further controls over transferred girls nor those against could claim the facts supported them and them alone. He therefore considered that

> the conflicting views should be subject to the test of trial and experiment; if opponents of the reform should prove to be right, no harm would have been done and the inestimable boon to the social conscience of the Colony that here there was no 'problem' to solve would have been achieved; if the advocates for the reform should prove to be right, then a great blot on the fair name of the Colony would have been removed.[73]

On passage of the bill, the Secretary of State was confident that "no administrative effort will be lacking to ensure this efficient operation". The number of registered *mui tsai* fell from 1,141 in November 1938 to only 127 by May 1941.[74] After 1945, *mui tsai* virtually ceased to exist in Hong Kong[75] and, in 1969, the Female Domestic Service Ordinance, introduced by Stubbs in 1922 with so much trepidation, was repealed as being "obsolete, spent and unnecessary".[76]

Northcote exhibited the attributes of a leader. It was he who persuaded his senior cadets and sympathetic unofficials to support the Minority Report's recommendations. He decided the policy he wanted, worked hard to win wide political support and ensured it was implemented effectively. Within a short period, he was able to exercise autonomy from the sovereign power and from the power of the local elites whose influence, as shall be seen, continued to grow. This required leadership and could only have come from the Governor. Although a very different milieu from the 1920s, as many now viewed the keeping of *mui tsai* with distaste, it was nonetheless a very real achievement. It also brought a stop to the concerted campaign against *mui tsai* in Britain that had continued throughout the 1930s.

War Revenue Ordinance 1940

The prospect of an income tax was not new to Hong Kong. It had first been mooted by the Colonial Treasurer in 1917 to help raise funds for Britain's war effort but was shelved as being too difficult and inappropriate for Hong Kong.[77] In 1922, an Interdepartmental Committee in London chaired by the Colonial Office suggested that colonies without an income tax should implement one. This was to try and establish a common income tax policy throughout the colonial empire although why, apart from resolving certain technical issues, was unclear. It proposed a Model Income Tax Ordinance which it suggested "be used as a guide by all Colonies which may in the future find it necessary to introduce an income tax".[78] Hong Kong considered an income tax unsuitable because of its "peculiar circumstances ... and the Chinese attitude towards Income Tax".[79] Also, in most years since 1916, it had been making a comfortable surplus of revenue over expenditure and there would have been little political incentive to try and find new sources of revenue.[80] The Colonial Office seemingly accepted that "some temporary shortcoming in this direction [was] fully understood"[81] and did not press Hong Kong on the matter.

In 1938, the prospect of an income tax was again raised obliquely by the Governor, Northcote. He wanted to secure additional permanent and more stable sources of revenue to pay for new although unspecified social services.[82] He established a Taxation Committee to examine how best this could be done. Its Chairman, Caine, the Financial Secretary,[83] strongly advocated the imposition of a full income tax.[84] Its members were two unofficial Legislative Council Members, M. K. Lo and J. J. Paterson of Jardines, an Executive Council Member and three others, Grayburn, also an Executive Council member, D. J. Sloss, Vice-Chancellor of the University of Hong Kong and a confidante of Northcote's, and J. Fleming, a partner in the accountants' firm Lowe Bingham and Mathews. It concluded, *inter alia*, that "the advantages of an efficiently administered income tax over other forms are overwhelming from the point of view of equity" and recommended that an expert be sought to advise on the feasibility of its implementation in Hong Kong.[85]

When the Legislative Council debated the Committee's recommendations in October 1939, Britain was already at war with Germany. The government now proposed that revenue from an income tax should be offered as a free gift to the British war effort. Nevertheless, the question of whether an income tax should be implemented was hotly debated in what has been referred to as one of the most contentious Legislative Council debates held up to that time.[86] The unofficials argued that an income tax would be costly; that it could not be levied on an equitable basis given the changing nature of the Chinese population; that the unwillingness of many Chinese to divulge details of their business and personal arrangements would make it unworkable; that it would drive capital and investment away from Hong Kong; and that it would be easily evaded. The Hong Kong government had to tread warily since the Governor had said he could hardly use the official majority to impose taxes whose proceeds were to be offered as a free gift.[87] In view of this opposition, the Governor referred the matter to another committee, the War Revenue Committee. This was a much larger Committee. It consisted of four government officials and representatives from the business community, including British expatriates, local Chinese and local non-Chinese. It did not recommend a full income tax but instead recommended that separate taxes be levied upon business profits, property and salaries. In March 1940, after further debate in the Legislative Council, the committee's recommendations were passed as the War Revenue Ordinance. It included a clause to repeal its provisions the year after war ended. A tax on interest was added the following year.[88]

Whose policy was this? This is perhaps less clear than might be imagined from the evidence. Firstly, it could be argued that it was Northcote's policy. Although he did not specifically refer to income tax in the Legislative Council in October 1938, it was most likely that he was aware that this was the only practicable option. He might have been influenced by an imperial need for Hong Kong to contribute towards Britain's impending defence needs rather than a desire to improve Hong Kong's social services.[89] However, Northcote was consistent in his support for the development of social services in Hong Kong. This was a constant theme throughout his time as Governor: in a speech to the Social Service Centre of the Churches in 1940; in a private letter to Lord Moyne, Secretary of State; in speeches he made shortly before his departure and in the valedictions he received from the local press on his departure.[90] An increased reasonably consistent tax yield would have been a necessary prerequisite for this goal.

It could also be argued that the policy to impose an income tax was Caine's. It is difficult to assess whether the proposal originated from Northcote and was faithfully implemented by Caine, or the extent to which Caine influenced Northcote's views. Caine was described as a "keen advocate of income tax" by a member of the Taxation Committee[91] and it is clear from that Committee's report that he strongly favoured an income tax. Caine was certainly a modernising influence on Hong Kong government policy. He had earlier supported greater spending on education in Hong Kong.[92] He was also identified as the originator of an ingenious proposal to make use of the Exchange Fund to fund the development of social housing in Hong Kong.[93] The eventual solution of the scheduler system of taxes would also appear to have been largely Caine's creation. After the November 1939 Legislative Council debate, and shortly before he left Hong Kong in December 1939, he had adeptly combined the elements that the unofficials could agree on in terms of a property tax, a corporation tax, a business profits tax and what was in effect a salaries tax designed to be paid largely by the Europeans in Hong Kong. This was the origin of the scheduler system of taxes in the War Revenue Ordinance.[94]

The role of the unofficials in the formulation of this policy is complex. Their principal role was the formulation of the detail of the policy. They were intrinsically opposed to any form of income tax. For the Chinese unofficials this was based mainly on their opposition to anyone prying into the private business affairs of their compatriots. For the British unofficials, their opposition was based more on their utter conviction that there would be widespread evasion and that it could not therefore be levied equitably. The advent of war brought a very different complexion to the debate and made it difficult for the British unofficials to continue to oppose it. Their desire to find a way out of their previous opposition would have helped in reaching their agreement to the eventual form of taxation. The importance of their role was also enhanced by Northcote's statement that he would not use the official majority to push this measure through. Their agreement to something therefore became an integral part of the decision-making process. The Colonial Office also accepted that for this reason the use of the official majority was "out of the question". The Colonial Office was also looking ahead to the situation after the war when the provisions of the War Revenue Ordinance would lapse. It thought that any post-war permanent income tax would have to be agreed to with the "express approval" of the unofficial members.[95]

Hong Kong was being pushed to modernise through the leadership of the Governor and a particularly competent Financial Secretary. To succeed, however, they needed the acquiescence of the unofficials, and indirectly of the leading members of the Chinese and European communities they represented. To obtain this, the formulation of the details of the policy was dictated by them.

Evacuation

In 1940, the unofficials showed very clearly that they were prepared to use their power to refuse to authorise expenditure even when this was needed to comply with a British government directive. In order to remove all unnecessary civilians from Hong Kong, the British War Cabinet had ordered the evacuation of all women and children unless the women were performing essential services. This did not apply to the whole population but only to that very small proportion that were of "pure" European descent. On receipt of this instruction, Norman Smith the Officer Administering the Government, had simply asked the Finance Committee to approve an initial token sum of HK$10,000 to help pay for this.

The unofficials unanimously opposed this request. The European members did so because they thought it unnecessary and pointless and that it smacked of "deportation". The Chinese members disliked it because it was discriminatory and because the taxpayer was being asked to pay for something which would benefit only a small proportion of the population. As Leo d'Almada e Castro warned, "an appreciable strain" had been put "on the loyalty of a large section of the community". M. K. Lo, however, set out a more fundamental concern,

> This [Legislative] Council was never consulted on the question of compulsory evacuation. The Finance Committee is now being asked to give a blank cheque in respect of an expenditure which this Council has never approved and for an object which has dumbfounded the Colony and caused universal complaint and criticism.[96]

Although he sympathised with the plight of those who had been unwillingly required to leave, the Chinese unofficials, as representatives of the majority of the population for whom no plans had been made, could not vote for the proposed item of expenditure.

Smith seemed at a loss. The item was ostensibly held over to another meeting but eventually the British government paid for the evacuation.[97] The unofficials had learned that their views could prevail over those of the British government when they concerned issues about which they felt keenly and where their arguments were strong. They also learned that, under such circumstances, they could force the Hong Kong government to renegotiate matters with the sovereign power.

Conclusions

The Hong Kong government's ability to formulate policy was very limited. Currency was a closed book to Peel and his government and even the otherwise erudite Clementi seemed to want little to do with the subject. Southorn showed more of a grasp of the issues when he became OAG on Peel's departure. Without Caine, Northcote would not have had expertise within government to formulate policy on income tax. Nor would he have had anyone as persuasive as Caine to push it through and be able to best Grayburn in debate. As a result, Governors relied heavily on external agents to help formulate policy. Peel seemed to have been in thrall to Grayburn's advice on how to respond to the various currency crises that arose. Northcote had to respond to the two Woods Commission reports on *mui tsai*. Without Caine's involvement it is questionable how much progress would have been made in formulating policy over income tax. At this level, it would appear that the Hong Kong government had little autonomy; its dearth of policy formulation capacity resulted in it being dictated to by others. Within this, however, lay the seeds for future autonomy. The implementation of these policies resulted in the production of a future capacity for policy implementation. Governors could then talk persuasively about the current *mui tsai* situation. Once the Exchange Fund was established it had a very clear mechanism through which to manage the currency. The establishment of the provisions of the War Revenue Ordinance created a department with personnel who gained experience of assessment and collection of revenue from direct taxation.

The role of the unofficials was also brought into sharp focus. They played a decisive role during the income tax debates. They had to agree to something that they would have preferred not to agree to. In this, the Hong Kong government was able to get its own way, but at a cost. It also had to be flexible enough to agree to something that it would have preferred not to have. It also set the scene for the implementation of what became permanent direct taxes after the war. Here, the Governor and Caine played a role akin to that of Carpenter's "bureaucratic entrepreneurs". This was also evident when Peel and Northcote worked hard to obtain unofficial support for the extension of statutory regulation over *mui tsai*. Without Northcote's advocacy of the need for an income tax, even Caine's policy formulation skills may have been insufficient.

The role of the senior cadets in these episodes seems less clear. This may have been due to the absence of pre-war Hong Kong government records and the fact that official correspondence with Britain was issued in the name of the Governor. There is, however, some circumstantial evidence which would suggest they played little role in the formulation of policy. As has been seen, Northcote, had not, at least initially, persuaded North of the need to extend regulation over *mui tsai*. Smith had seemed at a loss over the handling of the evacuation issue with the Finance Committee. He was also to be superseded as OAG by General Norton because the Admiralty persuaded the Colonial Office that he was not of the calibre to cope with emergencies likely to arise during the war. The cadets' lack of innovative policy making capabilities can also be deduced from the various modernising innovations which Caine was able to institute during his time as Financial Secretary, changes which had somehow eluded the long-serving cadets. What impact this had on planning for the post-war future of Hong Kong is the subject of Chapter 5.

5

Autonomy and the Threat to Sovereignty

> I find it more and more difficult to believe that the nature of our administration in Hong Kong will not be radically changed in all sorts of ways if and when it returns to British occupation.
>
> Sidney Caine,
> Head, Economic Department, Colonial Office,
> 13 February 1942[1]

The British Crown Colony of Hong Kong was captured by the Japanese army on Christmas Day 1941. British civil government was restored on 1 May 1946 in a form very similar to that of the pre-1941 government. So were many of its policies and personnel. This was not what the Colonial Office had envisaged in 1942. It had concluded then that a restored Hong Kong government should be different in both form and substance. This desire for change had later to be sublimated to wider pressures and constraints. The US and Chinese governments had pressed for Hong Kong's return to China after Japan's defeat. The British government, after slight internal equivocation, remained firm in its resolve to recover Hong Kong. Detailed planning for the restoration of government in Hong Kong had been carried out in co-operation with other British government departments. It had also been conducted within the constraints of an agreement with the US on the administration of liberated overseas territories which had been under the administration of an allied power before capture by the enemy.

The nature of desired changes, why they were so desired, and why they could not be realised will be examined in this chapter. This will include an assessment of how the Hong Kong Planning Unit (HKPU), established to plan the restoration of government in Hong Kong, was able to exercise a degree of autonomy; how the Colonial Office's ability to exercise power over it was constrained; and what impact, if any, the British Military Administration's relative freedom from Colonial Office control had on the longer-term development of Hong Kong's autonomy.

Identifying the need for change

Hong Kong's surrender, followed shortly by the fall of Malaya and Singapore, was a major blow to British prestige in Asia. It was felt especially hard in the Colonial Office.[2] Officials began to consider what might have gone wrong and what changes might be needed in a post-war Hong Kong government. An initial catalyst was the energetic Anglican bishop of Hong Kong, Ronald Hall,[3] who was renowned for his support of the under-privileged. He was in the US when the Japanese invaded Hong Kong. In London in January 1942, he left a detailed note at the Colonial Office setting out what he thought should happen in Hong Kong after the war. His observations on the cadets were particularly revealing and insightful. They were, he wrote, "excellent material [who] inevitably became parochial after 10 or 12 years confinement in the very limited and particular sphere of Hong Kong". He thought they should become less of an exclusive club whose "social knowledge was dated by their 'year'[4] at Oxford or Cambridge". There should be women, Chinese and Eurasians in the Hong Kong cadet service (provided they were British subjects) as well as graduates of other universities of the empire. There should also be a professional Town Clerk "with experience ... as a Town Clerk ... in an English industrial city."[5]

Sidney Caine, Hong Kong's Financial Secretary from 1937 to 1939, largely corroborated the Bishop's views. He thought that although the cadets were intellectually sound "they went to seed very badly owing to the conditions under which they worked, and the close circle in which they moved". Junior cadets were given too little responsibility and "nobody of less than twenty years seniority had any business to express any views about high policy which was a matter for his seniors and betters". Although the cadet service had successfully achieved its original goals of establishing a high-quality, efficient and incorrupt administration, it had also engendered a "tradition of superiority [which] has ... lingered on and the Cadet Service still remains very separate from the rest of the Government Service". This outlook was now obsolete because other branches of government had improved enormously. He also felt their mores and ways of thinking were at least twenty years behind the times, the result of the limited and infrequent contact they had with Britain. Like Hall, Caine thought, if somewhat vaguely, that the loss of Hong Kong was an opportunity to implement radical change and found it difficult to believe this would not happen. In April 1942, the Colonial Office Committee on Post-War Problems re Malaya and Hong Kong accepted that "the arrangements existing before the Japanese occupation would not be restored. We have to envisage a new deal."[6]

Wider concerns

These views reflected a growing unease over whether Britain's loss of its Far Eastern colonies had been due to deficiencies in colonial government. More fundamentally, exactly what Britain expected from its colonies and what role its senior colonial civil servants should play in achieving these expectations was being questioned. In September 1942, the Colonial Office established a committee to examine what lessons could be learned from the loss of Malaya and Hong Kong.[7] Its Chairman was Sir William Battershill[8] with Gent and Colonel Rolleston[9] as its members. It found there was a need to adopt a "wartime mentality" which it defined as

> an alertness of mind to a new situation, a sense of grim realism and unhesitating recognition of the new values ... and a readiness to see a change of tempo and method in administration.

In the longer term, the Committee realised that administrative procedures should be simplified and that it should also be made easier to dismiss or require the retirement of under-performing senior personnel. It was also necessary to devolve more authority to lower levels which included giving Governors more financial freedom to authorise additional expenditure. Such measures were thought to be equally important in facing the new challenges expected upon the restoration of peace. The Colonial Office Director of Recruiting, Sir Ralph Furse, thought that "the cutting out of dead wood is not only a war problem. It is highly important for the efficiency of the Service in the post-war era".

The Committee also considered the more fundamental question of the purpose and goals of colonial administration. Colonial officials, they considered, were too busy focusing on day-to-day routine administration when they "should have been thinking in terms of high policy". There was also the question of the relationship between a colonial government and the people it governed, especially when "Government was alien to the whole of the population save to the small minority of Europeans". It noted too the absence of "that sentiment of common purpose between the administration and the people which is so essential to all progressive government".[10]

In the summer of 1942, David MacDougall, a Hong Kong government senior official[11] had already addressed these issues in two articles in *The Times*. In the first, he had praised the efficiency and rectitude of British colonial administration in Hong Kong and Malaya. These attributes, he wrote, had "in a troubled era ... stood as exemplars of order, peace and decency". But in the second he asked what it was all for. He felt there was "something ... missing from both Government and governed which prevented the fusion of the community into a living whole". The material aspects of colonial administration, although "wholly desirable, brilliantly conceived and ably executed" were not enough. There needed to be a common purpose and that was patently lacking. The blame for this, he thought, lay squarely with the lack of interest shown from home. In response, N. L. Smith, Hong Kong's recently retired Colonial Secretary, claimed there had been no popular demand for reform from Hong Kong's Chinese population. The Hong Kong government had even had to deflect criticism from leading expatriates that it was too helpful and idealistic towards the local Chinese population. He did not, however, make mention of the Hong Kong government's general lack of direction or strategic view. It was as if he had failed to fully comprehend the broad nature of MacDougall's criticisms and, in failing to do so, had helped substantiate them. The Colonial Office did not even consider Smith's views merited a response.[12]

By the end of 1942, Colonial Office officials had begun to display a quiet determination that Hong Kong should be governed differently after the restoration of British administration. Planning for Hong Kong's recovery, however, was not to proceed on this basis. By mid-1942 it was being overshadowed by disputes with the US and China over the more fundamental question of whether Hong Kong would remain British after Japan's defeat.

The threat to Britain's sovereignty

Britain's defeat in Hong Kong quickly caused reverberations in China. In 1942, people close to the Chinese government expected Hong Kong to return to China after the war. Similar Chinese views were reported from Washington although officially the Chinese government's view continued to be that Hong Kong was a British colony. The US government was critical of British colonial policy in Asia and blamed Britain's defeat on "inherent faults of 'Imperialism' and selfish exploitation of the territories and peoples concerned". Foreign Office officials were so concerned about the US view that at a meeting in June 1942, Ashley Clarke, a senior Foreign Office official, told Gent that "we must be prepared to give-up the non-essentials in order to maintain the really important things". Gent took a different stance. He thought Britain's views

> must be based on what we believed to be right rather than solely on what would be the best moves from the point of view of foreign politics.

At ministerial level there was a stronger sense that Hong Kong must remain British after the war. Secretary of State for the Colonies Lord Cranbourne, thought that Britain's record of administration was "not one of which we need be ashamed. We created Singapore and Hong Kong, two of the greatest ports in the Pacific, out of nothing".[13] The one exception he made was defence. Here Britain had clearly failed its colonies. The blame, however, could not be Britain's alone. The US, he thought, would have to take some responsibility for its previous inaction. He was prepared to take a flexible line on Hong Kong's future if necessary. At a Cabinet-level meeting, chaired by Clement Atlee, at that time Secretary of State for the Dominions, Cranbourne stated that

> we should declare our readiness to discuss Hong Kong in return for certain advantages. If conditions in China were not favourable to such discussions or if such advantages were not forthcoming, the proposal would naturally fall to the ground.[14]

Over the remaining months of 1942, the Colonial and Foreign Offices attempted to produce a charter on colonial policy to counter American criticism. Churchill expressed his determination that Britain would remain a colonial power very clearly. In his Mansion House speech of 10 November 1942 he famously announced that he had "not become the King's First Minister in order to preside over the liquidation of the British Empire".[15] This determination was again shown in the latter part of 1942 during negotiations between Britain, the US and China over a treaty to abolish extra-territorial rights in China. China had tried to include the reversion of Hong Kong's New Territories, leased from China in 1898, in this treaty. At Foreign Secretary Eden's insistence, Britain resisted saying that the New Territories was outside the treaty's scope. The US supported Britain and, without US support, China acquiesced. After its signing in January 1943, the Chinese passed a note to the British ambassador in Chungking stating they reserved the right to raise the issue at a later date. The British side merely acknowledged receipt of this note[16] but it was a question mark which was to hang over Hong Kong's future in the immediate post-war years.

Both Eden, the Foreign Secretary, and the newly appointed Secretary of State for the Colonies, Colonel Oliver Stanley,[17] were quietly determined that Britain should recover Hong Kong after the War. Stanley told the House of Commons that there would be no change in Hong Kong's status and that it was not involved in the extra-territoriality question. Eden instructed his officials that in any question about Hong Kong they should "keep their cards up". At the end of 1942, Britain's policy was not to raise the future of Hong Kong but, if questions were asked, to respond saying there would be no change in the colony's status.[18]

Between early 1942 and early 1943, therefore, policy thinking on Hong Kong had ranged from the need for change after its post-war recovery, to fears it might not even remain British, to a quiet determination to recover it. Hong Kong, however, was within an American, and not a British area of military responsibility. It was within this context that during 1943 the Colonial Office, and, in particular Gent, began to consider the concrete steps necessary to ensure Britain's post-war recovery of Hong Kong.

Origins of the Hong Kong Planning Unit

Planning for the restoration of government in Hong Kong was a complex and tortuous process. The Colonial Office had to negotiate with other British government departments, particularly the War Office and the Foreign Office. It had also to obtain the agreement of the US within the context of an Anglo-American agreement on the administration of former colonies on their liberation. As Hong Kong was in a US strategic sphere, an American would be the head of a military administration upon its liberation. Gent wished to ensure, however, that as far as possible its policies and staff would be British. This was to constrain the opportunities for change in Hong Kong's post-war government structure.

War Office concerns

In February 1943, at the Colonial Office's instigation, consultations started with the War Office on arrangements for a post-war military administration in Malaya. In July 1943, this culminated in the establishment of the Malayan Planning Unit within the War Office. The War Office accepted this because Malaya was within the British strategic sphere and on liberation would have a military administration under a British military commander. However, because Hong Kong was in an American strategic sphere, the War Office was "reluctant to accept the task of planning for territory for which it had no responsibility".[19] This prompted Gent, in June 1943, to start similar planning for Hong Kong, and for North Borneo and Sarawak. He understood that because the War Office could not establish a planning staff for a colony outside a British sphere of influence that the Colonial Office would have to do it.

The War Office did not object but thought

> for the present it would be best for the Colonial Office Planners ... to remain on the Colonial Office establishment and plan in a civilian capacity.

At one point the War Office even tried to evade responsibility for the eventual militarisation of the Hong Kong planning staff because Hong Kong was outside the British strategic sphere.[20] This rather frustrated the Colonial Office. After further consultation, it was agreed that Civil Affairs officers for these territories would only be given military commissions nearer the time when they would be needed in the field. It was also agreed that the War Office would be primarily interested in "the preparation of plans for the immediate re-establishment of administration" whereas the Colonial Office would be responsible for "... the formulation of future policy". As the ultimate aim was the re-establishment of British colonial administration in these territories "all planning for military administration was required to conform so far as possible with civil policy".[21] The Treasury also authorised the Colonial Office to incur expenditure on the Hong Kong Planning Unit but with the proviso that costs should later be recovered from Hong Kong wherever possible.[22]

Foreign Office concerns

The Foreign Office was "entirely in favour" of the Colonial Office's proposal to start planning for the recovery of Hong Kong.[23] Their reply was given in the context of the Civil Affairs Charter under discussion with the Americans and the Dominions on the treatment of Allied territories on liberation from the enemy. A Combined Civil Affairs Committee had been established in Washington in July 1943 to implement this Charter followed by a London sub-committee in February 1944. Article VI, read

> When an enemy occupied territory of the US or the UK or one of the Dominions is to be recovered as the result of an operation combined or otherwise the military directive to be given to the Force Commander concerned will include the policies to be followed in the handling of Civil Affairs as formulated by the government which exercised authority over the territory before enemy occupation.[24]

The Foreign Office thought that the Colonial Office's initiative was essential because under this Article Britain would be responsible for providing directives for the civil administration of recovered British territories. Although there was some ambiguity over the extent to which military commanders of liberated former colonies would be bound by these directives, the existence of staff and policies

> would ... put us in a better position to claim that the civil administration of the territories should be handed back to His Majesty's Government as soon as military considerations permitted.

The British embassy in Washington, DC supported this view. They thought it better if trained British civil personnel were ready with a plan to administer any British territory recovered by the US military and that the US would be likely to accept this. The alternative was that the US might put their own staff in place, already under training in the summer of 1943. The Colonial Office thought this all "most useful".[25]

Despite this support, the Foreign Office refused to participate in discussions with the Colonial Office on Hong Kong's longer-term future. Gent had wanted to consider whether, if post-war the New Territories were under Chinese control, British administration of the remainder of Hong Kong would be viable. Gent had also wanted to discuss the possible impact of the state of Anglo-Chinese relations on Hong Kong's future. This meeting did not take place. The Foreign Office declined to attend because "we would be unable to make any addition to the official viewpoint" and other departments followed this line. The Colonial Office thought "this is a pretty myopic line for the Foreign Office to take". It later transpired that this had been because of Foreign Office officials' interpretation of Eden's earlier instructions to "keep their cards up" and not discuss Hong Kong's future. This did not derail the Colonial Office's efforts to establish the Hong Kong Planning Unit, to which the Foreign Office had, just shortly before, given their support.[26]

Agreement with the US

As part of its agreement with the Colonial Office, the War Office had agreed it would seek the agreement of the US to Britain's provision of civil affairs staff for Hong Kong. Later in 1944, a memorandum on policy in Hong Kong and Borneo was sent through the London Sub-Committee to the Combined Civil Affairs Committee in Washington. This set out that the administration of British Territory in Hong Kong and Borneo should be entrusted to a civil affairs staff comprising mainly British officers. It requested that Military Directives to Force Commanders should include instructions on these lines and informed the US that planning units had already been set up in London. This was agreed to with only slight amendments.[27]

Recruitment and staffing

Gent's strategy in finding personnel to man a Hong Kong Planning Unit was to recruit former or serving Hong Kong government civil servants. For Gent "an essential part for us to play is to do our best to ensure that any Hong Kong personnel available up and down the world is queue'd up in time". Hong Kong officers were "too rare to be disposed of otherwise than on Hong Kong work".[28] There never seemed any doubt that this was the only viable option.

The first head, appointed in August 1943, was N. L. Smith. He had thirty-one years' service as a Hong Kong cadet and had retired on the eve of the Japanese invasion in 1941 after five years as Colonial Secretary and two spells as OAG.[29] It was never intended that he would become Hong Kong's eventual Chief Civil Affairs Officer. He was, however,

> of the personnel available, the most suited to undertake this work since he has had experience in practically all the chief departments of the colony's administration.[30]

By mid-October 1943, Smith had recruited Dr Fehily,[31] a Hong Kong government medical doctor and an engineer, H. S. Rouse[32] recently retired after twenty-seven years' government service in Hong Kong.[33] By December 1943, he had also recruited Dr T. W. Ware[34], a former Hong Kong government medical officer, W. M. Thomson,[35] a cadet with invaluable experience in supplies, and P. C. M. Sedgwick,[36] another cadet. In September 1944, David MacDougall replaced Smith as Head of the HKPU. As well as being a cadet, MacDougall had also had experience overseas representing the Colonial Office in Washington, DC and, in December 1942, had attended an international conference in Mont Tremblant, Quebec on the future of Hong Kong. He had not only had much administrative experience in Hong Kong but had also gained broader exposure in London and overseas.

Recruitment of suitably qualified personnel was an important and difficult part of MacDougall's work. Staff with Hong Kong experience serving in the armed services could not simply be transferred in as would have been the case had the HKPU been under the War Office. Recruitment remained slow and, although the Treasury approved an increase in its establishment to twenty-eight officers in November 1944, by March 1945 only seventeen were in post with one temporary officer working part-time.[37] Of these, fourteen were serving or former Hong Kong government civil servants.[38]

Directives

An important part of the HKPU's work was the drafting of policy directives. These would guide Hong Kong's military commander on liberation on the conduct of civil affairs. This was a new area for the Colonial Office as experience gained to date was to be found in the War Office. No-one in the Colonial Office was clear what the directives should contain or how they should be drafted. Nor could the Colonial Office decide whether the directives should only guide the military commander in the short-term or set out longer-term policy.[39] It seems the former view prevailed as the title "Long-Term Policy Directive", which appeared on initial drafts, was soon replaced by "Civil Affairs Policy Directive".

The directives gave a clear indication that the Hong Kong government was to be re-established much as it had existed prior to 1941. They contained no hint of any changes designed to meet the concerns expressed in 1942. Most directives included interim measures to be implemented immediately or soon after liberation. Pre-war departments and systems were to be restored. The Administration Directive required the re-establishment of the Legislative and Executive Councils on resumption of civil administration, the appointment of a Secretary of Chinese Affairs and the restoration of the Urban Council. The Medical and Health Directive stated that "the organisation of the Medical Department existing in December 1941 should be restored as soon as possible" and that "essential health services should be restored to their former level as early as possible". The Postal and Telecommunications Directive stated that postage rates were to "approximate as closely as possible … the rates in force in 1941". The Financial Policy Directive required that "in general, the pre-occupation financial system should be revived" except as specifically directed otherwise. In particular "all revenue from the date of occupation should be collected in accordance with the legislation in force at the date of the enemy occupation". Hong Kong would remain a free port with retention of duties only on alcohol, motor spirit and tobacco. It also required that "as soon as the situation permits, Budgetary Control and estimates of revenue and expenditure should be re-established in accordance with colonial regulations". The Banking Policy Directive focused on the re-establishment of the banking system and the issue of currency. It instructed that the three note-issuing banks be re-opened immediately and that banks of Allied nations should be permitted to re-open as soon as possible. The Land and Survey Directive stated that "the leases and titles in force at the date of enemy occupation should be recognised as valid" and made detailed provisions for handling land transactions made during the Japanese occupation.

Some new policies reflected a change in Colonial Office policy on labour, social welfare and opium and had been approved by the corresponding Colonial Office Advisory Committee. The Labour Policy Directive required that factory legislation and international labour conventions "should be strictly enforced" and that legislation on workmen's compensation, right of association for employers and workers and fixing of minimum wages should be introduced "as soon as practicable". The Social Welfare Policy Directive required the appointment of a Social Welfare Officer and of a central Social Welfare Advisory Committee which was to co-ordinate the efforts of other government departments providing services "which are directly concerned with the social welfare of the people". One directive required the Hong Kong government to ban the use of opium and abolish the government monopoly.[40]

By August 1944, the draft directives were all complete. They were seen initially by Arthur Creech-Jones, the Under-Secretary of State for the Colonies who thought that "these directives seem to ... be on sound and right lines. Most of the things I looked for are included, including mui tsai". They were not confirmed by the Secretary of State until 8 October 1945, a month after the British Military Administration (BMA) had been established, and then they were delivered to MacDougall in Hong Kong. As an afterthought, Sir Mark Young, who was to be reappointed as Hong Kong's first post-war Governor, was consulted shortly before he left for Hong Kong in April 1946. He was told that "they indicate in consolidated form approved Colonial Office policy on the various matters referred to". Young thought simply that "they will be very useful". The directives might have been of more practical value if Hong Kong had had a US military commander after liberation. MacDougall, who had taken drafts with him when he went to Hong Kong in September 1945,[41] found them less than useful in his tireless efforts to rehabilitate Hong Kong in the months after liberation.[42]

HKPU and the proposed Municipal Council

Until the spring of 1945, the Colonial Office had been focused on the practical task of ensuring Hong Kong's recovery as a British colony. It had established the HKPU whose existence as both a planning unit and a future civil affairs administration under a military government had been accepted by the Foreign Office and the War Office. It had also been accepted by the United States government that, if Hong Kong was recovered as a result of military operations, Hong Kong would be governed by an American military commander who would operate with a British civil affairs staff implementing British policies.[43] The HKPU had produced a blueprint setting out the policies that would be followed and which would restore a government remarkably unchanged in structure and form from that of 1941. Hong Kong's immediate material needs had been assessed and provision made for the requisite funding. The return of British administration to Hong Kong thus seemed assured.

Gent, however, had not forgotten the need for change, so clearly voiced in 1942. He had a plan that would have greatly changed the Hong Kong government's structure, constrained the Governor's autonomy and reduced the power and influence of the cadets. This was a proposal for a partially elected municipal council. It appeared as if it came from a small group formed within the Colonial Office. This consisted of

Colonial Office officials responsible for Hong Kong and MacDougall of the HKPU. It also included Arthur Morse[44] from the Hongkong Bank and G. W. Swire[45] from Butterfield and Swire who had been nominated, at the Colonial Office's request, by the China Association[46] as their liaison representatives. This group had been formed for "informal and confidential" discussions on Hong Kong matters including "future long-term administration". Whether the proposed municipal council was discussed remains unknown as it had been agreed no record of these meetings would be kept.[47]

Between May and August 1945 it met three times to discuss not whether Hong Kong should have a municipal council but how one should be implemented. The China Association representatives favoured a council elected on a narrow franchise with a wide range of responsibilities and able to hire its own staff. It would have had nine elected European members, representing commercial, professional and local Portuguese interests; seven Chinese members "to be nominated, or selected ... by the registered Chinese Guilds" and seven members nominated by the Governor to reflect interests not represented by elected members. It would have been responsible for a wide range of government functions, such as housing, medical services, sanitation, poor relief, some aspects of education and public works. The range of functions could be increased as it became more experienced. The Legislative Council would also be reformed and would be composed of five official and two ex-officio members with four Chinese and two European unofficial members and one Portuguese unofficial member. The Legislative Council would have an unofficial majority although in total there would still be a majority of European members. The Executive Council's functions would be undertaken by a committee of the Legislative Council.

MacDougall and senior HKPU staff, on the other hand, favoured a council elected on a wider franchise with a more limited range of responsibilities. A detailed paper written by T. M. Hazelrigg[48] of the HKPU, argued that Hong Kong's existing hierarchy of consultative committees had operated effectively as a channel of communication with the Chinese population and that there was no demand for change. He proposed that the Urban Council's role be extended and that the Chinese members should be directly elected on a wider franchise, possibly on the basis of the Jury List. Hazelrigg thought that, because this would be a detailed task

> no useful action can be taken before full civil government has been re-established in the Colony, when detailed study of the implications of the principles now under discussion will be possible.

On 1 August 1945, at the next meeting, the China Association's views became clearer. Both Morse and Swire attacked the HKPU's proposals with some vehemence and revealed why they had supported the original proposals. They wanted a municipal council which "would provide a more economical and efficient way of carrying out the administration of local affairs". Morse railed against the high cost of government pensions and welcomed the opportunity to employ more local, and therefore cheaper, staff for whom a provident fund could be instituted. He felt that this would

> make it possible to engage such senior European staff as would be required on relatively short term contracts thus facilitating the vitalisation of the administration by a freer flow of persons from the United Kingdom

He also thought that "a bold approach" was needed and disparaged claims that existing consultative arrangements had worked efficiently.

Neither did Paskin endorse HKPU's approach. He made clear that Hazelrigg's paper did not represent Colonial Office thinking and reminded the Committee

> that the purpose of these discussions was to explore the possibilities of 'liberalising' the constitution of Hong Kong and that the proposal to set up a Municipal Council with extensive functions had emerged as the most effective means of giving a greater voice in the management of their own affairs to the population of the Colony.

He did not explain, however, why a municipal council had emerged as "the most effective means" of achieving this. The only consensus reached was that no final decision could be made in London and that local leaders would need to be consulted if it was to be successful. Here the matter rested as far as the HKPU was concerned. Japan's sudden capitulation required them to repair immediately to Hong Kong where they became totally immersed in rehabilitation work.[49]

The two different approaches have been described as contrasting sharply with each other.[50] The Colonial Office proposal, supported so strongly by the China Association, may not, however, have been as "liberalising" as it was presented. The nine British European members were to be elected by the European community by unknown means to represent the commercial, professional and local Portuguese interests. Given the specific sectors which would have been represented, however, they would have been likely to elect a staunch pro-business lobby in favour of the cost-cutting measures favoured by Morse. The seven Chinese members were to be nominated by their representative guilds. Smith had pointed out to MacDougall that as these would have been very "elitist", they would also have been likely to produce a pro-business lobby. Both the Colonial Office and the China Association representatives also wanted a wide range of functions transferred to the municipal council. Their strategy of maximum delegation of powers to a municipal council elected under a restricted franchise was the opposite of that proposed by the HKPU and would have considerably strengthened the business sector's sway over government. As Hazelrigg pointed out, it would have left "hardly anything of importance within the responsibility of the central government".

Although the Secretary of State had approved the involvement of the China Association representatives, he was not aware of the details being proposed.[51] Nor had Gent yet won broader support for them within the Colonial Office. He had told Gater, the Permanent Under-Secretary, somewhat disingenuously, that

> we have met with a general recognition on the part of those that knew the Colony, not only the officials of the HKPU but also our two confidential consultants from the China Association ... as well as other unofficials ... that it is ... not only ... practicable, but will be expected, that there should be an extension of democratic reforms in the new era.

He recommended to Gater that the Secretary of State make a public statement of Britain's intention to pursue reform upon the restoration of civil administration in Hong Kong.

Gater was sceptical. He sought Caine's view, not only on the financial implications "but also because of your previous experience in Hong Kong". On the one hand, Caine thought the overall aim of increasing "the element of popular participation in the administration of Hong Kong ... can be best done by developing a Municipal Council." On the other a diarchy was being proposed which although "not necessarily a bad thing ... it is certainly something rather novel in our experience and I think we must be prepared for unexpected difficulties." He did, however, think that it would be open to criticism that "the European community is over-represented". He was also prescient enough to ask if the proposed municipal council's employees would be members of the colonial service.[52] The Secretary of State, however, does not seem to have been consulted.

There the matter rested until December. Colonial Office officials then started to push the issue again after it was known that Sir Mark Young would continue as Hong Kong's Governor.[53] When Young was first briefed on the proposals, he expressed reservations about the range of functions to be given to the proposed municipal council. He also warned against deciding everything in London without knowledge of local conditions and views. Some Colonial Office officials, however, remained determined that this issue should not be allowed to slip. The return of a post-war Governor was seen as "a moment of ... psychological significance ... which is unlikely to recur". They were aware of reports which told of "a general expectation as well as hope that the post-war era will bring in a more democratic form of government in Hong Kong". They understood that it was for the Governor, in consultation with local leaders, to decide how to implement reforms. This, however, should not stop Britain from agreeing in principle that Hong Kong's inhabitants

> must be given a fuller and more responsible share in the administration of the affairs of the Colony and that this must be done soon.

Gater remained ambivalent and wanted reassurance from someone who had been in Hong Kong "in recent months" to review the Secretary of State's proposed announcement. This task fell to MacDougall who wanted to leave as much scope for manoeuvre for the Hong Kong government as he could. It was left to Miss Alice Rushton of the Colonial Office to try to explain the "sharp cleavage of opinion", between "... members of the Hong Kong government (represented by the HKPU) and views of unofficial leaders in Hong Kong (represented by Morse and Swire)". This was the first explicit attempt to tease out the wider implications of the proposed municipal council and the "unexpected difficulties" Caine had previously mentioned. She pointed out that vesting power in a municipal council would mean "a corresponding reduction in the civil establishment of the Central Government". It could, therefore

> hardly be expected that officials of the Central Government will be able to take a completely detached and unbiased view of this issue which so closely concerns them ... this may perhaps have accounted for the 'conservative' attitude of members of the HKPU as opposed to the more 'liberal' attitude of the non-officials who took part in our discussions.[54]

Sir Mark Young resumed his Governorship on 1 May 1946 when civil government was restored in Hong Kong. On that day, both he and the Secretary of State made public announcements in Hong Kong and London respectively that the British government had

> under consideration the means by which in Hong Kong, as elsewhere in the Colonial Empire, the inhabitants of the Territory can be given a fuller and more responsible share in the management of their own affairs.

A municipal council was mooted as "one possible method of achieving this end". This would be examined by the Governor over the next few months in consultation with the "representatives of all sections of the community" who would then submit a report to the Secretary of State "at an early date".[55] The outcome of the consultations and further developments are discussed in Chapter 7.

Possible reasons for a proposed municipal council

Gent was most likely the main promoter of the proposed municipal council in its originally proposed form. There is, however, no surviving documentary evidence to indicate why he thought it necessary to "liberalise" Hong Kong's constitution at this particular time. Nor is there any record to indicate why he thought a municipal council would have been the best way of achieving this. Only circumstantial evidence is available. Gent would have been aware of the comments made by Bishop Hall and Caine on the Hong Kong government and the cadets in 1942. He had remarked on

> the need (which we have for some time felt here, and which Sir Geoffrey Northcote himself was particularly concerned with) for widening the horizon of the Hong Kong Cadet.[56]

This would have been further evident to Gent during his membership of the Battershill Committee in 1942. That Committee's polite observations on the performance of civil servants in Malaya and Hong Kong may well have masked stronger views.

A municipal council, in the form favoured by the Colonial Office and the China Association, would have had implications for the future of the cadets. Such a council would have been able to hire its own senior staff, and offer its own terms and conditions of service. It was therefore tacitly apparent they need not have been members of the Colonial Service and would not have had their terms of service protected by the Secretary of State. The new municipal council would not, as far as Morse and Swire saw it, have been under any commitment to employ any cadets they did not wish to accept. The more functions the municipal council would have become responsible for, the fewer would have been left to central government and fewer cadets would have been required. Their power and influence would have been considerably diminished. The implications, if apparent to Miss Rushton, would have been equally clear to Gent and to Morse and Swire.

Gent's proposals would have circumvented one of the barriers to tackling the problem of under-performing Hong Kong cadets. As members of the Colonial Service, they were appointed and promoted by the Secretary of State under Colonial Regulations. It would have been difficult to tackle this issue within the strictures of the colonial service without highlighting Hong Kong's particular problems in the process. Bringing in a new form of government, with no need for members of the colonial civil service, would have addressed the problem. A mechanism would then have been found to meet the criticisms of Clementi and Peel, Hall and Caine.

British Military Administration

In September 1945, MacDougall arrived in Hong Kong with nine members of the HKPU to form the Civil Affairs Unit of the British Military Administration. On 7 September, he was appointed Chief Civil Affairs Officer (CCAO) with the military rank of Brigadier. On 13 September 1945, by proclamation, Admiral Harcourt, the British naval commander, delegated him wide powers. This included the authority normally vested in the Executive and Legislative Councils and the power to amend any existing ordinance or suspend its operation.[57] The task facing him and his team of civil affairs officers was daunting. Hong Kong, he said "was dead—deserted streets, unvexed harbour, shuttered shops".[58] MacDougall's initial priorities were food, currency, labour and public health. He tackled these problems expeditiously and efficiently. On 13 September 1945, two days after newly printed Hong Kong currency had arrived, he demonetised the Japanese Military Yen and reintroduced the Hong Kong dollar. The Japanese surrender had come too quickly for the supplies indented for in London to arrive until the following April[59] and he had to rely on the resourcefulness of his staff. In October 1945, he sent out one senior officer to Borneo for firewood, one to Shanghai for coal and another to Hongay for coal, peanut oil and "anything else he could lay his hands on". Much ingenuity was needed to source and secure essential supplies.

Admiral Harcourt gave MacDougall a free hand in running civil affairs and, as CCAO, he was able to exercise a remarkable degree of autonomy. He admitted that

> as regards executive decisions, I have been exercising a form of personal government through the Admiral, who takes the possibly optimistic view that I was sent out because I knew the job and the Colony, and he shows every disposition to accept my advice on all save service matters.[60]

MacDougall also managed to limit the Colonial Office's scope for interference in his work. He persuaded Admiral Harcourt to agree that naval signal traffic to London was so busy, and of such high priority, that he could only allow MacDougall to communicate with the Colonial Office once a month. This typified MacDougall's outlook. He felt that as both

Head of the HKPU and as CCAO "we were almost floating free" from the Colonial Office. They had, he claimed "no rules!" He felt it vital to preserve this autonomy from the Colonial Office simply to get things done. Approvals from the Colonial Office would have taken time which, because of the sheer immediacy of the problems facing him, was something he did not have.[61] In December 1945, MacDougall summed up his work in a letter to Gater.

> The task has proved far simpler and more difficult than I envisaged during the London planning. Once on the spot you quickly perceive there are a few things you must handle or perish. Socrates or Will Hay or somebody said one becomes a builder by building and a harpist by harping: similarly one becomes a rehabilitator by rehabilitating. Currency, labour, public health and food admit of no mistakes. In the first six weeks I bitterly resented anything that destroyed concentration on these and the amiable advisors who descended on us from time to time were not wholly welcome. Nor were the people who quoted directives at awkward moments.[62]

More Hong Kong government civil servants joined the British Military Administration in Hong Kong on release from internment[63] and others joined from retirement in Britain. By Christmas 1945, some 150 former expatriate internees were still working in the British Military Administration or in the utility companies and had yet to return home for recuperation.[64] The Hong Kong government was well on its way to being re-established much as it had existed in 1941.

Conclusions

Despite having clearly identified a need for change, the Colonial Office had to accept the restoration of a Hong Kong government remarkably similar to the one that had existed before 1941. The need to restore British sovereignty had become more pressing than a desire for change in the way that sovereignty was exercised. As the war progressed, the need for a plan to re-establish British administration quickly and effectively in what were likely to be uncertain circumstances became paramount. The quickest and surest way to achieve this was to recreate the pre-1941 government and this is what the directives, with some exceptions, set out to do. The simplest way to implement the directives was to recruit serving or former Hong Kong government staff. They became the mainstay of the HKPU and the British Military Administration, as did Hong Kong civil servants who joined the BMA from internment or retirement and who provided additional continuity. It is hardly surprising that the Hong Kong government they recreated was so similar to the one they had known. If an American Force Commander had been in charge of Hong Kong after the Japanese surrender, he would have had a very clear picture of Britain's policies and intentions. He would have also had to rely on British staff to implement them. Ironically Britain's desire to re-establish its sovereignty in uncertain circumstances reduced its ability to change the way in which that sovereignty could be exercised.

The HKPU became the Hong Kong government in waiting and undertook most of the preparation work. They provided the first drafts of most directives and were left to decide whether they were to address long- or short-term policy goals. Apart from directives on issues like currency, in which the HKPU had no expertise, Colonial Office comments were mostly drafting niceties. Policy changes were introduced, notably in education,[65] social welfare, labour and opium but these were in line with changes in colonial policy generally and would have been introduced in the normal course of events. There was no suggestion or hint that old government departments would be reformed or that pre-1941 laws would not come back into force.

The municipal council proposal posed the severest challenge to the Hong Kong government's autonomy. It also delineated the boundaries of the British government's ability to exercise sovereignty. On the one hand, the Colonial Office wanted to change the nature and structure of the Hong Kong government dramatically. On the other, they could not achieve this without relying on the people whose power they sought to curtail. The HKPU response reflected an attempt to mould proposals into a form they preferred and thought were right for Hong Kong. The Colonial Office's power, and the proxy power of the unofficials exercised through Morse and Swire of the China Association, was curtailed by the need to rely on the HKPU's capacity to undertake the prime goal, simple in concept but complex in execution, of restoring British sovereignty in Hong Kong.

The considerable degree of autonomy from the Colonial Office exercised by the HKPU and the British Military Administration arose from the challenging situation they faced and the drastic steps they had to take. This was not the time to simply follow procedures. These would not have achieved the over-arching goal of the restoration of British sovereignty. Once that had been effectively re-established and the normal structures of civil government restored, this type of autonomy, as shall be seen in the following chapters, was to fall away. Gent achieved a small but crucial victory. The decision to consult local leaders on the return of civil administration, cemented by the joint public statement, ensured that constitutional change was firmly on the agenda. How this played out, and what its impact on the Hong Kong government's autonomy was, is explored in Chapter 7.

6
Income Tax and Treasury Control

> The Governor's power of veto and the official majority in both Councils give the superficial appearance of complete control of legislation and taxation.
>
> Mills, op. cit., p. 396

> Bureaucratic entrepreneurship is the process by which agency leaders experiment with new programmes ... and gradually convince diverse coalitions of organised interests ... and politicians of the value of their ideas ...
>
> Carpenter, op. cit., p. 30

The need to win support from politicians is an integral part of a democratic system. In the closed political world of post-1945 Hong Kong, however, this kind of support might have been thought barely necessary. It has already been seen how malleable local views could be or how a Secretary of State could even disregard them. It has also been shown how a Governor with strong convictions, such as Northcote, could persuade unofficials to support proposals they would probably have preferred not to. After 1945, this became a more important part of the political process. Why was this so? This will be considered by examining how new and permanent direct taxes were introduced into Hong Kong and how the Governor, Young, won at least some unofficial support for them.

The unofficials' growing importance in the political process will also be examined in a case which brought them into direct conflict with the British government. This was over whether Britain or Hong Kong should pay for items of expenditure. They also wanted the abolition of British Treasury control over Hong Kong's finances. The controls had been imposed because Hong Kong had received advances from Britain when it had no funds of its own. How these disputes affected the unofficials' increasing influence over policy, and how their growing ability to use it altered their relationship with both the British and Hong Kong governments, will be examined.

Tackling the deficit

Britain expected her colonies to be financially self-supporting.[1] In May 1946, on the restoration of civil government, Hong Kong was not. The British Military Administration (BMA) had recognised the scale of this challenge when it estimated that in 1946–47 a re-established civil government would have expenditure of HK$104.1 million but revenue of only HK$41.5 million. The BMA noted pessimistically that "the future held out small hopes for the re-establishment far less expansion of hard-hit social services and for development generally".[2] On 16 May 1946, Young told the first full sitting of the Legislative Council that the need to tackle the Hong Kong government's dire financial situation was "of the first importance". He admitted frankly that

> I wish it were possible for me to present to you not only a clear picture of our present financial position but also a reasoned and probable estimate of our prospects for the coming year. But there are at the present time so many unknown factors that it is impossible to speak either of the present or the future, save in very general terms.[3]

The entire pre-war surplus had been "more than swallowed up" by expenditure since Hong Kong's fall to the Japanese. The government's total liabilities could not be fully ascertained as they might include the cost of the military administration[4] and "other uncertain factors". Even when all that had been clarified a budget deficit was still expected in the current fiscal year and, most probably, in the next one as well.

On 25 July 1946, the Financial Secretary in his budget proposed expenditure of just over HK$160 million, of which about HK$80 million was expenditure on rehabilitation. Apart from this, there was the need to replenish all government departments; to pay as much in cost-of-living allowance to civil servants as in salaries; to meet the cost of a temporary increase in the number of staff employed as many expatriates were recuperating in their home country; and to pay final leave salaries to a larger than normal number of officers whose retirement had been delayed by the war. Estimated revenue was HK$51.3 million, excluding receipts under the War Revenue Ordinance (see below), which left a deficit of HK$115.4 million. He pointed out that

> deficits can only be met by increasing revenue and by cutting down expenditure ... it seems clear therefore that we must have increased revenue and that I fear means increased taxation.

He felt sure, however, "that the Government may count on the support of Honourable Members in any measures which may prove necessary to augment our revenue".

His confidence appeared well founded. On 5 September 1946, during the Legislative Council budget debate, the unofficials were not opposed to raising additional revenue to balance the budget. Dr Chau Sik-nin[5] thought the budget was "not as harsh or burdensome as might have been feared". They accepted the need for the large expenditure proposed; they had, after all, endured the Japanese occupation and the need for rehabilitation was plainly apparent. What was in dispute was whether additional revenue should be raised through an income tax. The Financial Secretary had said one was being considered to replace the War Revenue Ordinance. Five out of six unofficials made their opposition very clear. They emphatically stated that an income tax could not be levied equitably in Hong Kong and should not be imposed. How this gap could be bridged was to be one of Young's major challenges.

Taxation Committee, 1946

Young summed up the debate by presenting Hong Kong's financial position in stark and uncompromising terms. The deficit, he said, simply "signifies increased taxation". He noted that, in their speeches, members had

> expressed with something approaching unanimity their opinions on what I regard as the most important revenue question before us today ... whether an Income Tax on the normal model shall be substituted for the existing War Revenue Ordinance.

He could not regard the issue as closed by the same arguments raised in 1939 and which the unofficials had reiterated during this debate. He set up a Committee to examine how additional taxation should be raised, including whether an income tax should be introduced. He reiterated the Financial Secretary's point that there was a need to balance the budget and to remove Hong Kong from dependence upon the British Treasury for financial assistance. He undertook that there would be "every opportunity for full weight to be given to every objection and every difficulty which may be held to militate against this or that method for raising revenue".[6]

A Committee with eleven members[7] and chaired by Financial Secretary C. G. S. Follows,[8] was quickly appointed. Members included Arthur Morse, now an unofficial Executive Council member and two unofficial Legislative Council members, M. K. Lo and R. D. Gillespie.[9] Its Secretary was E. W. Pudney,[10] later the first Commissioner of Inland Revenue. Its terms of reference were to advise on how to reduce the deficit and balance the budget in 1947–48; to review all taxes; and to make interim recommendations on immediate measures to increase revenue. It first met on 18 September and held its ninth and last meeting on 4 December before submitting its report to the Governor.

The committee held rather ambivalent views on income tax. At its first meeting, M. K. Lo, supported by two others, referred "to its complicated nature and the feelings of resentment with consequent evasions, which its provisions might arouse". Gillespie, however, thought an income tax the best form of taxation "provided it was equitably collected". The Chairman, with the Secretary's support, wanted the committee to focus on areas where agreement was more likely to be reached.[11] Over the next few meetings, various other proposals to increase revenue were agreed. On 5 November, when it became clear that HK$15 million was still needed to balance the budget, an income tax was again discussed. A brief, and seemingly rather subdued discussion ensued. It was accepted that an income tax

> would theoretically result in the most equitable distribution of the burden of taxation, and that a tax on incomes is inevitable here if the budget of the Colony is to be balanced and if Hong Kong is to conform to the standards generally expected of the middle of the 20th century.

However, the Committee recommended instead that, with some updating, the provisions of the War Revenue Ordinance should be continued. It was estimated this would produce HK$15.5 million in revenue which, with the yield from other proposed taxes, would produce the additional HK$45 million needed to balance the budget.

The Committee did not recommend a full income tax because, it claimed, this would take too long to prepare.[12] This stance has been lambasted as "nonsense" because several model ordinances already existed which could have been adapted for Hong Kong. It has also been argued that the government reluctantly accepted this recommendation because "there was not enough time to argue the point".[13] However, it was the Committee Chairman, Follows, and not the unofficials, who proposed the re-enactment of the War Revenue Ordinance provisions. It was unlikely that Follows would have made this suggestion without having discussed and agreed it with Young beforehand. Given the muted discussion in Committee on this point, it begs the question whether a consensus had not been arrived at with the unofficials beforehand.[14]

As in 1939 and 1940, the Taxation Committee played an important political role by bringing influential unofficials into the government's decision-making process. Although government had not pressed the case for a full income tax, it had made clear the need for additional revenue. The unofficials on the Committee, aware of the remaining deficit to be met, were prepared to support the continuation of the separate taxes of the War Revenue Ordinance. The Committee was a way of forming a coalition of support on this potentially contentious issue. The unofficials on the Committee were nudged towards agreeing to something they would probably rather not have agreed to, aware that this was the only viable way of raising the needed additional public revenue.

Colonial Office view

Pudney visited London in December 1946 and January 1947 to discuss the Taxation Committee's proposals with the Colonial Office and the Inland Revenue Department. Colonial Office officials accepted the Taxation Committee's recommendations that the four scheduled taxes of the War Revenue Ordinance taxes be continued. They were also pleased that there was provision for a taxpayer to opt for a personal assessment and have all his income assessed for tax and, in return, receive personal allowances. They were disappointed that without a full income tax that a surtax could not be levied. Caine, however, considered that this was the best that could be achieved under the circumstances. He thought that because a surtax could not be imposed, the standard tax rate should be set "as high as possible", with lower rates and high allowances to benefit people earning lower incomes. This would encourage higher rate taxpayers to opt for the personal assessment and achieve as nearly as possible the intent of a full income tax. It was also left to the Governor to decide the rate at which the tax should be levied.

Caine, however, left Pudney in no doubt that the Colonial Office expected rates to be set as high as possible. This was reiterated to Young who was told of the importance that the Secretary of State attached to putting "the standard rate at as high a level as you consider practicable". With this advice, Pudney returned to Hong Kong in mid-January 1947 with a revised draft ordinance. Young was told that this had the Secretary of State's, or at least his officials' approval in principle. The standard rate was proposed by Pudney to be 25% and this was agreed by Government. However, by the time the bill came to be published on 7 March, the standard rate had been left blank.

Inland Revenue Bill

The publication of the Inland Revenue Bill on 7 March 1947 did not stop opposition to an income tax. In an attempt to counter this, Young referred the bill back to the Taxation Committee and increased its membership to include all unofficial Legislative Council members. They "agreed in principle that direct taxation should be imposed" but with two caveats. One was that its imposition should be delayed and the other, supported by all except three members, was that "it was imperative that the standard rate should be low and that it should not exceed ten per cent".[15] They also felt the bill required further detailed examination and that this should be done by another committee.

Young was not going to allow these tactics to delay implementation. He promptly agreed to the formation of an expert committee to consider the bill's details and agreed a tax rate of 10%. A new Committee was quickly formed under Arthur Morse's chairmanship with bankers, lawyers and chartered accountants, rather than political unofficials, as members. They made a number of technical recommendations concerning the operation and the scope of the bill which Young accepted. Young thought, however, that the most important concession he made was agreeing to a standard rate of tax at 10%. For Young,

> There was no doubt in my mind that [setting up a second committee], together with the prior acceptance of the figure of 10% for the standard rate, was responsible for the breakdown of the united front against the Bill which had hitherto been evident.[16]

On 26 April 1947, when the bill was introduced into the Legislative Council, Young showed his determination that it should pass. In a straight-talking address he recognised that opposition "was due to a conviction held by many people in this Colony that this is not the best or the most appropriate form of taxation for Hong Kong". This opinion had been expressed vociferously by the local press and in particular by the local Chinese business community. There had been complaints that the measures were unfair, that the tax would not be equitably collected and that the taxpayer would have little or no control over how the tax yield was to be spent.[17] Young, however, was not prepared to accept such criticism. He stated that the measures contained in the bill were "the most appropriate method of providing for some of the essential expenditure of this Colony in present circumstances". He also made clear this was not a view imposed from outside "regardless of local opinion and local conditions". He pointed out that the proposals had been twice supported by the Taxation Committee, nine of whose twelve members were unofficials. It had been referred to a committee of experts who had also supported it. He poured scorn on the notion that matters were being hurried when nine months had passed since the proposal had been first mooted in the Legislative Council. It was now time to proceed, partly because the financial year to which this tax would apply was already a month old and, secondly, because he considered it "my duty to this Colony to see that the question does not remain undetermined at the time of my departure"[18] due in May that year.

He had not been without public support for his views. In March 1947, Arthur Morse, the Chairman and Chief Manager of the Hongkong Bank, Executive Council member and Chairman of the expert Taxation

Committee and Vice-Chancellor of the University of Hong Kong, D. J. Sloss,[19] both gave their public support to the measures at the Hongkong and Shanghai Bank's AGM in March. R. D. Gillespie, Legislative Council member representing the Chamber of Commerce, gave them his public support at the Chamber's AGM in April and received the unanimous backing of its Members.[20] In opposition had been a vociferous group called the HK & Kowloon Chinese Anti-Direct Tax Introduction Commission who had petitioned both the Hong Kong and British governments against it. Numerous petitions from other local Chinese organisations had also been received.[21]

The Legislative Council debated the Bill at its next meeting on 1 May. Three members, Chau Tsun-nin,[22] Leo d'Almada e Castro[23] and Dr Chau Sik-nin stated they would vote against it. Chau Tsun-nin thought the widespread opposition to the Bill arose "solely because (people) feel that it is not the best or most appropriate form of taxation for Hong Kong." He conceded the Chinese community could "very reluctantly" support three of the four proposed direct taxes but could not support the tax on business profits. This, he claimed, would violate the privacy which formed the centuries-old basis of Chinese business tradition.[24] Leo d'Almada e Castro thought it was not the time to introduce such taxes because individuals and businesses still had to rehabilitate themselves after the losses of the war years. With the advent of a proposed new form of government, it was also not the time for another major new initiative. Dr Chau Sik-nin agreed there was a necessity to raise additional revenue but thought this was not a proper form of taxation for a traditional Chinese society. He considered that such a direct tax should only be imposed where those being taxed have "an effective voice in its imposition as well as in the control of its expenditure". However, he did not at the same time advocate greater popular representation. The British unofficial members—Landale, Gillespie and Watson—gave their support with seeming reluctance. Landale thought that there were inherent dangers of malpractices and was sceptical of government's ability to implement the new taxes "equitably, economically and incorruptibly". Gillespie was concerned government might have no qualified staff to collect them and Watson, and the JPs he represented, said they would support the new taxes if they could be equitably raised.

The statesmanlike M. K. Lo displayed the greater breadth of vision and supported the measures. He was now convinced that, regardless of government's financial situation, it would need to spend money on a wide range of social services as presaged by the pre-war Governor, Northcote. Lo had a vision of a Hong Kong

> in which its people, aided by sound education, will assume progressively and in ever increasing measure, the responsibility of self-government; in which social services, like adequate hospitalisation, medical and sanatorium care, universal education, old age pensions, unemployment insurance, workmen's compensation, etc., etc., will gradually become available to its citizens, and in which the burden of providing for the expense of government and for these services will be equitably distributed amongst all. In any such picture direct taxation, based however approximately on ability to pay, must occupy a place.[25]

The bill was passed by a majority of ten. Young told the Secretary of State that, even with three unofficials voting against it, this was "a very satisfactory result". He considered it was important that the measure had been carried with at least some unofficial support, and had not added to the burden on the local community. They were coping with very high costs and higher rates of tax would only add to this burden. In Young's view

> the main consideration is to establish the machinery for direct taxation. Once that is accomplished any adjustment in rate which may be necessary to meet a change in conditions does not present so much difficulty.[26]

The Colonial Office were very pleased and thought that

> the Hong Kong Administration are to be congratulated on the fact that, in spite of very considerable earlier opposition, the Bill was finally passed without the use of the Official majority

They agreed that "the essential thing at this stage is to establish machinery of direct taxation, and secure the necessary measure of support for it in principle". [27]

Colonial Office and Treasury influence

Some in Hong Kong believed that the Colonial Office had been behind the introduction of an income tax.[28] Had London simply issued instructions as in the case of *mui tsai*? Or had a tax on incomes been introduced solely on the Hong Kong government's initiative? Why had London been so concerned that Hong Kong institute an income tax?

That colonies in general should introduce direct taxes concerned both the Colonial Office and the British Treasury. In 1945, the Colonial Development and Welfare Act had provided for "increased financial assistance towards the continuation and expansion of the policy of colonial development". Britain's concern about the lack of development in its colonies had helped to pass the first Colonial Development Act in 1929. This concern continued during the 1930s and led to the Colonial Development and Welfare Act, 1940 which made £5 million p.a. available from Britain over 10 years for colonial development. A further Act in 1945 increased this amount to £120 million over ten years of which Hong Kong's share was £1 million.[29]

The problem was that in 1945 Britain itself could hardly afford this sum. This was why the Secretary of State told colonies that it was

> important that direct taxation borne mainly by the richer members of the community should be reviewed, if this has not been done recently, so as to ensure that local revenues are making an adequate and fair contribution towards the cost of the development and advancement of the territory.[30]

This was reinforced by a further circular telegram from the Secretary of State in July 1946 advising that "it should be long-term policy in most colonies to develop direct taxation, particularly income tax on progressive basis". The Secretary of State clearly felt that it was only with this locally raised additional revenue that improved social services could be provided in Britain's colonies.[31]

The Treasury was also very concerned at what it saw as Hong Kong's expectations that the British taxpayer would meet its projected deficits regardless. The Treasury was also annoyed at the Colonial Office which had failed, in its eyes "to give the local administration adequate guidance on financial policy and particularly on such matters as taxation and borrowing". In July 1946, after MacDougall had met with Colonial Office and Treasury officials to discuss Hong Kong's finances, the Colonial Office told Young in a telegram that

> provided revenue is increased it is possible that the Colony should, apart from special expenditure, be approaching the position of a balanced budget in 1947–8. To this end it is desirable to increase revenue to as great an extent as possible ... pending introduction of a full Income Tax Ordinance as soon as staff can be made available.

The reference to a full income tax reflected Caine's views that "Hong Kong should come into line with all other important colonies and adopt a regular income tax".[32] Caine was also very aware of the disparities between the tax burden in Britain compared to Hong Kong's much lighter tax, and higher incomes and lavish lifestyles that some, though by no means all, in Hong Kong were enjoying. He may have been concerned that this could become a domestic political issue in Britain and one which would have been very hard to defend in the midst of Britain's dire post-war austerity.[33]

The telegram to Young crossed with a despatch from the Governor to the Secretary of State sent on 24 July in which Young admitted that

> the question of resuming the collection of taxes under the War Revenue Ordinance or of introducing Income Tax on normal lines has been engaging my attention.

He was aware, however, of the difficulties of implementing an income tax in Hong Kong, especially the dangers of evasion. He told the Colonial Office that he wanted to assess how much evasion there might be when members of the War Taxation Department had returned to Hong Kong after recuperation in Britain.[34]

Young was therefore contemplating the introduction of an income tax before the Secretary of State had suggested it. Both government and unofficials knew that Hong Kong could not continue to run on deficits. It was this which had influenced the Hong Kong government and not the hectoring circulars from the Colonial Office. The only credence they were given was a passing acknowledgment that the Secretary of State's July 1946 telegram had been "kept in mind when framing general fiscal policy for 1947/48".[35] The need for an income tax in Hong Kong came from the realisation of the impossibility of reducing expenditure under prevailing circumstances and the need, realised by all parties, to increase revenue. The Colonial Office's advice, therefore, was probably unnecessary; it was Young's steely leadership and determination which secured the implementation of the new Earnings and Profits Tax.

Young's action in implementing the pre-war taxes rather than a full income tax and not setting a higher rate of tax has been characterised as both "a serious failure of leadership"[36] and "the best [he] could do under the circumstances".[37] Could Young simply have implemented a full income tax and set the standard rate at the 25% he was initially considering? Later events in Singapore might have been instructive. In November 1947, Singapore's Governor, Sir Franklin Gimson, proposed an income tax to his Advisory Committee, a temporary legislature with an unofficial majority, to meet an estimated S$34 million budget deficit. It had rejected his proposal and Gimson, after consultation with the Governor-General in Kuala Lumpur and his fellow Governor of the Malay Union, Sir Edward Gent, decided to impose an income tax by decree. In protest, two leading Chinese members of the Advisory Council resigned. The widespread and keenly felt opposition may also have precipitated increased Chinese support for eventual independence.[38]

These events post-dated the passage of Hong Kong's income tax legislation by some months. The not entirely dissimilar nature of the two communities, however, may help provide some insight into what might have been possible reaction in Hong Kong had Young acted in a similar fashion. The lukewarm support of Hong Kong's British businessmen, who may have feared they would have ended up paying a disproportionate amount of tax, may have evaporated. The opposition of the Chinese businessmen would probably have been even more vociferous than it was. It would hardly have helped garner support in the Legislative Council for a proposed new municipal council which would have tended to lessen the powers of both these groups.

Young does not seem to have considered following Gimson's example in Singapore of circumventing the legislative process. This may have reflected Young's background in Ceylon with its responsible government. When it became apparent that if he wanted to receive at least some unofficial support he would have to introduce a standard rate of 10%, this is what he chose to do. It was the price he paid for the unofficial support he received. Both Young and Colonial Office officials clearly felt it was important to win at least some unofficial support. Gent's view, expressed in 1940 in respect of the need for explicit unofficial support for a possible post-war income tax, would still have been considered valid.

Young had achieved the passage of this legislation through a combination of strong leadership and determined coalition building. He had made the government's position and determination very clear and worked hard to build support among the unofficials: the very public support given by Morse, Sloss, Gillespie and the entire General Chamber of Commerce were testament to this. Without this support, he may have had the support of fewer or even none of the unofficials. The alternative would have been to pass the bill using the official majority, something he was very reluctant to do and which, over such a fundamental issue, would have been considered a marked failure of leadership. It would have brought the Administration into conflict with the unofficials when their support was needed for a number of difficult issues arising from the war and for the constitutional reforms which had recently been under public consideration. Young had now shown that the Hong Kong government had the capacity to set the agenda and to act to remove the looming budget deficit. Direct taxation in Hong Kong was now here to stay. The unofficials, however, had shown how hard a Governor had to work to win their support.

Financial dispute with Britain

With the chaos of war and its aftermath, some decisions were made and expenditure committed which, had there been time for greater deliberation, might not have been. There was also the question of authorisation of expenditure on the Hong Kong Planning Unit and the British Military Administration during and just after the Japanese occupation. Some of this expenditure had been met from income from the Exchange Fund[39] and some from funds advanced by the British government. Expenditure had, by necessity, been incurred and committed without the due authorisation of the Legislative Council's Finance Committee. It was some of these items which unofficials felt strongly should be paid for by Britain as the imperial power and not by Hong Kong. These items included payments for return passages to Hong Kong for people, mostly Europeans, who had been repatriated to their country of domicile on liberation; payment of salaries and pensions to members of the Hong Kong Volunteer Defence Corps and the Hong Kong Royal Naval Volunteer Reserve on their disbandment; maintenance and relief payments; and payments to civil defence workers and temporary civil servants. There was also the question of payment for goods and property requisitioned and destroyed to deny them to the enemy or lost or damaged as a direct result of war. These became known as "denial claims". The terms of Britain's £3.25 million advance to Hong Kong had also yet to be decided. Also to be decided was the question of whether Hong Kong should pay for the cost of the military administration.

Public concern

During the debate on the 1947–48 estimates in March 1947, unofficial members started to raise concerns over these still undefined claims against the Hong Kong taxpayer. The Financial Secretary reported, fleetingly, that "the Colony may be faced with claims for very considerable amounts indeed in respect of past events". Landale expressed concern that the size of this contingency had still to be determined. M. K. Lo warned that the Chinese community held "very strong views" in respect of these items. He asked for "an assurance that none of these claims will be settled by the local Government without assent of this Council". Young assured him that payments already made in respect of disputed items had been entered into a suspense account and he undertook "that no future transfers from these suspense accounts to our general expenditure account shall take place without prior reference to this Council".[40] In the Legislative Council on 16 October 1947, M. K. Lo asked about the "nature and extent of the financial aid rendered to the Colony and when it was so rendered". The acting Colonial Secretary replied that Hong Kong had received advances from the British government totalling £3.25 million. No repayment had yet been made and Hong Kong "was still subject to general Treasury control". He also enumerated the items that had been paid for since the end of the military administration, either in Hong Kong or London, and that, as at 30 September 1947, approximately HK$15 million had been placed in a suspense account. On 6 November 1947, Lo further asked under what authority the £3.25 million advance had been spent and how it had been divided between expenditure charged to Hong Kong's account and that charged temporarily to a suspense account. The Financial Secretary replied that £2.5 million had been received before 30 April 1946. The balance of the advance had been received after the resumption of civil government to make good the deficit for 1946–47. As expenditure up to April 1946 had totalled £4.5 million, and income from the Exchange Fund during the war had amounted to £2 million, the balance had been met from the £2.5 million advance from the British government. Of this, just over £4 million had been spent and charged to Hong Kong's account. An additional £1 million had since been spent and charged to a suspense account. In the absence of a functioning Hong Kong government, these payments had been made on the authority of the Secretary of State. The Financial Secretary added that this authority was exercised "largely in accordance with commitments approved in previous years by the Hong Kong legislature".[41] The odd situation seems to have arisen whereby the Secretary of State based his authority on that delegated by the Crown to a colonial legislature rather than on his own direct authority from the Crown.

Grantham's despatch

In December 1947, Sir Alexander Grantham, who had replaced Young as Governor in July, sent a long and detailed despatch to the Secretary of State with an assessment of Hong Kong's financial position. It was a detailed and, in places, hectoring despatch in which he had the temerity to lecture the Secretary of State. He was, however, very clearly making the point to the Colonial Office, and no doubt the Treasury too, that this was a serious political problem in Hong Kong which could only be resolved with the co-operation of the British government. The crux of his argument was that,

> If, as a result of being overrun by the enemy, a Colonial Government has ceased to exist and had been cut off from its normal sources of revenue, it is for the mother country to meet any liabilities which may arise, until the Colony can be restored to its former status as a member of the British Commonwealth.

He made clear that there was no prospect of increasing taxation in Hong Kong if the purpose was to raise revenue to spend on these disputed items. He understood there was an economic crisis in Britain but if the matter was resolved to both parties mutual satisfaction this would "influence the unofficial attitude for years to come".

Grantham proposed a settlement totalling almost £7 million, rather mild after the arguments he had just made. He proposed that Britain should be responsible for:
- all funds advanced to meet expenditure incurred by the British government between the capitulation and return of civil government, taking account of income from the Exchange Fund;
- all expenditure placed in a suspense account and all further claims arising from the war;
- all claims in respect of requisitioned foodstuff and funds borrowed and refunded for purchase of supplies for internees; and
- a grant and loan to the University of Hong Kong.

If a settlement were to be generous, then "both officials and unofficials will go forward along the path of political development in a real spirit of co-operation". This was a reference to the proposed constitutional reforms which would have seen more power devolved upon unofficials. But

> if a niggardly attitude is displayed, this will be remembered in the years to come when the unofficial element is exercising a much greater degree of control.

Although not specifically asked for, a free grant for reconstruction was "still hoped for by the general public" and

> would not only have a value politically out of all proportion to its intrinsic cost but would be received with profound gratitude by the people of Hong Kong.[42]

Colonial Office and Treasury response

Both the Treasury and the Colonial Office had been grappling indecisively with Hong Kong's uncertain post-war finances since the re-establishment of civil government. To be fair, it was known that Hong Kong would be running a deficit during its first financial year and there was scant information upon which to base any meaningful forecasts. Other factors were how broad commitments made by the British government to provide compensation and assistance for rehabilitation to colonies affected by the war should apply to Hong Kong, if at all. An important underlying feature was the severe pressure that Britain's post-war finances were under with the need to keep expenditure to a minimum. Despite this, a free grant of £30 million grant was made to Malta in view of the devastation wrought upon it by the war. As the Colonial Office had feared,⁴³ this gesture was not lost upon other colonies. In July 1946, Young asked the Secretary of State to consider making a similar type of grant to Hong Kong to cover the cost of its war damage and rehabilitation.⁴⁴ The Colonial Office thought that because Hong Kong's conditions were very different from Malta's and its earning capacity infinitely greater, it was not worthwhile even approaching the Treasury. It was decided to do so only if specific grounds arose to justify such a request.⁴⁵

The Colonial Office had been slow to appreciate the political considerations in Hong Kong which Grantham's despatch helped bring into focus. In March 1947, the Governor was asked whether relief payments of HK$8.8 million made by the Foreign Office in Macau during the Japanese occupation to Hong Kong civil servants and pensioners could be included in Hong Kong's recurrent expenditure "provided that you are satisfied that there would be no political objection to such a transfer". Young replied that

> There would be very great political objection to the proposal that these Macao relief payments should be met from recurrent expenditure ... Feeling is growing locally that it is inequitable that Hong Kong should be required to meet this type of claim.⁴⁶

The Colonial Office had now begun to realise the Governor's political difficulties. It told the Treasury that, subject to asking Hong Kong for more details on their projected financial position, "there are good grounds for supporting the Governor's request [made on 24 July 1946] for a grant from HMG on the lines of the £30 million grant to Malta". The Treasury warned the Colonial Office that there was "very little likelihood of HMG being able to agree to [such] a grant" but also said they would "examine ... with interest" Hong Kong's report.⁴⁷

This was the context within which Grantham submitted his despatch of 12 December 1947. On its receipt, the Colonial Office responded with unusual alacrity. A copy was quickly sent to the Treasury and by early February the Colonial Office had formulated its own proposals for a detailed and comprehensive settlement. The Treasury were already familiar with this concept as they had already agreed the basis of a settlement for Burma and were considering one for Malaya. The Colonial Office reminded them of feelings in Hong Kong and stressed that "the goodwill of the unofficials will become increasingly important to us in Hong Kong, especially if our political difficulties with China ... increase and intensify".

It was not clear whether Colonial Office officials fully understood why Hong Kong's unofficials held such strong feelings. Nor whether they realised that, in the absence of an agreement, the Hong Kong government would have had to use its official majority in the Legislative

Council to authorise expenditure the unofficials would not. This was a question implicitly asked in Grantham's despatch. Caine took a wider view and thought that,

> There can be no dispute ... that the Colony has a valid claim for substantial assistance in meeting the immense burdens resulting from its fate as an outpost of the Empire which could not be defended. The individual items must inevitably lose their identity in assessing that claim in terms of cash.

The Colonial Office proposed that Britain waive repayment of the £3.25 million loan-in-aid; make a free grant of £5 million in respect of matters arising from the war, providing the Hong Kong government takes responsibility for other liabilities arising; and make a £250,000 grant to the University of Hong Kong. This would have made a total free grant of £8.5 million. Caine thought this was "moderate measured by what Hong Kong has experienced" and also comparable to what Malaya was asking for. In addition, the Colonial Office recommended that Britain make an interest-free loan available to the Hong Kong government for the construction of a new airport at Deep Bay. [48]

Britain's offer

The Treasury agreed that the cost of the British Military Administration be waived, that the £3.25 million loan-in-aid be treated as a grant, that a £3.25 million loan be made available for construction of a new airport at Deep Bay and that a £250,000 grant be made to the University of Hong Kong.[49] In presenting this comprehensive offer to Hong Kong, the Secretary of State took care to balance several conflicting factors. He emphasised Britain's generosity in the face of its present austerity and Hong Kong's "rapid recovery and present prosperity". He made clear that Britain could not accept any further contingent liability in respect of Hong Kong. He hinted that no more could be expected from Britain and that he could rely on Grantham

> to make every effort to ensure that HMG's action in these difficult times (the gravity of which have not perhaps always been fully appreciated) shall be taken by the population of Hong Kong as evidence of the good-will which it is in fact intended to be.

Once the package had been agreed to he would then he would "consider the relaxation of the present financial control over the finances of Hong Kong".

Negotiating a free grant

What was missing was an offer of a free grant from Britain. Grantham thought the package offered would be unacceptable to the unofficials without it. He told the Secretary of State that he was "deeply appreciative of the spirit of goodwill manifested by His Majesty's Government".[50] However, this had to be seen in the context of strongly held local opinion which had been made clear by M. K. Lo during the budget debate in the Legislative Council in March. Lo had pointed out that Hong Kong had already made a great contribution to the war effort and that unofficial members

> should not agree to regard as a liability of the Colony War expenditure sanctioned by the Imperial Government in relation to the Colony as a unit of the British Empire.

Such views had been made very plain to Lord Listowel, Minister of State for the Colonies, during his recent visit to Hong Kong.[51] Grantham replied to the Secretary of State to ask if the package could include an ex-gratia payment of £1 million to cover the amount in the suspense account. If Hong Kong had to meet this expense, over which there was such strong feeling, then "in spite of any effort of mine, gesture of His Majesty's Government will completely lose its value". Grantham was careful not to ask for more than was being offered; he simply asked if the offer could "be modified in some degree". He was

> convinced that something on this line would go far to meet criticism by appealing to local pride and it could no doubt be justified by emphasis on grave difficulties which His Majesty's Government are now facing.[52]

Grantham's request was quickly considered by the Treasury, probably helped by a desire to make a simultaneous announcement on settlements for Malaya and Hong Kong at the end of April 1948. The Treasury was unable to increase the overall package but took Grantham's hint and reshuffled it. They agreed to make a £1 million grant to Hong Kong by reducing the maximum loan for the proposed airport by the same amount. The financial implications of this move were minimal and would achieve the original aim of "getting the maximum political capital out of the gesture".[53] On 24 April, the Secretary of State informed Grantham of this revised offer. He emphasised that Britain "cannot contemplate any further assistance" in respect of any other possible claims. He hoped this would enable Grantham to overcome "the difficulties referred to in your telegram". Grantham replied immediately accepting the package "with gratitude".[54]

This exchange revealed, however, what appears to have been a genuine misunderstanding between Grantham and the Colonial Office. Grantham had asked that what were to become known as "denial claims" should be met by the service departments concerned. These were claims for losses as a result of requisitioning or destruction of goods, including vessels, during the battle for Hong Kong in December 1941 to deny them to the enemy. The claims were estimated to be about HK$25 million. Grantham's request had been overlooked by the Colonial Office but when it came to their attention, they were adamant that Britain could not be expected to meet them. The matter was to remain unresolved until 1950.[55]

The unofficials' response and acceptance

On 27 April 1948, a simultaneous announcement was made in Britain and Hong Kong setting out the terms of the financial settlement. On 26 May 1948 what this meant for Hong Kong became clear when Leo d'Almada e Castro asked a question in the Legislative Council. The Financial Secretary replied that with the £1 million grant, and Hong Kong's current surplus of HK$30 million, the government would be able to meet all liabilities arising from the war.[56] The unofficials, however, were privately very unhappy and considered Britain's offer to be simply Hong Kong's due. The Hong Kong taxpayer would still need to meet a large contingent sum which they considered was

> the responsibility of HMG ... any other view must be contrary to the whole conception of the responsibility of HMG towards one of its Colonies which was overrun by the enemy in war where its Government ceased to exist during the enemy occupation, and when all its assets outside its territories were utilised on its behalf for payments arising out of the war.

Grantham was aware, however, that rather more than this lay behind the unofficials' antipathy. Britain had still not made any public statement about Hong Kong's future and this had resulted in "the general critical view which they [the unofficials] take of HMG so far as HK is concerned". They feared that "in a showdown with the Chinese, HMG would climb down and desert the Colony". The unofficials were realistic enough to realise that, given Britain's current economic condition, no better offer would be forthcoming. They also did not wish to give comfort to "critics of the British Empire" by voicing such concerns publicly in the Legislative Council. They were therefore prepared to accept the proposed settlement "as representing a very real proof of sympathy and goodwill of HMG towards the Colony".[57] They also asked that Hong

Kong be immediately removed from British Treasury control and that a speedy resolution of all the "denial claims" be made.

On 2 June 1948, Landale introduced a motion to this effect into the Legislative Council. During the debate, it was M. K. Lo who most eloquently summed up the arguments. He stated that, although one could argue the finer points of the claims made by Hong Kong against Britain, on this occasion they were concerned with "the much more general question of a broad settlement of War expenditure". On such a matter "although dollars and cents must have their say in this mundane world, sentiment cannot be altogether excluded from our consideration". He referred to the sacrifices Britain had made during the war and to Hong Kong's healthy finances. In the worst, and most unlikely, scenario Hong Kong would be left with a HK$15 million deficit which, in view of the HK$30 million surplus of the year just past, appeared to be manageable. Only Landale mentioned Treasury control during the debate when he said,

> Before the war the Colony had reached the age of discretion and had achieved a certain degree of financial autonomy, but as a result of the war ... our finances deteriorated. However, during the two years since the war I submit that we have proved that we are capable of being re-instated to that same degree of financial autonomy that we enjoyed before the war, and it is the sincere hope of all my Unofficial Colleagues that our request will be acceded to.

The Colonial Secretary informed Council that the Secretary of State had recently said that he supported relaxation of Treasury control in principle and that "methods of achieving that end are now already in hand".[58] The motion was carried.

Treasury control

When a colony could not support itself and was in receipt of financial support from Britain, its finances came under British Treasury control. This was to safeguard the interests of the British taxpayer whose money was being used to support that colony. This required extensive financial reporting by the colony concerned and supervision by Treasury and the Colonial Office. Even after its finances were restored, Treasury would normally continue to exercise control for a further three years.

Hong Kong's case was different. It had been in receipt of imperial funds because it had been lost to the enemy. After the restoration of civil government, a very loose form of control had been exercised which had not in practice been onerous.[59] For the Colonial Office, it never amounted to more than securing "Treasury agreement to any particular class of fresh expenditure". It had also sought Treasury agreement to the Secretary of State's approval of Hong Kong's annual estimates. Although the Treasury was always reluctant to concede control, it had strangely never been willing to clearly or formally define it.[60] It was so nebulous, Young thought that because Hong Kong was forecasting a surplus, it had already been lifted.

Oddly, the Treasury left it to the Colonial Office to propose the nature of controls and, in 1947, they tried to do so. They did not want the standard level of control applied because Hong Kong did not have the capacity to produce the detailed financial reporting required. The Colonial Office did not want to "put any work on to the Government which is not absolutely necessary".[61] The Treasury's concern, however, was the Hong Kong government's financial policies and its urgent need to increase revenue. This would have helped ensure that Hong Kong would be able to balance its own budget without British help. It was also a prerequisite on which the Treasury insisted before it would consider financial assistance for rehabilitation.[62] Treasury control also concerned the unofficials. M. K. Lo first expressed concern to the Hong Kong government when he sent a draft of a Legislative Council question to the Financial Secretary in September 1947. He was concerned both at what Hong Kong's liabilities might be and at continuing Treasury control. He also referred to Treasury control during the budget debate in March 1948. His concern was based on his erroneous belief that it was the outstanding disputed items which resulted in this.[63]

Binding their acceptance of Britain's financial offer to the abolition of Treasury control proved, therefore, rather a hollow victory for the unofficials. Both the Colonial Office and Treasury were moving away from the concept of detailed control of a colony's finances. The Colonial Office thought it had "always proved to provide nothing but endless friction". It was also seen as desirable to remove it in view of the proposed constitutional changes which would have given more political power to the unofficials. The Treasury was also becoming more resigned to the fact that stringent financial control of colonies was counter-productive. During the war, colonial governors had been able to decide more for themselves in respect of financial matters when the Treasury had been unable to exercise its customary control. With remarkable candour, the Treasury realised "that the exercise of Treasury control involves the colony, the Colonial Office and the Treasury in much tiresome and often futile correspondence, the cost of which, in man-hours and money, would be difficult to justify".[64]

When, on 20 October 1948, Grantham announced in the Legislative Council that British Treasury control would cease retrospectively from 1 April that year this did not mean the removal of all financial controls from Britain. They were to be replaced by controls exercised by the Secretary of State whose approval would be required for the annual estimates, for expenditure involving important points of principle and for the terms of issue of government loans. Losses or write-offs would become a matter for the Legislative Council. The Secretary of State was to be "kept fully informed of the Colony's financial position and of the general trend of its financial policy at least quarterly". It was emphasized that "the key-note of the proposed arrangements is consultation rather than control".[65]

Conclusions

Young's determination to implement some form of income tax with at least a modicum of unofficial support is an example of how a Governor could operate effectively as a bureaucratic entrepreneur. It is also an example of how a Hong Kong Governor could act decisively in the face of opposition from unofficials with different policy preferences. Young won the support of all but three unofficials on the basis of his own authority, arguing strongly for the need to balance the budget. He skilfully built a coalition of unofficial support through the creation of committees. This allowed concerns to be addressed, support to be gradually built up and opposition whittled down. To ensure passage of the new tax, Young was prepared to take an incremental approach by agreeing to a minimal tax rate and to the continuation of separate pre-war taxes. His policies were also differentiated from those of the Colonial Office who, in the guise of Caine, would have preferred a full income tax as well as a higher tax rate but who was prepared to accept a lesser result. Perhaps, most importantly, Young's public resolve never wavered and he remained adamant that the tax must go ahead. In pushing through a new policy, when it was so clearly seen as the right thing to do, he was acting in a long-established tradition of British colonial governors.[66] It is also how Carpenter would have expected a bureaucratic entrepreneur to act.

The question remains why it was so important to gain at least some unofficial support. From a local perspective, this was a major new policy initiative which would have affected not only business but also the interests of the unofficials and the circles from which they came. Without at least a modicum of unofficial support it would have been difficult to implement the new taxes effectively. With some support, the unofficials could explain to Hong Kong's British and Chinese business communities why it was necessary to have such taxes and why there was no alternative. If Young had received no unofficial support then the matter would have had to have been referred to the Secretary of State.[67] This prospect does not seem to have perturbed the Colonial Office but it would have put them in a quandary. They would either have had to tell the Governor to pass legislation using the official majority or recall him.

The power of the Governor to influence opinion can also be seen in Grantham's handling of the disputed financial items. He had to persuade the Colonial Office, and through them the British Treasury, that there were real political concerns and that a financial settlement was necessary. He had also then to win the support of sceptical unofficials for a proposal to which they were, *prima facie,* opposed. Why, however, was unofficial support now so important? There were three factors accounting for the unofficials' influence. Firstly, they had the power to approve or not approve expenditure items. Ever since Stubbs had reformed the Finance Committee in 1920, it had had an unofficial majority. By the late 1940s it was, by custom, recognised that the Hong Kong government would not use the official majority in the Legislative Council to overturn this. If the unofficials had not been prepared to accept London's offer, the matter would have had to be referred back to the Secretary of State. Given the widespread feeling over these payments, simply replacing the unofficials would not have changed views in unofficial circles and the Colonial Office's only real option would have been to find a negotiated solution.

Secondly, there was a strong sense that these expenditure items were an imperial responsibility. There was a clear sense that while Hong Kong had been under Japanese occupation, expenditure relating to its recovery and the restoration of British administration was a matter for Britain and not Hong Kong. The fact that Hong Kong had made such a fast economic recovery, especially compared to Britain, seemed irrelevant to most unofficials. It was also related to the third factor, alluded to by Grantham, and that was the doubt felt in many unofficials' minds over Britain's commitment to Hong Kong if the Chinese or the American governments exerted pressure for the return of the colony to China. This may well have inculcated a view that there was "nothing to lose" in taking the stance they did over this issue which became a proxy for the real source of their discontent.

What does the unofficials' growing influence say about the Hong Kong government's autonomy? In both these cases the unofficials were able to wield almost extraordinary influence. It showed more clearly than the issue of *mui tsai* that if Hong Kong were to adopt new modernising measures, for example, increasing public revenue to pay for a broader range of public services, then unofficial support was essential to give them the necessary legitimacy. This was underscored by Young's efforts to secure unofficial support and the Colonial Office's relief that he had been able to do so. In the case of the disputed items, the unofficials were in disagreement with the British and not the Hong Kong government. This was by no means the first time they had been so but, apart from the 1940 evacuation case, it was the first time they had been able to influence so publicly a British government's decision in their favour. The pressure exerted upon an, albeit not unwilling, British government must only have served to increase the unofficials' standing, at least in their own eyes but also, as shall be seen, in Grantham's.

The imposition of income tax, the achievement of a financial settlement and the abolition of Treasury control are indicative of the development of a more complex power relationship between the British government, the Hong Kong government and the unofficials. This had come about as a result of the war and its disturbance of the routines of pre-war colonial administration and of the introduction of modernising measures. There was a growing need for the Hong Kong government, and indirectly the Colonial Office, to form an effective coalition with the unofficials in order to implement new policies. How the unofficials' growing influence was to be felt in this tripartite relationship will be examined in Chapter 7.

7
Constitutional Reform and Its Demise

In May 1946, on his return to Hong Kong, Young stated publicly that it was British and Hong Kong government policy to introduce changes to allow "the inhabitants of the territory ... a fuller and more responsible share in the management of their own affairs".[1] Six years later, the Secretary of State announced the time was "inopportune" for major constitutional reform.[2] In the interim, the Hong Kong government had presented four different proposals to the Colonial Office. Why was there such prolonged consideration? Why were there so many different proposals and what were their origins? Whose policy was reflected in the final decision not to proceed?

This chapter examines the origins of these proposals, how they were formulated and the barriers to their implementation. It reviews the interplay between the Governor and the Secretary of State on the one hand and the Governor and the unofficials on the other. It charts the growth of the unofficials' influence and examines their role in policy formulation. It compares the differing degrees to which Governors Young and Grantham were willing or able to define policy goals and their skills in influencing Hong Kong's unofficials, Colonial Office officials and successive Secretaries of State.

It also examines the extent to which these policies were unique to the Hong Kong government. It considers whose policies—the Governor's, the Secretary of State's or the unofficials'—eventually prevailed. It examines the Hong Kong government's capacity to implement and formulate policy and the growing influence of the unofficials in policy formulation. It also looks at the balance of political support between Britain and Hong Kong for these various proposals and the influence this had on the outcome.

Young and constitutional reform

The public statements made by the Governor and the Secretary of State on 1 May 1946 committed both the British and Hong Kong governments to constitutional reform. These statements added that one way of achieving this was through "a Municipal Council, constituted on a fully representative basis".[3] The Secretary of State stated his preference for a body elected on a wide franchise, responsible for important functions of government and with power over its own finances. This superseded the China Association's favoured format of a municipal council established on a narrow franchise and with extensive powers. Young was told to formulate plans, consult widely and report back to the Secretary of State with his findings and recommendations by the end of October.[4]

Constitutional reform was not one of Young's top priorities. There were the more pressing issues of finance, supply and housing.[5] In late May, however, Young appointed Hazelrigg as special adviser on constitutional reform. He was a lawyer with long experience in the Hong Kong government who had worked on this issue twelve months previously when with the Hong Kong Planning Unit. Young and he seemed to share a common outlook; there were similar themes present in both Hazelrigg's June 1945 paper and Young's detailed proposals submitted in October 1946.

Young demonstrated the same determination and single-minded devotion to consultation and planning as he was later to show in respect of the passage of income tax legislation. By the end of May 1946, he had sent letters to Chinese and non-Chinese organisations seeking their views on proposed constitutional reform. He asked them whether the establishment of a municipal council and the transfer to it of some of government's functions would be the best way of doing so. Notices inviting the submission of views were published in the local English and Chinese language press and the *China Mail* asked its readers to respond to a survey on the issue.[6] By the end of August, Young had formulated his proposals and announced them in a broadcast on Hong Kong radio in both English and Chinese. During September, he consulted further on these revised proposals which included having twenty private interviews with the entire committee of the Hong Kong General Chamber of Commerce (HKGCC).[7]

In October, when Young responded to the Secretary of State, he recommended the establishment of a municipal council of thirty members. It would represent all of Hong Kong Island, Kowloon and New Kowloon and its seats would be divided equally between Chinese and non-Chinese. Two-thirds of its members would be directly elected. The Chinese elected members would represent wards in Hong Kong Island and Kowloon and the non-Chinese ones would be elected from a central list. The remaining members would be chosen by selected representative organisations, again equally split between Chinese and non-Chinese organisations. The franchise would be based either on property or jury service qualifications. It would not be restricted to British subjects but there would be a residential qualification. Non-British subjects would also be able to stand for election subject to a longer residency requirement. Young wanted his proposed municipal council to be widely representative.

Young also proposed reforms to the Legislative Council that would have given it an unofficial majority excluding the Governor who would have both an original and casting vote. He proposed that the number of official members in the Legislative Council be reduced from four to two with the five ex-officio members being retained. He recommended formalisation of the convention that the Hong Kong General Chamber of Commerce and the Justices of the Peace nominate one unofficial member each. He also proposed that the municipal council nominate two of its members as unofficials.

Confidentially, Young admitted to the Secretary of State that there was a great deal of apathy and apprehension towards constitutional reform. He had received only a dozen replies from the public and the *China Mail* had received less than a hundred responses to its survey. Little space was devoted to the subject in the local press and many organisations had commented on the indifference of their members. He also admitted that his recommendations "cannot be said to represent the unanimous wishes of the community or even the strongly expressed desire of any large section of it". This did not deter him. Young saw constitutional reform as necessary if Hong Kong was ever

> to develop an active sense of citizenship and to become capable of openly expressing and giving practical effect to the general desire of its inhabitants to remain under British rule and to resist absorption by China.

This "general desire" was constrained by widespread apprehension over whether Hong Kong would remain British or would shortly be returned to China. The proposed constitutional changes were seen as a way of prolonging British rule in Hong Kong. Anyone supporting it, therefore, might be thought a British collaborator. It was also feared a municipal council could come under the sway of the Kuomintang and become embroiled in Chinese politics. Young thought such fears could be overcome by careful design of the structure of the council.

Colonial Office reaction

Sir Thomas Lloyd, Gent's successor in the Colonial Office, supported this view. He accepted Young's and MacDougall's arguments that to allay fears Britain would abandon Hong Kong, local Chinese should be given a clear lead by government. Such a lead could be given through the proposed constitutional reforms. In MacDougall's view, this would help overcome apathy and fear by showing Britain's sincerity in allowing local people more participation in their own government. Young also thought his proposed measures were

> the main hope ... for the future of Hong Kong as a British possession. Constitutional reform will aim at augmenting the number and strengthening the hands of the citizens with an actual stake in the Colony

Having made a public commitment to change, it now had to happen.[8]

Caine continued to harbour doubts about the suitability of a municipal council. His views were vindicated by the Governor's observations that there was no real support for his proposals or demand for change. Caine favoured greater democratisation of Central Government as the best way of "introducing an element of greater democracy into the real Government of the territory". Caine's colleague N. L. Mayle, was simply against reform as "there is apparently no substantial body of opinion in favour of constitutional advance". In December, a consensus emerged within the Colonial Office when it was agreed that, in view of the public announcements made on 1 May, "there was no going back". The Secretary of State should be advised to suggest that Young drop his proposal for a municipal council and instead focus on reform of central government to include election of some Legislative Council members.

Creech-Jones, Secretary of State since 7 October 1946, favoured Legislative Council reform. He did not favour communal representation and supported election of some members by a non-communal electorate and others nominated by the Governor. He supported an equal number of official and elected members with an unofficial majority created by members nominated by the Governor. Some unofficials should serve on the Executive Council and they should "... gradually assume some responsibility in the Executive". His was also concerned about the possible impact of shortly to be announced changes to Singapore's Legislative Council which would allow for direct elections on a broad non-communal franchise. If it was thought that Hong Kong's municipal council was being established to avoid greater liberalisation of the Legislative Council, this announcement might exacerbate the decided lack of enthusiasm on the part of the inhabitants of Hong Kong for any constitutional changes.

He thought there would be more opportunity to control Kuomintang influence in a reformed Legislative Council with its official membership than in a municipal council with none. He also preferred changes to central government rather than creating something new which, if it went wrong, could prove difficult to rectify.[9] Creech-Jones was probably a bit over-concerned about the impact of Singapore's reforms on Hong Kong. Singapore's politics were less communally based than Hong Kong's were and there was local support in Singapore for such an approach. There also turned out to be little enthusiasm for elections to Singapore's new Legislative Council or its reformed Municipal Commission.[10]

Young was not in favour of abandoning his proposals. After allegedly consulting only four of his officials, who probably included MacDougall and Hazelrigg, both in favour of his scheme,[11] Young quickly rejected the Secretary of State's counter-proposals. He thought that Kuomintang influence would be difficult to counter in a partly elected Legislative Council. He also thought that Singapore was an inappropriate analogy because of Hong Kong's more transient population and much closer connection with China.[12] Creech-Jones acquiesced and, in March 1947, announced in the House of Commons that he had accepted the Governor's recommendations in principle.[13]

The China Association's views seem not to have changed since the discussions in the Colonial Office in 1945. After the Secretary of State's announcement in the House of Commons in March 1947, the Association had further discussed the nature of the proposed municipal council with the Colonial Office. They made a last-ditch attempt to secure the kind of small European-dominated council, modelled on the pre-war Shanghai Municipal Council, which had originally been mooted in 1945. Creech-Jones told the China Association, however, that

> we should find it impossible to defend any system which, in the circumstances of a territory such as Hong Kong, appeared to have the intention of ensuring a permanent European majority on the Municipal Council.[14]

Young remained disappointed that he never received formal notification of this acceptance before he left Hong Kong on retirement in May 1947. This was not sent until July,[15] by which time Hong Kong's new Governor, Sir Alexander Grantham, had arrived.

Young and autonomy

To what extent had the Hong Kong government under Young exercised autonomy over this issue? Would Young have had the capacity to implement it? Could he have won the unofficials' support?

By the time Young was chosen as Governor, a decision in principle to institute constitutional reform had already been taken by the Colonial Office. Although Young had been able to contribute to debate on the issue before arriving in Hong Kong, he was, in effect, faced with a *fait accompli*. His instructions had been clear. He was to consult on constitutional reform and to develop detailed proposals accordingly. During his twelve months in office, however, Young proceeded to make these proposals his own. It was he who fleshed them out and who consulted widely. He defended them vigorously despite a lack of support for them in Hong Kong and in the face of the Secretary of State's preference for Legislative Council reform. So much were the proposals identified with him personally, they became known as the "Young Plan". As Louis argues, he may have "... succeeded in committing the Colonial Office to the principle of municipal self-government".[16] Young's policy was unique inasmuch that the Secretary of State acquiesced to it when he insisted it was the correct one. It could be argued, that when he left Hong Kong in May 1947, it had also become the politically differentiated policy of the Hong Kong government.

Could Young have implemented his proposals? Although both Young and MacDougall were confident they could have, it would have taken their concerted strong leadership to have succeeded. Judging from Young's efforts to secure passage of his income tax legislation, he would probably have been equally persistent in canvassing support for constitutional reform. Would he have succeeded? He showed, in his handling of both income tax and constitutional reform, that he was willing to compromise on detail if his principles remained intact. Compromise had been reached with the unofficials over income tax because additional public revenue was clearly needed and no viable alternative had been identified. Young was now proposing to dilute the long-established and publicly recognised oligarchic influence of the elite through his proposed municipal council. This was the group that government had relied upon to govern the local Chinese community since at least Lockhart's reforms in the 1890s. Winning unofficial support for his proposed council would have been a more difficult battle than he had faced over income tax.

The absence of unofficial support for Young's proposed reforms does not seem to have concerned the Colonial Office. Given the fundamental changes proposed, it would have been awkward if the official majority had been required to carry the reform legislation. Recalling the Governor would have achieved little and replacement of the unofficials would not have changed the scheme's underlying unpopularity. The Hong Kong government's autonomy under Young on this issue was therefore never put to the ultimate test of implementation. Young's proposals resulted in neither the creation of a more autonomous form of government or in the implementation of his preferred policy. He had no opportunity to show whether the Hong Kong government really had the capacity, or the ability, to build the necessary coalition to implement this policy in the face of such strong local opposition.

Grantham and constitutional reform: The initial months

Sir Alexander Grantham arrived as Governor in Hong Kong on 27 July 1947. The Secretary of State's despatch approving Young's recommendations had just been published the day before. On his arrival, Grantham publicly expressed his full support for them. He stated that they represented

> a great step forward on the democratic path by the establishment of a municipality and ... the creation of an unofficial majority in the Legislative Council.

He even thought that

> it would be a very great mistake ... if there were to be a new policy, because that would mean the stopping of everything that was being done and starting all over again.

This would "at best mean a long delay".[17]

On the surface, matters looked as if they were proceeding in accordance with the Secretary of State's instructions to "proceed forthwith with all detailed preparations including the drafting of the necessary legislation".[18] Shortly after his arrival, Grantham told the Secretary of State that the municipal council bills were ready for publication and asked for his further views on external control. Young had argued that the proposed municipal council should have "the most complete control over its own affairs" and that the Governor should have no power of veto over it.[19] Grantham disagreed and the Secretary of State also had concerns which he wished to consider further. It was not unreasonable for Grantham to ask the Secretary of State to clarify his views on such an important issue as external control: any bill which omitted to address such a crucial point would have been considered incomplete The Secretary of State also had reservations over Young's recommendation that the council should have control over its own finances which he was considering further.

Grantham sent a reminder in October and said the bills had been printed and were about to be considered by the Executive Council.[20] The following month he sent the draft ordinances to Mayle in the Colonial Office.[21] He had also appointed a cadet, J. H. B. Lee,[22] a long-serving but passed-over junior cadet, to replace Hazelrigg who had retired the previous May. Despite these appearances of progress, Grantham must have started to have doubts about the proposed reforms. In early August, he had met representatives of the Hong Kong General Chamber of Commerce who, he later claimed had, "never been in favour of it [the Young Plan]". He also claimed that, when Young had met its committee members separately in September 1946, eight of them had expressed their opposition to it.[23] It is unlikely that by August 1947 they had changed their views.

Grantham and constitutional reform

The Colonial Office did not reply to Grantham on the questions of finance and external control until 27 March 1948.[24] They had been delayed five months awaiting the Treasury's comments. Grantham was told that the Municipal Council would need to submit estimates to the Hong Kong government for approval and any additional revenue required would need to be given as a grant-in-aid from Hong Kong's general revenue. There would also have to be some form of external controls and by-laws would need to be confirmed by the Hong Kong government as municipal by-laws were by the Minister of Health in England.[25]

The first signs of obfuscation and delay by Grantham began to appear during the Legislative Council meeting of 19 March 1948. Constitutional reform was clearly not one of his priorities; Grantham gave it only one paragraph at the end of his long and comprehensive annual policy address at this meeting. Delays, he said, had been caused by practical problems of implementation such as organising the voting arrangements and the preparation of the various bills. He made no mention of his wait for a reply from the Secretary of State on the issues of financial and external control. One clue to his deliberate obfuscation was when he said he was awaiting the Colonial Office's reply on the draft bills.[26] When the Colonial Office read of this in June they were taken by surprise because in his letter of the previous November, Grantham had said he had sent the bills for information only. It said they would now respond but Grantham replied, rather insouciantly, that it should not bother and that he would send them complete bills shortly.[27]

The Colonial Office's changing perceptions

From June until November 1948, it appears neither the Hong Kong government nor the Colonial Office took any further action. There was also a growing awareness within the Colonial Office of the disquiet felt in Hong Kong over the proposals. There had been a stream of visitors, both official and unofficial including Dr Chau Sik-nin, an Executive and Legislative Council member. From them, the Colonial Office had learnt that "there is little or no enthusiasm in Hong Kong for these constitutional changes at all". There was also an awareness that inaction could lead to criticism. Lord Listowel, the Under-Secretary of State for the Colonies, believed there was a "risk that political capital may be made by the Chinese out of inaction". However, the changing situation in China, particularly the communist victories over the Kuomintang, concerned Colonial Office officials. They wondered whether a municipal council might be "captured" by one or the other of the two warring parties. Grantham was asked whether he should therefore "go slow, or indeed ... mark time" over the proposed council and constitutional reform and where he thought the "balance of advantage lies".[28]

This was just the opening Grantham had been waiting for. Only now, in November 1948, did Grantham formally discuss the Secretary of State's secret telegram of 27 March, with its comments on financial and external control, in the Executive Council. He then told the Colonial Office that he now had "grave objections to Government going back on its word and political capital would be made out of any such withdrawal". He also took the opportunity to start redefining the debate. He made clear that

> there are many fundamental points in proposals already published regarding which criticism has been publicly voiced and, when [*sic*] Municipal Council Bill [is] ... published, there will probably be counter proposals from Unofficial Members which would oblige me to defer proceeding further with the bills pending consideration of counter proposals in consultation with you.

This was a tacit recognition that the original proposals could not be implemented. Grantham also made clear, as he was again to do later, that the Secretary of State had his part to play in deciding on this issue. Grantham's views were portrayed rather more starkly by J. B. Sidebotham who commented that

> the Governor ... is pretty sure that, when the Bills come up for [consultation] in the Legislative Council, there will be sufficient criticism of them from the Unofficial side to necessitate a considerable

amount of 'back peddling' and delay and even, possibly, the abandonment of the Municipal Council project entirely.[29]

The campaign to prepare the Colonial Office for the abandonment of the Young Plan continued during the first few months of 1949. In January, the unofficials told J. J. Paskin, a senior Colonial Office official visiting Hong Kong, that

> there is an extremely strong and absolutely unanimous opinion amongst the Unofficial Members that the scheme ... is on quite the wrong lines ... it was much too complicated.

The unofficials called for publication of the bills to allow the public to judge for themselves. They assured Paskin that "unofficial members were confident that ... there will emerge a fairly solid public opinion against the proposals".[30] The Colonial Office soon afterwards started to begin to accept that publication of the draft bills would result in further change.[31]

The unofficials' role

Grantham allowed the unofficials a seemingly more independent role in the formulation of policy on constitutional reform. On 30 March 1949, during the budget debate in the Legislative Council, the senior unofficial member, D. F. Landale, raised this question. He took Grantham's cue that the Colonial Office was to blame for the delay in publishing the proposed reform legislation. He poured ridicule on its somnolent attitude and compared it to a scene from *Alice in Wonderland*. He made clear that the unofficials would use their position on the Finance Committee to block funds for preparation work for the proposed municipal council until "an opportunity should be given to this Council to debate the advisability, or otherwise, of the new Constitution taking the form of a Municipal Council". He felt opinion was strongly in favour of "a larger and more representative Legislative Council working in conjunction with a larger and more representative Urban Council". He thought that "the cumbersome machinery of the proposed Municipal Council ... would overlap a lot of the functions of the Colonial Government". As draft legislation would be required to bring these reforms into effect he asked that the draft bills be published soon and that unofficial members had at least two months

> to ascertain whether the proposals meet with ... the general approval and, if not, whether they should be wholly rejected or amendments considered.[32]

Grantham closed this debate by setting out a road map which the unofficials were largely to follow. A municipal council, he told them, "can only be brought into effect by an Ordinance". However, changes to the Legislative Council required changes to the Royal Instructions made by the Secretary of State. Government would therefore publish the draft bills and if the unofficials disagreed with them, they should "bring forward alternative proposals" best done by bringing "a resolution forward in this Council with those alternative proposals". If there were

> more than one set of alternative proposals ... it would obviously be better ... if the Unofficial Members could agree amongst themselves as to what alternative proposals they would like.

He assured Members that it was

> not the intention to steam-roller through the Legislative Council the existing proposals and any alternative proposals that have the backing of the Unofficial Members of this Council will receive my fullest consideration and will be forwarded to the Secretary of State for the Colonies with my recommendations.[33]

This was a direct affirmation that the official majority would not be used to pass unwelcome reform proposals through the Legislative Council. It also signified that if the unofficials preferred reform of the Legislative Council over creation of a municipal council, this was for the Secretary of State to decide and not Grantham.

This exchange smacks of some prearranged understanding between Grantham and the unofficials. The closeness of that relationship may have reflected Grantham's background and the circumstances leading to his appointment. He had joined the Hong Kong government as a cadet in 1922 and had served mostly in the Colonial Secretariat.[34] He was a sociable and outgoing officer who mixed easily in both government and business circles[35] and had made something of a mark for himself.[36] He was ambitious and, seeing little immediate prospect for promotion in Hong Kong, had taken the unusual step of asking the Colonial Office for a posting elsewhere. He had gained experience as Colonial Secretary in Bermuda, a stepping stone to further promotion, and in Jamaica and as Chief Secretary in Nigeria before becoming Governor of Fiji in 1945.[37]

It is unclear why Grantham in particular was chosen for Hong Kong. His contemporaries in Hong Kong had not expected him to become Governor and some had thought he had been appointed through friends in London.[38] In December 1946, the China Association had lobbied for a "really good man" and a "first class Governor" to replace Young. Lloyd later commented that most of the Association's doubts would be set at rest by the news of the selection ... of a fairly young and thoroughly experienced officer and preferably one known to them by repute.[39]

Such an officer would have to have been a member of the Colonial Administrative Service who had served in Hong Kong, or perhaps in the Straits Settlements or Malaya. Grantham's name would have arisen as someone of the right age (mid- to late forties), familiar with Hong Kong and Hong Kong business people (through his previous service) and qualified for the job through experience (in other colonies and as a colonial Governor). He may not have lobbied for the position because he was then Governor in Fiji and claimed to be looking forward to a further three years there.[40] However, he was probably later aware of the China Association's lobbying for appointment of someone like himself as Governor. This would have cemented his already good relations with Hong Kong's expatriate British business community.

Unofficials' motion

Events now began to gather pace. Grantham further warned the Colonial Office of growing popular disquiet over the delay. He claimed that local feeling was in favour of "an enlarged Legislative Council with a greater unofficial representation".[41] On 27 April, Landale tabled a motion in the Legislative Council.[42] He pointed out that,

> For a year or more ... all my Unofficial colleagues have been far from convinced that [Sir Mark Young's] proposals ... were what the genuine inhabitants of the Colony desired.

His motion, tabled on behalf of all unofficials, referred to their disquiet over the proposed constitutional changes since the publication of the Secretary of State's despatches last July. He also claimed that insufficient consideration had been given to other options. He stated that the best way of "giving to the inhabitants of the Colony a fuller and more responsible share in the management of their own affairs" was to undertake a "more fundamental modification of the Constitution of the Legislative Council."

The unofficials' motion set out to do this. It proposed that the establishment of a municipal council be "abandoned" and that the Legislative Council should be reconstituted with an unofficial majority of one. The Legislative Council proposed that it should consist of twenty members, of whom nine, including the Governor, would be official and eleven unofficial. Of the latter, some would be "elected by qualified residents of British Nationality" and others would be nominated by the Governor. Only when the Legislative Council had been so reconstituted should consideration then be given to the reform of the Urban Council, with a view to giving it "a greater measure of direct representation and an increase in its financial and administrative powers in municipal affairs".

The motion was tabled early to allow time for public opinion to be expressed.[43] Grantham also explained to the Secretary of State that it was tabled before the publication of the draft bills, which he had earlier said was a crucial first step, as he claimed that Landale would be retiring shortly and leaving the colony.[44] The draft Municipal Council Bills were not published until 3 June 1949 which Grantham thought might "help quieten public agitation over constitutional reform". It elicited some comment from the local press. The *Wah Kiu Yat Po* thought the Municipal Council Bills did not meet most people's aspirations but conceded that it would provide for an expression of public opinion. The *Ta Kung Pao* was disappointed that the Municipal Council would have very limited power.[45]

The motion was debated in the Legislative Council on 22 June 1949.[46] MacDougall had already left Hong Kong on early retirement and been replaced by J. F. Nicoll.[47] In Landale's absence, the motion was introduced by Sir Man-kam Lo. He outlined in more detail a slightly revised proposal which now called for a slightly smaller reconstituted Legislative Council with an unofficial majority of five members. Of seventeen members, six would be official, including the Governor with a casting vote and normal reserve powers, plus eleven unofficials. Six of the unofficials would be Chinese, four elected and two nominated by the Governor. Five would be non-Chinese, three elected and three nominated by the Governor. One of these should be Portuguese if none of that community had been elected. Only British subjects would be eligible to vote. There would be separate electoral rolls enabling Chinese electors to vote for Chinese members and *pari passu* for non-Chinese.

Lo made it clear that the motion had the full support of all unofficials who considered that "their proposal represents a fair and acceptable compromise". He indirectly rebuked the Hong Kong government and the Colonial Office when he said that,

> If it commands a general measure of popular support and will receive the urgent consideration of Your Excellency and the Secretary of State for the Colonies, they [the unofficials] see no reason why it should not be practicable to implement it within a very short time—even a matter of a few months.[48]

The motion would also appear to have been authored by the unofficials themselves. M. M. Watson[49] stated that,

> For many months past and at many meetings of the Unofficial Members of this Council, the subject of the reform or modernisation

of the constitution of the Colony has been discussed. Needless to say they have also discussed the matter with a large number of the residents of the Colony.

There had been little public enthusiasm for reform. He had to admit that the public had shown a "somewhat surprising lack of interest in the subject". Nor had he been able

> to find any definite trend of opinion for either the one or the other method of the forms which have been suggested; that is to say, the changes in the Legislative Council proposed in this Motion or the establishment of a Municipal Council as set out in the proposals of Sir Mark Young and which have now been embodied in the draft Municipal Council Bill.

Despite this, the proposed reforms had unanimous unofficial support and "there is no hesitation on their part in recommending them to the public".[50]

This somewhat odd almost contradictory view was echoed by Leo d'Almada e Castro. He cast doubt on whether any wider support for reform existed among Hong Kong's long-established Chinese residents. He could

> see no evidence over the last six weeks since this motion was first tabled, no evidence that the large majority of residents of long standing in this Colony want any reform at all.

Yet he finished by saying,

> I am strongly of the view that delay in this matter is neither necessary nor desirable and I can see no reason why reform as tabled in this motion should not come into being in 1950.

Chau Tsun-nin thought the Urban Council should be reformed as soon as possible after reconstitution of the Legislative Council. Dr Chau Sik-nin, in opposition to all other unofficials, supported extension of the franchise to all Hong Kong residents, subject to a residence and property qualification.[51]

The motion was carried. The unofficials gave their unanimous support and the officials all abstained. This helped underscore Grantham's delegation of policy formulation on constitutional reform to the unofficials. In closing, Grantham merely summed up the debate. He made clear that the final decision lay with the Secretary of State whom he would consult "as soon as possible", putting forward his own views and recommendations.[52]

Grantham's despatches

In August, Grantham sent two lengthy despatches to the Secretary of State, one open and the other secret. The secret one was particularly illuminating. In it, he set out the recent history of the "Young Plan". According to Grantham, this was a story of things that went wrong and for which everyone but himself was to blame. He tried to show that all along there had been little if any local support for Young's proposals. The Hong Kong General Chamber of Commerce, with close ties to the China Association, had never supported it. He thought the unofficials were justified in their motion when they claimed that "sufficient consideration was not given to alternative methods". This was because Young had only consulted four officials on Creech-Jones's alternative proposal to limit reforms to the Legislative Council.[53]

He also blamed MacDougall,[54] though not by name, for agreeing to a suggestion by the Secretary of State. This was that anyone who was not on the Jury List because he could not understand English should be allowed to vote.[55] Grantham was also not above using rather intemperate language to criticise the Secretary of State. As he rather graphically put it, "such a franchise was open to the whole semi-illiterate mass of the population and the danger of packing of such an electorate by interests outside the Colony is self-evident." Again, criticising the Secretary of State, he told him the matter had been

> held in abeyance for several months while your further observations ... on external control over the affairs of the Municipality were awaited ...

Further delay had been caused by the need to await comment from the Colonial Office's legal adviser and by pressure of work in the Attorney-General's Chambers and the Attorney-General's absence on leave. When, in November 1948, the Executive Council had eventually considered the matter

> it was clear from this discussion that there would be strong opposition to the scheme from the Unofficial Members when the Bills were introduced into the Legislative Council.

Grantham recommended acceptance of the unofficials' motion. He claimed, without explanation, that having an unofficial majority was something which "must come sooner or later, and the advocacy of it by the Unofficials had brought it to the front now". He stressed that the motion did not mean abandoning the municipal council proposal but merely postponing its implementation. It would be considered by a Commission to be established for the purpose, and then by "the newly constituted Legislative Council with its unofficial majority". He finished by stressing the importance of two things. First, "that this matter should be dealt with urgently". He conceded that delay in implementing the Young Plan proposals "was perhaps fortunate in that it gave an opportunity for a complete reconsideration of the scheme". Second, he stressed to the Secretary of State that the decision belonged to him, and him alone, and that he should not refer it back to Hong Kong for further discussion. He lectured him by saying that

> I trust that you will make your decision a final one after further consultation with me if necessary—in no way subject to reconsideration in the Colony.

He continued to distance himself from this decision by adding that

> moreover, it seems to be accepted here that the decision will be yours. I was careful to stress this point in my speech at LegCo on 22 June.[56]

The Colonial Office's response

There was division within the Colonial Office over Grantham's new proposals. The officials were loath to contemplate such a large unofficial majority in the Legislative Council or to have to rely upon reserve powers to maintain government control. Under the former, there was the risk that the government might be outvoted in the Legislative Council and could not always rely upon the preponderance of European unofficials to vote for the government. The latter was intended only for use in extreme circumstances and was not suitable for dealing with routine matters. There was also awareness among unofficials of the changes taking place in China which could affect Hong Kong. The incident where HMS *Amethyst* was fired upon by Chinese communist forces in the Yangtze River in April 1949 had seriously affected British prestige in China and Hong Kong. The approach of the Communist forces in Southern China, and the Cabinet decision to reinforce Hong Kong in mid-1949 all pointed to the need for caution. Sir Charles Jeffries[57] summed up the Colonial Office's position by saying that

> political developments in China have ... killed the Young Plan. It would be impossible now to hand over effective control of key services to a municipal body which might quite easily be anti-British in character.

Creech-Jones, however, was prepared to accept Grantham's recommendations but was not keen on them. He wondered how Grantham could justify allocation of a disproportionate number of Legislative

Council seats to Europeans when there were some 1.8 million Chinese in Hong Kong and only some 14,000 non-Chinese. He thought the problem was

> not only one of counting heads of British subjects but also of reconciling to this principle racism and other interests in Hong Kong.[58]

There had been several parliamentary questions on Hong Kong's constitutional reform in the latter part of 1949 but these did not seem to pose much of a political threat to Creech-Jones. They may have helped him agree with Grantham's proposals as, although he might not have liked them, they would at least have shown that action on reform was under way.

In January 1950, Paskin wrote to Grantham to tell him that the Secretary of State generally agreed with his proposals. It was now some six months since the unofficials' motion. Hong Kong, and its recently reinforced garrison, was braced for any possible threat from the new Chinese government. Ostensibly, in view of these factors, Paskin asked Grantham whether he would "still consider that this matter of constitutional reform is urgent". Paskin's query may also have been a ploy to play for time and hope that they could change Creech-Jones' decision as Paskin warned that the forthcoming British general election would make

> consultation with Ministers more difficult on anything except the most urgent business. This may well ... delay final decisions on your proposals.

Grantham agreed the matter was not urgent but neither did he want undue delay. Over the next two months feeling grew in the Colonial Office that now was not the time for major constitutional reform. Comments from recent Hong Kong visitors led Jeffries to believe that

> constitutional reform is not a burning question with the general public, and that the introduction of some elected members and a raising of the unofficial side to equality with the official side of the Legislative Council would give general satisfaction.[59]

Grantham's revised scheme

In June 1950, Grantham suddenly produced revised proposals. This was on the eve of his return to Britain on leave and for meetings at the Colonial Office. He had discussed his new proposals with Executive Council members just the day before he left. He claimed that

> 'liberal' elements had got 'cold feet' and that the wind was now blowing against constitutional advance to the extent envisaged in the 1949 proposals.

This change was probably because Nicoll, on his return from Britain just before Grantham left, had updated him on the Colonial Office's latest thinking on constitutional reform. This was that a bare official majority in the Legislative Council would now suffice. Grantham now proposed that the Legislative Council should have fifteen members with an unofficial majority of five. There would now be indirect rather than direct elections for some of the unofficials. The Unofficial Justices of the Peace would nominate one European and one Chinese member and the Chinese Chamber and General Chambers of Commerce would nominate one member each. The Urban Council would also be allowed to nominate two members. Four unofficial members would be nominated by the Governor, at least two of whom would be Chinese. There would be five official members, including the Governor, with an original and casting vote, who would retain the usual reserve powers.[60]

Colonial Office officials were prepared to accept Grantham's new proposals but the new Secretary of State, James Griffiths, was not happy with them. He preferred the Young Plan as he thought this the best way of Hong Kong remaining as a British colony. By now the Korean War had broken out and he decided to wait for six months before replying. However, Grantham and the Colonial Office officials wanted to move forward as they were concerned that without some progress they would be subject to local criticism in Hong Kong for their inaction. There had been some such response but Grantham seems to have paid this scant attention. Before progress could be made, however, Griffiths had to be persuaded to reply to Grantham's despatch of August 1949. To try and persuade him to do so, Grantham and Colonial Office officials tried to meet his concerns by modifying his proposals slightly to expand the representation of the Urban Council. He now proposed to extend the electorate for the Urban Council by including non-English-speaking British subjects and increase to three the number of unofficial members they could nominate to the Legislative Council. Hong Kong's unofficials would not agree with this as they wanted to retain their influence in the Legislative Council and not see the expansion of the Urban Council. Grantham eventually persuaded them to accept a modified arrangement. The Legislative Council would have one more member nominated by the Governor and the Governor would no longer have an original vote but would retain a casting vote. The problem was how to manage the change from the 1949 proposals to the new ones. Paskin thought,

> that it should be contrived that the new proposals should appear to be put forward on the initiative of the unofficials in Hong Kong.

Another difficulty was that before this could happen, the unofficials wanted the Secretary of State to reply to Grantham's despatch of the previous August.[61] Nicoll, the Officer Administering the Government during Grantham's absence, reported that

> the Unofficials would ... have preferred that they should not be asked to put up another motion but they appreciate the difficulties.

There had been a growing feeling in the Colonial Office and the Foreign Office that it was not an opportune time to implement major constitutional reform in Hong Kong. At the end of 1950, the Foreign Office had advised strongly against doing so. The Chinese Communist Party had been very quiet over Hong Kong and the Foreign Office did not want to give the new Chinese Communist government "an excuse to raise the question of the retrocession of Hong Kong to China".[62] Grantham, who was asked if he would object to postponing the reforms, thought that Hong Kong people would be too concerned with "more immediate and material problems". He proposed leaving matters as they were until the situation became clearer. Jeffries and Griffiths both concurred[63] and there the matter rested for the remainder of 1951.

Grantham's second proposal

In October 1951, the Conservatives returned to power and Oliver Lyttelton became Secretary of State for the Colonies. In December, he made the first ever visit of a Secretary of State to Hong Kong.[64] He met local organisations and unofficial members of the Executive and Legislative Councils[65] with whom

> some sensible and gradual developments of the constitution were ... discussed, and I found little difficulty in giving the affirmative impression that I felt without committing myself too far upon the details.[66]

He was also "inclined to go no further in the direction of constitutional reform than the minimum which might be considered necessary".[67]

Little popular support for reform was expressed during the Secretary of State's visit.[68] Although the Executive Council unofficials were not in favour of reform they agreed the time had come for action. Grantham told the Secretary of State in Hong Kong that both he and the unofficials felt that the mere fact that nothing had happened

> was beginning to lead to agitation; that he would find it increasingly difficult to hold the position for very much longer; and that the consequent restiveness in Hong Kong itself would become more embarrassing.[69]

In early January 1952 Grantham, whom Lyttelton later described as "one of the ablest and most successful of all the colonial Governors",[70] submitted a new proposal for reform. This was little different from the one he had made in 1950. He now proposed a Legislative Council of sixteen members with the Governor, four officials and eleven unofficials. The Governor would nominate five of the unofficials. The Justices of the Peace would elect one Chinese and one non-Chinese member, the Hong Kong General Chamber of Commerce and the Chinese Chamber of Commerce would each elect one member each and the Urban Council two. All members would be British subjects but the members of the electing bodies need not be. The Governor would have a casting but not an original vote. Because the Governor would not now have an original vote, this would increase the size of the unofficial majority from five to six. Senior unofficials proposed the Urban Council should consist of six nominated and four elected members.

In February 1952, Nicoll reinforced Grantham's and the unofficials' view that there was a need for action when he attended a meeting at the Colonial Office. He reiterated that inaction was now a worse option than proceeding with reform. Nicoll thought the Hong Kong government could still "carry the day" on any important issue even with the unofficial majority now proposed for the Legislative Council. The problem was still how to manage the implementation of the reforms. Grantham had suggested two approaches to the management of the public perception of change. Firstly, that the Secretary of State should reply to his August 1949 despatch and he commended a draft he had sent the previous March. Secondly, both his August 1949 open despatch and the Secretary of State's reply should be published. Then "after a short interval the senior unofficial member of Legislative Council would give notice of a motion in the Legislative Council recommending revised proposals".[71]

The Foreign Office, whose objections had stayed Grantham's 1950 proposals, was this time given little room for manoeuvre. In a strongly argued letter, they were told that the Secretary of State had accepted the Governor's view that it was now desirable to proceed with the "programme which was put into cold storage in March 1951". That was why he had told the Reform Club of Hong Kong that "a measure of constitutional reform was under sympathetic consideration". The Foreign Office was also told that Grantham's latest proposals had already been discussed in the Executive Council which had agreed "that the balance of disadvantage would now lie on the side of continued inaction". The Secretary of State trusted the Foreign Office would accept his views "that we should now go ahead with these proposals". However, as if to assuage the Foreign Office, they were assured that

Constitutional Reform and Its Demise   131

> If ... the situation in the Far East should deteriorate to a point where it would clearly be impolitic to proceed ... there would be no great difficulty in devising some reason for putting the whole matter into cold storage again.[72]

The Foreign Office acquiesced to this toughly worded approach. The next question was whether the Cabinet should be consulted. The Cabinet Office thought that the Prime Minister would want to discuss this and asked for a short paper. This made it very clear that the Governor's 1949 proposals had been stalled because of Foreign Office objection which had now been withdrawn. It would now be difficult not to implement these proposals. Britain could be accused of inaction with potentially greater adverse effects than any Chinese Communist Party propaganda. The Secretary of State was also prepared to say that if the situation in the Far East again deteriorated the proposals could be further deferred.[73] The Cabinet agreed to the proposal without apparent comment. Grantham agreed that the Secretary of State, in reply to his 1949 despatch, should ask him to consider broadening the franchise to include non-British subjects and encourage him to consider the possibility of indirect elections.[74]

Volte-face

On 26 June 1952, Grantham recommended to the Secretary of State that the proposed Legislative Council reform be completely scrapped.[75] At the Executive Council meeting on 17 June, members advised that the publication of the despatches be delayed and that Grantham should discuss the matter with the Colonial Office when he returned shortly to Britain on leave. At the following meeting on 24 June, members concluded that "any far-reaching changes in the constitutional set-up in Hong Kong at the present time were inadvisable" and should be limited to increasing the number of elected members of the Urban Council to four and giving them more financial autonomy. When Grantham wrote to the Colonial Office to tell them about this complete change of view, he said that any reform to the Legislative Council now posed a "danger".[76] The Colonial Office viewed this about-face with some equanimity. Jeffries thought that although "it is awkward ... I have always felt that it would be very much better if we could avoid making major constitutional changes while the emergency is on".[77] Lyttelton decided that the matter would need to go back to Cabinet but decided to await its return from recess in September. When tabled, it was agreed with no discussion.[78] When the demise of the reform proposals was made known publicly in Hong Kong in October there was barely a murmur. The *South China Morning Post* thought that the decision was correct and would be accepted now whereas it would not have been three years earlier. Much of the Chinese-language press was silent. The *Sing Tao Jih Pao* lamented the lack of progress but understood the present difficulties. It thought, however, that "a more decisive step forward might have been taken at the present stage".

Why the *volte-face* in June 1952? During his visit to the Colonial Office, Grantham had explained that "since the Secretary of State's visit in December 1951 ... unofficial opinion ... had steadily crystallised and was now strongly against any major constitutional change". As there was

> only a small but vocal minority [who] now viewed reform with favour, he considered that this minority could be held in check, particularly as it had recently suffered a setback in elections to the Urban Council.[79]

In March 1952, the Executive Council had advised that elections to the Urban Council should be held for the first time since the end of the Japanese occupation. They took place on 30 May and Brook Bernacchi[80] of the Hong Kong Reform Association and William S. T. Louey of the Kowloon Residents' Association were duly elected. There had been nine candidates for two seats and the electorate had been restricted to members of the Jury Lists, membership of which required a sufficient knowledge of the English language. About one-third of the 9,704 registered electors voted. This was interpreted by the unofficials as a sign that support for major constitutional reform had weakened and they then moved to curtail major reforms altogether.

What was the "danger" that Grantham foresaw? It was that, if the reforms were introduced, some Chinese members might use the Legislative Council as a platform for communist propaganda and might seek to cause embarrassment, or even disaffection, among other Chinese members and thus put them in a difficult position. Perhaps the Urban Council elections were also seen as a proxy for what could happen during future Legislative Council elections. Even though the proposed indirect elections to the Legislative Council may have returned "safe" members, they would have shown it to be considerably less "democratic" than a reformed Urban Council.

Grantham and autonomy

Grantham did not exercise the same degree of ownership over constitutional reform as Young had done. Under Grantham, responsibility for policy formulation seemed to shift from the Hong Kong government to the unofficials. Why did Grantham allow this to happen, especially over something as fundamental as constitutional reform?

Grantham's aim seemed to be to make the stalled reforms London's problem rather than his. Shortly after his arrival in Hong Kong, he must have realised the difficulty of his position. He may have been deterred from advising the Secretary of State of these difficulties as the despatches approving the new policies had just been published and Grantham had publicly committed himself to their implementation. As an ambitious Governor, it is unlikely he would have wanted to portray himself as an ineffectual one, particularly so soon after his arrival. As the creation of a municipal council required the passage of a bill through the Legislative Council, this needed at least a modicum of unofficial support. Otherwise the issue would have had to have been referred back to the Secretary of State[81] which again would have brought Grantham's capabilities as Governor into question. By shifting the focus to reform of the Legislative Council, requiring revision of the Royal Instructions by the Secretary of State, Grantham deflected the solution to the problem away from himself.

Grantham's most effective role was in the management of the process of policy formulation rather than the formulation of policy itself. This was an area in which he was alleged to excel and he was careful not to put a foot wrong. He did not approach the Colonial Office directly until he was fairly sure of his ground beforehand. He was thus able to gradually change the focus of the argument to suit the views of the unofficials or the Colonial Office as circumstances changed and their respective views shifted. In doing so he showed more skill in the handling of Secretaries of State than either Stubbs or Clementi had done. He did not challenge Creech-Jones directly and it was not until Lyttelton assumed office that he felt able to make a more determined push towards the total abandonment of reform.

Grantham's policy, however, was not his own but was tailored to fit the political support that existed. Young had done this, too, with income tax but there had been a crucial difference. Young had compromised on matters of detail but had stuck to important points of principle. By contrast, Grantham left the crucial question of principle as well as detail to the unofficials. Leaving so much to the unofficials might have reflected a lack of policy-making capacity on Grantham's part. The competent Hazelrigg had gone and, in the absence of the availability of the Hong Kong government files, there is little evidence of any role MacDougall may have played. Grantham's approach was so much the opposite of Young's that MacDougall must have found his position under Grantham very difficult. His apparent silence sits uneasily with his great activity during the military administration and, as shall be seen in the next two chapters, on housing and squatter issues. He did not approve of Grantham always siding with "the strongest side", as the unofficials were in this case; they were not, he felt, always correct.[82] In the Colonial Office there was no-one of the calibre of Gent to take charge. Creech-Jones, the Secretary of State, was distracted by Palestine[83] and, from his handling of Hong Kong's reforms it would appear he had insufficient faith in his own judgement to overrule his officials. Nor was there any sustained British domestic pressure for Hong Kong's constitutional reform. Despite parliamentary questions, no civil society group had been mobilised as had been the case over *mui tsai*. Both Young and Grantham played "a pivotal role" in the development of this issue.[84] The centrality of Grantham's role was, however, in the management of the policy formulation process rather than, as in Young's case, in developing his own uniquely differentiated policy. It was Grantham's unwillingness or inability to stake out exactly what he wanted in terms of policy, as well as the lack of any similar clear delineation from the Colonial Office, that created a void which the unofficials, opposed at heart to any reform, were only too willing to fill.

Grantham and the unofficials were able to get their way with the British government only partly because the balance of political support in Hong Kong had swung the pendulum their way. The turbulent situation in China and concern over the Chinese Communist Party's intentions and the potential threat this posed to Hong Kong's future also had an effect. Grantham, and the unofficials, like MacDougall when head of the Hong Kong Planning Unit, took advantage of this uncertainty in the minds of Colonial Office officials to have their own way: it was once more the autonomy of crisis. This autonomy, however, was not autonomy for the Hong Kong government but more autonomy for the unofficials. It was akin to the position of Stubbs being in thrall to the Chinese elites over the question of the regulation of *mui tsai*. Grantham was adept at manipulating and promoting these policies but they were neither his nor the Hong Kong government's. The Hong Kong government's policies were not, therefore "politically differentiated from the actors who" sought to control it[85] and it could not be said to have acted autonomously in this matter.

How further policy voids were left to be filled by others, how the threat of British domestic pressure could still be brought to bear upon Hong Kong government policy and the implications these factors had on the development of the Hong Kong government's autonomy will be examined in Chapters 8 and 9.

8
Post-war Housing Policy and the British Government

> Am I right in assuming that there is no social policy in Hong Kong at all ... the Housing Policy seems non-existent. Why has the Department allowed this drift to go on?
>
> Arthur Creech-Jones,
> Secretary of State for the Colonies,
> December 1949

The exasperation and frustration in Creech-Jones' remarks was palpable. He had been asked about Hong Kong's housing policy by the Archbishop of Canterbury and the Colonial Office official responsible for Hong Kong had told him, perhaps not very tactfully, that Hong Kong's policy was to leave housing to the private sector. For Creech-Jones this only "confirm[ed] what the Archbishop told me", although what that was remained a mystery even to his senior officials.[1] Just over one year later, however, Creech-Jones' successor had issued detailed and comprehensive directions to Hong Kong on what housing policy it should adopt. It was instructed to establish a Housing Authority whose duties should include "the preparation and execution of a programme of house building ... and the management of low-cost housing".[2]

The ability to influence the outcome of Hong Kong's policy issues continued to swing between Britain and Hong Kong. Local politics had played a major part in the demise of Hong Kong's proposed constitutional reform. The potential influence of British domestic pressure on Hong Kong, however, remained an important factor. The threat of domestic political pressure on a British government was to galvanise the Secretary of State's concern over Hong Kong's apparent lack of a housing policy. His specific instruction to form a Housing Authority appears, *prima facie*, similar to that given by Churchill to Stubbs or Passfield to Clementi over *mui tsai*. But there were differences on this occasion. It was not simply a case of Grantham being told, as Stubbs and Clementi had been, to do something he believed was inappropriate for Hong Kong. Although Grantham may have solicited directions from the Secretary of State, it was not apparent that Grantham wholeheartedly thought this was the right policy for Hong Kong. Indeed, it was not clear exactly what Grantham thought should be done by government in respect of the provision of subsidised housing.

The development of the Hong Kong government's housing policies from 1946 to 1954 will be analysed in this chapter. It will examine how, in the early post-war years, the Hong Kong government had some capacity to develop a response to Hong Kong's dire housing situation. This, however, was to be constrained by a lack of resources and by the British Treasury's extreme caution. After MacDougall's departure, Grantham seemed unable to formulate a housing policy in the face of indifference from Legislative Council unofficials. This was despite the all-pervasiveness of the problem, the limited resources available to local initiatives and the sound policy advice for government action from his senior officials. Into this policy void stepped the Secretary of State with his directions which proved to be the unlikely seed of a future autonomy.

The view from London

Colonial Office officials showed considerable empathy towards Hong Kong's desperate housing situation. During his visit to Hong Kong in January 1949, Paskin, had been

> appalled at the slum conditions in which even Chinese clerks in Government service had to live. That, living in such conditions, they were able to appear in office in clean clothes and to do a useful job of work was recognised as astonishing by the European officers of the Secretariat with whom I discussed this question.

Paskin realised that the Hong Kong government could no longer rely on the private sector to supply all Hong Kong's housing needs. He felt it was time for the Colonial Office to "take up with the Governor the question whether the Government itself should not now on a large scale, enter the field of housing". He recognised, however, this would "involve the expenditure of very large sums of public money".[3]

The Colonial Office was aware of the constraints Hong Kong faced. Firstly, there was the problem caused by Hong Kong's traditional policy of allowing free ingress and egress to Chinese nationals. In the six months from November 1948, over 110,000 refugees had arrived in Hong Kong. Some 40,000 had arrived in May 1949 alone although after that the rate began to decline.[4] Sidebotham believed that as long as this policy remained then to provide on a large scale better and newer housing accommodation in Hong Kong ... merely means providing an added inducement for more and more Chinese to flock into Hong Kong from the even worse conditions in China.

Secondly, there was the pressing issue of Hong Kong's defence in the face of the uncertain intentions of Communist forces in southern China. In the summer of 1949, as a result of a Cabinet decision, Hong Kong's garrison had been massively reinforced. This, in turn, was to divert the limited resources of the Public Works Department to provide necessary facilities for the military which had led to the diversion "of the capacity of private building contractors". Lastly, there was the question of the Hong Kong government funding any large-scale housing programme. This issue had several dimensions. Colonial Office officials recognised Hong Kong's unofficials' discontent over Britain's refusal to meet "denial claims" and other expenditure items which they felt were the British government's responsibility. There was also the question of Hong Kong's reluctance to contribute towards the cost of reinforcing the garrison which unofficials also considered was Britain's responsibility. These factors helped account for the Hong Kong government's reluctance to try and increase taxes. There was little hope that the unofficials' would approve tax increases if they were to pay for items they believed were Britain's responsibility. Colonial Office officials also realised that under Grantham's recent proposal to create an unofficial Legislative Council majority it was

> even less likely that she will be willing to submit to increased taxation except to meet the expenditure which she herself can be persuaded to consider desirable.[5]

There followed an exchange between ministers and Colonial Office officials which reflected a Secretary of State's difficulty in imposing his wishes upon an unwilling colony. To Creech-Jones and his Parliamentary Under-Secretary of State, Rees-Williams, who had recently visited Hong Kong, the solution was simple and straightforward. To Rees-Williams, seemingly oblivious to the role of local officials and unofficials in Hong Kong,

> Our responsibility is plain and to my mind we have neglected to give a clear lead. In my view neither the unofficials, European and Chinese, nor the officials can be relied on to take the necessary enlightened view and back it with resolute action. The lead must come from this office and cannot be left until after constitutional changes have been made ... The way is clear. What needs to be done is obvious. What is required is a strong boost from this end.

Creech-Jones agreed but also showed a rather wider appreciation of the situation. He was prepared to

> make all fair excuses for the preoccupation of Hong Kong and the emergency. *But this Office must now give a strong lead.* Otherwise we are in for the same bad criticism. [emphasis in original]

The Permanent Under-Secretary, Jeffries, and his fellow officials were more aware of the delicacy of this task. They had to both show an understanding of Hong Kong's situation and move it in the required direction. This had to be a gentle and subtle process. If directions were to be too strongly worded

> the Governor might well feel that a despatch in these terms, which he would have to lay before his Executive Council, constitutes an unmerited reflection on his administration.

But on the other hand

> unless the Governor receives an official despatch which he could lay before the Legislative Council ... it is most unlikely that he would be able to persuade the legislature to vote the necessary increases in taxation.

A draft despatch to the Governor was prepared as a basis for discussion with the Colonial Secretary, Nicoll, due home on leave.[6]

Had the despatch been sent, it would have helped meet the Secretary of State's and his Parliamentary Under-Secretary's views. It stressed that existing policies to encourage private housing development

> had not ... been satisfactory; progress alike in reconstruction and in the building of additional accommodation has been too slow, and with the return of a large measure of prosperity in Hong Kong the time has now, I consider, arrived when the Government of Hong Kong should itself take an active part, and endeavour to set a much faster pace in this matter.

How the Legislative Council was to be persuaded to vote the raising and expenditure of the necessary funds was left unclear except for an exhortation that this

> was a public duty, incumbent on the legislature of Hong Kong, who in this way would be showing a proper appreciation and awareness of a state of affairs in relation to Housing which calls for prompt remedial measures in a Colony under British administration.

The despatch would have been an indictment of the Hong Kong government's lack of leadership and the Colonial Office's lack of awareness of developments in Hong Kong. On 26 January 1950, at a meeting in the Colonial Office, Nicoll outlined the difficulties caused by the rapid influx of refugees and its effect on housing. He described action already taken by the Hong Kong government not only on housing but also on education, social welfare and finance as well. He pointed out the difficulty of increasing income tax and the concern that if increased tax receipts might be used to pay for increased defence contributions and outstanding war claims there would be little left for social services.

Jeffries now realised that "more is in hand than we knew about" and told the Secretary of State that any despatch would "have to be carefully thought out". Creech-Jones wanted to add his own views but did not have time because of the impending general election. In London, this was where the matter rested until Grantham's visit in June 1950. The Labour government won the subsequent election, but Creech-Jones lost his seat. The Colonial Office's attitude mellowed. Sidebotham thought that because

> the Governor has got so much 'on his plate' at the moment ... we should do everything possible to avoid adding to it unless it is vitally necessary to do so.[7]

The housing problem had been sorely exercising the British Military Administration and the Hong Kong government since 1945. It had also become a pressing issue for the unofficials. What was the nature of the problem, what measures had actually been taken and how effective had they been?

Housing under the British Military Administration

The shortage of adequate housing, and the subsequent overcrowding, had long been seen as a problem in Hong Kong. It had been the subject of several housing commissions, the last one having reported in 1938. Northcote was keen to approach the problem through systematic town planning and Caine had suggested a way to finance the provision of housing through making use of the Exchange Fund. However, no action transpired: the free flow of people into Hong Kong and in particular the sudden inflow of refugees escaping the Japanese; the distractions caused by the onset of war; and Northcote's own failing health all transpired to prevent further action on the housing problem in the years just before 1941.[8]

On his return to Hong Kong in September 1945 however, MacDougall quickly realised that although housing would be a major problem it could not be an immediate priority. In September 1945, a housing survey estimated that about 60% of European-style housing had been destroyed or damaged. Chinese-style housing had been less severely affected but the situation quickly worsened with the rapid influx of people from China. Repairs to the housing stock proceeded very slowly due to the severe shortage of materials. As there was no new building, the British Military Administration (BMA) instituted rental controls to prevent landlords taking undue advantage of the situation. MacDougall recognised that housing was likely to be "a burden upon the Civil Government for many months to come".[9]

This view was corroborated by the Building Reconstruction Advisory Committee, appointed by the BMA to quantify the housing problem and propose solutions to the housing shortage. It found that, in respect of non-Chinese housing, accommodation for 7,000 to 10,000 people had been damaged or destroyed and that 160,000 Chinese had been displaced by war damage. This situation was worsening as the population recovered. Other factors were the shortage and high cost of building materials, qualified personnel and labour, a lack of finance and

> the Rents Ordinance which prevents property-owners from increasing rents although building costs have risen considerably.

This discouraged property owners from repairing or rebuilding their premises. It recommended that government should purchase and import building materials which should then be allocated to owners seeking to rebuild. Alternatively, government should subsidise the cost of repairs. It also recommended that government should build accommodation for its own staff.[10]

Young's policy on housing

Although housing was only Young's third priority, the housing shortage was a contentious local issue.[11] In public, his response to the Committee's report was uncharacteristically vague. He accepted the Committee's recommendation that he should appoint a senior officer to take charge of "co-ordinating and directing the work of reconstruction and housing". Otherwise, all he did was promise government would consider the Committee's recommendations carefully and would shortly make a public announcement. He also stressed the limitations of what the government could do and that the "the problem ... can only be satisfactorily solved by the co-operation of the whole community". Young's other two priorities, finance and supply,[12] also constrained what he could do to alleviate the housing situation. Until these were satisfactorily addressed, government had no material capacity to do more about housing even if it wanted to.

Policy issues and capacity constraints

In July 1946, Young rejected the Building Reconstruction Advisory Committee's proposal that it should interfere with the workings of the market. He considered that co-ordination of the importation of building materials was best left to the Hong Kong General Chamber of Commerce. Government "should not usurp the normal functions of commercial importers and thereby delay their recovery".[13] He agreed that "so long as the housing shortage remains acute" rent control legislation should remain and private development of new accommodation should be encouraged by the granting of long leases rather than short-term permits.[14] Without prior reference to the Secretary of State, Young announced a policy whereby government would renew 75-year leases under modified terms. Many of these leases were due, or soon due, to expire. Normally, before renewal could be considered, the leaseholder had to have a building erected and maintained on site in accordance with the building covenant. However, many buildings had been destroyed as a result of the war or enemy occupation and had only a few years of the lease left to run. It was not worthwhile for leaseholders to re-erect or repair a building unless they knew that the lease would be renewed and on what conditions.

Young had undertaken to decide as soon as possible the terms upon which these leases would be renewed. In June 1946, after consulting the Executive Council but not the Secretary of State, government announced that leases would be renewed on the basis of 1941 premium and Crown Rent valuations. For those who applied within the following twelve months, premium payable on renewal would be remitted by up to half the cost of rehabilitation or reconstruction. Both these decisions represented considerable concessions. However, grantees would also be required to develop their sites to the maximum permitted in order to ensure that "all available land should be developed to the utmost".[15] Young's aim was to facilitate the provision of much-needed new accommodation as soon as possible.

The Colonial Office seemed to realise the necessity for independent action in Hong Kong's peculiar circumstances without prior reference to London. Mayle thought that renewing leases on the basis of 1941 values had been too generous and that remitting half the premium in certain cases would be inequitable. Caine, who as Hong Kong's pre-war Financial Secretary had proposed a way to finance a housing policy, took a more sanguine view. He pointed out that whatever the rights or wrongs of the matter, it was important to encourage the rapid redevelopment of much needed accommodation. MacDougall agreed. However, the Colonial Office and the Hong Kong government stipulated that only applications received in the following twelve months would be considered. Thereafter, the Colonial Office should be consulted if Hong Kong still wished to renew leases on these terms.[16]

The Hong Kong government took another initiative in July 1946 but this time asked for the Secretary of State's prior approval. It requested that, over the next twelve months, the Governor should be allowed to grant land by private treaty to see if "private interests can be induced to develop housing estates rapidly". The problem was that Crown Land could only be sold for private residential development at public auction. A prospective developer had to undertake much preparatory work before he knew whether a proposed development would be viable or not. If that site then had to be sold by public auction, it could be bought by another purchaser with a higher bid, quite possibly a speculator. Prospective developers had insufficient incentive to undertake the necessary preparatory work and this acted as a disincentive to private development. In August 1946, the Secretary of State approved the Governor's request on condition that action would be taken to prevent undeveloped land from being held by speculators.

Such schemes were difficult to bring to fruition. Even if a developer was eligible for a private treaty grant, problems of finance prevented most such schemes from proceeding. In mid-1946, a proposal to build 200 concrete houses on a site in Jardine's Lookout on Hong Kong Island was made. This would have required the government to take a 51% share in order to make it viable. MacDougall was keen to try and make it work and thought that government could ask the British Treasury for a building loan. He remarked, in some frustration, that "sooner or later the Treasury must realise that in Hong Kong houses must be erected in a hurry".[17] The scheme foundered on uncertainties over site formation costs: extensive site formation work was required which could not be accurately costed at such an early stage. The target market of lower middle-class Hong Kong residents was also not expected to be able to afford the rental level needed to make the scheme financially viable. It was considered, therefore, that the British Treasury would be unwilling to authorise the Hong Kong government's involvement and no request was made. Reluctantly, Young agreed to drop the project.[18]

Housing and the unofficials

Housing was of much concern to the unofficials. On 16 May 1946, M. K. Lo asked in the Legislative Council "will Government make an announcement regarding the housing problem and how it is proposed to be dealt with?" The Financial Secretary replied that it would, but later after it had worked out details.[19] On 21 November 1946, in reply to a follow-up question by Lo, the Acting Colonial Secretary R. R. Todd,[20] said there had been progress on the repair of buildings and that the supply of building materials had increased. Landlords were unwilling to build at present because of the high costs involved.[21] On 19 June 1947, Lo asked for a further report on housing. The Acting Colonial Secretary, again Todd, tried to paint a picture of steady progress. Over the past seven months some 200 to 300 applications a month had been received to reinstate old buildings or construct new ones. Progress, however, had been delayed by a world-wide shortage of building materials. Of some 80 applications for renewal of 75-year leases, terms had been offered to 40 of which 18 had accepted. Some private applications for housing schemes had also been received but they had not yet proceeded because of the unavailability of building materials and a lack of finance. He thought that although there had been some improvement of late

> it is more evident now than twelve months ago that no quick solution is more likely here than it is in other parts of the world.

He even went as far to say that government itself might also build housing

> on a large scale, uneconomic as that might be, if it had access to supplies of building materials in sufficient quantity.

Motion debate

The Acting Colonial Secretary finished his statement by saying that

> Government is deeply conscious of its obligations to the citizens of this Colony in the present prolonged housing crisis ... housing is and for the past year has been this Colony's number one problem. It is hoped that Council will appreciate that the fact that no satisfactory solution has yet been found is not due to lack of effort. Honourable Members can rest assured that these efforts will not slacken in the months to come.[22]

This precipitated one of the Legislative Council's most hotly contested motion debates. It may have been that unofficial members found this a suitable opportunity to vent their ire upon government for all its perceived shortcomings over the previous year. The absence of a permanent Governor between Young's departure on 17 May and Grantham's arrival on 27 July might have allowed them to speak more freely. Whatever the reason, the Acting Colonial Secretary's statement served as a red rag to a bull. A motion was moved by the senior unofficial, D. F. Landale, who called upon government to treat the housing issue "as one of utmost urgency". It should "without delay, plan and vigorously pursue" its own accommodation and offices. Government was enjoined to actively encourage private building to the utmost extent possible and ... remove all unnecessary Government impediments to private enterprise ... in particular modify its present unfair and repressive policy in regard to the renewal of 75-year Crown Leases.

M. K. Lo devoted his lengthy address almost entirely to a defence of the perceived rights of leaseholders of 75-year leases. Landale complained that Todd's reply had been "complacent and misleading". Another member roundly disparaged government's claim that there was a shortage of building materials. R. D. Gillespie thought that

> not only has Government failed to do anything to relieve the housing situation, but through procrastination and lack of decision has in several cases ... stopped private enterprise from building houses.

He gave examples of government's alleged perfidy and thought that these showed that

> not only is Government not deeply conscious of its obligations to the citizens of this Colony in the present prolonged housing crisis, but is, in fact, not conscious of them at all.

Dr Chau Sik-nin was perhaps closer to the mark when he accused the Hong Kong government of having no

> person or department of Government charged with the power and duty to initiate measures for building and housing, and to co-ordinate departmental views and to reconcile conflicting ideas with the paramount policy of Government.[23]

The OAG, MacDougall, and his colleagues took the unofficials' concerns very seriously. Preparatory meetings were held in Government House to co-ordinate the officials' reply and the Acting Colonial Secretary's reply was especially cleared by the Attorney-General. Such an ad-hoc approach tended to bolster Dr Chau's criticism that no one senior civil servant was in overall charge of this important policy issue.[24] When the debate resumed one week later, Todd proposed amendments to the unofficials' motion which would remove all criticisms of government. He pointed out that a leaseholder had no legal right to the renewal of a 75-year lease when it expired. It was a matter for government to offer such terms as it saw fit. As a guiding policy, the government had taken this to mean it would re-grant 75-year leases on condition the site was re-developed to the maximum permissible to provide much needed additional accommodation. In any case, their contribution to solving the shortage of accommodation was negligible.

The Director of Public Works denigrated unofficials' arguments when he claimed that he had

> looked forward with great interest to hear from the addresses of Honourable Unofficial Members, clear and practical suggestions for the quick solution of the Colony's No. 1 problem, namely housing ... I regret to say I left this Council on Thursday last no whit wiser than when I entered it.

He portrayed the unsuccessful promoters of potential housing schemes as speculators and opportunists. Recent prices at land auctions had shown that prices asked by government for private treaty grants for housing schemes were only one third of the current market price. He portrayed potential developers as incompetents, submitting ill thought out schemes which, on detailed examination, turned out to be impracticable. One such potential developer had even complained that the Public Works Department was "rushing" him to submit revised plans. He disputed the contention that there were large stocks of building materials in Hong Kong. If that was the case, he "was surprised that the keen merchants of this city have not come forward and offered them for sale in large quantities".

MacDougall's address brought everyone back to earth. No matter what was said in Council, the situation of those in need of housing would not be improved because of what had been said that afternoon. He stated, categorically, that "Government has accepted the responsibility for tackling this emergency". The solution, he felt, lay both with government and the private sector working together and that they were "busy with a number of schemes, at least one of which, and it is a big one, looks entirely practical".

His address was appreciated for its sincerity. M. K. Lo thought it put "the matter very impressively". D'Almada e Castro thought "if its sincerity could not be gauged from its language ... that sincerity was clearly conveyed by its tone". The unofficials refused, however, to accept government's counter-arguments and could only reply in the most petulant of tones. When the motions were put to the vote, the official majority ensured that government won the day.[25]

"The Lee's [sic] are building!"[26]

Determined to keep the initiative, MacDougall thought it important to "... retain the impetus we gained from the recent housing debate".[27] Action focused on a proposed scheme at Lee Gardens on a site owned by the Lee Hysan Estate Co Ltd (Lee Hysan). This was for apartment blocks containing 58 four-roomed flats and 22 three-roomed flats. The main issue was the need for government financing. For the scheme to proceed, Lee Hysan proposed that government provide a building fund of HK$3.6 million. Flats would be sold on a 25-year lease for an average price of HK$68,000. All net proceeds would be paid to government to offset its financing. The balance remaining would represent government's investment in the scheme. Lee Hysan's investment would be HK$1 million in respect of site formation costs.

This arrangement needed the Secretary of State's approval. However, Hong Kong's finances were still under British Treasury control. When MacDougall wrote to seek permission, he set out clearly the need for government involvement for any housing scheme of this nature to go ahead. He stated bluntly that,

> Private enterprise has neither built nor in present conditions plans to build new houses. If Government is not prepared to enter into partnership as suggested, thus driving the scheme back to private enterprise alone, the overwhelming probability is that the scheme will have to be postponed. The indisputable fact is that the Colony must be provided with additional accommodation, and that private capital is and for some time will be unwilling to undertake building. The use of public funds as proposed ... enables a start to be made.[28]

The Colonial Office was hesitant to accept MacDougall's proposals. All it was willing to concede was that the Hong Kong government might offer a guarantee for a bank loan. Nor was it prepared to consider MacDougall's further request that the government could similarly invest in other schemes. The Governor, by now Grantham, was slightly disingenuous in his response to the Colonial Office. He said that, if this scheme was seen to be a success, then "there will be no further hesitation on the part of private enterprise to launch building schemes on their own initiative". On the other hand

> if only a small percentage of flats is taken up other schemes will automatically be dropped by their promoters. It is unlikely that Government assistance in this case will give rise to any embarrassment in regard to future schemes.[29]

Grantham also accepted that he was only likely to obtain approval to offer a government guarantee for a loan. This would reduce the amount of interest the bank would charge the developer. The Secretary of State agreed but baulked at the possibility of the Hong Kong government taking equity in the company if the guarantee was taken up. He insisted that this could only be considered a loan to the company.

Despite MacDougall's impatience to proceed, the agreement with Lee Hysan was not finalised until January 1948. The Secretary of State also constrained the Hong Kong government's future policy making capacity when he made clear his approval did not mean Hong Kong could

> commit itself in any way to accepting any financial responsibilities for providing residential accommodation in the Colony in future.[30]

This was to limit the government's capacity to make housing policy until after Grantham's meetings at the Colonial Office in the summer of 1950.

Housing schemes

In August 1947, at the Governor's behest, the Secretary of State extended the policy of granting land for housing schemes by private treaty for a further twelve months. The lack of building materials, especially steel, and high labour costs had made progress slower than hoped. Young was optimistic that some schemes would shortly proceed although the cost of land remained an issue.[31] Up to August 1947, twenty applications had been received under this scheme of which nine had complied with the government's conditions. There had been complaints that processing of applications took too long but the Director of Public Works explained that it took time to prepare the "preliminary conditions" under which leases could be granted and to examine their practicability.[32]

Government did not seek to renew this provision when it expired in August 1948 because it thought there had been sufficient time to take advantage of it. Instead, Grantham proposed to allow the grant of land for comprehensive workers' housing schemes. With many large commercial undertakings coming into Hong Kong, particularly from Shanghai, the workforce had increased. Without adequate housing, they would squat on Crown or private land near their employer. It was thought,

> Proper housing schemes for workers and their families sponsored by industrial concerns would not only benefit industry by securing a contented labour force, but would also be a great boon to the workers themselves, and ... would provide housing for large numbers who might otherwise become additions to the already numerous squatters who are such an embarrassment.

The Secretary of State agreed. This policy also included "banks, mercantile companies and other large-scale employers already established in the Colony".[33]

Policy hiatus

After this initiative, the Hong Kong government seemed unable to formulate and decide on policy. Their scope for action had been limited by the Secretary of State's prohibition on government participation in any private housing scheme, including schemes to house government staff. For such schemes to be viable, interest on loan capital had to be no more than 3½% rather than the commercial rate of 6%. This could only be achieved with a government guarantee. As the Acting Financial Secretary pointed out

> it was made clear to us in connection with the Lee Hysan Estate scheme that that was the first and last occasion on which a Government guarantee would be approved by [the UK] Treasury.[34]

The unofficials also opposed government involvement in the provision of subsidised housing. M. K. Lo, in making the only reference to housing in the Legislative Council in 1949 thought that

> If ... the rent is to be fixed as to include an element of subsidy, then all I can say is I do not see why the taxpayers who include the humblest artisan who smokes a few cigarettes should be made to pay this subsidy.[35]

There was sympathy for the poor standard of housing in which many junior government staff lived. One proposal was that government should build housing for its staff and provide an example to other major employers in Hong Kong. Although the Financial Secretary thought there was some merit in this, he could not support it on the grounds that the colonial government did not house local staff, except when they were required to live near where they worked. There were also budgetary constraints as "departments' expenditure estimates as submitted must be cut by at least $70 million to produce a balanced budget". The government's already proposed programme of works would also keep government busy "for a long time to come".[36]

In January 1949, there was a further attempt to galvanise the development of a housing policy. The Chairman of the Urban Council, Fehily, suggested setting up an interdepartmental committee "to explore all possibilities and all angles of this very complex problem". Over the next two months, Fehily's proposal was circulated among officials in the Colonial Secretariat and Public Works Department and produced a rather pessimistic response. A typical comment was that,

> Such committees ... put in a lot of hard work and time. If their deliberations are to involve anything in the way of Government expenditure, or alternatively a loss in Government revenue, the personal attention of the Hon F[inancial] S[ecretary] should be drawn to the proposals before they go too far and much time is wasted.

Unsurprisingly, the Deputy Financial Secretary agreed with such views. The Deputy Colonial Secretary, Barnett, commented that the first question was always "who puts up the money to build the houses?" MacDougall exercised his customary leadership and pointed out that

> a group of people have the idea that houses for low-paid workers can be built without subsidy from public funds other than remission of premium and Crown rents in respect of ... sites.

He warned that "none of the difficulties and dangers glooming" in these views "can be allowed to prevent the further exploration of this idea". He asked Fehily to "abandon the Committee idea" and asked him to come up with proposals for housing schemes on the basis that "land will be forthcoming very cheaply".[37]

The debate on housing continued within government and pointed a very clear way forward. In May 1949, the acting Director of Public Works, Andrew Nicol,[38] told Fehily that the era of flatted tenements had come to stay and this applied equally to the poor man's house as to that of the well to do. The problem was the extreme shortage of sufficiently level land for such schemes in the urban area. The cost of site formation was also going to be expensive and the only way to ensure a return was to build "multi-storey blocks of tenements". Because of this expense he argued that "if houses for the workers are to be constructed they can only be done under the guidance and control of Government and some form of Housing Trust". Whatever the form, "the crying need for cheap serviceable workers quarters is undeniable".[39]

Neither Grantham nor MacDougall seemed to be at the heart of discussions on housing policy. Nor did they play that vital leadership role which could have carried the issue forward. MacDougall gave a clear lead but did not seem to follow through: perhaps, by March 1949, he was becoming distracted by his impending retirement.[40] It was only after he had left that housing seemed to come to Grantham's personal attention. In June 1949, just three weeks after Nicoll, MacDougall's replacement, had arrived, Grantham commented that "I understand that he [Fehily]. Dr Willis and some others have schemes for inexpensive bungalows or flats for the white-collared workers." He told Nicoll, who seemed particularly interested in housing, that it was "a v[ery] serious problem, so that anything we can do to alleviate it should be done". He should ask the Chairman of the Urban Council "to put up his proposals and have them examined". On 15 June 1949 Nicoll met with Fehily and Melmoth, a junior cadet who was also one of the joint secretaries of the Hong Kong Housing Society, and concluded that "there is much need for coordination with the Hong Kong Housing Society which I have arranged".[41]

Housing societies

There was little progress in policy formulation on the provision of low-cost housing between the 1947 Legislative Council housing debate and MacDougall's departure in 1949. The Secretary of State had effectively neutralised the Hong Kong government's private treaty grant policy by prohibiting it from providing financial support to private developers. The policy of granting land to employers had not had sufficient time to make an impact. There was now a policy vacuum. No housing was being provided and the institutional mechanisms for future provision had not been created. Into this void stepped a group of people in the social welfare sector who believed that something should be done and who also had some means of trying to help.

In 1947, the Lord Mayor of London's Air Raid Distress Fund donated £14,000 to the Hong Kong Social Welfare Council, the forerunner of the Hong Kong Council of Social Service. It agreed that it should be used to provide housing for workers and their families. On 17 April 1948, a Sub-Committee convened by Bishop Hall met for the first time to consider the best way to proceed. Without much preamble, it decided to form "The Hong Kong Housing Society".[42] The Lord Mayor's £14,000, however, was insufficient to finance any housing scheme in full. The Hong Kong government could not lend them funds or guarantee a bank loan because the British Treasury would not approve it. The Hongkong and Shanghai Bank would not lend money for one-room units for fear they would quickly turn into slums. It would, however, lend money for two-room units if government was prepared to grant a site on King's Road, North Point at nil premium. On 29 March 1949, the Executive Council approved such a grant; the Secretary of State's approval was considered unnecessary because it was covered by his blanket authority to grant land for comprehensive workers' schemes. However, it ran into problems in September when it became clear the Hongkong and Shanghai Bank would lend money only if the project

> was not subject to the active participation in the management by other members of the Society, so that the Bank could rely on the Society being managed in a business-like way.

As Morse told Grantham, he was convinced that otherwise over the next two to three years the Hongkong and Shanghai Bank would have to

> call in the loan and ... then ... either Government would have to replace the money or the property would pass into some private individual's hands.

Morse would lend money if the Society's two Trustees, Dr S. N. Chau and J. H. Ruttonjee and senior government officials were made responsible for the project.[43]

This was eventually arranged over the next few months but necessitated the creation of a new society to run the project and receive the loan. This was the Hong Kong Model Housing Society, a company limited by guarantee with Memorandum and Articles of Association prepared by J. R. Jones, the Hongkong and Shanghai Bank's legal adviser. Because the Model Housing Society was not connected with the Housing Society, it lost the benefit of the Lord Mayor's £14,000 grant and the Hongkong and Shanghai Bank therefore agreed, exceptionally, to fund the total construction cost. The Executive Council also agreed to re-grant the site to the Model Housing Society rather than to the original grantees, the Hong Kong Housing Society, and the Secretary of State's retrospective approval was sought.[44]

This arrangement resulted in the Hongkong and Shanghai Bank's almost total ability to dictate the terms of the land grant to ensure complete protection of its loan. Government was forced to include the land in this security so that in the case of default it could be sold to repay any outstanding part of the loan. This was unusual as normally lease conditions would prevent assignment of land granted at nil or nominal premium for a special purpose. It also transpired that the Model Housing Society project was unable to cater for the lowest paid workers, its original target group. Rents had to be set at about $160 per month rather than the originally estimated $50–$60 per month. Account had not been taken of rates and property tax in the original calculations. Such a rental level was still thought acceptable because there was still a demand for affordable rental accommodation in this sector. It also left the Housing Society a niche for their slightly lower-cost housing projects.[45]

Although referred to as a "clash of personalities", it later became apparent that the problem lay with the antipathy of the Hongkong and Shanghai Bank, and probably more particularly Morse, towards Bishop Hall. He was a man admired for his intentions and ideals but not for his administrative skills or for his political judgement.[46] The Housing Society was never formally told that the North Point site was to be granted instead to another body.[47] However, to its credit, the Society persevered with other projects and was destined to play an important role in the provision of low-cost housing. The Hong Kong Housing Society's tenants could afford to pay higher rents than future Housing Authority tenants. This more realistically reflected the additional costs involved and the higher quality of accommodation provided.[48] It was also to prove a more resilient and effective body than many may initially have expected with a strong emphasis on housing management.[49] As MacDougall commented shortly before he left Hong Kong "there is ample room for everyone who has an idea of how to solve the housing problem on a non-profit basis".[50]

Policy co-ordination

Policy co-ordination machinery did already exist although it operated in a somewhat disjointed fashion. A Hong Kong Colonial Development and Welfare (CD&W) Committee[51] had been established in 1946. The Secretary of State had required this of all colonies under the British government's CD&W policy which had set aside £120 million to be spent over ten years. Hong Kong's share was £1 million. Each colony benefiting had to set up its own local CD&W Committee to draw up a plan and advise on how the funds should be spent.[52] A Hong Kong Committee was formed in 1946 which consisted of both officials and unofficials and established several Sub-Committees. In January 1947, it formed the Housing and Town Planning Sub-Committee whose terms of reference were,

> Generally to consider and report on the needs of the Colony for improved housing and town planning over a 10-year period and to make recommendations on the action required to meet these needs having regard to the relative urgency of the various problems.

It met only once, on 12 April 1950, and then only at the Colonial Secretary's behest: he wanted it to consider and agree to the formation of a Town Planning Unit within government.[53] A new Housing Committee was formed in 1950, shortly before Grantham left on leave for London. Its Chairman was W. J. Carrie[54] and it had both official and unofficial members, including one lady.[55] It was tasked to consider the type of housing that should be provided and what type of organisation should provide it. At its first meeting on 7 July 1950, Carrie explained the background to its formation and the Governor's hope that it

> should consider whether the remainder of Hong Kong's Colonial Development and Welfare allocation might not best be spent on housing for the underprivileged.

Although Grantham may have formed this committee to pre-empt criticism, it did provide a forum for consideration of appropriate forms of low-cost housing schemes. On health grounds, it rejected a plan proposed by the Hong Kong Housing Society to erect barrack-style accommodation. It was prepared, however, to recommend a scheme incorporating one and two-roomed units. It also recommended that government should grant HK$200,000 to the Hong Kong Housing

Society and that it should lend them the balance required, approximately HK$700,000. The government, however, did not respond to the Committee's suggestions.[56]

Grantham's meetings in the Colonial Office, 1950

In June 1950, Grantham attended meetings in the Colonial Office concerning Hong Kong's social policies. On 21 June, at the first of these, Paskin stated that

> Mr Creech-Jones had given instructions that the Office should investigate what could be done to improve social conditions in Hong Kong; particular stress had been laid on bad housing conditions and this matter had also been raised by the Archbishop of Canterbury.

The meetings were not the showdown that could have been expected had Creech-Jones still been in office. The Secretary of State only attended two meetings and Grantham was the most senior official present at others. They were held in an almost dispassionate manner, discussions were civilised and exchanges measured rather than heated. The underlying impression was that they were more important to the Colonial Office than to Grantham.

When asked about housing, Grantham agreed that "little was going ahead" but referred to a recently started "private housing scheme ... which would cater mainly for white collar workers". He thought that "Government's task must be to provide housing for the lower paid manual workers" and agreed that "the matter should be pursued with urgency". He also thought that

> it would be useful if a despatch were sent to Hong Kong suggesting that provision of adequate housing should be started urgently using Colonial Development and Welfare funds and that in the first instance a pilot scheme should be worked out.

This, he was later reported as thinking, would be a way whereby "his hand would be strengthened".

On 30 June, housing was again discussed though rather inconclusively at a meeting chaired by the Secretary of State, Griffiths. Grantham explained that the Hongkong and Shanghai Bank was not prepared to finance a scheme for lower paid workers because it did not provide it with good security. He thought that

> it was in this connection that Bishop Hall had brought the housing situation to the notice of the Archbishop of Canterbury as the Bank would not agree to advance money for one of these schemes if Bishop Hall took any part in its management and this annoyed him.[57]

However, the housing problem was not discussed in any great detail. Indeed, the whole wide-ranging meeting seemed to be conducted in the absence of the kind of fervour that might have been expected had Creech-Jones been there.

A flurry of action

Upon Grantham's return in November 1950, there was a great flurry of activity in Government House. Papers on housing were called for and urgent meetings were held with the Colonial Secretary and the Financial Secretary. Grantham was not going to wait for the Secretary of State's despatch before starting to formulate what he wanted to appear as his own policy. He commented, without any irony, that

> we seem to be drifting. The first thing to be done is to examine whether or not a housing scheme or schemes, in a big way, are prima facie sound and the best method of using the un-earmarked balance of our CD&W Fund allocation.

On 18 December 1950, the Colonial Secretary held a meeting to discuss a detailed paper on what government could do. It concluded that the cost of housing a large number of residents would be extremely high, probably about HK$150 million to house 100,000 people. As there was no likelihood that government would be able to "better the conditions of more than an arbitrarily selected few" there was no argument in favour of subsidies. However, these could be avoided if housing was financed through long-term loans and if land premium could be paid by annual instalment.[58] On 20 December 1950, the issue was further discussed at a meeting at Government House with the Colonial Secretary, Financial Secretary and Carrie, the Chairman of the Housing Committee. It was decided that the Secretary of State should be asked to agree in principle that CD&W funding should be used to meet site formation costs and that government could make interest bearing loans to a future improvement trust to meet building construction costs. It was also agreed that applications for grants should be made to cover site formation costs for two pilot projects, including one proposed by the Hong Kong Housing Society. Government would also consider setting up an improvement trust.[59]

Secretary of State's despatch: A housing blueprint

These decisions pre-empted receipt of the Secretary of State's detailed and comprehensive despatch. This was sent on 28 December 1950 and received on 3 January 1951. Although the Secretary of State said his aim was "to offer certain advice" about housing development in Hong Kong, Grantham was told categorically that "a housing authority is required" which should also be a "representative body". The Secretary of State presented this in the context of meeting both planning and housing needs. The most important short-term need was "to provide rapidly a very considerable quantity of low-cost housing for low paid workers" as well as a need to house both "the artisan and lower middle classes". The reasons for this were to clear "unsightly and insanitary squatter areas" and "improve built up areas in the city to accord with the longer term planning needs of Hong Kong". A Housing Authority established under the auspices of government was required as the private sector would be unlikely to provide such housing. The Secretary of State also pointed out the need for multi-storey development, the need to build quickly and the need for efficient estate management. In the short term, there would be a necessity to accept that initially housing quality would be low. There was also a need to consider longer-term financing.[60]

Grantham's reply to the Secretary of State on 10 February was his own blueprint for Hong Kong's housing. This also accorded with the decisions made at the Government House meeting held on 20 December. He took care to claim that these proposals "were formulated prior to the receipt of your despatch ... but I do not think that they conflict with your advice". It presented a coherent plan for the development of subsidised housing. Grantham stressed it was important "politically and psychologically to produce results as soon as possible" but equally that "it will be advantageous to have the experience gained by a Pilot Scheme before embarking on developments on a larger scale". He set out how he intended to finance housing through the recent creation of a Development Fund which would allow up to $15 million to be spent on housing over the next two years. Rehousing had to be in the urban areas to allow residents to be near their employment. This meant the preparation of difficult and expensive sites which would amount to "as much as 25% of the total cost of housing schemes which would be considered quite out of proportion in most other countries". As this cost could not be recovered from rents paid by low-income tenants, he argued this justified a grant rather than a loan from the CD&W Fund. As a first instalment, he said, he would ask for a grant of £13,500 to develop two blocks of workers' flats as a pilot scheme. He then slipped in that the Hong Kong Housing Society would be the body to undertake this development and asked the Secretary of State's approval to lend it $2 million from the Development Fund. He also proposed that

> a Housing Authority or Improvement Trust should be set up which would have considerable unofficial representation although being subject to strict financial control and supervision by Government.[61]

Formation of the Housing Authority

The problem facing Grantham was how to establish a Housing Authority. He then had to decide what issues it was going to tackle. He also had to work out, and seek support for, the complex task of establishing a major new organisation in the face of disagreement both from unofficials and from some of his senior officials. It thus took another three years before an Authority was created. It took this time for Grantham and his officials to study the issue and work slowly towards building a consensus on the form a future Housing Authority should take and the role it should play.

In July 1951, the Executive Council agreed to grant a site to the Housing Society which had become incorporated by ordinance on 10 February 1951. This was for a pilot scheme to build 370 small flats at Sheung Li Uk. The Executive Council also agreed in principle to the establishment of an improvement trust, despite having been told nothing about what form it would take, what its responsibilities would be or how it would operate.[62] It took the government a further year to develop more detailed proposals on how a Housing Authority should be constituted and organised. A senior officer was sent to Singapore to study the workings of the Singapore Improvement Trust. The Hong Kong government then decided to recommend the establishment of a Housing Authority for the provision of housing alone. This was in preference to a broader improvement trust which would also have engaged in slum clearance.

On 13 May 1952, the Executive Council was told what must have been obvious for some time that

> the problem of housing the population of Hong Kong has now assumed such proportions that it cannot be solved by the activities of the two Housing Societies. It is, therefore, considered a matter of urgency that a Housing Authority should be constituted to speed up the provision of housing for the less well-paid members of the community.

Such an Authority would be

> responsible to Government for the provision of adequate housing for the lower paid members of the community at minimum economic rents.

As housing was, in most large cities, a municipal responsibility, the Executive Council was asked if this responsibility should be given to the Urban Council, constituted as a Housing Authority.[63] The Executive Council was "generally in favour" that the Chairman of the Urban Council should become incorporated as a Housing Authority but asked that government consult local land companies on practical issues and report back.

Government formed a small ad hoc committee chaired by the Colonial Secretary, now Robin Black, with four officials and three unofficials from private development companies as members. This was another example of including unofficials in the policy making process. It met three times in June and July 1952 to consider

> the extent to which housing can be provided for about half a million persons, not including those who would be dealt with by the Squatter Resettlement Scheme.[64]

Members agreed that the Urban Council should be constituted as the Housing Authority; that it should be able to appoint a Select Committee on housing to which non-Urban Council members could be co-opted; that the day-to-day administration would be carried out by a sub-department of the Urban Services Department under a cadet officer; that the Public Works Department should be the Housing Authority's architectural agents; and that properties managed by the Housing Society and the Model Housing Society should eventually be transferred to it. Government should also fund its operations through low-interest, long-term loans. Two members were concerned that once government assumed a responsibility for housing that it would become a major political issue. They were also concerned that once assumed, "this liability might grow to excessive proportions and require expenditure beyond the resources of the Colony". They proposed that the Housing Authority should be a completely independent body in the perhaps rather naive hope that it "would not be subject to political pressures".[65]

In August 1952, the Executive Council considered the Committee's findings in their continued debate on housing and whether the Housing Authority should be an independent corporation. The Council accepted the committee's majority view, with one unofficial dissenting, that the powers of the Housing Authority should be vested in the Urban Council. Government control should be retained through the power to approve individual housing schemes.[66]

The Financial Secretary, Arthur Clarke,[67] however, continued to believe strongly that trying to solve the housing problem in this way would be totally inadequate. He thought that the government would be eternally committed to the provision of subsidised housing in Hong Kong and that it would be impossible to satisfy public expectations. He favoured instead a "Development and Housing Corporation" which would be financially independent from government. It would be solely responsible for planning and implementing development projects and it would engage mostly in slum clearance. It would have to rely on government guarantees and the use of government's powers of resumption and town planning.

Grantham was not prepared to overrule his views within the confines of the administration. Rather unusually, his views were included as a separate annex to a memorandum to the Executive Council which was discussed on 28 April 1953. One Executive Council member supported the Financial Secretary's proposals because he thought that the Chairman of the Urban Council was already very heavily committed. He also thought that a Housing Authority should operate on strict commercial lines and that any shortfall should be funded by an "open subsidy".[68] However, after discussion, the Council reaffirmed its previous decision that the Urban Council should be constituted as a Housing Authority. Now that the matter had been decided at a policy level, it could go to the Legislative Council.

Legislative Council debate

On 7 April 1954, the Housing Authority Bill was introduced into the Legislative Council. In moving the first reading, the Colonial Secretary explained the history of government's housing policy since 1946 and pointed out that

> the establishment of such an organisation is no light undertaking. The most searching investigations and the most careful deliberations have been necessary.

He set out the government's proposals in detail, admitting that the public had been very patient in waiting for them. He emphasised that the Housing Authority alone would be unable to solve the housing problem. The other housing societies would still have a role to play, a view at odds with the Ad-Hoc Committee who thought that the Housing Authority should subsume the other Societies projects.[69]

When the debate resumed on 28 April 1954, the only unofficial member to speak on the bill was M. W. Lo, who had been appointed to the Legislative Council on the resignation of his brother, Sir M. K. Lo. He supported the bill but with misgivings. It had "far reaching consequences" and was of "revolutionary character". He pointed out that Hong Kong was not alone in facing a severe housing problem, but what was distinctive was

> the staggering number of people over whose admittance in the Colony we have no control, and on the duration of their stay we have no idea.

Some 300,000 people sought rehousing, not including 300,000 squatters for whom a costly rehousing programme was already under way. He stated his support of the government's bill in the most grudging of terms,

Sir, frankly, I have my doubts and misgivings in this enterprise of Government. But I am aware Government has proceeded cautiously and has taken great pains before this Bill was brought into being. I am prepared therefore to accept the principles underlying this Bill.[70]

The bill was passed and the Housing Authority came into being.

Conclusions

The development of Hong Kong's housing policy from 1945 until 1954 can be divided into three periods. Firstly, from the re-establishment of civil administration in 1946 until the end of 1948, the Hong Kong government was trying to find innovative ways to address the housing problem. It had to do so within policy constraints imposed by Britain and when resources available to both the public and private sectors were limited. It tried to modify and adapt land allocation and management policy, as far as it could, to encourage private housing development. Anything which required expenditure, or the foregoing of revenue, had to be approved by the Secretary of State who, after agreeing to one such case, made clear he would not contemplate others. Nevertheless, this period was marked by the government's relatively innovative approach within this constrained framework. Again, it was MacDougall who tried to create policy-making capacity within the Hong Kong government. He was able to keep the Hong Kong government's housing policy differentiated not only from policies preferred by the unofficials but also from policies some Colonial Office officials would have preferred. The Hong Kong government was, therefore, able to exercise a limited form of autonomy although it was able to achieve little as a result of it.

Secondly, from 1949 until Grantham's return in November 1950, the government's housing policy went through a more uncertain stage. It was a period marked by a seeming policy paralysis and lack of leadership which showed Grantham's limitations as a leader in policy formulation. MacDougall seemed to play a less active role, or perhaps was constrained from doing so by his relationship with Grantham. Even when it was a recurring subject of comment and debate among middle and upper civil servants, Grantham was unable, or unwilling, to harness and develop their ideas into public policy. Given the unofficials' dislike of government subsidy or of direct government involvement in the provision of low-cost housing, it was left to what are now called non-governmental organisations, or NGOs, to try and fill this void. Resource limitations, however, hampered their effectiveness as much as it had the private sector's. Eventually, even Grantham realised that government would need to get involved. His steps in this direction, however, with the establishment of a Housing Committee, were tentative and seemed to happen only after the Secretary of State's outburst over the Archbishop of Canterbury's remarks. Again, Grantham was reacting and not leading and the Hong Kong government, under his leadership, seemed to exercise little effective autonomy over this issue.

The final period started with Grantham's meetings in the Colonial Office in 1950 which led to the Secretary of State's despatch in December. Did Grantham elicit the Colonial Office's support to bolster his desired housing policy or was he required simply to implement a policy decided in London as Peel had been required to do in 1930 over *mui tsai*? It is difficult to know what Grantham's desired or favoured policy was. At the Colonial Office meetings, he was recorded as simply "agreeing" that housing was an "urgent matter", almost admitting by his lack of fervour or initiative in first raising it, that he did not really think so. Nor did he request the Secretary of State's support for a housing policy, but seemed to acquiesce to a suggestion that a despatch "would be useful". By his lack of action when action was needed, a policy void had been created. This void had to be filled by the Secretary of State issuing explicit instructions on exactly what Grantham was required to do. Grantham also seemed simply to accept what was suggested. He appeared to be supporting the strongest side and, when attending a meeting in the Colonial Office chaired by the Secretary of State, it would have been clear who the strongest side was. Again, there is very little evidence of the exercise of autonomy.

On his return to Hong Kong, Grantham was faced with a situation similar to that faced by Peel in 1930 when he arrived in Hong Kong with instructions from the Secretary of State to start registering *mui tsai*. Like Peel, Grantham now started to implement the Secretary of State's instructions. Like Peel, he was able to exercise a considerable degree of autonomy in doing so but there was a subtle difference. Grantham took care to be seen to act before the formal receipt of the Secretary of State's instructions and seemingly before anyone else in government was aware of them. He was also keen to point out that the policies he was implementing were his own while assuring the Secretary of State that they "did not conflict" with his instructions. In addition, the Secretary of State who, from October 1951 was Grantham's supporter Lyttelton, chose not to follow up on the issue. As housing was also being visibly tackled, albeit by the two housing societies, this seemed sufficient to placate Bishop Hall. Grantham, therefore, had greater freedom of movement in the implementation of the Secretary of State's instructions than had Peel who had had to submit reports every six months to the Colonial Office. *Mui tsai* had also been a source of continuing pressure from groups in Britain in a way that housing never was. Grantham was thus able to exercise a degree of autonomy by default and managed to avoid creating a further policy void into which unofficials, or the private sector may have moved.

No matter how much Grantham may have welcomed the Secretary of State's instructions and no matter how much he wanted it to appear this was his own policy, the fact remains that it was not. The decision to establish a Housing Authority was not therefore a "politically differentiated" policy of the Hong Kong government. Grantham had not shown that he had the capacity to formulate an effective housing policy on his own. He had also shown the limitation of his political skills. It took him over three years to develop detailed plans and forge the political support necessary, inside and outside government, to ensure the passage of legislation. He was unable to provide the leadership required to build support in a timely fashion either within the Executive Council or within his own administration: he could only placate his Financial Secretary by allowing his proposals to go before the Executive Council and be rejected by them. He was at least astute enough to ensure that the Secretary of State could be satisfied with his immediate action by ensuring that the Housing Society was able to proceed with its pilot project at Sheung Li Uk. Grantham and his administration, therefore, had hardly shown that they were entirely their own masters.

In his December 1950 despatch, the Secretary of State had referred to the need to use a housing trust to solve the growing squatter problem. This was not to be a matter for the Housing Authority but remained an issue in Hong Kong. How this was tackled is discussed in Chapter 9.

9
Squatter Resettlement

> [T]he Governor had called a meeting at Government House ... on Boxing Day ... I was able to tell the ... gathering that it would be impossible ... to try to build temporary shelter for some sixty thousand people. The Governor ... then turned to the Director of Public Works and asked him to make proposals for some permanent shelter. So the momentous step was taken for the government itself to build something for the fire victims.[1]
>
> Denis Bray[2]

The Shek Kip Mei fire on Christmas Day 1953 left upwards of 60,000 people homeless. Four months later, a decision had been taken to resettle them into permanent multi-storey accommodation provided at public expense. Within a year, it had become government policy to rehouse all cleared squatters in this manner. This marked a major shift in policy. Prior to this, the Hong Kong government had never seriously contemplated the provision of permanent subsidised housing for squatters. Sites for temporary resettlement had been provided which allowed squatters to erect their own huts. How had this decision been taken? Did the Hong Kong government have to seek the Secretary of State's approval or rely upon him for advice, direction or resources? Did the Hong Kong government have the capacity to formulate and implement such a programme on its own and, if so, how did this capacity develop? What influence did the unofficials in the Legislative and Urban Councils have on this decision? Was this a step forward taken by the Hong Kong government in the exercise of autonomy?

The development of the Hong Kong government's squatter resettlement policy from 1948 will be examined in this chapter. It will assess the government's ability to formulate and to implement this policy and will consider how it reinforced the government's authority and reputation for effectiveness. It will then examine how, because of the policy's unintended consequences, and in the face of a sudden ten-fold increase in squatter numbers, the Hong Kong government quickly reviewed it.

Government's inability, however, to implement this new policy effectively, the increasing involvement of unofficials in the policy making process and the impact of the Shek Kip Mai fire are then reviewed. Finally, this chapter examines the effectiveness with which the policy of permanent resettlement was implemented and what impact this had on the development of the Hong Kong government's autonomy.

Early policy development

Influxes of migrants were not new to Hong Kong. Traditionally, better economic prospects in Hong Kong attracted migrants looking for work and, conversely, improving economic conditions in China attracted them back again.[3] There had been a major influx of squatters in 1938 when large numbers of refugees entered Hong Kong to escape the depredations of the Japanese. They had posed a major problem and relief efforts were organised by the Hong Kong government.[4] Many only left Hong Kong when the Japanese restricted rice supplies during the occupation. The population then dropped from about 1.6 million in 1941 to an estimated 600,000 by August 1945. By the end of 1946, it was estimated to have risen back to 1.6 million and to 1.8 million by December 1947.[5]

Squatters were not seen as a major problem in the years immediately following 1945. The number of squatters in the main urban area was comparatively small in 1948.[6] The issue was not considered sufficiently pressing by unofficials to raise it in the Legislative Council even though squatter areas posed problems to the authorities. The Hong Kong Police considered them to be centres of gambling and prostitution and places where criminals could seek refuge almost with impunity. Normal policing methods did not work and the police felt that the only effective measure was their total removal.[7]

The removal of illegal squatters became a politically sensitive issue in 1948 during an attempted clearance of squatters from the Kowloon Walled City. Under the Convention of Peking, 1898, Britain had leased the New Territories from China for 99 years. Although the Kowloon Walled City was to remain under Chinese jurisdiction, Britain abrogated this provision shortly after it came into effect. This, however, was never recognised by China. During their occupation, the Japanese demolished the walls to extend the runway at the airport and the area was subsequently occupied by squatters. The Hong Kong government wanted to remove them because Grantham wished to revive a pre-war scheme to turn the area into a public park.[8] The Chinese government protested and when in January 1948 the squatters resisted eviction the situation got out of hand. The police opened fire and killed one protester.

Others were arrested but the Hong Kong courts rejected an argument from their defence counsel that the government had no jurisdiction in the Walled City. This resulted in anti-British riots in Shanghai and the burning of the British Consulate in Canton.[9] Britain, therefore, decided not to press what it saw as its rights in the Walled City and the issue was left unresolved. The exercise of British jurisdiction inside the Walled City remained a sensitive area in Sino-British relations until 1987 when both Britain and China agreed that it should be cleared and turned into a public park.[10]

Government was concerned that these sensitivities could spill over into a land dispute at Kai Tak. When the Japanese had resumed land to extend the airport runway they had not paid any compensation.[11] After the war, government was willing to offer land exchange to the former owners, if suitable sites could be found, but otherwise would only offer cash compensation. Government received a petition in January 1948 which "insisted" upon land exchange and threatened trouble if none was offered. Although the request was not unreasonable, both the Secretary for Chinese Affairs and the Deputy Colonial Secretary were concerned at the petitioners' belligerent tone.[12] They thought the matter could escalate if the petitioners and their supporters attempted to connect it to the Kowloon Walled City incident. The Executive Council agreed and advised that the introduction of a bill to provide for compensation could "lead to an aggravation of the Kowloon City problem [and] that it would be better to wait until this problem has been settled".[13]

In January 1948, against this backdrop, MacDougall received a letter from the General Officer Commanding Far East Forces in Hong Kong. He complained about a squatter area in Hong Kong Island and quoted at length from a report by the local police commander. This described the police's inability to tackle the problems caused by the squatters, particularly the operation of brothels, unless concerted government action was taken. The letter was circulated to departments "for enquiries". Shortly afterwards, Fehily, Chairman of the Urban Council, told MacDougall he had established a small committee of representatives from concerned departments. They would consider the issue of squatters and make recommendations to government.[14] This all seemed to happen with remarkable speed. MacDougall, in replying to the General, was cautiously optimistic that it might be

> possible to undertake a programme of progressive improvement of these spots ... all this sounds incredibly cautious but you know that squatters have become dynamite.

It seems a little odd that the General Officer Commanding should raise such an issue in this way and that a committee to review the matter was established with such alacrity. MacDougall had always had good relations with the armed services. He had also known Fehilly from before the war and had worked closely with him in the Hong Kong Planning Unit in London and later in the British Military Administration. He was aware of the problems of policing squatter areas and the sensitivity of clearing them after the Kowloon Walled City incident. He may have wanted to ensure that the government's writ still ran within other squatter areas and did not wish them to become hostage to future relations with China. He also thought that the handling of the squatter problem had become one of "increasing urgency and Government is anxious to tackle the problem in the immediate future".

Grantham, however, seemed unaware of the wider importance of this issue. MacDougall did not approach him on the matter until June 1948 when he told him that the issue was now under investigation. He played up the urgency of the matter, almost as if Grantham was unaware of it, by saying that

> there have been some letters recently in the newspapers about squatters: the anxiety of these correspondents marches hand-in-hand with ours. I hope to have some new and definite plan by next week.[15]

It was possible that MacDougall solicited a letter from the General Officer Commanding as a ploy to ensure that Grantham focused on this issue and that government developed an effective squatter clearance and resettlement policy. Grantham could hardly have ignored a complaint from such a senior figure or a report from the Chairman of the Urban Council backed by a number of senior officials. MacDougall would not have wished the Hong Kong government's autonomy to be lost to the Chinese government or to lawless elements among squatters. To prevent this, he may have wanted to ensure the Hong Kong government had the capacity to formulate and implement its own effective policy towards squatters.

Chairman of the Urban Council's report

On 30 June 1948, the Committee's report was submitted to MacDougall. It was the first defining post-war statement on squatters and established the Hong Kong government's initial policy towards their clearance and resettlement. It sought both to identify the nature and scale of the squatter problem and make policy recommendations to deal with it. It was, as Fehily admitted, an "extremely difficult and complex" problem.[16] The Committee estimated there were 20,000 urban squatters in Hong Kong Island and 10,000 in Kowloon. They were to be found on Crown land,

War Office land and on roofs of private premises. Some huts were made of "miserable collections of rags and matting". Others appeared to have been mass-produced wooden structures. Surveys had shown that

> about 30% of the inhabitants of most squatter colonies are respectable artisans, some of whom have lived in Hong Kong for some years, are gainfully employed and could afford more orthodox accommodation if they could find it. The majority are newcomers to the Colony and many are destitutes or bad characters the Colony could well do without.

The report also found that overcrowding, extremely poor sanitary conditions and fire risks were grounds for clearing them. This would require careful planning because as soon as squatters were evicted from one site, they would squat again elsewhere. In the long term, the only solution was an adequate supply of housing. In the short term the Committee recommended that, "Government should allot certain areas on which the controlled building of squatter shacks should be officially permitted."

The report recommended action by several departments. It recomended that the Crown Lands and Survey Office should identify resettlement areas; that the Urban Council should issue permits for a small fee to approved squatters for sites within these areas and that the Social Welfare Office (SWO) should help with screening. Clearances should be undertaken gradually rather than all at once to avoid causing political problems or economic hardship. The Committee realised that not all squatters could benefit. Some, it was surmised, would go into normal accommodation, and some would continue to squat where they could. It was important, however, to institute squatter patrols to discourage and prevent people from re-squatting on sites just cleared. The hope was also that it would present a stark choice to squatter families. They would have to realise that "they must either find proper accommodation, go to a government site or leave the Colony". This policy was described candidly as "a short term policy of gradual attrition followed up by measures to ensure that sites once cleared are kept cleared". It was also hoped that this course "offers the best hope of success" and, perhaps equally importantly, would keep costs low.

The report also recommended that a housing scheme for four-storey blocks of workers flats proposed by a Health Officer, Dr J. S. Willis should go ahead. The Committee recognised, however, that this could not be done on a strictly commercial basis. It recommended that government should provide land to private developers on favourable terms to build these flats. They should be let to tenants screened by the Social Welfare Officer at government controlled rents.[17]

Government's response

Once MacDougall had received the report, he lost no time in taking action. He recommended to Grantham that the report should go to the Executive Council, saying that "this whole business of squatters is of paramount importance". The Governor agreed without demur and went further by instructing the Director of Public Works to simultaneously prepare estimates for water supply and latrines in readiness for submission to the Finance Committee.[18] On 13 July 1948, the Executive Council agreed that the report's recommendations be approved in principle and that the Finance Committee should be asked to authorise the expenditure, which it duly did.[19] Details were not finalised until January 1949 when further Executive Council approval was sought[20] and the policy could start to be implemented. This included identification of sites for approved areas where squatters could erect huts of a standard pattern. The Social Welfare Officer also established a screening process through which those eligible could be selected. As there would only be space for limited numbers in the approved areas, only those who could either afford to pay, or borrow, the $800 required to erect a hut would be selected.[21]

Only cleared squatters were to be offered a site in a resettlement area. Spaces were not to be allocated to non-squatters, no matter how deserving. It was recognised that many of the police and Urban Services Department staff engaged in clearances were themselves squatters or lived in accommodation which should have been condemned. The concern was that increasing the number and size of resite areas for single-storey cottage development would prevent permanent development for many years to come. The answer was felt to lie in the provision of "cheap housing schemes rather than on the resettlement of squatters in approved areas" for such staff. The Chairman of the Urban Council thought the best answer to the problem of sub-standard housing was "to request Government to foster the development of cheap housing schemes of a more permanent nature".[22] The Director of Public Works was also sympathetic to this view.[23]

Implementation of 1948 policy

The operation of the policy went more smoothly than anticipated. By the end of 1949 the Chairman of the Urban Council reported that some 45,000 squatters from 8,500 huts had been cleared. There had been little trouble because "once the squatters knew that they really had to go, they went quite peacefully and displayed no signs of rancour". It was, however, only a qualified success. Many cleared squatters simply moved and squatted further away from the main urban area "where they continue to form a serious health danger and a grave fire menace". There they replicated the overcrowding and insanitary conditions which had caused government Health Officers such concern in the first place. Moreover, many squatters screened as being eligible for resiting in an approved area did not take up the offer. According to a Social Welfare Office survey, the reasons were mostly financial. Many cleared squatters could not afford the cost of erecting a hut as they did not earn enough and had no capital to fall back upon. The approved areas were also too far away from places of employment and they could not afford the travelling cost. The capacity of approved areas was also now seriously constrained by the lack of an adequate water supply. This could often not be improved without compromising the supply to adjacent residential users.[24] In some areas too there had also been site formation problems. Despite these problems, government had shown that, after the Kowloon Walled City debacle in 1948, it had re-established its right to clear squatter areas as it thought necessary. This was accepted by the squatters and resulted in no complaints or agitation from the Chinese government. The capacity of the Hong Kong government to exercise its authority over any area in the colony had been quietly re-established.

Review of 1948 policy

The massive influx of refugees from China in 1948 and 1949 posed a major challenge which caused great concern to the Hong Kong government. In August 1949 W. J. Gorman the Chief Fire Officer, Kowloon, wrote to the Colonial Secretary about an increase of several hundred squatter huts in the outskirts of Kowloon. These posed a serious fire hazard and looking after those made homeless by fire would result in much additional government expenditure. He wanted to create fire lanes to help stop fires spreading. He was "aware that the situation bristles with difficulties but ... I must earnestly recommend that some drastic action be taken". The Chairman of the Urban Council realised the need for action but could not support Gorman's proposal. He was concerned it might have been construed as recognising a legal right of squatters to occupy the land upon which they were squatting illegally.[25] This debate continued within government during the course of 1950, fuelled by a disastrous fire in the Kowloon Walled city squatter area on 11 January 1950 which destroyed the huts of over 17,000 squatters. However, neither the Colonial Secretary nor the Financial Secretary were prepared to countenance the expenditure of large sums of money as proposed by Gorman for ameliorative measures to reduce the fire risk in squatter areas.[26]

The worsening situation led to a review of squatter resettlement policy by the Social Welfare Officer, J. C. McDouall.[27] He did not make far-reaching recommendations. He recognised that the success of the 1948 policy in clearing squatters from much of the inner urban area had meant the problem had been pushed to the outskirts. McDouall also believed that

> political as well as economic reasons led the majority of the 1948 squatters who were dispossessed to believe that at all costs it was better to stay in Hong Kong than to attempt to return to China.

The situation was exacerbated by a large influx of refugees from China pushing total squatter numbers to an estimated 330,000. Very few further clearances could be contemplated because they would only worsen the situation in outlying squatter areas.[28] McDouall recommended there should now only be a limited amount of squatter clearance in the main urban area. Otherwise, apart from the provision of thirty feet wide fire lanes, no other infrastructure or social services should be provided. As Deputy Colonial Secretary, K. M. A. Barnett, rather acidly commented, this amounted to the government taking

> all possible steps to persuade new arrivals to leave the colony by making them as uncomfortable as possible. Having driven squatters to the outskirts of the urban area, to try to pen them in still closer and again to make them as uncomfortable as possible.

He was concerned that in doing so "we may be in danger of losing the basic claims of humanity" and feared that whatever the Hong Kong government did would lead to accusations of brutality similar to that experienced during the Japanese occupation.[29]

On 5 December 1950, the Executive Council considered McDouall's report and instructed that a more detailed survey be conducted. This should identify sites where squatters could erect huts of approved design; identify other sites where they could be tolerated; and identify sites "where quarters could be built for Government employees on the permanent establishment or by local utility companies, etc". The Chairman of the Urban Council, or the Social Welfare Officer, was also authorised to approve allocation of sites in approved areas to "reputable" persons who were not already squatters. In respect of areas which were impracticable to clear, the Executive Council agreed that fire and safety lanes should be provided and that there should be,

> Discouragement of squatters from staying in these areas by a policy of attrition, the aim of which would be to make them as uncomfortable as possible in the hope that they will return to China. No social services of any sort would be encouraged.[30]

Wakefield report

This detailed survey was conducted by J. T. Wakefield,[31] a cadet officer who recommended what was in effect an extension of the existing policy. He proposed that the overall objective should be "the complete clearance of squatters from existing areas which are objectionable". This would require the clearance of some 210,000 squatters from the main urban areas of Hong Kong Island and Kowloon. He proposed that the whole of the urban area in both Hong Kong Island and Kowloon be gazetted under the Public Health (Sanitary Provisions) Regulations, 1948, providing the legal basis for clearances to take place. He further proposed that there should be one "approved" area and one "tolerated" area in both Hong Kong Island and in Kowloon. Squatters in "tolerated" areas would, for a small fee, be allowed to erect huts to minimum construction standards with controls on their size and siting. "Tolerated" areas would also be administered by the Chairman of the Urban Council who was confident that, even in as large a "tolerated" area as Hung Hom, containing some 30,000 squatters, "further entries into this area can be, and are being, controlled by the Urban Council".

On 3 July 1951, the Executive Council approved Wakefield's findings and recommendations. Beyond consideration of the staffing requirements there was no mention in the Executive Council memorandum of the government's ability to implement these recommendations nor how long it would take to complete. When the Executive Council considered further details six months later, they were only told that

> although it is of course hoped that the "tolerated" settlements will not be permanent it would be unwise to assume that they will have a life of less than five years.[32]

Slow progress

If the Hong Kong government had shown some capacity to reformulate policy on squatter control, it rapidly became clear that it had only limited ability to implement it. In November 1952, barely ten months later, the Chairman of the Urban Council, by then Barnett, candidly admitted as much. In January 1952, the Executive Council had been told that some 23,000 resettlement huts would be constructed by the end of December; by the end of October, only just over 7,000 were ready. Barnett identified two difficulties. Firstly, there had been delay in providing a water supply to two "tolerated" areas, including a large one at Ngau Tau Kok. Secondly, there was the problem of the rate at which squatters could be screened by the Social Welfare Officer. By October 1952, both these issues had been addressed and Barnett hoped that progress would improve.[33]

However, only one month later he identified further problems. One was "the absence of a single controlling authority" and the other was "the reluctance of squatters to be resettled". The problem of co-ordination was that five departments were involved in the clearance and resettlement process—the Urban Council, the police, the Public Works Department, the Social Welfare Office and the Resettlement Office. Barnett complained that "to co-ordinate the work of five departments without power to give overriding orders is impossible". He argued that the Director of Public Works should become the co-ordinator as he was the land authority and the problem was one of illegal occupation of land, be it Crown or private land. The other was the reluctance of squatters to move for which Barnett adduced two principal reasons. The first was the delay in utilising the sites cleared for their proposed permanent use which encouraged re-squatting on the cleared site. More importantly, there was lack of employment close to resettlement areas. This, he thought, was "the crux of the whole matter" and steps should be taken to encourage the establishment of factories in these areas.

The Commissioner of Police thought that the whole programme should be slowed down. Clearances should only proceed when a site had to be cleared for serious health reasons or was required for development. Otherwise squatters should be left where they were. Although squatter areas were not easy to police, it was more difficult to police squatters who had been cleared and become street sleepers or who had squatted on rooftops. He also thought it was a waste of time in some of the bigger areas to erect single-storey huts. Six to seven story tenements should be erected instead. The Secretary for Chinese Affairs, Todd, agreed that it was time for a serious review. He thought they could either "concentrate on tidying up existing squatter areas" as suggested by the Social Welfare Officer or "embark on substantial housing schemes with Government leading the way to encourage other big employers".[34]

On 12 January 1953 the Colonial Secretary, Black, called a meeting to discuss these views and decide on what to do. He was already aware of the problems of squatter clearance having had to reluctantly postpone resumption of land in a squatter fire site in October 1952.[35] Black supported a more pragmatic approach and agreed the Executive Council should be advised that,

> Squatter areas should only be considered for clearance if the area occupied was required for development or was a very serious health risk; at the same time there must be an area available immediately for re-settlement and the area vacated must be put to immediate use. Squatter areas remaining undisturbed must be cleaned up and administered as tolerated areas.[36]

Squatter resettlement and the Urban Council

In mid-January, Grantham agreed a paper should go to the Executive Council.[37] This was before the programme's lack of progress became a matter of public criticism from both elected and appointed unofficials on the Urban Council. They had become concerned at the slow pace of resettlement and were frustrated by the division of responsibility for clearance, resettlement and management of resite areas between different departments. In December 1952, Brook Bernacchi, an elected member, had asked the Chairman at a Council meeting about squatters who had been cleared but who had chosen not to move into approved or tolerated resettlement areas. Barnett publicly castigated him for asking questions on matters outside the Urban Council's jurisdiction but the following day it was Barnett who was strongly criticised in the local press.[38]

On 10 February 1953, matters came to a head. They centred round an awkward legal arrangement which government had put in place. The statutory powers concerning squatter resettlement had been conferred not on the Urban Council but on the Urban Council Select Committee on Resettlement. This remained separate from the main Council to which it was not accountable. Neither was the Council informed about its workings nor was it able to discuss the Select Committee's work or reports. D. J. Ruttonjee, an appointed unofficial Urban Council member, tabled a motion demanding that the Council meet in committee after each regular session to discuss the work of its Select Committee. Ruttonjee argued that it was now necessary for the whole Council to become involved as there was growing public criticism of the Council over the slow pace of squatter clearance. This was despite the fact that it was an issue over which they exercised no responsibility and over which they felt they were being unfairly criticised. Even the Select Committee itself had little control over the resettlement programme. Several members spoke in support of the motion which was unanimously adopted.[39]

It is likely that this very public airing of his government's shortcomings was not lost on Grantham. The following day, the *South China Morning Post* published an editorial scathingly critical of the programme's slow progress and the secrecy surrounding it. The next day, Barnett "had the benefit of a further discussion with His Excellency the Governor". He received instructions that the clearance of squatters was to continue and that it should be done according to a six-month programme. It should be co-ordinated by the Director of Public Works with the Social Welfare Officer, Chief Resettlement Officer and the Commissioner of Police providing input. Clearances would need prior approval from the Deputy Colonial Secretary or, if departments disagreed, from the Colonial Secretary.

On 19 February Grantham clarified these instructions at a meeting with senior officials. He reiterated that the squatter clearance programme would continue, subject generally to availability of suitable resite areas. A six-month programme, co-ordinated by the Director of Public Works, would be "communicated to the Urban Council Select Committee on Resettlement as a confidential document". The Public Health (Sanitary Provisions) Regulations should be re-drafted to reflect these changes. The Executive Council were not to be involved until the new regulations were ready.[40] This was expected to take some time because of pressure of work on the Attorney General.

The Colonial Office, although concerned at the number of squatter fires, had begun to feel rather impotent. The usual telegram that the Secretary of State sent to convey his sympathy after each major squatter fire was now wearing a little thin. As such statements were made public in Hong Kong, Sidebotham thought that they were a useful way of showing sympathy publicly. To help understand the issue better, he asked Grantham

> if you could let us have a brief note of what preventive measures and precautions are already in force or are contemplated if, as we assume, the only permanent means of prevention is the long-term solution of clearance and resettlement.

As a reflection of how the Colonial Office viewed its position, Sidebotham finished his letter by saying,

> I hope you will not find us tedious in pressing points which have probably worried you for some time, but we feel the role of the Impotent Chorus of tragedy growing upon us.[41]

The following month Grantham replied explaining the impossibilities of controlling fires effectively in congested squatter areas, the challenge of resettling some 300,000 squatters, the shortage of suitable land and the need to find employment for them near their place of abode. Hinting that he felt he should not be entirely blamed for such matters, he claimed it would take several years to find a solution.[42]

Grantham also sought to put the public mind at ease during his annual address to the Legislative Council on 4 March 1953. He took care to spell out who in government was responsible for what but was not prepared to risk giving offence to the Urban Council by depriving them of their responsibility for resettlement. He emphasised the enormity of the problem and that it would take several years to resolve. He made clear that "Government's policy remains the same—to clear the squatters with as much expedition as possible and to resettle them, if possible in fireproof buildings, but at least under proper control".[43]

Shortly after this, Barnett seems to have made his peace with the Urban Council by re-organising the Select Committee on Resettlement. He proposed that the Chairman of the Urban Council should also become the Chairman of the Select Committee which would now have four unofficials as members. It was also agreed that each unofficial Urban Council member should be responsible for visiting squatters in a specific geographic area. Colonel Douglas Clague endorsed these proposals. He also proposed that the Select Committee should consider what steps could be taken to speed up the resettlement, reduce the cost of erecting huts and prevent abuses.[44]

Grantham had shown his usual political astuteness in trying to head off growing unofficial criticism of the government's squatter clearance and resettlement programme. He had taken care to say publicly that everything was on track, if a little behind, that it was a large problem and would take time to resolve. He was aware that failure to implement this policy effectively was tarnishing the government's reputation. His response to this was to give greater credence to the unofficials' views rather than to address the practical problems raised by his officials. Privately, he had simply told them to make the policy work. He sought to restore the government's reputation by trying to re-build confidence in his administration's ability to deliver, but without ensuring that it had the capacity to do so.

Further delay

During the remainder of 1953, the resettlement programme continued its slow progress. The total number of resettled squatters gradually increased from 35,000 in April to 43,000 in November.[45] This caused the Colonial Secretary to comment, in some exasperation, that,

> Whatever may be said ... in explanation of delays, the fact remains that H.E.'s [the Governor's] orders for action to be taken ... have *not* been carried out ... squatter resettlement policy is a matter of major importance for political, social welfare and health reasons and it must not be allowed to drift. [emphasis in original]

But this is precisely what had happened. It was not until November 1953 that a draft directive was sent to the Director of Public Works. This had been prepared in the Colonial Secretariat by Bray and the Deputy Colonial Secretary, C. B. Burgess, who thought that

> the main trouble at the moment is that there has been *no* co-ordination and no assumption of overall responsibility for clearances.[46] [emphasis in original]

The Colonial Secretary had to admit that "a directive should, in fact, have issued from this office after the meeting at Government House last February". What was now needed was "a strong directive to infuse new life into squatter clearance and resettlement". On 16 December 1953, after a further inter-departmental meeting chaired by Black as the Governor's Deputy,[47] a directive was eventually issued. It sought to streamline co-ordination by appointing the Director of Public Works as the co-ordinating authority on squatter control. The government's squatter resettlement policy was to be brought into sharp relief by the biggest civil disaster to befall the colony to date, the 1953 Christmas Day fire in Shek Kip Mei, the largest squatter area in Hong Kong.

Shek Kip Mei Fire

The fire started in the Shek Kip Mei squatter area late on the evening of Christmas Day 1953. It was, according to Denis Bray,

> much more severe than anything we had seen. Shek Kip Mei was the largest squatter area by far. It might have contained up to one-third of all squatters.[48]

The fire started about 9:30 pm when a kerosene lamp was knocked over into a bucket of rubber solution used for making shoes. It had got a firm hold at the back of the squatter area before the Fire Brigade was even called. When they arrived, their access was impeded by thousands of people fleeing from the fire down the narrow alleyways. The fire's heat, fanned by a stiff breeze, carried it deeper into the squatter area. The fire burned for five hours[49] and could be seen clearly from across the harbour on Hong Kong Island.[50] Only 40 people were injured and there were only three fatalities. The police cordoned off the area and prevented people from entering the fire site; it was estimated that 10,000 came just to watch. When the damage could be assessed, it was calculated that 41 acres had been burned out and 60,000 people made homeless. The Social Welfare Office was mobilised and immediately opened up two kitchens which started working 24 hours a day. Assistance was offered by the army and by Hong Kong's many voluntary organisations, including the Civil Aid Services, St John's Ambulance and the Boy Scouts. Come daylight, the Social Welfare Office started to register the homeless. The initial screening, which took four days, was rather basic because about a third of the 58,000 registered homeless had lost their identity cards in the fire. Of these, only about 5%–10% were reckoned to be impostors.[51]

The government's reaction was swift. Grantham, held a meeting with his senior officials at 10:30 the following morning.[52] It was agreed that temporary housing was impractical "because the numbers were so large". Instead, the homeless were to be allowed to sleep on the streets of Sham Shui Po, sheltered by the many verandahs, and provided with sanitation facilities by the government. It was also decided that the remaining private land on the fire site should be resumed, that the whole site should be cleared and that the homeless should be allowed to resettle on the site. This was not, however, permanent resettlement with subsidised accommodation provided by government. Government would only provide "assistance in the form of housing materials to individual families". The exact form of assistance would depend on the advice of the Public Works Department but the scale was to be "about $200 a family" and was in line with past practice.[53] The site was already earmarked for the development of low-cost housing in five years' time and when it was needed "the inhabitants will be moved".

When the Executive Council was consulted three days later the government's policy had quietly but materially changed. Instead of providing building materials, government now proposed it would

> build lines of small temporary housing units. Each unit consisting of a room 10' by 10' with door and window. Houses will adjoin each other and be fire proof ... [and] will cost in the order of $800 each.[54]

These would be "constructed on the cheapest basis consistent with considerations of public health and fire prevention". Although the Executive Council advised that the units should be built "as rapidly as possible at the site of the fire", they baulked at the estimated total cost of $16 million. They wanted the Secretary of State to consider establishing a relief fund in Britain to defray at least some of this cost. The Governor had already warned the Colonial Office that "there will be a serious financial commitment". He had perhaps been encouraged by their initial reply asking him to let them know "if you need any help from here".

The Governor's report later that day by telegram to the Secretary of State implied it was unfair that the burden of paying for rehousing should fall upon the Hong Kong taxpayer. After all, he claimed, "the victims of this fire are not Hong Kong people". Nor was the government responsible for them either as "they are persons who have taken refuge here in face of recent developments in China". Even without the fire "they would have imposed on this Colony a continuing burden in all the varied fields of finance, social services, housing, employment and security".[55] The government, therefore, felt it "necessary to urge that a contribution of say $3 million should be made by Her Majesty's Government" which would go towards defraying the cost of rehousing. Such a contribution would, the Colonial Office was advised "create an excellent impression here" and would help counter any propaganda the Chinese government may try and make out of the situation. Much to the Colonial Officer's relief, Grantham had already been able to deflect an offer of financial assistance from the Bank of China. The Secretary of State replied quickly agreeing to a free grant of £200,000 as a contribution towards rehousing.[56] This generosity had by no means been a foregone conclusion. Hong Kong's healthy financial position was well known to the Colonial Office. As one official had remarked,

> I do not know whether ... Hong Kong may approach H[is] M[ajesty's] G[overnment] for a grant: I think not, however, unless the cost of providing accommodation, etc is so enormous that even Hong Kong's ample reserves cannot stand the strain.[57]

Policy review

The Hong Kong government was, however, about to lose the political initiative. Its emergency and relief response to the fire had been admirable. The problem of fire-prone squatter areas and the need for an effective policy to tackle them still remained. Into this gap stepped Colonel Douglas Clague,[58] a distinguished war veteran and prominent local businessman who was a nominated unofficial Urban Council member. The Chairman of the Urban Council, Barnett, had asked members to suggest how the Council should respond to the disaster. Clague responded promptly and at length. He thought that the prime objective should be

> to provide, if possible, more permanent homes for the squatters and it follows that every semi-permanent ... dwelling put up, makes a direct contribution to the overall housing problem.

It was essential that action should be taken immediately although the problem would not be solved "by means of building cottages only". This would incur great cost but Clague seemed not overly concerned "provided we ensure that good value is received for the money expended, then I believe it is a sound policy".[59] Clague was appointed Chairman of the Urban Council's Emergency Resettlement Sub-Committee at a meeting of the Committee of the Whole Council on 5 January 1954. It is unclear how or why he was appointed. The minutes of meeting simply state that "it was agreed that" he be so appointed. They leave the impression that the Urban Council Chairman, Barnett, did not play a key role in this appointment.[60]

Over the next three months, two concurrent reviews of squatter resettlement policy took place. One was conducted under Clague's Emergency Resettlement Sub-Committee. It had three officials as members, the Director of Public Works, his deputy, and the Chief

Resettlement Officer. Its two unofficial members were R. C. Lee and P. D. Au and Barnett also attended meetings. Its terms of reference reflected the current thinking on resettlement. It was to look for land for cottages for resettlement of squatters, make recommendations for the early development of undeveloped sites, and "make further recommendations on a long-term basis for the acceleration of the resettlement scheme".[61]

The other review turned out to be a more tentative one conducted by government and not the speedy one that Grantham later liked to remember.[62] Its review started in January and began promisingly with an able analysis by the Deputy Colonial Secretary, Burgess.[63] He thought that three factors made it appropriate to review resettlement policy. Firstly, the redundancy of the old policy had been put clearly into focus by the resettlement policies adopted for the Shek Kip Mei squatters. Whereas it had previously taken three years to rehouse 40,000 squatters, some 60,000 from Shek Kip Mei would be rehoused in six months. Secondly, land was not available to rehouse 200,000 squatters in one-storey cottages with ready access to the urban area. Lastly, the Director of Public Works had drawn up estimates for six-storey resettlement blocks and this could overcome the difficulty of "moving people from the area which they themselves have freely selected as their home". Burgess also outlined the problems of co-ordinating the work of different government departments. Perhaps most importantly, he considered a crucial factor in the policy's previously slow progress had been the "lack of a sense of urgency in the general approach to the problem".

On 8 February 1954, the Governor discussed Burgess' proposals with his senior officials. The meeting recognised that one of the main problems of existing resettlement policy had been "Government's reluctance to finance and implement resettlement schemes directly". However, despite the fact that action after Shek Kip Mei had shown that large numbers of squatters could be resettled quickly, the meeting still felt it

> to be very doubtful whether Government would be justified in applying to the whole squatter resettlement problem the direct action which had been forced upon it as a result of the Shek Kip Mei disaster.

The solution "appeared to be" the construction of multi-storey blocks on a limited number of suitable sites. It was tentatively mooted that problems of "inadequate co-ordination" could be addressed by appointment of a senior cadet as a Commissioner of Resettlement. He would take over responsibility for the resettlement functions allocated to the Director of Public Works only two weeks before the fire. The Director of Public Works should also consider the possibility of allocating up to one-third of the Shek Kip Mei site for multi-storey development with a view to increasing the number of families that could be housed on the site already prepared.

Despite clearly identified shortcomings in the existing squatter policy, Grantham took no brave new decisions. Instead, small, cautious steps were taken. Nothing was to be decided until Clague's Committee had reported. Yet again, the Hong Kong government had let a policy void appear into which Clague had stepped. The government committee also agreed that

the Urban Council should continue to concern itself with the general policy of resettlement, but that the responsibilities of the Council as Housing Authority should be regarded as a separate function until ... the problems of squatter resettlement and low-cost housing merged. [64]

It was soon to become apparent that government could no longer deny the Urban Council a role in policy-making on squatter issues.

Clague's Sub-Committee

Clague's Sub-Committee was more decisive. An interim report issued on 10 February recommended that government should improve its screening methods and that

a single senior officer should be charged with the overriding executive control of screening, clearance and resettlement.[65]

Clague's produced its final report at the end of March. It stated clearly that the "present routine of huge fires every year is quite unacceptable". This was the "overriding consideration at present". The immediate solution was the driving of fire lanes through existing large squatter sites before the onset of the dry season in October. Even if fire lanes and other palliatives could be implemented "a sufficiently serious fire risk will remain until the whole problem has been permanently solved". The Sub-Committee also supported the Director of Public Works' view that in respect of the Shek Kip Mei fire site, an "alternative layout ... including eight six-storey blocks, should be accepted".

The Sub-Committee was also decisive in its analysis of the squatter problem and how government should tackle it. Hong Kong Island, apart from Chai Wan, was not a priority; the numbers and size of the squatter areas were smaller there, and the fire risk correspondingly less. The situation in Kowloon was more serious. The main problem was the serious shortage of suitable sites to resettle existing squatters under present squatter resettlement policy. The committee concluded that "the Kowloon problem was virtually insoluble by present methods". The long-term answer was "decanting". This was to clear a squatter area and rehouse the squatters in buildings constructed on only part of the cleared site, necessitating rehousing at a far greater density. Further similar development could then take place on the remaining undeveloped portion of that site. This would require the construction of "multi-storey structures whenever the site is suitable". It was only by increasing density that more squatters could be resettled on less land, freeing up land for other permanent uses. The Sub-Committee was also "much impressed" by the Director of Public Works' plans for six-storey "convertible" structures. These could be used initially to rehouse squatters at a higher density. Later, individual units in these blocks could be combined together to create larger units for slightly lower density low-cost housing.

The Sub-Committee considered the alternative of doing nothing except to create fire lanes in existing squatter areas. After all, "why ... should squatters, who have no particular claim, be rehoused on land worth in some cases $30-$40 per square foot?" Their conclusion was that to leave squatters *in situ* would, in the longer-term, create a vested interest and prevent permanent development on those sites. If they were rehoused in multi-storied buildings, then some land presently occupied by squatters would be freed up for permanent development. If the Sub-Committee's recommendations were accepted, then a senior government officer should be appointed "as a temporary and emergency measure, to be solely responsible for these matters". He should have the authority to carry out his responsibilities and should become a temporary member of the Urban Council. The Emergency Resettlement Sub-Committee should be disbanded and replaced with a Select Committee, preferably with the temporarily appointed government officer in charge of resettlement as Chairman and it "should proceed as a matter of urgency with the preparation of detailed plans for the resettlement of squatters".[66]

Government and the Urban Council

Even before Clague's Sub-Committee submitted its final report, government had to concede a role in squatter clearance and resettlement policy to the Urban Council. D. R. Holmes[67] was selected as Commissioner for Resettlement. During March he had been in the Colonial Secretariat planning the establishment and mode of operation of the new department. He wanted to remove responsibility for resettlement from the Urban Council and preferred instead to establish a separate resettlement board. Interested Urban Council members could sit on this board. He sounded out Clague privately on this proposal but Clague insisted that the Urban Council "as such" had to be involved. Holmes lamented that

> it is perhaps unfortunate that resettlement was ever made the concern of the Urban Council but that for 'political' reasons the authority of the Council must now be widened to include overall responsibility for the planning, co-ordination, and carrying out of clearance operations, as well as for the administration of resettlement areas.

Holmes was still reluctant to accept this situation. He thought it relied on ground the Urban Council had already won from government through "the deliberations of Colonel Clague's emergency sub-committee of the Urban Council, the appointment of which is inadequately documented in Secretariat files". He thought that "this argument should be most carefully examined before it is accepted" although he rather ruefully admitted that "we need all the support and help we can get".[68]

Clague, however, had already prepared his arguments. He was critical of the Hong Kong government which he thought "should have been prepared to devote more resources to resettlement before the drastic lesson of the Shek Kip Mei fire" and that "if Government had listened to the views of the Urban Council, stronger action would have been taken sooner". He told Holmes quite frankly that if the government did not involve the Urban Council, it would "forfeit the goodwill of the unofficial members". He presented his case very carefully and skilfully. He did not claim that the Urban Council would oppose government but he made it clear that government would need their support. He had very carefully assessed government's position and knew how much they had relied upon him to bring together the policy proposals his committee had made. All Holmes could do was again lament, without any apparent irony, that

> I do think it is unfortunate in the present 'political' circumstances if the Urban Council is able to extend its authority into a new sphere of administration merely by persistently expressing an interest and thus establishing some sort of squatters' rights.

The situation also caught officers in the Colonial Secretariat by surprise. Burgess, the Deputy Colonial Secretary, found the whole situation "surprising and confusing". He thought that Barnett's behaviour as Chairman of the Urban Council had also been less than helpful. Clague had claimed to Holmes that

> the unofficial members feel, rightly or wrongly, that the Chairman of the Urban Council has to some extent frustrated their efforts to

interest themselves in the fundamental aspects of resettlement or to influence the course of Government action in that field.

Burgess expressed annoyance that Barnett had not kept "Government informed of the significance, and the details, of developments within the Council".[69] The Colonial Secretary seemed to tacitly accept that the government would have to work through Clague and involve the Urban Council. He told Holmes to produce his own recommendations on the basis of the Clague Sub-Committee's findings. Holmes was also told to assist the Clague Sub-Committee in producing its report and then make recommendations on the running of his new department, including its relationship with the Urban Council. On 18 March, Holmes attended a meeting of Clague's sub-committee and Clague's views again held sway in the face of opposition from three senior officials attending. In summing up the meeting, Holmes remarked,

> I think we are moving slowly towards an arrangement which would be acceptable; but the progress seems to consist of haphazard and disconcerting steps. The meeting referred to above was somewhat embarrassing to me ... and the whole atmosphere is quite novel.[70]

Whether squatter resettlement should be a responsibility of the shortly to be formed Housing Authority was also considered. It was thought they would eventually merge but, given the urgency of the resettlement problem, the two should remain separate for the time being. Grantham, in what might also be a reflection of his overall political philosophy, thought that

> resettlement and Low Cost Housing probably would merge, but let it come about naturally in the light of experience, whether it be soon or whether it be late.[71]

Towards multi-storey resettlement

The Executive Council accepted the Clague Sub-Committee's recommendation that six-storey blocks be built on the Shek Kip Mei fire site to rehouse squatters made homeless by the fire.[72] The Finance Committee subsequently approved the financial implications. On 6 April 1954, the Executive Council considered the Clague Sub-Committee's short- and long-term recommendations on squatter resettlement. Members agreed that a temporary resettlement department should be established and that fire lanes be driven through squatter areas with the consequential resettlement of some 18,000 squatters. They baulked, however, at the long-term recommendations. They were not yet convinced that government should accept this as a general policy of how resettled squatters should be housed. Instead, members asked the Commissioner for Resettlement to prepare

> one specimen plan for the resettlement of squatters, if possible those dispossessed in the clearance of the fire lanes, in multi-storey structures in order that the long-term policy of the Emergency Sub-Committee of the Urban Council may be examined in more detail.[73]

On 14 April 1954, the Colonial Secretary introduced legislation into the Legislative Council to make the Commissioner for Resettlement a temporary member of the Urban Council. He took the opportunity to review the government's existing squatter clearance and resettlement policy. He admitted that more rapid results might have been obtained had government "taken over a landlord's duties". The concern had been to limit the government's expenditure whether on staff salaries, the cost of site preparation or on loans to organisations which built cottages in resite areas. He admitted that co-ordination between the three departments involved with clearance, screening and resettlement "would have been more effectively co-ordinated and have ensured more rapid progress if they had been the concern of only one department". He explained that the government's long-term policy consideration was that it "should accept the need to construct, at public expense, multi-storey accommodation and let it to squatters". This had still to be examined in detail before being accepted. Perhaps the most far-reaching and fundamental change he announced was to publicly recognise that

> squatters can no longer be regarded as just refugees temporarily seeking shelter in Hong Kong. Many of them are certainly displaced persons from across the border, but many of them are also displaced persons from our own over-crowded urban areas. The problem has become a domestic one and our immediate responsibility, therefore, is all the greater.[74]

On 22 July 1954, the continuing threat of fire was underlined by another large squatter fire in Kowloon Tong which left an estimated 25,000 people homeless.[75] If all these people were to be resettled on the same site "to even minimal acceptable health standards" they would have to be rehoused in government built multi-storey blocks. In August, government announced that this is what it would do for those made homeless by this fire.[76] There was another big fire at Li Cheng Uk in Kowloon in early October 1954. The Commissioner for Resettlement had now realised that squatters could only be resettled quickly and effectively in multi-storey resettlement blocks. He told the Executive Council that he thought this was

> a practical, successful and permanent solution to the squatter problem . . . Many distinguished and well-informed visitors have already seen the occupied buildings at Shek Kip Mei and it is safe to say that the six-storey resettlement programme is making an important contribution to the prestige of the Colony as well as to the standard of public health and public order.[77]

Hong Kong's reputation in dealing effectively with squatter resettlement had spread internationally with requests for information being received from the United States and Philippines governments in November 1954.[78]

The Executive Council was sufficiently convinced and agreed that the Director of Public Works and the Commissioner for Resettlement should

> examine the possibilities of anticipating squatter fires by means of a considerable extension and acceleration of the six-storey resettlement programme and should report as urgently as possible how much money could be spent on six-storey blocks within the next 18 months.

This review was conducted quickly. On 9 November 1954, the Executive Council was told that over the following eighteen to twenty-four months multi-storey blocks to rehouse 120,000 squatters could be built for $40 to $50 million. This was in addition to the 85,000 squatters for whom permanent multi-storey resettlement blocks were either already under construction or under planning.[79] Practical constraints to achieving this goal were the finding of sufficient supplies of aggregate, piling contractors, water supply and staff. Further complications were clearing squatters from sites required for their rehousing and the uncertainties arising from further large squatter fires. The standard of accommodation to be provided was low with only 24 square feet provided for each adult and with the provision of communal lavatory and washing facilities.[80] On 17 November 1954, the Executive Council approved these recommendations and the Finance Committee the financial implications shortly afterwards.[81]

The government's general acceptance of the need for permanent rehousing of squatters cleared for development can be dated from this point. It was made public in a press release issued by Holmes on 31 December 1954. He pointed out that, with the success of permanent multi-storey rehousing at Shek Kip Mei, the government had agreed to "a considerable extension of the multi-storey programme".[82] The policy formulation process had been slow and incremental, pushed forward by the gradual realisation that this was the only realistic option. The government's caution can be summed up by a remark made by the Commissioner for Resettlement some eighteen months after he had been in post when he said "we now know that resettlement in multi-storey buildings . . . can be successfully carried out on a very large scale (we were far from being certain of this 18 months ago)".

The policy was justified not on the basis of a humanitarian concern for squatters. Public money was to be spent "on resettlement, etc, only when the interests of the community *as a whole* demand that we should do so" (emphasis in original). Using the Shek Kip Mei fire as an example, Holmes thought that if government

> had not taken vigorous and effective action, the streets of Kowloon and the fire area itself would have been in a state of chaos for an indefinite period and the fire area would eventually have been res-quatted [*sic*] on ready for another fire. Considerations of public health, public order and public prestige made this quite unaccept-able and the *general* interest therefore demanded that we embark on the construction of semi-permanent and permanent resettlement accommodation.[83] [emphasis in original]

The government's recovery of the initiative was not only marked by such statements, it was also evident from the visible and almost immediate success of the resettlement programme. This was measured in terms of the speed at which resettlement blocks were constructed and the relative ease with which people were moved into them. This success has been ascribed to both the government's financial, administrative and technical resources and the fact that those moved into them had very low expectations. Resettled squatters felt the biggest advantages were that their new premises would not burn down in a fire or blow away in a typhoon.[84] This was also a very clear manifestation of the government's capacity to implement a major new policy. It enhanced its reputation for effectiveness and helped it towards restoring its pre-eminence over policy. After just a year as Commissioner for Resettlement and Chairman of the Urban Council's committee monitoring resettlement policy and its implementation, Holmes reflected that,

> The most delicate of my duties is the Chairmanship of the three Resettlement Select Committees of the Urban Council. These Select Committees exercise a real and effective control over every aspect of resettlement. It has not proved easy to ensure that they should do so without causing delay and friction.[85]

Conclusions

Did the Hong Kong government have its own distinct policies towards squatters and, if so, did it have the capacity to execute them? Firstly, from 1948 until 1950, it can be argued that MacDougall, and not Grantham, ensured that the government had an effective policy towards the clearance and resettlement of squatters from the main urban area. The government's authority had been challenged in the Kowloon Walled City incident. Given the complications with China, it could not have risked squatters in other areas using this as a precedent to challenge its authority. Grantham and the unofficials had been relatively uninterested in squatter resettlement and MacDougall may have rekindled this. The policy decided upon enabled government to show its determination and ability to clear squatters as and when it wished to do so. Given the relatively small number at the time, it was successful in achieving its objective of clearing squatters from the main urban area. It was, therefore, a uniquely differentiated policy which government had the capacity to implement and whose success enhanced its reputation for effectiveness in this field.

The second phase, from 1950 to late 1953, was an extension of the previous policy. It attempted to make most squatters return to China by trying to make conditions in Hong Kong too unpleasant to remain. However, as most squatters had no economic prospects whatsoever in China, they stayed put in Hong Kong. The tenfold increase in numbers over less than three years, with the attendant increase in the size and scale of squatter areas, created an enormous fire and public health risk. The ineffectiveness of government's policy was reflected in the slow pace of clearance and resettlement and the fact that most squatters cleared re-squatted elsewhere under similar conditions. A lack of urgency and coordination meant that by the time of the Shek Kip Mei fire government had not maintained its capacity for effective policy implementation and had lost its reputation for efficiency. Here it had a unique political preference but not the capacity to implement it. Its reputation suffered accordingly.

The last phase, from Christmas 1953, was marked by a considerable loss of autonomy to Clague and the unofficials of the Urban Council. The government's initial vacillating response had left a vacuum which Clague, and through him the Urban Council, had been quick to fill. Nothing decisive was happening when it should have been and Clague had stepped in to fill the breach. The government had, through Grantham's lack of decision and leadership, lost the initiative to Clague who had become a temporary "Secretary for Resettlement". Grantham, through a lack of leadership, had allowed others to lead the policy-making process, much as he had allowed to happen during the various debates on constitutional reform.

Two further factors. Firstly, the Colonial Office and the Secretary of State both played a negligible role in the development of policy on squatter resettlement Apart from the £200,000 grant, they effectively left Hong Kong to handle the issue itself. They offered no advice on resettlement policy nor issued any instructions to Grantham. Unlike constitutional reform and the Housing Authority, the Hong Kong government had acted completely autonomously from the sovereign power. It had not been a policy over which Britain had shown much interest. Whereas in a previous era, Hong Kong would have had to obtain approvals for expenditure and the creation of posts, in this case it was left to tackle the issue on its own. Squatter resettlement, unlike *mui tsai*, constitutional reform and housing, was not a matter of deep personal interest to a Secretary of State. Nor was it, as in the case of *mui tsai* and housing, a matter of concern or potential concern to domestic political interests in Britain.

Secondly, after MacDougall's departure in 1949, Grantham lacked a strong and experienced chief of staff to co-ordinate policy formulation and ensure its effective implementation. His replacement, Nicoll, had no previous Hong Kong experience and was in post for only about two years. His successor, Black, also had no Hong Kong experience and spent a comparatively short time as Colonial Secretary. That is not to say that they were not diligent or committed to their responsibilities. It would, however, have made their dealings with the long-established senior cadres of the civil service, with many years of Hong Kong experience, more challenging and less effective. They were also, for reasons not clear, unwilling to respond effectively to the advice given them by senior officers in the Urban Services Department and Public Works Department that the only way forward was to build multi-storey housing blocks.

Were the reasons behind the Hong Kong government's decision to provide permanent multi-storey resettlement for squatters, as one scholar has argued, to achieve "social integration and political control?"[86] Was this a necessary pre-condition to obtaining "political stability, low costs of living, and land [that] were all urgently needed for organised industrial and urban growth?"[87] M. W. Lo argued during a Legislative Council debate that "our Government is organized and, rightly so, to ensure order, peace, due administration of justice, education and public health".[88] It was on the grounds of so ensuring order, peace and public health that the Hong Kong government justified its actions or, as Smart describes it, to "overcome potential chaos".[89] The sheer scale of the problem, the enormous risk posed by the threat of large-scale fires and the threat to public health resulted not in a move away from the concept of minimal government but in an extension of what minimal government now entailed.

The government's response to the 1953 Christmas Day fire may be seen to have been an autonomous act by the Hong Kong government.

It was not, however, the defining moment it might have been. Rather, it was the start of a realisation that government needed to take more direct action and that it was capable of doing so without going bankrupt, risking thousands more squatters pouring into Hong Kong from China, or facing open rebellion from leading business unofficials reluctant to spend public money. Initially, it failed to realise that the drastically changed circumstances it faced required a rapid expansion of the notion of minimal government. When it did change, government found it had done the right thing and had almost inadvertently established a reputation for efficiency and effectiveness in squatter resettlement. The government had been pushed somewhat unwillingly into creating the capacity to deal with a problem and had then found, somewhat to its own surprise, that it had found a more effective way of coping with it. In doing so, it had unwittingly enhanced its own reputation not only within Hong Kong but also internationally. The conditions had now been created for the further development of the government's autonomy in the years to come.

10
Financial Autonomy

> The Secretary of State has now informed me that, in view of the good standing, financial and administrative, of the Colony, he will further relax his control and will no longer require the Estimates to be submitted for his approval; nor will he require supplementary provisions to be authorized by him.
>
> Governor Robin Black, Legislative Council, 6 March 1958[1]

> The fact that there has been no pressure for financial devolution from Hong Kong since 1949 may be because they have largely taken the law into their own hands without, it should be noted, any comments from us so far.
>
> J. T. A. Howard-Drake, Colonial Office, 5 October 1955[2]

Britain's formal granting of financial autonomy to Hong Kong in 1958 had the air of an important turning point in relations between the two governments. Officials in both governments knew, however, that Hong Kong had been exercising *de facto* financial autonomy for several years beforehand and that the Colonial Office had done nothing to stop it. How had the Hong Kong government come to exercise such autonomy? The controls instituted in 1948[3] had, after all, set out which matters needed the Secretary of State's approval and on which issues he was to be consulted. Had Hong Kong sought such autonomy for itself? Was it the culmination of steps taken, along the lines of those advocated by Carpenter, to develop the capacity, political support and legitimacy to acquire autonomy over its own finances? Or had the controls simply become largely irrelevant and been allowed to fall into disuse?

How the Hong Kong government had arrogated financial autonomy to itself is examined in this chapter. This will be done by reviewing the extent to which Hong Kong adhered to the 1948 financial controls and how it managed, seemingly, to disregard them as evidenced by a case study of the arrangements for the funding of a major, much-needed reservoir project at Tai Lam Chung. How Hong Kong was able to exercise a considerable degree of financial autonomy in respect of an annual cash contribution to Britain to defray defence costs will also be examined. Lastly, the considerations of Colonial Office officials will be reviewed to understand why they agreed to grant Hong Kong formal financial autonomy.

Hong Kong government and the 1948 controls

In the beginning, with Sir Geoffrey Follows as Financial Secretary, the Hong Kong government was careful to comply almost to the letter with the more clearly defined parts of the 1948 controls. It sought the Secretary of State's approval of the annual estimates and supplementary provision. Telegrams outlining Hong Kong's budget proposals were sent to the Secretary of State usually in February before the Legislative Council budget debate in March. The telegram sent in February 1949, for example, was a detailed two and a half pages long. It set out the estimates of revenue and expenditure. It expressed concern at the "scale of expenditure particularly on personal emoluments" and at how the deteriorating international situation required additional expenditure on security. It explained how expenditure on rehabilitation arising from the war had to be met from recurrent revenue because of the poor take up of the Rehabilitation Loan; that it was the Hong Kong government's policy to build up adequate reserves, although "adequate" was not defined; and it set out the government's and Finance Committee's views on the raising of additional revenue. It also asked for the Secretary of State's views "on the question of further borrowings". A similarly detailed telegram was sent in February 1951.[4] The required quarterly financial reports were also sent regularly to the Secretary of State.

Follows successor, Arthur Clarke, was capable of interpreting for himself what compliance with the 1948 controls meant. The 1952 telegram shrank to a rather sparse one page. Clarke told the Governor beforehand, rather insouciantly, that

> it seems to be the practice to inform the Secretary of State of our budget proposals in advance, usually by telegram. I submit a brief savingram for your approval.[5]

Clarke did not seem to have taken too seriously the Secretary of State's injunction that the keynote to the arrangements was

> consultation rather than control and ... you will ... appreciate that I shall need to be kept as fully as possible informed of financial trends in the Colony and be consulted at an early stage regarding proposals for expenditure which require my approval[6]

It also seems to have become standard practice that detailed estimates were sent to the Secretary of State only after their approval by the Legislative Council.[7]

Hong Kong also interpreted for itself when to seek approval for expenditure under supplementary provision. It was aided by what one official described as "rather carelessly worded" conditions.[8] One of these was the definition of "capital" and "recurrent" when it came to seeking supplementary provision for expenditure of $680,000 in emergency relief by the Social Welfare Office. This expenditure was neither recurrent, as it would not necessarily arise every year, nor was it capital expenditure. It was also rather inconveniently above the HK$250,000 limit for local approval of recurrent expenditure but within the HK$1 million limit for local approval of capital expenditure.[9] The Deputy Financial Secretary commented, rather robustly, that

> it is clear that the Secretary of State's consent is required for the lower figure of $250,000 only when we are assuming a recurrent charge. As we are not in this case, his consent is not required, even if it stretches the word "capital" pretty far.

When asked two years later, the Secretary of State concurred with this view.[10]

Hong Kong officials also seemed to have had their own understanding of the nature of the 1948 controls. It was, thought Follows

> largely a question of psychology and I think that the Colonial Office, and still more the Treasury, like to feel that they have some measure of financial control over Colonies without Unofficial majorities, even though that control may exist more in theory than in practice.

A junior Hong Kong government official had wanted to streamline procedures by including large items of supplementary expenditure in quarterly financial reports to the Secretary of State. This, thought Follows, would be unacceptable to the Colonial Office "as there would then be no pretence at control as the expenditure would already have taken place".[11] He preferred to defer any review of the existing system until Hong Kong had an unofficial majority.

Colonial Office concerns

Hong Kong's own interpretation of the controls did eventually irk Colonial Office officials. They began to bemoan the sparseness of information Hong Kong provided on the estimates and their inability to influence them before they were approved by the Legislative Council. By 1955, the Secretary of State's approval of the estimates had become "a simple business" in which we [Colonial Office officials] are given no opportunity to comment ... before they have been finally approved in Hong Kong. As far as this important provision goes, Hong Kong in practice seems to enjoy 'financial devolution'.

Neither, it was felt, had the Secretary of State been kept informed of Hong Kong's financial position, or of general financial trends, or been consulted on "expenditure involving important points of principle". The Colonial Office felt it had been unable to keep the Treasury informed "of all important matters affecting Hong Kong's finances". The Colonial Office's main concern seems to have been how the Treasury might view their failure to implement the 1948 controls and how this might affect their own standing with the Treasury.

Hong Kong's unilateral decision to proceed with an amended and more expensive version of a major infrastructure project without first consulting the Secretary of State drew the Colonial Office's "attention to Hong Kong's failure to adhere to the 1948 despatch".[12] The Tai Lam Chung Reservoir was needed to meet the increasing demands for water from a continually growing population. The shortage of water had been a perennial problem in Hong Kong and, even after the completion of the Shing Mun Reservoir in 1937, there was still only sufficient water to meet current needs. In 1938, the Tai Lam Chung area in South-West New Territories was identified as a potential site for a reservoir and its feasibility was confirmed by surveyors in 1940. Survey work had restarted in 1947 when the total cost of construction and water distribution was estimated at HK$100 million. This was too much for a government faced with other competing post-war priorities and the project was shelved.[13]

In 1951, growing demand for water caused the project to be reconsidered and a revised scheme was proposed. The dam and supporting infrastructure would be built in two stages. In the first stage, the dam would be constructed 150 feet high with provision for it to be later raised to 200 feet. Stage I would cost only HK$40 million spread over the several years it would take to construct the dam. In Stage II, the dam would be raised to its full height of 200 feet. On this occasion, the Hong Kong government gave the Colonial Office no cause for complaint. After the Finance Committee approved it in principle[14] and agreed that it should be funded from the Development Fund, Hong Kong asked the Secretary of State for his approval which was given without apparent demur.[15]

It was the Hong Kong government's failure to seek the Secretary of State's prior approval to a major revision which upset Colonial Office officials. In April 1953, the Director of Public Works told the Governor that he now considered it would be impracticable to build the dam in two stages. It would instead be more sensible to build it to its full height in the first stage. Additional works should also be incorporated to enable the increased water supply to be distributed. Otherwise, the dam would have to be emptied before it could be raised to its full height and other works then constructed to distribute the additional water. This would have meant even tighter water restrictions than currently in force while this was being done. Grantham accepted this view and the Finance Committee approved the additional cost.[16] However, Hong Kong chose merely to inform the Colonial Office of this decision in a short one-page note rather than to seek the Secretary of State's formal approval.[17]

Officials in the Colonial Office were unhappy at being told about important changes to a major project in such an off-hand manner. They felt that

> something more than this very brief savingram was called for in informing the Secretary of State of what is, after all, a major decision to proceed with the full 200' Tai Lam Chung Scheme at considerable extra expense. I think we might reasonably have expected the Governor to explain the various considerations which led to this decision.

They were also concerned whether the Development Fund had sufficient funds to pay for the additional cost of the Tai Lam Chung Reservoir on top of its other commitments. There was also confusion over whose authority was required to approve expenditure from the Development Fund. Colonial Office officials conceded that they probably could not "claim a 'legal' right to be consulted about expenditure from the Development Fund" but, given the financial implications involved in this case, they thought they still had such a right. Everyone in the Colonial Office also agreed that Hong Kong had "a very grave water problem" and that consequently "there can be no question of *not* approving what has been decided" [emphasis in original]. Officials felt, however, that this was also a case for "a little frank speaking" with the Governor.[18] Grantham was asked to explain the decision, how he would build up the Development Fund again and if the Finance Committee now felt "reasonably confident that the Budget surplus for 1953–54 will considerably exceed the approved Estimate".

Further changes were made to the project before Grantham could reply. In January 1954, the Director of Public Works estimated that the cost of the scheme had risen from HK$60 million to HK$80 million. Surprisingly, this was because "no comprehensive estimate has previously been prepared since the details of the scheme were not finalised" and "the original estimates were undoubtedly in some cases too low". It was also now apparent that it was necessary to construct additional associated works to enable the additional water that could be stored to be distributed. In addition to the initial revised expenditure of HK$80 million, yet further works would necessitate estimated expenditure of HK$15 million per annum for several more years after the reservoir's completion. If only the originally estimated HK$60 million for Stage I was to be spent, additional water capacity could be provided but not the means to distribute it.

On 19 January 1954, Grantham replied to the Colonial Office. If Colonial Office officials had known how routinely it had been prepared they might have been even more incensed. The Deputy Financial Secretary thought that "in view of the increased cost, [the reply] is somewhat fuller than might, perhaps, otherwise have been considered necessary". Clarke did not seem to consider it very much out of the ordinary and simply told the Governor that he agreed that Stages I and II should be combined as "to proceed only with Stage I will still leave us short of water". Apart from a query about wage increases, Grantham accepted the draft and it was sent.

Clarke also advised Grantham to tell the Colonial Office that the Tai Lam Chung scheme was to be funded from general revenue and not the Development Fund. He had always felt this was "the more appropriate course"[19] and had said so in conversation with a Colonial Office official. It was not surprising that he took this view. The Development Fund had been established from profits from trading in essential commodities undertaken by the government after 1945. On its establishment, it had been agreed that it would be used only to fund development projects whose future recurrent costs would not be a charge on Hong Kong's ordinary revenue raised through taxation. Nor would the Development Fund fund projects directly but would lend money to other organisations for their own developments.[20] Funds had already been lent to the Hong Kong Housing Society and loans were also to be made to the Hong Kong Housing Authority. Directly funding the Tai Lam Chung Reservoir, which would have recurrent expenditure implications for general revenue, was not in compliance with the Development Fund's stated aim.

Grantham's reply caused much heart-searching within the Colonial Office. Everyone agreed he had made a good case for combining the two stages, providing Hong Kong had funds over the coming years to meet the additional expenditure. There was also a consensus that the project should be funded from general revenue. Otherwise the Development Fund would be too severely depleted and have nothing left for other much-needed development projects, particularly housing. Colonial Office officials, however, continued to think that the Governor should have consulted them first and not merely informed them after a decision had been taken. One official remarked in some exasperation that "Hong Kong has enjoyed virtual freedom in matters of financial policy since 1948". It was also realised, however, that "it would not be easy to insist now on a degree of consultation with which we have dispensed during the last few years".

Defence contribution

From 1950, Britain and Hong Kong conducted annual negotiations over how much Hong Kong should contribute towards the cost of reinforcing its garrison. These were to constrain the Colonial Office's considerations of how it might limit Hong Kong's growing financial autonomy. Hong Kong's contribution was based upon what it could afford to pay. The Colonial Office was therefore conscious that any steps it took to limit Hong Kong's other expenditure might be interpreted as trying to increase its defence contribution. It was concerned that if they insisted on the Tai Lam Chung Reservoir being funded from the Development Fund it

> might be regarded in Hong Kong as attempting to manipulate the Colony's finances to suit the United Kingdom book ... it might be said that one of our motives was to ensure a higher Defence Contribution from general revenue.[21]

During the annual negotiations, Hong Kong usually managed to limit its defence contribution to how little it thought it could get away with. There was little the British government, principally the Treasury and the War Office acting through the Colonial Office, could do to persuade it otherwise. These negotiations serve, therefore, as an illustration of Hong Kong's ability to exercise a high degree of autonomy over an important financial matter which directly affected both governments. Their importance was threefold. Firstly, it showed how Hong Kong could exercise a considerable degree of autonomy in effectively deciding for itself how much it would pay. Secondly, and conversely, it showed how little power and influence the British government had in influencing how much Hong Kong should pay. Lastly, the negotiations influenced Colonial Office thinking as officials considered what to do about Hong Kong's financial autonomy.

Hong Kong's post-1945 defence

Hong Kong may have been able to exercise a degree of autonomy over how much it contributed to the cost of reinforcing its garrison but defence policy was firmly in the hands of the British Cabinet Defence Committee. The War Office had most influence although Hong Kong government and Colonial Office persistence helped put paid to some of its more extreme proposals. In March 1946, on the Chiefs of Staff's recommendations, the British Cabinet Defence Committee had already concluded that Hong Kong could not be defended against attack by a major power in occupation of the Chinese mainland. Hong Kong's garrison would remain at two brigades plus supporting arms for internal security purposes until the police force was back up to strength. It would then be reduced to one brigade. In 1948, the Committee decided that the garrison should consist of one infantry brigade, a major artillery unit and supporting arms "except in the event of a threat from a major power in occupation of the Chinese Mainland".[22] This was an unspoken reference to the Soviet Union. The implications were that the garrison would then be withdrawn although the Governor was not made aware of this until 1949.

In December 1948, Britain had started to consider its defence response to the Chinese communist advance southwards towards Hong Kong. It was thought that by the third quarter of 1949 the situation in China might have deteriorated. It might pose a potential threat internally from strikes and externally from lightly armed guerrilla forces. Reinforcements of one battalion might then be required. The situation continued to be monitored closely and in April 1949 the Cabinet decided to reinforce Hong Kong with an additional brigade. It also agreed that the Chiefs of Staff "should keep the development of events in the Far East under close and regular review".[23]

By the middle of May 1949 the potential threat to Hong Kong had become more immediate.[24] In response, the Chiefs of Staff supported by the Minister of Defence proposed that Hong Kong should be massively reinforced. Field Marshall Slim, the Chief of the Imperial General Staff stated bluntly that

> a decision should be taken to defend Hong Kong against all-comers and to make a firm announcement to this effect ... we should then consider the necessary arrangements to provide the forces required.

Malcolm MacDonald, the Secretary of State for Defence, felt it would have an important effect on local morale. This had been shaken by the belief that "it was not our real intention to defend the Colony". He also hoped that reinforcements would act as a deterrent. On 26 May 1949, the Cabinet agreed to reinforce Hong Kong's garrison.[25]

Reinforcements started to arrive in June 1949.[26] By the end of the summer, Hong Kong's garrison had been increased by two additional brigade groups and a Royal Marine Commando brigade. This represented a significant additional commitment to Britain's already tight defence budget. This included the costs of providing additional troops and equipment and the capital costs of maintaining such an unexpectedly large force in Hong Kong for an indeterminate period. Although no-one knew how long the additional troops would be required, steps had to be taken to improve the facilities available for them in Hong Kong.[27] Britain was under tremendous financial strain in 1949 and could barely afford this additional commitment. The Chancellor of the Exchequer was trying to keep annual defence costs below £700 million. However, the Defence Secretary was not prepared to submit any estimates below £800 million, of which some £16 million went towards defence of the colonies.[28] Hong Kong was relatively prosperous compared to austere postwar Britain. It was eagerly eyed by the service departments and by the Treasury as a source of funding to help defray this additional cost, estimated at between £2–3 million per annum. When other Commonwealth countries declined to help pay for Hong Kong's reinforcement, the Treasury could only look to Hong Kong. Even with a garrison of the size agreed in 1948, the Treasury had already been hoping that Hong Kong would contribute towards its defence as it had done before the war.[29]

Background and initial discussions

Before 1941, Hong Kong had paid an annual defence contribution to the British government. In 1900, this had been set at 20% of Hong Kong's gross revenue, less a small number of agreed items. This formula continued to be applied until 1938 when Caine, Hong Kong's Financial Secretary, successfully negotiated a revised formula whereby a fixed sum was paid.[30] No defence contribution was requested immediately after the war because

> until the effort of rehabilitation was completed and the stability of the Colony's economic position restored, it was not feasible to reopen the question of its defence contribution.

Hong Kong's unofficials had been aware that Britain might seek to re-impose a defence contribution on Hong Kong. In October 1948, the Finance Committee voted funds for the reconstitution of local defence forces. Members emphasised this was to be Hong Kong's sole contribution to the cost of its defence. Britain should not, as before the war, request a cash contribution. Grantham so informed the Colonial Office and asked it to intercede on Hong Kong's behalf if the issue was ever raised in London.[31] The Colonial Office told him that he could

> safely make it plain to your Legislative Council that while no promise can be given that Hong Kong would not be asked at some future date to make some additional contribution for defence purposes it is quite certain that no such request will ever be made which does not take fully into consideration Hong Kong's general financial

position at that time, the fact that Hong Kong has assumed financial responsibility for the initial phases of the Hong Kong defence force, and also the possibility which you envisage that the development of the force will involve Hong Kong in further financial provision.

The Treasury and the War Office had other ideas and thought it

> Important ... we should not allow much time to elapse before we let the Hong Kong government know that we expect them to bear a part of this additional [defence] expenditure.

On 5 July 1949, even before all the reinforcements had arrived, inter-departmental discussions started in London over how much Hong Kong should pay. Clear lines were drawn between departments, the War Office and the Treasury on the one hand, which thought Hong Kong should pay a cash contribution, and the Colonial Office on the other which thought that it should not. The War Office was not slow to remind the Colonial Office that Hong Kong had paid a defence contribution before the war. It maintained that a colony should pay for its own internal security and local defence, and that if it did not have the money to do so, the Colonial Office should find it.[32] The Colonial Office, unsurprisingly, emphasised the imperial interest in maintaining the defence of Hong Kong and said that, "there should be a distinction between what a Colony can contribute and what it should contribute". Hong Kong had already made a "considerable provision" for defence expenditure in its 1949–50 budget. The Colonial Office thought that Hong Kong should be asked not to charge for services it provided to the armed forces or for the cost of providing requisitioned buildings, in so far as such "would not result in any extra cost to the Hong Kong government".[33] The Treasury took a more pragmatic view. It observed that Hong Kong was very lightly taxed and had no heavy government debt, implying that it could afford to pay more. It also thought that, as Hong Kong would only be able to pay what it could afford, there was little point in talking about any particular principle on which an amount could be based.

The Colonial Office was unable to resist the calls that Hong Kong should be asked to make a cash contribution towards its defence. It told Grantham informally that Hong Kong would be asked to make such a contribution and that it would be

> Impossible ... to resist in principle the contention that Hong Kong ... should do the utmost it reasonably can in its present financial position, to contribute towards the cost of internal security and Commonwealth defence.

The Colonial Office said it would be unable to argue that Hong Kong "ought to get off scot-free". It also pointed out that Hong Kong could afford to tax itself more heavily and that 80% of additional defence expenditure would be spent in Hong Kong.[34]

In October 1949, Grantham was told that the scale of additional defence expenditure on Hong Kong was "of grave concern to HMG, especially in light of UK's present financial position". Additional expenditure was now estimated at £5 million in 1949–50 with total recurrent expenditure estimated at £2 million per annum thereafter. The Secretary of State was

> sure you will agree that it would be scarcely equitable if Hong Kong were not to take some share (according to her means) of this heavy burden.

Grantham was reminded of the benefits to Hong Kong of the stability provided by its defence. Much of the additional expenditure would also be spent in Hong Kong, "with consequential benefits to trade and revenue". The hope was expressed that

> you will be able to put forward proposals for a contribution representing the maximum possible effort by Hong Kong in her present circumstances.[35]

He was free, however, to suggest how best payment should be made, whether for specific items or as a lump sum as before the war.

Settlement of outstanding claims

The unofficials were not prepared to consider any defence contribution "until [the] slate had been wiped clean in respect of [the] last war".[36] Grantham quickly reminded the Colonial Office there was still much continued dissatisfaction in Hong Kong over contingent liabilities, the "denial claims" arising from the war. This issue had still not been satisfactorily resolved. In 1948 the Colonial Office had clearly told Grantham that no further financial assistance could be offered and the settlement of any "denial claims" was a matter for the Hong Kong government. The unofficials disagreed and still felt these outstanding items should be met by Britain. The Colonial Office was not completely surprised by this response. It knew that "although these claims tend to be quiescent, they are revived whenever discussions take place on current claims between HMG and Hong Kong". They were thought to amount to HK$25 million or £1.5 million. No claims had been made in court probably because Hong Kong had had no formal war damage compensation scheme. It was also thought that

> the extraordinary commercial prosperity which has been enjoyed by commercial firms since the liberation has enabled most of them to recover financially in spite of any losses arising out of the war.

The Colonial Office was initially not prepared to accept the linking of payment of a defence contribution to settlement of outstanding claims. It thought this should be assessed only on Hong Kong's ability to pay.[37] The proposed linkage alarmed the War Office who blamed the Colonial Office for "stalling indefinitely" and the Hong Kong government for "drag[ging] in claims relating to the last war". It thought that unless there were new ways of bringing pressure to bear on the Hong Kong government, the matter should be referred to Ministers. The Treasury realised that

> as there is no evidence of any recalcitrance, to put the question before Ministers at present appears ... [to] be quite pointless.

Unlike the War Office, the Treasury realised Hong Kong could not be treated as merely another Whitehall department. This was because

> constitutionally the Hong Kong government is something of an independent body and Ministers could do no more, I imagine, than instruct the S[ecretary] of S[tate] for the Colonies to exert his maximum possible influence for expedition.[38]

The Treasury was also aware that Hong Kong was working on this matter and that time was needed to consult unofficials before any result could be expected. It was also beginning to accept that, despite their best efforts, it was unlikely a defence contribution would now be included in the 1950–51 estimates.

Both the Colonial Office and the Treasury began to see that linking the defence contribution to a settlement of denial claims might help resolve both these issues. The Colonial Office realised the claims were

> a constant source of friction between the two governments and rightly or wrongly are regarded by Hong Kong as sufficient reason for refusing to agree on other financial points until the incidence of charge of the claims is settled.

It wanted to resolve these issues as their "continued existence ... leads to accumulated misunderstanding and ill-will".[39] The Treasury looked somewhat further ahead and realised that the claims "have all engendered a certain amount of warmth and they are no doubt politically difficult to the colony". Although they would have preferred the two issues be kept separate, the defence contribution was the more important and

> it would be a good thing ... to get her [Hong Kong] back into the habit of making a general contribution ... and that it might be worth making some concessions on the 'once for all' war time claims in order to achieve this result.

Negotiations now proceeded in this direction. The Treasury was keen to get both Hong Kong's Financial and Colonial Secretaries to visit London to reach a comprehensive settlement.[40] This would also help the War Office to "hear the case expounded as only those direct from Hong Kong can expound it". There was little controversy or disagreement at the series of meetings held in April 1950 in London where the atmosphere was described by one Colonial Office official as "extremely co-operative".[41] The British government agreed to accept Hong Kong's claims of £998,000 which should be offset as Hong Kong's defence contribution for 1949–50. No money need change hands in that financial year. The Treasury pushed for a payment of £1.5 million for 1950–51 but Hong Kong would only agree to pay £1 million in four quarterly payments in addition to £231,000 as the cost of military works already included in the estimates.

Hong Kong's unofficials were prepared to agree to this "provided that no additional taxation will be imposed this year other than that already contemplated". The Treasury and the Colonial Office agreed Grantham could tell them that "no additional taxation will be forced through this year by the official majority". The caveat was that Hong Kong could not use the excuse of financial stringency to reduce the defence contribution later in the year. On 15 May 1950, Ministerial approval was given to this agreement.

For the Treasury, this agreement had three advantages. Firstly, now that denial claims had been resolved they would no longer be a stumbling block to any future financial discussions with Hong Kong. Secondly, the claims made by Hong Kong could now be written off without having to ask Parliament, or the Legislative Council to vote. Lastly, although the Treasury had obtained no commitment from Hong Kong to pay any contribution beyond 1950–51, there seemed

> a good prospect that, unless there is any marked change in circumstances a substantial Defence contribution will continue to be forthcoming. This is more than can be said for most of the colonies.[42]

On 24 May 1950, the Legislative Council approved the financial settlement by resolution. The Financial Secretary presented it as a saving to the Hong Kong taxpayer. He also pointed out that it was

> a matter of considerable satisfaction that we have at long last wiped the slate clean and no longer have hanging over our heads a number of unknown liabilities. We can now close all our files on this class of claim which has taken up such a disproportionate amount of time in the Secretariat ever since the liberation.

He suggested, rather disingenuously, this represented a saving to Hong Kong. Otherwise it might have had to pay as much as £4–5 million towards defence costs in the current year. He also said that Hong Kong could not meet the demand for a defence contribution of £1.5 million for 1950–51. This was because of Hong Kong's heavy commitment to development projects and because a surplus was committed against loan advances. He had agreed instead that Hong Kong would pay only £1 million plus the cost of two military roads. He had resisted attempts to commit to paying a defence contribution in the following years as circumstances were too unpredictable. He also told the Legislative Council that he had been

> much impressed by the very fair and reasonable attitude of the Treasury delegation and indeed some members of that delegation were of the greatest assistance to us in our dealings with other departments.

The settlement was a little higher than he may have liked and, unless tax receipts were higher than anticipated, would result in a small deficit for the current financial year. The unofficials approved the settlement, with some reluctance. Their spokesman, Sir Man Kam Lo, explained that

> since the terms now before this Council must be regarded as the most favourable which the Colony could obtain, I feel that they should be accepted by this Council if for no other reason than that of putting an end finally and once and for all to all outstanding financial questions arising out of the last war.

Lo also stated that £1 million per annum could not be taken as a yardstick and that each year would have to be negotiated on the basis of Hong Kong's financial position at that time. Follows agreed.[43]

Defence contribution: 1951–52

The 1951–52 negotiations started off with the Colonial Office treating Grantham in a friendly and collegiate fashion. He was not sent a despatch, the most formal means of communication, but a semi-official letter. Grantham, was addressed as "Dear Grantham", in the manner of the day and the letter ended "Yours ever". The style was informal, even conversational, never instructing, but suggesting or recommending for consideration. Yet, it clearly set out the parameters within which the issue should be settled. It referred to the previous April's meetings in London, to Hong Kong's fiscal surplus but also acknowledged the pressures Hong Kong's finances were under. It explicitly asked Grantham, "What are we bid?" The letter's implications were clear. Firstly, it was unlikely the

Secretary of State would instruct the Governor to use the official majority to secure a defence contribution. Secondly, neither could Grantham expect to argue that Hong Kong should pay either nothing or less than the current year. It was a reminder that, despite local political difficulties, Grantham was still answerable to London for his actions.

Grantham's tactics were twofold. Firstly, he delayed replying to the Colonial Office for four months,[44] blaming the delay on the retirement of the Financial Secretary, Follows. These were deliberate tactics on Hong Kong's part. Follows, admitted as much when, after his discussions with Grantham, he wrote that

> if we put in $16 million there can be no hope of getting off with anything less. Moreover, the balance of advantage lies in postponing negotiations regarding the amount of the contribution as long as possible, as the indications are that our financial position will deteriorate in the course of the next few months.[45]

Secondly, he offered only $8.5 million instead of the $16 million expected by the Treasury. He explained how Hong Kong would incur local defence expenditure of HK$16.5 million; that he could only budget for a reserve of 10 months' expenditure which, he felt, was not enough and that he expected trade to be badly hit by the US trade embargo with China.

Both the amounts and the arguments put forward by the Governor were given little credibility in London. The Colonial Office thought he had not given them "a very full picture".[46] The War Office thought the amount offered was "quite inadequate". The Treasury thought Hong Kong could easily afford at least £1 million and suggested the Colonial Office ask them for at least the same as last year. The Secretary of State told Grantham that he could not, therefore, understand why the proposed contribution was only half that agreed for the current year. He could not accept Grantham's arguments and told him that he expected Hong Kong's contribution to be much the same as for 1951–52. Grantham could hardly ignore the Secretary of State's injunction to

> reconsider this matter in the light of the foregoing observations and furnish me with your comments as soon as possible.

The implication was clear: he was expected to improve his offer.

Grantham replied quickly. It was a distinctly odd reply. Despite setting out at length why Hong Kong could hardly afford to offer more, that is what he did. He said he would recommend to the Legislative Council that Hong Kong should contribute $16 million. This, after deducting the cost of other military related expenditure, would reduce the cash amount to HK$14.3 million. The Treasury, however, remained unimpressed and thought Grantham's response "a rather poor effort". It thought Hong Kong should pay at least £1 million, which it could afford, and that it would not need to seek financial aid from Britain if it did.[47] Sir Charles Jeffries, the Colonial Office Permanent Under-Secretary, was more cautious. He thought asking Hong Kong for more would risk rejection by the Legislative Council. He was perhaps influenced by the Secretary of State's forthcoming visit to Hong Kong[48] when this issue could well have been raised by the Governor or the unofficials. He proposed instead that the Governor's offer be accepted with expressions of disappointment and hopes for better things the following year.

Unfortunately, the Colonial Office's stance had been undermined by Grantham's increased offer. The difference between this and what the Treasury wanted was only HK$2 million. Sir James Crombie, Permanent Under-Secretary at the Treasury thought this comparatively small increase would hardly cause insurmountable political difficulties with the Legislative Council. The amount now requested was still less than the previous year's. Grantham told Paskin, then in Hong Kong, that he was prepared to approach the unofficials on the basis of a HK$16 million contribution, and other expenditure in kind, though he could not guarantee the outcome. He also thought it "imprudent" to include a figure in next year's estimates higher than the HK$8.5 million already included in the current year's estimates.[49] The Colonial Office was prepared to accept Grantham's counter offer. The Treasury, the War Office and the Air Ministry, reluctantly agreed but stressed they expected a better offer the following year. Nor were they prepared to accept that only $8.5 million should be included in the next year's estimates and remained unconvinced by the Governor's alleged political difficulties.[50] The Colonial Office told Grantham that although it agreed with his proposals, it lectured him that to include only HK$8.5 million in the following year's estimates

> would be incommensurate alike both with Hong Kong's financial ability to contribute and with HMG's vastly increased defence commitments and would merely lead to repetition of arguments exchanged throughout 1951.

The Treasury may well have been right when they claimed that Grantham had overestimated the political difficulties. In February 1952, the Finance Committee agreed to the higher level of defence contribution but "not without demur".[51] When the Financial Secretary referred to this during the subsequent Legislative Council budget debate, there was no dissenting voice from the unofficials.[52] So far, Grantham's tactics had succeeded. Hong Kong's contribution remained about the same, despite Treasury and War Office rants and he maintained the same low starting point for next year's round of negotiations.

Defence contribution: 1952–53

The following year's negotiations were less fraught. Hong Kong, however, would only offer to contribute $16 million. This irritated the Treasury[53] which noted Hong Kong's "extremely comfortable surpluses" now totalling $200 million. It expressed hope that the Colonial Office would press Hong Kong "quickly and emphatically for a substantial increase in the offer of HK$16 millions".[54] Such hope was fulfilled when, on 31 December 1952, the Legislative Council, with all unofficials supporting, approved a free gift of HK$8 million to Britain in addition to the HK$16 million already included in the estimates. This was because, firstly, on the basis of tax receipts to date, Hong Kong's finances could support it and secondly, as a member of the Commonwealth and in view of Britain's increased defence commitments around the world, it would be an

> appreciation of the efforts now being made by Her Majesty's Government, and by the people of the United Kingdom on behalf of the free world of which this Colony is a part ... to relieve in some small degree the burden now being borne by the United Kingdom.[55]

Such a move had been presaged the previous summer when an increase in Hong Kong's defence contribution had been discussed with Grantham. It had been agreed he would consider an increase in the light "of the present extremely comfortable state of the Colony's surplus balances". The Treasury considered the outcome for the year "pretty satisfactory".[56]

Defence contribution: 1953–54

The next round of negotiations started the following July. The Treasury forecast that as Hong Kong was likely to have a surplus of HK$20.4 million that year,[57] it should be asked for a defence contribution of HK$24 million. Grantham deployed his usual delaying tactics. He thought that even though "the arguments for an additional contribution may be as cogent this year as last" it would not be politic to try and include them in the estimates just yet. He advised waiting until November "when the Colony's financial prospects can be more accurately judged".[58] When Hong Kong sent its half-yearly financial report to the Colonial Office in November, Grantham was told it left little room for doubt that Hong Kong's financial position is such that the Colony can well afford to make an additional defence contribution this year over and above the $16 million already provided in the estimates.

Grantham, however, was not to be persuaded. He declined to approach the Legislative Council to increase the contribution to HK$24 million.[59] He feigned surprise on being told that simply because Hong Kong's surpluses were higher than expected the defence contribution should also be increased. He suggested that if any additional defence contribution was to be contemplated, it should be spent in a way clearly beneficial to Hong Kong and proposed three areas where this might be achieved. The Colonial Office "regretted" that Grantham felt unable to approach the Finance Committee about an unconditional increase but reluctantly agreed he approach the unofficials on his conditional offer. The unofficials were prepared to accept a conditional increase but wanted to be consulted before funds were disbursed.[60]

In April, Grantham withdrew this offer. He did so after the Executive Council had considered the Clague Committee report on permanent rehousing of cleared squatters. This was because of the estimated cost of between HK$6 million to HK$8 million to clear fire lanes in squatter areas before the next dry season in October. Grantham could not now contemplate any increase in the defence contribution. This claim met with considerable scepticism by the Treasury which thought Hong Kong could afford to pay both for clearing fire lanes as well as an additional defence contribution of HK$8 million.[61]

Cabinet decision

On 16 February 1954, the British Cabinet decided to drastically reduce the size of Hong Kong's garrison.[62] This was to restrict considerably the British government's ability to demand an increased defence contribution from Hong Kong. It also strengthened Grantham's and the Colonial Office's hand in resisting such calls. No decision was made on the timing of the reduction which was to await a forthcoming five-power conference in Geneva. It was also hoped the planned reduction could be undertaken in tandem with a reduction of troops in Korea to help try and allay any public concerns in Hong Kong. The Treasury and the Colonial Office realised this would make it more difficult to press Hong Kong for an additional HK$8 million in defence contribution. The Treasury, although sceptical of Grantham's claims of parsimony, became more circumspect in pushing him to reconsider his position.[63] The Colonial Office thought it unrealistic to press him further and preferred to wait for a few months. Even then, the Colonial Office was reluctant to press Grantham for an additional contribution. They felt they would have been "morally on pretty weak ground" if they had done so.[64] It was even reluctant to ask Grantham for the full HK$16 million contribution for 1955–56 in view of a Cabinet decision on 5 November 1954 to delay the garrison rundown. The Colonial Office told Treasury that

> local politics apart ... some people might question the morality of squeezing large sums for defence out of a Colony whose defence is bound to be a very problematic affair.[65]

They were eventually persuaded by the Treasury to do so on the grounds that the reduction was unlikely to take place in the current financial year. Grantham, who had had to keep news of the planned garrison reduction confidential from unofficials, roundly rejected this. He pointed out that

> if this argument could be put to unofficials, the result would be antagonistic and any subsequent reduction would undoubtedly give rise to accusations of bad faith against both HMG and this government.

Colonial Office officials agreed that it was not worth while taking this matter up further with Grantham.[66]

In December 1954, Sir John Martin, the Permanent Under-Secretary, met the unofficials during his visit to Hong Kong. Their strength of feeling on this issue and the return of the Naval Dockyard site and Murray Barracks to the Hong Kong government was brought home to him. He concluded that as long as they held a "strong sense of grievance" over these matters there was little hope in them agreeing to an additional defence contribution.[67] By January 1955, both the Treasury and the War Office had given up trying to secure any additional contribution for 1953–54 in addition to what had become the standard annual contribution of £1 million. During the remainder of 1955, the Treasury began to focus more on reduction of the garrison. The savings to be obtained from this greatly outweighed any additional contribution Hong Kong might make. They still made further attempts to press Hong Kong to increase its contribution but the Colonial Office now refused to press Grantham to do so. They claimed Hong Kong had too many development commitments, a claim the Treasury refuted, and that Hong Kong would do well if it was even able to maintain its defence contribution at HK$16 million.[68] There the controversy over Hong Kong's defence contribution seemed to rest, to be overtaken by the Grantham's concerns over the planned reduction of the garrison.

Defence contribution and implications for autonomy

Why did Hong Kong agree to pay a defence contribution? Firstly, by the latter half of 1949, any doubts over Britain's commitment to defend Hong Kong must have dissipated. That commitment had now been made manifest through the quadrupling of the size of the garrison during the summer of 1949. Secondly, the Treasury and the Colonial Office had seized the opportunity to resolve the outstanding claims and get Hong Kong back into the habit of making an annual defence contribution. The unofficials were prepared to accept this as it was the best deal they were likely to get and would finally resolve the issue of outstanding claims. Thirdly, under the potentially overwhelming threat from Chinese communist forces, it was hardly the time for a rancorous dispute with Britain over who should pay for Hong Kong's defence. The previous year, Landale had privately told the Governor that the unofficials did not wish to parade their disquiet over the proposed financial settlement for fear of giving comfort to "critics of the British Empire".[69] It was likely similar sentiments still held sway.

The argument, put simply, was that Britain needed the money and Hong Kong could afford to pay. Hong Kong's unofficials were likely to have been aware of Hong Kong's relative prosperity compared to Britain's. If they had refused to pay a defence contribution, especially at such a delicate time, they would have risked appearing parsimonious and small-minded. It would also have been difficult to keep such a dispute from becoming public which would have harmed Britain's and Hong Kong's interests even more. These factors help explain why the meetings of Hong Kong's Financial and Colonial Secretaries held with the Colonial Office, Treasury and service departments in April 1950 went so smoothly.

In subsequent years, there was more of a purely business feel to the negotiations. After agreement in 1950, Hong Kong could only claim they should no longer pay a defence contribution if they could not afford it. It was obvious that they could. It was therefore a question of how much they should pay. Here Hong Kong had the upper hand because it could say what it could afford and what the unofficials were likely to agree to. Grantham was also adept at securing agreement to the amount he wanted Hong Kong to pay rather than what Treasury would have liked. Despite the War Office's protestations, there never was any cause to involve ministers, other than to ratify what their officials had agreed. It would have caused ministers to expend more political capital than it was worth to insist that Hong Kong pay more by instructing Grantham to use the official majority. Grantham also ensured matters never got to this stage. It was a careful balancing act which he played with considerable precision.

Granting of financial autonomy

The promised review in 1949 had been a very brief one conducted solely within the Colonial Office. It had concluded there was no need for change. This was because Hong Kong might, without warning, be subjected to what officials referred to as "Cold War" tactics from China and this might result in pressure on Hong Kong to pay more for its defence. It would be difficult then to deal with the Treasury on Hong Kong's behalf if more financial control was devolved to Hong Kong. It was also felt that financial devolution went hand-in-hand with constitutional reform[70] then still under discussion with Britain. The 1949 review had not been a full review inasmuch that the controls had not been extensively debated within the Colonial Office or with Treasury. There the matter had been left to stand.

By 1955, Colonial Office officials had begun to realise the need to do something about Hong Kong's failure to comply with the 1948 controls.[71] One reason for doing so was because of the direct linkage between the Colonial Office and Treasury created by the annual discussions on the defence contribution. On no other issue did the Colonial Office intercede with the Treasury on Hong Kong's behalf. It was thought that for this reason alone the Treasury would be sensitive to any possibility of financial devolution for Hong Kong.[72] This was despite the fact that Colonial Office officials had become much more assertive on Hong Kong's behalf with Treasury. They had begun to question under what authority or principle colonies could be required or expected to contribute towards their own defence.[73] It was also thought that because the 1948 controls had needed Treasury's concurrence, Treasury would also need to be involved in discussions to modify or abolish them. The Colonial Office was concerned that because of the paucity of financial information provided by Hong Kong, Treasury was not as well informed about Hong Kong's finances as it might have liked—and it might discover that Hong Kong had not kept the Colonial Office well informed either.[74] Perhaps unknown to the Colonial Office, the Treasury was well aware of the state of Hong Kong's finances, to the extent that it was able to forecast what surpluses it was likely to make.

The Colonial Office's main concerns were that the estimates were not seen until it was too late to change them; that expenditure on important points of principle was not referred to them; that no information was given to them other than that contained in the regular quarterly reports and that the Colonial Office was unable to keep the Treasury informed as they themselves knew little. The Colonial Office recognised that Hong Kong had, since 1948, been "rolling in money" and had "not the slightest chance of falling under Treasury control again for the usual reasons". It was thought that because of Hong Kong's defence contribution and management of its currency, Treasury had an interest in how Hong Kong's finances were being managed.[75]

Colonial Office officials felt they had to do something but were at a loss over what that should be. One rather petulantly expressed his irritation that Hong Kong had "taken the law into their own hands without ... any comments from us so far".[76] This reflected their sense of impotence because there were few, if any, effective means through which they could recover their authority. Officials discounted the option of continuing to tolerate the present situation and pretend as if nothing had happened. There was concern, however, that if financial autonomy were to be formally granted that this would somehow encourage agitation for further constitutional development. The Colonial Office could either, therefore, insist on the strict application of the 1948 controls or it could take steps to amend or modify them in some fashion. There was also the delicate question of how to approach the Governor. A despatch "would come rather out of the blue at this stage" and would have been too drastic a step. The best approach, it was suggested, would be "a pretty informal letter to Mr David [Hong Kong's Colonial Secretary)]".[77]

Gradually, it was realised that Hong Kong could manage its own finances competently and responsibly. It had, after all, built up its reserves to the equivalent of one year's revenue and had kept public debt to less than two month's revenue. The role of the unofficials was recognised in this. It was thought

> these achievements go to the credit of a responsible Government with a nominated Legislative Council ... and to a responsible climate of effective public opinion (really business opinion) which has preferred private enterprise to an expensive public enterprise. There is no reason to suppose that any of these factors favourable to a responsible conduct of the colony's financial affairs will change for the worse in the foreseeable future.

Public opinion, albeit defined in this narrow way, would ensure that public expenditure, and taxation, would be kept to a minimum and that this

> should be the best safeguards of responsible and economical financial policy in the colony – certainly better safeguards than would be a Constitution giving the vote and influence to the working classes, as distinct from the business classes, because the working classes might be expected to require more of a welfare state and hence a great increase in government expenditure.[78]

The granting of financial devolution would not, it was thought, encourage any more pressure than could be managed for "more democracy" and the Colonial Office would also probably be happier seeing less rather than higher expenditure. These statements were made without any sense of irony. Only ten years previously, some Colonial Office officials had been extolling the virtues of a more popular form of government in Hong Kong.

The question of how to approach the Governor was resolved when it was simply put to him during a visit to the Colonial Office in the summer of 1956. Officials planned to tell him they were unhappy with the operation of the 1948 controls. They would then allow him either to accept they should be implemented in full or, alternatively, let him make proposals for greater financial autonomy. It turned out there was no need for such a meeting as Grantham agreed to greater financial autonomy when this was first informally discussed with officials. The Treasury's views were sought and, after a two-month delay, they seemed to accept the Colonial Office's proposals quite readily.[79]

Eighteen months later on 6 March 1958, the Governor, by now Black, announced the granting of formal financial autonomy to the Legislative Council.[80] A despatch sent on 14 January 1958[81] had removed the need for the Secretary of State's formal approval of the annual estimates. This recognised the Hong Kong government's and the unofficials' capacity to manage Hong Kong's finances effectively and responsibly. It also recognised what had been apparent for some time which was the Colonial Office's lack of capacity to intercede effectively. As an official commented,

> it is not going to be very easy to intervene in Hong Kong's affairs because they do not require financial assistance from the UK, and on present form are unlikely to do so ... for some time to come. We must therefore recognise that in the more extensive correspondence now contemplated with the Financial Secretary of Hong Kong we may not in normal circumstances be called upon to do more than utter general and perhaps platitudinous observations on the information with which he has supplied us.[82]

When relaxation finally did come, the acting Financial Secretary thought it would allow for even more effective control by the Secretary of State. It would allow him to comment informally on the estimates before Legislative Council approval rather than be presented with a *fait accompli*.[83]

Conclusions

Yet again, Hong Kong had shown that, even when it had a policy imposed upon it by Britain, it could still exercise a high degree of autonomy in its implementation. Once it was agreed in principle that a defence contribution should be made, it was Hong Kong and not Britain who decided how much it would pay. This was simply a matter of politics, a game in which Grantham played the unofficials' card to the full. The Colonial Office, and the Treasury, had to accept whatever amount he thought the unofficials would agree to. How much this genuinely reflected the unofficials' views is hard to quantify, given that many discussions would have been conducted privately. Perhaps they may not have been quite as sensitive as Grantham liked to portray. In his exercise of autonomy, Grantham was probably somewhat less subtle and more forceful in getting his way than Peel had been in 1930 over how he would regulate *mui tsai*.

It was not just politics in Hong Kong that was important. The lack of political pressure in Britain had an equally important counter-balancing effect. The question of how much Hong Kong should contribute to the cost of its defence was of immense importance to officials in the Treasury and the War Office but of virtually none to Ministers or to Parliament. When War Office officials wanted to escalate Hong Kong's dilatoriness to ministerial level, the Treasury was more circumspect and knew that there was insufficient cause to do so. There is no evidence that any Minister took any more than a perfunctory interest in the issue. The political pendulum, therefore, had swung in Hong Kong's favour and when that happened, Hong Kong's views were again able to hold sway. Officials in London, no matter how cogent their arguments, could not counter the overriding political influence of Hong Kong's unofficials without the engagement of Ministers.

The question of Hong Kong's lack of adherence to the 1948 financial controls was again of more concern to officials than politicians, both in Hong Kong and in Britain. In Hong Kong, officials had sought Legislative Council approval of the estimates before the Secretary of State's. If Hong Kong had sought the Secretary of State's approval first, and he had delayed replying or there had been a serious disagreement, this may have become a political issue in Hong Kong. This did not arise. Hong Kong's officials simply presented their own proposals to the Finance Committee without seeking, or seeing the need to seek, the Secretary of State's prior approval, for example, over the Tai Lam Chung Reservoir project.

What seemed to concern Colonial Office officials most was not whether Hong Kong's finances were being competently managed but that their own authority was being so blatantly flouted. Treasury officials, on the other hand, were more concerned about how much Hong Kong could pay towards its defence. What galled Colonial Office officials was that there was little they could effectively do to counter Hong Kong's insouciance. When financial control was raised with Grantham in such a contrived and seemingly off-hand way, he seemed to have dismissed the matter as almost a bureaucratic detail that just needed to be tidied up.

What had the Colonial Office expected? Hong Kong now had the capacity to formulate and implement its own financial policies. This was a far cry from the position in 1932 when the Colonial Office complained of the low quality of Hong Kong's financial management. In 1935, the Colonial Office had instructed colonial Governors to create a new post of Financial Secretary to advise the Governor on all matters of financial and economic policy. In that year, Caldecott asked the Colonial Office to nominate a successor to the then Colonial Treasurer as he considered no-one in Hong Kong was suitably qualified. This resulted in the appointment of Sidney Caine, a Colonial Office civil servant as Hong Kong's first Financial Secretary from 1937 to 1939.[84] Follows, the first post-war Financial Secretary was highly regarded by MacDougall and his successor, Arthur Clarke, was a strong-minded cadet officer who had joined the Hong Kong government in 1937. The competent manner in which Hong Kong's finances were run in the 1950s was a logical outcome of the Colonial Office's desire in the 1930s to achieve this result. It was a testament to Hong Kong's financial management that sufficient surplus funds were available from which development could be funded and a defence contribution made. Efficient and competent officers, however, no longer needed the same kind of oversight that incompetent ones did. This helped make the 1948 controls less relevant than they might have been in a previous age. Now that Hong Kong had the capacity to manage its finances effectively, the Secretary of State was left with little room for manoeuvre.

By the 1950s, the financial responsibilities of the unofficials can only have been strengthened as Hong Kong's finances increased in scope and complexity. This, combined with the increased competence of Hong Kong's financial management, resulted in the Secretary of State's legitimising role being, *de facto*, superseded by the unofficials. The formal granting of financial autonomy in 1958 was, therefore, as Colonial Office officials were only too aware, belated *de jure* recognition of this. Provided Hong Kong managed its finances competently and needed no financial assistance from Britain, the Secretary of State would be under no political pressure to recover his role as arbiter of Hong Kong's finances. The legitimising function exercised by the Secretary of State on behalf of the Crown in respect of Hong Kong's finances had become obsolete and been transferred to the unofficials.

11
Conclusions

There was no clear linear progression in the development of the Hong Kong government's autonomy. There were too many variables for this to have happened. There were moments when it was able to exercise a degree, even a high degree of autonomy, and others when it was not. Much depended on the circumstances of the time, the political pressure that was brought to bear and how those in authority responded to it. The exercise of autonomy was as much the result of changing political pressures as it was of the personalities and the beliefs of the principal actors involved, in Britain as well as Hong Kong, and their willingness and determination to act upon them.

Carpenter sets out a clear exposition of the conditions necessary for government agencies to develop autonomy in a democratic political system. The Hong Kong government, however, was not democratically elected but was answerable to a British government that was and, in addition, it had to take account of local political opinion reflected by the unofficials. Nor was it, like the United States government agencies Carpenter studied, competing with other government agencies for power or resources. This concluding chapter will consider, therefore, what issues and factors, including those set out by Carpenter, were relevant to the development of the Hong Kong government's autonomy in this somewhat different milieu. Firstly, however, this chapter will examine whether Hong Kong's constitutional subservience to the British Crown had a major impact on the development of its ability to exercise autonomy.

Hong Kong's colonial relationship with Britain

Hong Kong's relationship with Britain provides only a limited context to understanding the changing power relationship between the two governments. Constitutional subordination provided the institutional framework within which the British government established a comprehensive series of reporting requirements and approvals. The formal appointment of the Governor, senior civil servants and unofficials by the Secretary of State on behalf of the Crown all provided an opportunity for Britain to exercise power over the colonial government. The workings of this relationship, within the rubric of colonial regulations, provided a framework within which political power could be exercised.

In practice, however, politics was the principal determinant of the balance of political power between the two governments. In some cases, it was politics in Britain that enabled the home government to prevail, as in the case of *mui tsai;* in others, it was local politics that enabled the Hong Kong government to determine the outcome, as in the case of the proposed municipal council. In others, the outcome was the result of more nuanced forces. The directive on housing, for example, was a consequence of the interplay of political forces in both places. This relationship, therefore, provided the context but not the driving force behind the nature and development of the power relationship between the British and Hong Kong governments.

Whose policies prevailed?

It is remarkable how few policies examined originated from the Hong Kong government: indeed, nearly all originated from elsewhere. The policy to regulate *mui tsai* was dictated by Churchill and Passfield to an unwilling Hong Kong government; the local government's preference was not to interfere. In 1946, Young was similarly told that he had to consult and plan for constitutional reform. The Secretary of State also instructed a not unwilling Governor to establish a Housing Authority and Hong Kong was given little option but to pay a defence contribution. Nor was it just from the sovereign power that policies emanated. The Hong Kong government under Stubbs and Clementi was strongly influenced by Chinese elite pressure over *mui tsai*. It was unofficial opposition, initially to the Young Plan and then eventually to any constitutional reform, which pushed Grantham to abandon constitutional change. More positively, one Urban Council unofficial, in the absence of direction from the Hong Kong government, took the lead in the early development of a permanent squatter resettlement policy.

The British government, in the form of the Secretary of State for the Colonies and his senior Colonial Office officials did not seek to "control" the Hong Kong government. It was expected to conduct its business in accordance with a set of common values tacitly understood by politicians and officials on both sides. Colonial Office officials tended to act more as supervisors and gave much credence to the views of the "man on the spot". The various approvals requested by Hong Kong governors were often readily agreed to by the Secretary of State.[1] The British government usually sought to impose its will only when domestic political pressure brought matters to ministers' attention and made it in their interests to act. Their intervention could then be decisive.

There were occasions, however, when policies were unique to the Hong Kong government. In 1936, Caldecott amended the law regarding *mui tsai* even when all Chinese unofficials opposed him. Northcote took care to win political support from Legislative Council unofficials for the implementation of the Woods Commission Minority Report recommendations when the Colonial Office had not expected him to do so. Young also developed his own detailed plan for a municipal council and defended it against attack from the Secretary of State. MacDougall persuaded the Colonial Office to allow the Hong Kong government to support the Lee Hysan housing scheme and ensured that the government had an effective policy to clear and resettle squatters from the main urban area in 1948. These all happened under the strong leadership of a governor or senior cadet.

The ability of the unofficials in the Executive, Legislative and Urban Councils to influence or even author policy was also an important influence. Sometimes the unofficials operated quite blatantly in their own interests as, for example, in seeking to pursue constitutional reform to create a Legislative Council within which they could exercise more power. Their lack of enthusiasm for the Hong Kong government to embark on a policy of building low-cost housing most probably delayed the introduction of a Housing Authority. Influencing events more indirectly, were "activists" such as the Haslewoods, Miss Picton-Turbervill, the pressure groups in Britain backing them and, to a lesser extent, Bishop Hall in Hong Kong. They mobilised public opinion in Britain in innovative ways and brought pressure to bear upon the Hong Kong government, mostly indirectly, through the British government.

Policy formulation and implementation

A recurring theme was the Hong Kong government's initial belief that it had no capacity to implement proposed new policies followed by the discovery that it had more potential to develop such a capacity than it thought it had. Once required to implement new policies, it was often able to do so quite successfully. There are two main aspects of this capability to consider. Firstly, there was the capacity to formulate policy in new policy areas and the ability, as Carpenter says, "to analyse, to create new programmes, to solve problems, to plan". This was, perhaps the weakest aspect of the Hong Kong government's performance. Carpenter thinks "nothing so distinguishes twentieth century bureaucratic government from its predecessors as its ability to plan, to innovate, and to author policy".[2] It was almost the lack of these capabilities that defined the Hong Kong government during this period. It held a very pessimistic view of its ability to attempt most things new. Both Stubbs and Clementi were convinced that the state had no capacity to regulate *mui tsai* and had no confidence in the effectiveness of a new inspectorate to implement regulations. There was an infinite belief in the immutability of Chinese mores and none whatsoever in the government's ability to act as an agent of social change and development. The government and the unofficials both gave lack of capacity as a reason for being unable to implement proposed new policies. It was one reason why Clementi believed he was unable to regulate *mui tsai* and Young's opponents adduced this as a reason for not introducing income tax. Young had to reassure the unofficials that that capacity could and would be created. Grantham also gave lack of capacity as an excuse for inaction on proposed constitutional reform.

A capacity to generate new policy proposals did exist within the civil service. Some senior and middle-ranking civil servants, concerned over Hong Kong's housing situation, submitted their recommendations to senior levels within government, proposing the building of permanent multi-storey housing blocks. In late 1949, the Deputy Director of Public Works was advocating the establishment by government of a housing trust as the only way to tackle the housing problem. After MacDougall's departure, however, Grantham seemed unable to pull together views expressed by civil servants and to develop a cohesive and viable housing policy. The loss of MacDougall's guidance was exacerbated by the absence of any institutional planning mechanisms which would have helped create the potential capacity preferred to formulate policy in new areas; there were no standing government planning or co-ordination committees nor standing policy committees which would play such an important part in policy co-ordination in later years.[3] It took, for example, the steadying hand of the Secretary of State and the Colonial Office before a firm housing policy was established.

The second aspect was the capacity to implement new policies efficiently and effectively. It was remarkable how well the Hong Kong government could implement new policies even if it was not adept at formulating them. Despite Stubbs and Clementi's forebodings, Peel established an inspectorate that, in spite of some criticism, was reasonably effective in administering the *mui tsai* regulations and enabled Hong Kong to provide Britain with authoritative-sounding statistics with which to confound its critics. That success was one reason why Caldecott and Northcote were able to proceed with their own distinctive policies.

MacDougall created the capacity for the British Military Administration to tackle the intractable problems facing it. In 1948, he was also able to ensure the effective formulation and implementation of a squatter clearance and resettlement policy. Under post-war Financial Secretaries, Hong Kong's finances were put on a more even footing and regular surpluses were accumulated. Even Grantham, once he had been given policy direction over housing, eventually managed to establish a Housing Authority, although it took him nearly four years to do so. This reflected the abilities of the cadets, and subordinate officers, to apply themselves effectively to a task even if they were less adept at formulating new policies in the first place.

Implementation was weak, however, when it required inter-departmental co-ordination. The 1951 squatter resettlement policy was stymied by poor implementation: the rigid lines of departmentalism prevented the effective inter-departmental co-ordination on which its success depended. Conversely, the implementation of the policy to resettle squatters in permanent multi-storey accommodation through the work of a single department was extraordinarily successful and rapidly became an international byword on the issue. Effective implementation allowed Holmes, as Commissioner for Resettlement, to eventually regain effective control of squatter policy from the Urban Council once he had shown that government, through the work of his department, had the capacity to build multi-storey resettlement blocks quickly and manage them efficiently.

Although government had policies imposed upon it from elsewhere, the creation of the capacity to implement them gave it the means to help make these polices its own. The act of creation of that capability forced it to study issues and thereby become more knowledgeable about them. Practical experience increased its ability and confidence in handling these issues. This, in turn, gave the government a certain authority in discussions with the Secretary of State and the Colonial Office which helped it respond as it wished rather than continue to be dictated to.

Legitimacy

Why were new policies imposed upon the Hong Kong government despite it having shown neither an ability to formulate them nor the demonstrated capacity to implement them? Firstly, the Hong Kong government was the only instrument through which the British government could exercise its sovereignty: it had no ready alternative means of doing so. The Hong Kong government was also not competing with other agencies for legitimacy as was the case in the United States. If it was having problems with issues it should have been facing up to—challenges over public order, safety and public health as in the case of squatters—it was the only body available to tackle them. There were no alternatives. If the government lacked the capacity to tackle new issues, then that capacity had to be created.

Secondly, it was the only body with access to the resources needed to tackle such problems. The Hong Kong government did not enjoy a "strong organisational reputation" nor had it consistently displayed "demonstrated capacity".[4] It was, however, the only body with the necessary powers and access to funds to tackle issues on a suitable scale. This was especially so for housing and squatter resettlement. The early attempts by the Hong Kong Housing Society and the Hong Kong Model Housing Society showed the difficulties of raising private finance to tackle the housing problem. Only the Hong Kong government could establish a fund, such as the Development Fund, from which loans could be made to the Housing Society and the Housing Authority on terms favourable enough to make low-cost housing projects viable. Only the colonial government could seek grants or loans from the Colonial Development and Welfare Fund, and only the government had the authority to clear squatters, make land available for their resettlement and, with the support of unofficials on the Legislative Council sitting as the Finance Committee, fund the construction of permanent multi-storey resettlement blocks to rehouse them.

There was also the question of why the imposition of these polices on the Hong Kong government did not derogate from its authority. The Hong Kong government was in the unusual position that no other political body or party or other sovereign power had any interest or desire to usurp or takeover its political power or authority. There was no opposition waiting in the wings for an opportunity to become the lawful government. There was no nationalist party agitating for independence as there was in other British colonies after 1945. The only possible alternative would have been if Hong Kong had reverted to China to be ruled by the Chinese government of the day. There was, however, no serious or popular agitation for this. As a result, if a serious issue needed to be addressed and if the Hong Kong government was not satisfactorily addressing it, it had then to be pushed or prodded into doing so. This was the pattern which emerged under Stubbs, Clementi, Peel and Grantham. It was this which helped create the Hong Kong government's capacity to implement new policies which, in turn, gave it the experience and expertise to begin to formulate further policies in these areas. This, in turn, enhanced its reputation for the effective provision of services and allowed it to exercise an increasing level of autonomy from Britain and from the unofficials.

Importance of the unofficials

The role of the unofficial, especially after 1945, was important for three reasons. Firstly, because the unofficials in the Legislative Council had power and had shown they were prepared to use it. They obtained control over government expenditure in 1920 when Stubbs created an unofficial majority in the Finance Committee of the Legislative Council.[5] In 1940, its unofficial members had shown they were prepared to use this power when they declined to vote $10,000 for the evacuation of European women and children from Hong Kong.[6] After 1946, they made very clear that they were not prepared to approve expenditure on items arising from the aftermath of the war which they thought should be borne by Britain. This had pushed even Young, who was otherwise prepared to stand up to the unofficials if he thought he was right, to agree that such expenditure be placed in a suspense account until agreement with Britain had been reached. This would have increased the unofficials' sense of what they could achieve *vis-à-vis* not only the Hong Kong government but also the British government. It was also the implicit power of the unofficials on the Finance Committee which helped Grantham in his annual negotiations over the defence contribution.

Secondly, the unofficials had a motive to wield this power. In the years immediately after the war, there was an underlying uncertainty over Britain's commitment to remaining in Hong Kong.[7] Britain had been loath to make any public announcement on the future of the colony for fear of triggering a request from the Chinese government to start negotiations over the colony's future.[8] If the unofficials had doubted Britain's determination to remain, they may have been encouraged to be more belligerent than they otherwise might have been. This was clearly the case during the July 1947 Legislative Council housing debate when one unofficial remarked that he had "never heard a debate in which more spirit was displayed".[9] Conversely, in 1949, Britain's manifest commitment to Hong Kong's defence would have constrained them from objecting in principle to making a contribution to the cost of Hong Kong's defence.

Thirdly, the unofficials were allowed to exercise their power and influence over government policy. If the various Governors discussed here are to be broadly classified, then Stubbs, Clementi and Grantham considered unofficials' views to be immutable while Peel, Northcote and Young considered them malleable. Stubbs and Clementi considered themselves unable to tackle the Chinese elites over *mui tsai;* Peel and Northcote managed to win their support and Caldecott simply disregarded them. Young persuaded some unofficials to support his income tax proposals and he was prepared to tackle them on the issue of constitutional reform. Grantham, however, acquiesced to their views and allowed them to lead the debate. His unwillingness to grasp the nettle over government provision of low-cost housing before receipt of the Secretary of State's instructions may have been due to the decided lack of unofficial interest in such a move. His willingness to allow Clague such a free hand in the development of proposals for squatter resettlement amounted almost to a derogation of gubernatorial authority to the Urban Council. The conclusion is that political support was an essential part of the process of policy development: the problem was that while some Governors sought the political support of the unofficials other Governors lent them their political support instead.

The culmination of these developments was the eventual realisation by Colonial Office officials that authority on financial matters had shifted from the Secretary of State to the unofficials. This was compounded when they realised they were unable to do anything to reverse this. No matter what formal regulations were in place, it was the unofficials who now had the final word. This was the culmination, and probably unintended consequence of granting them financial authority in 1920, the Colonial Office's attempts from the 1930s to improve the quality of financial management in colonies like Hong Kong and the Colonial Office's insistence in 1948 that Hong Kong build up its reserves.[10] The Secretary of State's financial authority had been rendered obsolete and irrelevant.

Political pressure from Britain

In Britain, political support and pressure upon the British government to implement policies in Hong Kong was issue specific; the abolition of *mui tsai*, for example and, somewhat more obliquely, for the provision of low-cost housing. There was no general pro-Hong Kong lobby. These were issues over which a British government was very susceptible to pressure; they could not defend the Hong Kong government's inaction against allegations of slavery nor defend the colony's dismal housing conditions. Faced with such criticism, political pressure led the British government to use its powers over Hong Kong to insist upon implementation of policies in these areas. Conversely, when there was no political pressure from Britain, the ability of British officials alone to impose their will on a reluctant, even recalcitrant Hong Kong was seriously constrained. This was shown over discussions on how much Hong Kong should contribute to the cost of its defence.

How could political pressure from Britain override opposing political views in Hong Kong? There were two reasons. Firstly, a Governor was unable to resist specific instructions from a Secretary of State backed by British domestic political pressure and by wider international concern. This could have brought him close to recall. Secondly, despite the Chinese elites' seemingly unwavering support of traditional Chinese customs, many were educated in the British liberal tradition both in Hong Kong and at leading British universities.[11] They were perfectly aware of the opprobrium that was attached to the keeping of *mui tsai*. Even although they tried to argue this was done with the best interests of the girls in mind,[12] they would most likely have been aware how indefensible such arguments would have been in Britain. Similarly, state provision of housing for the less well-off was a major plank in the policies of the newly elected Labour government after 1945.[13] Unofficials in Hong Kong, with their knowledge of Britain and British policies, would most likely have been aware of the difficulty of maintaining obdurate resistance to the public provision of housing in Hong Kong for the less well-off.

Leadership

The hand of a strong leader can be found in the development of most of these policy proposals. Some proved themselves very effective at building political support for their proposed policies. Northcote built up a political coalition among the unofficials in support of the Minority Report recommendations. He made some concessions but his main proposals were supported. Young also showed this approach could work with his strenuous efforts to win political support for his income tax proposals. MacDougall showed how, within the administration, he could formulate and win support for his proposed policy on squatter clearance.

Leaders were not always to be found within the bureaucracy. Some unofficials were able to exert influence over policy when policy voids appeared. These were created when the Hong Kong government failed to address pressing issues until they had reached crisis proportions. This was the case most explicitly after the Shek Kip Mei fire. The government's tentative approach allowed Clague, long a critic of the implementation of the Hong Kong government's squatter resettlement policy, to adroitly step in and persuade the Chairman of the Urban Council to establish a committee under his chairmanship. He acted, as one would have expected an entrepreneur to act, swiftly and skilfully, taking advantage of an opportunity which presented itself and then stoutly defending his position.

Grantham avoided entering the policy debate over the kind of constitutional reform, if any, which would be best for Hong Kong. He restricted his role to the management of process rather than the development of policy. Grantham gave his backing to policy proposals because the unofficials wanted them or because others had cold feet. He supported what was proposed but did not propose what was not supported; he did not lead the debate. In the absence of a leader within the Hong Kong government, others emerged, in this case the unofficials in the Legislative Council of whom Landale, the senior unofficial in Grantham's time, may have played a leading role.

It was also not in the nature of the Hong Kong government's leading civil servants, the cadets, to promote new policies or to be politically adventurous by expanding government activities into new areas. They were not the kind of proactive leaders who would "take action consistent with their own wishes".[14] They saw their role as administering a colony, maintaining public order, ensuring justice was administered, public works constructed and maintained and that regulations were enacted and enforced. Many cadets appeared to see this as their main function and were almost unable to see beyond their day-to-day responsibilities.[15] The Hong Kong government did not, therefore, cultivate the type of personnel who were, by nature, entrepreneurs. Such people when they appeared, such as Lockhart and MacDougall, were exceptions. However, events showed that, once cadets had to take on and implement new policies, they were generally capable of doing so provided they were implemented within the one department; inter-departmental co-ordination was not a strong point.

The other category of leader was the "social activist" like the Haslewoods in the *mui tsai* case and Bishop Hall in the case of housing. By astute manipulation of the democratic system in Britain, Hall and the Haslewoods managed to achieve changes to the Hong Kong government's policies. In both cases, this involved applying, or threatening to apply, pressure upon the British government over issues which it was unable to defend. This also showed how susceptible a democratic government was to public opinion and the very limited direct impact that public opinion still had upon the Hong Kong government. This impact could, of course, have been considerably reduced if Governors had recognised the need to address such issues promptly and decided for themselves how to respond rather than waiting to be told what to do.

As both Northcote and Young showed, however, a Governor's leadership could play a decisive role in the development of new policies. Whether or not this happened was greatly dependent upon the personality and outlook of the Governor of the day, how he chose to respond to issues as they arose and how he responded to the political views of the unofficials. Some had a very clear conception of what they wanted and were prepared to work to build the necessary political support to achieve it. Others, like Stubbs and Clementi, also knew what they wanted but were unable to counter political support for change in Britain, nor did they understand the impact that domestic political views could have upon the British government. They also underestimated their ability to change the views of unofficials and leading local elites in Hong Kong. A Governor like Grantham was not prepared to advocate change in the face of opposition from unofficials as had Young. Similarly, the personalities and political views of respective Secretaries of State also had a bearing. Creech-Jones' strongly held views over housing prevailed but were not shared by Lyttelton. Lyttelton was under no political pressure over the issue and was, by inclination, content to leave most matters to Grantham whom he trusted implicitly. Had the personalities been different, so might have been the outcome.

Sovereignty and the autonomy of crisis

The Hong Kong government was the representative of Britain, the sovereign power. If Hong Kong's position as a British colony was challenged, then the Hong Kong government's first duty was to preserve Britain's sovereignty.[16] This did not happen often. The threat posed by United States pressure to return Hong Kong to China after the war allowed the Hong Kong Planning Unit considerable freedom to plan for the post-war re-establishment of the Hong Kong government as it had existed before 1941. A challenge also occurred under the British Military Administration when faced with the dire circumstances it met upon its arrival in Hong Kong in September 1945. It was able to act under minimum supervision from the Colonial Office in order that it might quickly and effectively re-establish law and order, paving the way for the return of British civil administration and thereby the exercise of Britain's sovereignty. MacDougall also realised the need for speedy action to remedy the multiple problems faced by the post-war colony. The same factor also held sway after 1949 when the uncertainties over communist intentions towards Hong Kong influenced Colonial Office thinking towards constitutional reform. This allowed Grantham and the unofficials more leeway in their argument that constitutional reform should be diluted and then abandoned. However, autonomy of this nature lasted only as long as did the perceived crisis and was not a basis for the development of a more sustainable form of autonomy.

A sense of crisis also constrained the ways in which the British government was able to exercise its sovereignty. The British government felt unable to impose its policies upon the Hong Kong government when its own position there was perceived to be under threat and it had to rely on the Hong Kong government for the retention of its sovereignty. Reforms of the post-war Hong Kong civil service contemplated in the Colonial Office in 1942 were never introduced; the re-establishment of

British sovereignty after Japan's defeat was more pressing. In 1952, it had to accept that constitutional reform would not go ahead as originally envisaged; the retention of British sovereignty in the face of a possible threat from the newly installed communist Chinese regime overrode any desire for reform. However, conversely, when the retention of Hong Kong's British sovereignty depended on British action, and the expenditure of British resources, the balance of power shifted to Britain and Hong Kong had to agree to make a contribution towards the cost of its defence. Again, such factors held sway only as long as the crisis did.

The autonomy of the Hong Kong government

A reputation for the capacity to formulate and implement new policies effectively was not a necessary precursor for the adoption of new policies by the Hong Kong government. Indeed, the opposite was usually the case. Government was often required, as a result of external political pressure, to implement new policies without showing it had the proven ability to do so. That capacity, to implement new policies successfully, was created as a consequence. Incremental development of these new policies and programmes then began to develop in ways analogous to the Carpenter model. The intrinsic abilities of the cadets engendered new capabilities which allowed them to further develop policies on their own volition and achieve a degree of autonomy.

The Hong Kong government did not seek autonomy. It did not proactively develop brave new policies to address the challenges of a rapidly changing Hong Kong yet it was the only body which could tackle the pressing social problems that Hong Kong faced. It did not of its own volition seek to address them but had to be cajoled into doing so. Only then did it discover a capacity it never believed it had. This gave it the ability and confidence to decide for itself what it wanted to do and enhanced its scope for action independently of either the British government or organized interests in Hong Kong. Therein lay the origins of autonomy.

Notes

Chapter 1 Introduction

1. Article 3 (2) of the *Joint Declaration of the Government of the United Kingdom of Great Britain and Northern Ireland and the Government of the People's Republic of China on the Question of Hong Kong*, in Ian Scott, *Political Change and the Crisis of Legitimacy in Hong Kong* (Honolulu, Hawaii: University of Hawaii Press, 1989), p. 353; and Article 2 of *The Basic Law of the Hong Kong Special Administrative Region of the People's Republic of China* (Hong Kong: Joint Publishing [H.K.] Co. Ltd., 1991), p. 5.
2. Steve Tsang, ed. *A Documentary History of Hong Kong: Government and Politics* (Hong Kong: Hong Kong University Press, 1995) pp. 19–30.
3. *Colonial Regulations 1935*, amended 1945 (London: His Majesty's Stationery Office, 1945), Regulation 105.
4. Lennox A. Mills, *British Rule in Eastern Asia* (London: Oxford University Press, 1942), pp. 391–92.
5. Norman Miners, *Hong Kong Under Imperial Rule 1912–1941* (Hong Kong: Oxford University Press, 1987), pp. 50–51 and p. 109.
6. J. M. H. Lee, *Colonial Development and Good Government* (Oxford: Clarendon Press, 1967), p. 72.
7. See Miners, op. cit., pp. 50 and 284; Mills, op. cit., pp. 392 and 397; and Lee, op. cit., pp. 55, 60, 73 and 220.
8. Royal Instructions 29 and 3 in Tsang, op. cit., pp. 27 and 23 respectively and Letters Patent in ibid., p. 19.
9. Sir Cosmo Parkinson, *The Colonial Office from Within, 1900–1945* (London: Faber and Faber Limited, 1946), p. 139; Mills, op. cit., p. 397.
10. Scott, op. cit., p. 324.
11. Leo Goodstadt, *Uneasy Partners: The Conflict between Public Interest and Private Profit in Hong Kong* (Hong Kong: Hong Kong University Press, 2005), p. 49.
12. See, for example, Hurst Hannum and Richard B. Lillich, "The Concept of Autonomy in International Law", *The American Journal of International Law*, Vol. 74, No. 4, (1980), pp. 858–89; G. L. Clark, "A Theory of Local Autonomy", *Annals of the Association of American Geographers*, Vol. 74, No. 2 (June 1984), pp. 195–208; H. Wolman and M. Goldsmith, "Local Autonomy as a Meaningful Concept", *Urban Affairs Review*, Vol. 26, No. 1 (Sep 1990),

p. 3; Zeng Huaqun, "Hong Kong's Autonomy: Concept, Development and Characteristics", *China: An International Journal*, Vol. 1, No. 2 (September 2003), p. 315; and J. Richardson, "Dillon's Rule Is from Mars, Home Rule Is from Venus: Local Government Autonomy and the Rules of Statutory Construction", *Publius*, Vol. 41, No. 4 (2011), pp. 662–85.
13 Gordon L. Clark, op. cit., pp. 198–201.
14 H. Wolman and M. Goldsmith, op. cit., pp. 3–17, quoted in G. A. Boyne, "Central Policies and Local Autonomy: The Case of Wales", *Urban Studies*, Vol. 30, No. 1 (1993), pp. 87–101.
15 H. Wolman, R. McManmom, M. Bell and D. Brunori, "Comparing Local Government across States", in M. E. Bell, D. Brunori and J. Youngman, *The Property Tax and Local Autonomy* (Cambridge, MA: Lincoln Institute of Land Policy); quoted in J. Richardson, "Dillon's Rule Is from Mars, Home Rule Is from Venus: Local Government Autonomy and the Rules of Statutory Construction", *Publius*, Vol. 41, No. 4, (2011), pp. 662–85.
16 Miners, op. cit., p. 74.
17 Daniel P. Carpenter, *The Forging of Bureaucratic Autonomy* (Princeton and Oxford: Princeton University Press, 2001).
18 Ibid., pp. 4–21.
19 Ibid., pp. 5 and 14.
20 Herbert Kaufman, *The Administrative Behavior of Federal Bureau Chiefs* (Washington, DC: The Brookings Institution, 1981), pp. 161–74; James Q. Wilson, *Bureaucracy* (New York: Basic Books, 1989), pp. 183 and 227; and Carpenter, op. cit., Chapter 3.
21 For the difficulties faced by the British government in trying to persuade colonial service officers to innovate and plan and promote development in the colonies see Lee, op. cit., pp. 35–39; J. M. Lee and Martin Petter, *The Colonial Office, War and Development Policy* (London: University of London, for the Institute of Commonwealth Studies, 1982), pp. 170–72; D. J. Morgan, *The Official History of Colonial Development*, Vol. 1, *The Origins of British Aid Policy, 1924–1945* (Atlantic Highlands, NJ: Humanities Press, 1980), pp. 183–84.
22 Mills, op. cit., pp. vii–viii.
23 Parkinson, op. cit., Chapter 6, pp. 136–54.
24 G. B. Endacott, *Government and People in Hong Kong, 1841–1962* (Hong Kong: Hong Kong University Press, 1964). See particularly Chapters XIV and XV.
25 Steve Tsang, *A Modern History of Hong Kong* (Hong Kong: Hong Kong University Press, 2004).
26 Scott, op. cit., p. 324.
27 Goodstadt, op. cit.
28 Ibid., p. 56.

Chapter 2 Governor, Cadets, Unofficials and the Colonial Office

1 Sidney James Webb, Lord Passfield, OM, PC was born in 1859 and educated in London and overseas. He became a civil servant in the War Office in 1878, joined the Colonial Office in 1881 and resigned from the civil service

in 1891. He was an MP from 1922 to 1929 and served in Labour governments as Secretary of State for the Dominions in 1924 and as Secretary of State for the Colonies from 1929 to 1931. He was a prolific writer, helped found the London School of Economics and was a famed Fabian. He died in 1947.

2. Oliver Lyttelton, KG, PC, DSO, MC, LLD, 1st Viscount Chandos was born in 1893 and educated at Eton and Cambridge University. He served in the Grenadier Guards from 1914 to 1919 and subsequently had a career in the British Metal Corporation of which he became Managing Director. He became a government minister during the Second World War and, in 1951, served for three years as Secretary of State for the Colonies under Churchill. He died in 1972.

3. Malcolm John MacDonald, OM, PC, was born in 1901 the son of Ramsay MacDonald, the first Labour Prime Minister. He was a Labour MP from 1929 until 1935 and again from 1938. He served as Secretary of State for the Colonies from June to November 1935 and again from 1938 to 1940. He was instrumental in passing the Colonial Development and Welfare Act, 1940. In 1941 he was appointed High Commissioner to Canada and in 1946 became High Commissioner for South-East Asia. He died in 1981.

4. Arthur Creech-Jones was born in London in 1891 and educated at Whitehall Boys School, Bristol. He was a junior clerk in the War Office and was imprisoned during the First World War as a conscientious objector. He then became a trade union official and an MP in 1935. He lost his seat in 1950 but was re-elected in 1954. He became Under-Secretary of State for the Colonies in 1945 and Secretary of State from 1946 to 1950. In later life he retained an abiding interest in colonial affairs. He died in 1964.

5. Sir Gerard Edward James Gent, KCMG, OBE, DSO, MC, born 1895, educated King's College, Canterbury and Trinity College, Dublin. Appointed Assistant Principal, Colonial Office, 1920, Principal, 1927, Assistant Secretary 1939, Assistant Under-Secretary of State for the Colonies, 1946, Governor, Malayan Union, 1946 and Commissioner, Federation of Malaya, 1948. He died on 4 July 1948 in an air accident over London.

6. Sir Sydney Caine, KCMG, was born in 1902 and was educated at Harrow School and the London School of Economics where he graduated with First Class Honours. He joined the Treasury as Assistant Inspector of Taxes in 1923 and transferred to the Colonial Office as an Assistant Principal in 1926. He commented on a number of Hong Kong issues including *mui tsai* and currency issues. From 1937 to 1939 he was Hong Kong's first Financial Secretary. On his return to the Colonial Office he was often asked for his comments on Hong Kong affairs. In 1947 he was knighted and returned to the Treasury. In 1952 he became Vice-Chancellor of the University of Malaya and from 1957 to 1962 was Director of the London School of Economics. He died in 1991.

7. Tsang, *A Modern History of Hong Kong*, p. 109, and G. B. Endacott, *A History of Hong Kong* (Hong Kong: Oxford in Asia, 1964), p. 310.

8. Grantham, op. cit., p. 107.

9   Sir Alexander Grantham, GCMG, born 1899. He served in the army during the First World War and was afterwards educated at Cambridge University. He was appointed a Hong Kong cadet in 1922 and served variously in the Colonial Secretary's office and as Assistant Treasurer, Police Magistrate, Second Assistant Colonial Secretary and Deputy Clerk of Councils. He was appointed Colonial Secretary, Bermuda in 1935, Colonial Secretary, Jamaica in 1938 and Chief Secretary, Nigeria in 1941. He became Governor of Fiji and High Commissioner Western Pacific in 1944 and Governor of Hong Kong from 1947 until his retirement in 1957. He published his memoirs *Via Ports* in 1965 (Grantham, op. cit.) and died in 1978.
10 *Colonial Regulations, 1935*, amended 1945 (London: His Majesty's Stationery Office, 1945), Regulation 105, 138 and 142.
11 Miners, op. cit., pp. 43–44.
12 See Letters Patent, in Tsang, *Government and Politics*, pp. 19–21.
13 Parkinson, op. cit., p. 156 and Charles Jeffries, *The Colonial Empire and Its Civil Service* (Cambridge: Cambridge University Press, 1938), pp. 198–99.
14 Sir Charles Adderley, Parliamentary Under-Secretary of State for the Colonies commented in 1868 that "in distant Crown Colonies the Home Government can only supervise ... their original act is sending a good Governor, and their check is dismissing him". CO 273/18 dated 21 May 1868, quoted in Henry L. Hall, *The Colonial Office* (London: Longmans, 1937), pp. 113–14.
15 Martin Wight, *British Colonial Constitutions 1947* (Oxford: Clarendon Press, 1952), p. 17; Colonial Regulations, op. cit., Colonial Regulations 245 and 194; Miners, op. cit., pp. 97–100; Letters Patent, in Tsang, *Government and Politics*, p. 19; and Kathleen Cheek-Milby, *A Legislature Comes of Age* (Hong Kong: Oxford University Press, 1995), p. 26.
16 Sir Reginald Edward Stubbs, GCMG, born 1876 and entered the Colonial Office as a clerk in 1900. He was sent to Malaya in 1910 to investigate staff salaries. Appointed Colonial Secretary Ceylon in 1913, he became Governor of Hong Kong in 1919, Governor of Jamaica in 1926, and Governor of Ceylon from 1933 to 1937. He died in 1947.
17 Sir Francis Henry May, GCMG, born 1860, educated Harrow and Trinity College, Dublin. He was appointed a Hong Kong cadet in 1881 and became Captain-Superintendent of Police 1893. He was appointed Colonial Secretary in 1902. In 1910 he was appointed Governor of Fiji and returned to Hong Kong as Governor in 1912, surviving an assassination attempt on his arrival. He was the first Hong Kong cadet to become a Governor of Hong Kong. He retired in 1919 and died in 1922.
18 Sir Robert Brown Black, GCMG, OBE, known as Robin, born 1906, educated Edinburgh University, appointed cadet in Malaya in 1930. Posted to Trinidad as Assistant Colonial Secretary in 1939 and returned to Malaya in 1940. POW during the war and became Deputy Chief Secretary, Malaya in 1946. Appointed Colonial Secretary, Hong Kong on 13 February 1952. He later became Governor, Singapore and Governor, Hong Kong, 1958–64. He died in 1999.

19 Sir Cecil Clementi, GCMG, born 1875, educated St Paul's School and Magdalen College, Oxford. He was appointed a Hong Kong cadet in 1899 and became Land Officer and Police Magistrate, New Territories from 1903 to 1906. He was appointed Colonial Secretary, British Guiana 1913 and Colonial Secretary, Ceylon in 1922. He returned to Hong Kong as Governor in 1925 and became Governor of the Straits Settlements in 1930. He retired in 1934 and died in 1947.
20 Miners, op. cit., pp. 43–45 and H. J. Lethbridge, *Hong Kong: Stability and Change* (Hong Kong: Oxford University Press, 1978), pp. 31–51.
21 Sir William Peel, KCMG, KBE, born 1875. He joined the Colonial Service as an Eastern Cadet in 1898 and served in Malaya. He became Colonial Secretary there before being appointed Governor of Hong Kong on 9 May 1930. He retired in 1935 and died in 1945.
22 Sir Andrew Caldecott, GCMG, CBE, born 1884. He joined the Malayan Civil Service in 1907 and wrote the words to the Negeri Sembilan State Anthem. He was Colonial Secretary of the Straits Settlements from 1932 to 1934, Governor of Hong Kong from 1935 to 1937 and then Governor of Ceylon from 1937 to 1944. He was the author of several short stories and had three books published. He died in 1951.
23 Sir Geoffry Alexander Stafford Northcote, KCMG, born London 1881, educated at Balliol College, Oxford. He joined the Colonial Service in 1904 and served in Kenya. He was appointed Chief Secretary, Northern Rhodesia, in 1927 and became Chief Secretary, Gold Coast, in 1930 and Governor, British Guiana, in 1935. He was Governor, Hong Kong, from 1937 to 1941. He died in 1948.
24 Sir Mark Aitchison Young, GCMG, was born in 1886 and was educated at Eton and King's College, Cambridge. He joined the Ceylon Civil Service in 1910 and saw military service during the First World War. He was Colonial Secretary of Sierra Leone from 1928 to 1930 and then became Chief Secretary of Palestine. From 1933 to 1938 he was Governor of Barbados and from 1938 to 1941 was Governor of Tanganyika. He was Governor of Hong Kong from September to December 1941 and spent the remainder of the war as a prisoner of the Japanese. He returned as Governor of Hong Kong in May 1946 and served one more year until May 1947 when he retired. He died in 1974.
25 Miners, op. cit., Chapter 1, pp. 4–27 and pp. 45–53.
26 See Miners, op. cit., pp. 85–9 and Lethbridge, op. cit., Chapter II.
27 Sir Ralph Furse, *Aucupararius* (London: Oxford University Press, 1962), p. 164.
28 For a discussion on the pre-1941 Hong Kong civil service see Miners, op. cit., Chapter 5.
29 Sir Hercules Robinson, GCMG, PC, later 1st Baron Rosmead, was born in 1824. He was educated at Sandhurst and in 1843 embarked upon a military career. In 1848 he joined the Board of Public Works in Ireland and in 1854 went to Montserrat as President of the Council. From 1855 to 1859 he was Lieutenant Governor of St Kitts and was Governor of Hong Kong from 1859 to 1865. In 1865 he became Governor of Ceylon and from 1872 until 1879 was Governor of New South Wales. From 1880 to 1889 he was High

Commissioner of South Africa and was greatly involved in disputes with the Boers. He later returned to South Africa as High Commissioner and died in London in 1897.
30 Lethbridge, op. cit., pp. 31–32 and 37–38; Furse, op. cit., p. 239; and Miners, op. cit., pp. 85–89.
31 Sir Frederick Lugard, GCMG, CB, DSO, PC, later 1st Baron Lugard, was born in India in 1856 and was educated at Rossall School and the Royal Military Academy, Sandhurst. He was commissioned into the army in 1878 and saw active service in Afghanistan, the Sudan, Burma and East Africa. In 1888 he joined the British East Africa Company and from 1890 to 1892 was Administrator of Uganda. For the remainder of that decade he was active in colonial affairs in Africa. From 1900 to 1906 he was High Commissioner of the Protectorate of Northern Nigeria and in 1906 was appointed Governor of Hong Kong. He is remembered for establishing the Kowloon Canton Railway and for founding the University of Hong Kong. He was Governor of Nigeria from 1912 to 1919 and Britain's representative at the League of Nations Permanent Mandates Commission from 1922 to 1936. He died in 1945.
32 Quoted in Lethbridge, op. cit., p. 40.
33 Sir James Haldane Stewart Lockhart, KCMG, born in 1858 and educated at Watson's Academy and Edinburgh University. He was appointed a Hong Kong cadet in 1878. He became Registrar General in 1887, an Executive Council member in 1891 and, Colonial Secretary in addition in 1895. He was appointed Commissioner, Wei Hei Wei, in 1902 and served there until 1920. He died in 1937.
34 Kenneth Myer Arthur Barnett, OBE, ED, was born in 1911 and educated at Cambridge University. He was appointed a Hong Kong cadet in 1934 and served as a District Officer. He was also a Lieutenant in the Hong Kong Volunteer Defence Corps and saw active service during the defence of Hong Kong. He was a prisoner of war during the Japanese occupation. He served in the British Military Administration and as Deputy Colonial Secretary, Chairman of the Urban Council and Deputy Commissioner, New Territories. He became Commissioner for Census and Statistics in 1959 and successfully held the 1961 census, the first in thirty years. He retired in 1969 and worked for the United Nations in census work in Malawi and Bangladesh. He was a renowned Chinese linguist. He died in 1987.
35 Grantham, op. cit., p. 6 and CO 825/42/15, undated typewritten memo by Sydney Caine, January–February 1942.
36 Mills, op. cit., p. 398 and Scott, op. cit., pp. 63–64.
37 Scott, op. cit., pp. 60–65; Lethbridge, op. cit., pp. 104–29 and Elizabeth Sinn, *Power and Charity: A Chinese Merchant Elite in Colonial Hong Kong* (Hong Kong: Hong Kong University Press, 2003).
38 Lethbridge, op. cit., pp. 109–10 and 120–21 and Mills, op. cit., p. 399.
39 Quoted in Lethbridge, op. cit., p. 39.
40 CO 825/10/4, letter from Sir William Peel to Walter Ellis dated 1 December 1930 and minute by Calder dated 24 February 1931.
41 CO 129/523/6, letter from Swire to Colonial Office dated 29 January 1930 and CO 825/42/15, undated typewritten memo by Sydney Caine, January–February 1942.

42 Alexander Grantham, "Hong Kong", *Journal of the Royal Central Asian Society*, Vol. 46, April 1959, p. 121.
43 Steve Tsang, *Governing Hong Kong* (Hong Kong: Hong Kong University Press, 2007), pp. 27–31; Grantham, *Via Ports*, p. 6.
44 Lethbridge, op. cit., p. 38.
45 A. P. Thornton, *Doctrines of Imperialism* (London: John Wiley and Sons, 1965), p. 48.
46 Tsang, *Governing Hong Kong*, p. 84.
47 Sir Ralph Dolignon Furse, KCMG, DSO and Bar, was born in 1887 in London. He entered the Colonial Office in 1910 and served in King Edward's Horse during the First World War. He returned to the Colonial Office and rose to become head of colonial service recruitment. He retired in 1948 and in 1962 published his memoirs, *Acuparius*. He died in 1973.
48 Furse, op. cit., p. 239.
49 Miners, op. cit., p. 38; Parkinson, op. cit., pp. 136–39.
50 Ann M. Burton, "Treasury Control and Colonial Policy in the Late Nineteenth Century", *Public Administration*, Vol. 44 (1966), pp. 169–94.
51 Miners, op. cit., p. 35 and Steve Tsang's interview of MacDougall, 2 August 1979.
52 A. N. Porter and A. J. Stockwell, *British Imperial Policy and Decolonisation, 1938–64, Volume 1, 1938–51* (London: MacMillan Press, 1987), pp. 8–9.
53 George Henry Hall, 1st Viscount Hall, was born in 1881 in Glamorganshire and became a miner at the age of 12. He became an MP in 1922. He served in various minor ministerial posts and was Under-Secretary of State for the Colonies from 1940 to 1942, Under-Secretary of State for Foreign Affairs from 1943 to 1945 and Secretary of State for the Colonies from 1945 to 1946. He was elevated to the peerage in 1946 and served the Labour government until 1951. He died in 1965.
54 James Griffiths, CH, known as "Jim", was born in Wales in 1890. He was educated at Betwys Board School and went to work in the mines at the age of 13. He became a member of the Independent Labour Party and later became President of the Miners Federation of South Wales. He became a Labour MP in 1936 and was elected to the Labour Party's National Executive in 1939. He became Minister of National Insurance in 1945 and one of the ministers involved in the creation of the welfare state. He was Secretary of State for the Colonies from 1950 to 1951 and after the defeat of the Labour Government was Deputy Leader of the Labour Party. He became the first Secretary of State for Wales in 1964 under Harold Wilson and remained an MP until 1970. He died in London in 1975.
55 Philip Cunliffe-Lister, GBE, CH, MC, PC, 1st Earl of Swinton, was born in 1884. He was educated at Winchester College and University College, Oxford. He served in the army during the First World War. He was elected an MP in 1918 and served until his elevation to the House of Lords in 1935. He was President of the Board of Trade from 1922 to 1931 with two short breaks. In 1931 he became Secretary of State for the Colonies under the National Government of Ramsey MacDonald. He then became Secretary of State for Air under Stanley Baldwin, a position he continued to hold

until 1938 after being created Viscount Swinton in 1935. He was Minister of Aviation in the Second World War and also served as Minister under Churchill from 1951 to 1955. He was created Earl of Swinton in 1955 and died in 1972.

56 Miners, op. cit., p. 32; Porter and Stockwell, op. cit., p. 9; and Lord Passfield in a letter to his wife, 15 September 1930, quoted in Miners, op. cit., p. 32.

57 Chan Wai-kwan, *The Making of Hong Kong Society* (Oxford: Clarendon Press, 1991), pp. 221–22; T. C. Cheng, "Chinese Unofficial Members of the Legislative and Executive Councils in Hong Kong up to 1941", *Journal of the Royal Asiatic Society Hong Kong Branch*, Vol. 9 (1969), pp. 7–30.

58 Sir Robert Kotewall, CMG, was born in Hong Kong in 1880 and educated at Central School and Diocesan Boys' School. He joined the Hong Kong government and served until 1916 when he left to go into business and became an honorary adviser to the Chinese government. He was an unofficial Legislative Council member from 1923 to 1936 and an unofficial Executive Council member from 1936 to 1941. He was particularly helpful in assisting the Hong Kong government resolve the 1925 strike and boycott. He played a leading role in the Chinese community during the Japanese occupation, seemingly at the request of the Secretary for Chinese Affairs, but was not admitted back to public life after the return of British administration. He died on 1949.

59 Hong Kong Hansard, address by Stubbs on motion by Colonial Secretary dated 29 January 1920, pp. 3–4 and Miners, op. cit., pp. 64–65 and HKRS 170 1/472 (I), minute by K. M. A. Barnett, Principal Assistant Colonial Secretary, to the Financial Secretary dated 28 November 1947.

60 Mills, op. cit., p. 396.

Chapter 3 The Origins of Policy, 1917–30

1 Tsang, *A Modern History of Hong Kong*, p. 109.

2 *South China Morning Post*, editorial, 29 May 1919.

3 G. B. Endacott, *Government and People in Hong Kong* (Hong Kong: Hong Kong University Press, 1964), pp. 148–58.

4 Adam Gibson, MRCVS. He was born on 2 July 1871 and appointed Colonial Veterinary Surgeon on 9 January 1902. He arrived in Hong Kong on 25 April 1902. He was appointed Head of the Sanitary Department and, by implication also President of the Sanitary Board in addition to his other duties from 18 May 1918 to 16 March 1920. He retired on pension on 26 September 1920.

5 Francis Bulmer Lyon Bowley, born 24 January 1868 at Bristol and educated at Bristol Grammar School. Solicitor, London 1890. He arrived in Hong Kong in 1893 and joined Mr H. L. Dennys and became Crown Solicitor in 1900. He was one of the founders of the Law Society in 1907 and was a member of the Sanitary Board from 1915 to 1920. He died in 1953.

6 Miss Ada Pitts, MBE, was born around 1865 and came to Hong Kong in 1901 as an English missionary. She helped establish a home for Chinese prostitutes. She was also involved in working with *mui tsai* and was instrumental in raising that issue, and the issue of child labour, in Hong Kong.

7   Carl Smith, "The First Child Labour Law in Hong Kong", *Journal of the Royal Asiatic Society*, Hong Kong Branch, Vol. 28 (1988), pp. 46–47.
8   Susanna Hoe, *The Private Life of Old Hong Kong* (Hong Kong: Oxford University Press, 1991), p. 235.
9   Dr Alice Deborah Sebree Hickling, MBE, born in Madagascar in 1876 where her father was a missionary. She was educated at Oxford and the London School of Medicine for Women and at medical school in Glasgow. After two years practising in the UK she came to Hong Kong in 1903 with the London Missionary Society in the Alice Memorial Maternity Hospital as Hong Kong's first lady doctor. She later joined the Tsan Yuk Hospital which, under her guidance, became a teaching hospital. She left the LMS and returned to England in 1909, returning to Hong Kong the following year. She was appointed Acting Medical Officer of Health and became a member of the Sanitary Board. She died in Hong Kong in 1928.
10 Smith, op. cit., pp. 50–1.
11 Dr Ts'o Seen-wan, CBE, was born in Macau in 1868. He was educated in Shanghai and at Cheltenham College, England. He served his articles at two solicitors firms in Cheltenham and London and qualified as a solicitor in England in 1896 and returned to Hong Kong to practice the following year. He was a founder of St Stephen's Boys College in 1903. He was a member of the Po Leung Kuk Committee, of the Tung Wah Advisory Committee and of the District Watch Committee. He was a member of the Sanitary Board from 1918 to 1929. He was appointed Chinese Labour Controller during the 1925 strike and raised the Hong Kong Police Reserve in 1927. He was a JP and an unofficial Legislative Council member from 1929 to 1937. He died in 1953.
12 Chan Kai-ming was born in Hong Kong in 1859 and educated at Diocesan School and Central School. He taught there briefly before becoming an interpreter in the Magistracy. He then became a businessman, was manager of the Opium Farm and became director and chairman of Messrs Gande, Price & Co, wine and spirit merchants and a Director of the Tai Yau Bank. He was a Director of the Po Leung Kuk and Tung Wah and a Vice Chairman of the Chinese Chamber of Commerce and a life member of the University of Hong Kong Court. He was a JP, a member of the Sanitary Board and briefly an unofficial member of the Legislative Council. He died at his home at 16 Caine Road in December 1919 after a long illness.
13 Sir Chaloner Grenville Alabaster, OBE, KC, was born in 1880. He was a barrister who, by 1915, was practising in Hong Kong. He was a member of the Sanitary Board. He was appointed Acting Attorney-General in 1930 and Attorney-General in 1931. He was interned during the Japanese occupation and returned to Britain in 1945. He retired on pension in 1946. He died in 1958.
14 William Chatham, CMG, was born in 1859, educated in Edinburgh Royal High School and trained to be an engineer. He arrived in Hong Kong in 1890 as an Executive Engineer with the Public Works Department and became Director of Public Works in 1901 as well as becoming a member of the Executive and Legislative Councils and Vice-President of the Sanitary

Board. He retired in 1921. A valediction published in the Hong Kong Government Administration Report of 1921 stated that: "The majority of the Public Works of this Colony as they exist today are a standing monument to his energy and foresight."

15 Minutes of Sanitary Board meeting held on 27 May 1919 reported in the *South China Morning Post*, 28 May 1919.

16 Edwin Richard Hallifax, CMG, CBE, was born in 1874 in India and was educated at Blundell's School and Baliol College, Oxford. He came to Hong Kong as a cadet in 1897. He served in various posts including District Officer North before becoming Secretary for Chinese Affairs in 1913, a post he held until his retirement in 1933. He was reputedly a very conservative officer. He died in 1950.

17 CO 129/465, minute dated 17 December 1920, pp. 307–9.

18 CO 131/54, minutes of meeting of the Executive Council dated 24 March 1921, p. 637.

19 Stewart Buckle Carne Ross, OBE, known as Carne, was born in 1875 and obtained a BA degree. He joined the Federated Malay States as a cadet in 1899 and in 1900 was sent to Canton to study Cantonese. He transferred to the Hong Kong service in 1901 and served in a variety of posts, including a spell in the Colonial Office in 1912. He had been District Officer North and during the last seven years of his service was Postmaster General during which he also spent some time in China winding up postal affairs there on behalf of Britain. He had also acted as Secretary for Chinese Affairs and sat on the Executive and Legislative Councils in this capacity. He died in October 1923, probably in the UK, while undergoing an operation. He was regarded as a very capable and efficient officer and appeared to have been well liked by his colleagues. He died in 1923.

20 Dr Charles William McKenny was born in 1885 and qualified as a doctor at Trinity College, Dublin. He arrived in Hong Kong in 1912 and was appointed Medical Officer of Victoria Gaol. He held a variety of government medical posts thereafter, including, several times, Superintendent of the Civil Hospital and Lunatic Asylum.

21 The Rev. Herbert Richmond Wells. An agent of the American Bible Society in China, he joined the London Missionary Society in 1894 and after a few years in the Canton district came to Hong Kong, He was Warden of Morrison Hall at the University of Hong Kong in 1914. He helped revive the Ying Wa College and was active in other parts of Hong Kong public life, not least as Chairman of the New Territories Agricultural Association from 1927 until at least 1938. He was a Cantonese scholar of note and published a primer in the dialect and wrote regular articles in the *South China Morning Post* about Cantonese. He was still resident in Hong Kong in 1945.

22 Sir Shouson Chow was born in Hong Kong in 1861. He was sent by the Chinese imperial government to the US as a young man to study and on his return to China worked in many positions in China. He came to Hong Kong in 1911 and was an adviser to Tung Wah and Po Leung Kuk, was a member of the District Watch Committee and the Sanitary Board. He was an unofficial Legislative Council member from 1921 to 1931. He was very helpful in

23 Hoe, op. cit., p. 235.
24 The Officer Administering the Government or OAG was the title of the person acting as Governor while the Governor was absent from the colony. He was also referred to as "His Excellency".
25 Sir Claud Severn, KBE, CMG, was born in 1869 and educated at Selwyn College, Cambridge. He joined the Foreign Office in 1890 and in 1894 was appointed Private Secretary to the Governor of the Straits Settlements. He remained in Malaya for the next 17 years until he was appointed Hong Kong's Colonial Secretary in 1912. He remained in post until his retirement in 1925. He died in Oxford, UK, in 1933.
26 Hong Kong Hansard, 28 September 1922, pp. 85 and 94.
27 See Hong Kong Administrative Report, 1923, Annex C 14–15.
28 Report on the Census of the Colony, 1921, p. 159, section 6, second paragraph.
29 Census Report, 1921, Legislative Council Sessional Papers, 1921.
30 Hong Kong Hansard, 18 July 1921, address by Attorney General, p. 88.
31 CO 129/468, Attorney General's Report on the Rents Ordinance dated 22 July 1921, p. 440.
32 Hong Kong Hansard, 18 July 1921, address by Attorney General, p. 86 and 5 February 1920, p. 13.
33 CO 129/468, Attorney General's Report on the Rents Ordinance dated 22 July 1921, p. 440.
34 Miners, op. cit., p. 10.
35 Sir Paul Chater, CMG, an Armenian, was born in Calcutta in 1846 and came to Hong Kong at the age of 16 and worked in a bank before moving onto a more general business career, in particular founding Hong Kong Land with Jardines and helped found Hongkong Electric. He was arguably the most successful and influential businessman in the Hong Kong of his day. He became an Executive Council member in 1896 and remained so until his death in 1926.
36 CO 131/460, minutes of Executive Council meeting, 30 June 1921.
37 Lau Chu-pak was born in Hong Kong in 1866 and was educated at the Central School. He was a clerk at the Hong Kong Observatory. He later went into business and was a founding member of the Chinese Merchants' Bureau, the forerunner of the Chinese Chamber of Commerce of which he became Chairman. He was Chairman of the Po Leung Kuk and Tung Wah and a member of the District Watch Committee and the Sanitary Board. He was an unofficial Legislative Council member from 1913 until his death in Hong Kong in 1922.
38 Hong Kong Hansard, 23 June 1921, p. 62.
39 CO 131/460, minutes of Executive Council meeting, 30 June 1921.
40 P. Ramanathan, *Riots and Martial law in Ceylon, 1915* (London: unknown publisher, 1916, republished New Delhi: Asian Educational Services, 2003); Online Asia Times, 25 August 2001 at http://www.atimes.com/ind-pak/

helping to resolve the 1925 strike and boycott and was reputedly knighted for these services. He became the first Chinese member of the Executive Council in 1926 and served until 1936. He died in Hong Kong in 1959.

CH25Df02.html; P. T. M. Fernando, The British Raj and the 1915 Communal Riots in Ceylon, in *Modern Asia Studies* Vol. 3, No. 3 (Cambridge: Cambridge University Press, 1969), pp. 245–55; A. P. Kannangara, "The Riots of 1915 in Sri Lanka: A Study in the Roots of Communal Violence", *Past and Present* 102(1), pp. 130–64.
41 Literally, "little younger sister" but its real connotation would not have been lost on anyone familiar with the system.
42 Miners, op. cit., pp. 154–57.
43 CO 129/449, Governor, Hong Kong, to Secretary of State dated 9 August 1918 and minute dated 15 October 1918, CO 129/466, minute dated 6 April 1920 and Miners, op. cit., pp. 158–9.
44 Lieutenant Commander and Mrs H. L. Haslewood, *Child Slavery in Hong Kong: The Mui Tsai System* (London: Sheldon Press, 1930), p. 22 and Hoe, op. cit., pp. 237–38.
45 Letter published in Hong Kong English language press, 4 November 1919, printed in Haslewood, op. cit., p. 22.
46 The Anti-Slavery Society can trace its origins back to 1787. It claims to have played an important part in the abolition of slavery and the slave trade. Many of its early supporters came from the English non-conformist churches. It also claims to have been instrumental in the abolition of the *mui tsai* system in Hong Kong and Singapore. It now exists under the name *Anti-Slavery International.*
47 Hoe, op. cit., pp. 240–41.
48 CO 129/468, Stubbs to Secretary of State, despatch dated 17 October 1921; minute from Secretary for Chinese Affairs to Colonial Secretary dated 27 Jul 1921, p. 426 and Miners, op. cit., pp. 160–61.
49 Carl Smith, op. cit., pp. 91–113. The two Legislative Council members were Ho Fook, brother of Sir Robert Hotung, and Lau Chu-pak, compradore of A. S. Watson & Co.
50 Chau Siu-kai, educated Queen's College, manager Tung Wah, 1889, Chairman Tung Wah 1903 and 1914, Director Po Leung Kuk 1894 and 1902, member Legislative Council 1923–24, member District Watch Committee.
51 Chan Wai-kwan, op. cit., pp. 221–22 and Lethbridge, op. cit., p. 118.
52 CO 129/468, 27 July 1921, p. 426.
53 Smith, op. cit., pp. 99–100.
54 Colonel Josiah Wedgwood, born 1872, became an MP in 1906, first as a Liberal and then as a member of the Independent Labour Party. He served in the first Labour government in 1924 and was an MP until 1943 when he was elevated to the House of Lords. He died in 1943.
55 CO 129/478, pp. 297 and 315 and UK Hansard, House of Commons, 21 March 1922. Churchill was Secretary of State for the Colonies from February 1921 to October 1922.
56 CO 129/478, pp. 312–13 and Miners, op. cit., p. 164.
57 Legislative Council Sessional Papers, 1929, pp. 203–4.
58 Miners, op. cit., pp. 165–66.

59 Sir Gilbert E. A. Grindle, KCMG, Head of Eastern Department, Colonial Office. He became Assistant and then Deputy Permanent Under-Secretary of State for the Colonies in the 1920s.
60 CO129/478, pp. 764–66, letter to Sir Arthur Grindle, dated 16 September 1922 and 1 October 1922.
61 Hong Kong Hansard, 28 December 1922.
62 The bill was publicly supported by local trade unions hoping the unofficials would oppose it and allow them to claim a propaganda victory over the elite. The unofficials did not wish to allow them to do so and decided in consequence not to oppose the bill. See Miners, op. cit., pp. 166–67.
63 Miners, op. cit., pp. 167–68.
64 CO 129/514/2, letter and editorial from the *Manchester Guardian* dated 16 January 1929 reproduced as a pamphlet with a copy on this file, sent to the Colonial Office by Haslewood.
65 Legislative Council Sessional Papers 1929, p. 233.
66 CO 129/514/2, letter from Amery to Clementi, 20 April 1929 and Legislative Council Sessional Papers 1929, p. 249.
67 CO 129/522/6, Governor, Hong Kong to Secretary of State, dated 18 December 1929 and 21 January 1930.
68 Dr Sir Drummond Shiels, MC, born 1881 in Edinburgh and educated to primary level. He became a photographer and, after military service in the First World War, studied at Edinburgh University and became a medical doctor in 1924. He was MP for Edinburgh East from 1924 to 1931 and served as Under-Secretary of State for India in 1929 and then as Under-Secretary of State for the Colonies. He remained active in public life until his death in 1953. His biographer claimed he had an "abrasive and tough-minded manner, an urbane sense of humour and a conceit with which he regarded himself and his opinions" (see *Oxford Dictionary of National Biography* [Oxford: Oxford University Press], 2004).
69 Miners, op. cit., p. 174.
70 Lee and Petter, op. cit., Chapter 1.

Chapter 4 Britain's Influence over Hong Kong's Policy, 1924–41

1 G. B. Endacott, *A History of Hong Kong* (Hong Kong: Oxford University Press, 1973), p. 289.
2 T 160/1068/1, minute from S. D. Waley, British Treasury, to Sir F. W. Leith-Ross, dated 25 July 1930 and note by M. J. Breen, Acting Colonial Treasurer, dated 27 July 1929 in Colonial Office booklet, *Correspondence Relating to the Currency Position in Hong Kong 1929–1930.*
3 Report of the Currency Commission, London, HMSO, 10 May 1931, para. 10 and 132.
4 Michael James Breen was born in 1884 and educated at Royal University, Ireland. He arrived in Hong Kong as a cadet in 1907. He served as Assistant Postmaster General, Assistant District Officer and Assistant Colonial Secretary before being seconded for military service between 1916 and 1919. On his return to Hong Kong he served as Postmaster General, Chairman of the Retrenchment Commission and acted several times as

Colonial Treasurer. He was also Chairman of the Economic Commission of 1935. He retired in 1936.
5   T 160/1068/1, Note by M. J. Breen, Acting Colonial Treasurer, dated 27 July and 4 November 1929 in Colonial Office booklet, *Correspondence Relating to the Currency Position in Hong Kong 1929–1930*.
6   Ibid., Note by M. J. Breen, Acting Colonial Treasurer, dated 24 October 1929.
7   Tony Latter, "Hong Kong's Exchange Rate Regimes in the Twentieth Century: The Story of Three Regime Changes", HKMIR Working Paper No. 17/2004, September 2004, p. 8.
8   T 160/1068/1, letter from A. H. Ferguson, Manager, Chartered Bank to Colonial Treasurer dated 14 February 1930 in Colonial Office booklet, *Correspondence Relating to the Currency Position in Hong Kong 1929–1930*.
9   Hong Kong Legislative Council Sessional Papers, Report of the Currency Committee, 14 July 1930.
10 CO 323/1120/11, minutes of the first meeting of the Colonial Office Currency Committee, 5 January 1931.
11 T 160 1068 2, Report of Hong Kong Currency Commission, HMSO, 10 May 1931, para. 109, p. 29 and para. 83, pp. 129–31.
12 Ibid., minute to Waley from colleague who attended Currency Committee meeting, dated 25 July 1931 and minute from Waley to Sir F. W. Leith-Ross dated 12 November 1931.
13 CO 323/1165/11, despatch from Governor, Hong Kong to Secretary of State dated 22 April 1932.
14 Ibid., Conclusions reached by the Currency Committee at its meeting held on 14 July 1932.
15 T 160/1068/2, despatch from Secretary of State to Governor, Hong Kong, dated 11 February 1933 and the Governor's reply, dated 27 April 1933.
16 T 160/1068/3, as recorded in minutes of Currency Committee meeting held on 16 February 1934.
17 CO 323/1249/9, letter from Vernon, Colonial Office to Kershaw, Bank of England, dated 1 October 1934, letter from Ezechiel, Crown Agents to Clauson, Colonial Office, dated 4 September 1934 and letter from Kershaw, Bank of England to Vernon, Colonial Office, dated 10 October 1934.
18 Hong Kong Hansard, statement by Governor, Sir William Peel, 18 October 1934, p. 197.
19 *South China Morning Post*, editorial, 24 October 1934.
20 CO 323/1249/9, draft minutes of Currency Committee meeting held on 26 October 1934.
21 T 160/1068/3, minute to Sir F. Philips from unknown writer likely to have been written in early to mid-December 1934.
22 CO 323/1249/9, telegram from Secretary of State to Governor, Hong Kong, dated 21 December 1934.
23 CO 323/1312/11, minute from Caine dated 26 April 1935 and telegram from Governor, Hong Kong to Secretary of State, dated 26 April 1935.
24 *South China Morning Post*, 26 April 1935 and 17 April 1935.
25 CO 323/1312/11, telegram from Governor, Hong Kong to Secretary of State, dated 26 April 1935.

26 T 160/1068/4, minutes of Currency Committee meeting held on 2 May 1935 and 10 May 1935.
27 CO 323/1312/11, telegram from OAG, Hong Kong to Secretary of State, dated 26 May 1935, telegram from OAG, Hong Kong, to Secretary of State, dated 19 July 1935, report from Young dated 23 July 1935 and report from Young dated 23 July 1935.
28 Ibid., telegram from OAG, Hong Kong, to Secretary of State, dated 30 July 1935.
29 Ibid., note from M(alcolm) M(acDonald) (Secretary of State) dated 29 October 1935.
30 Ibid., telegram from Secretary of State to OAG, Hong Kong, dated 2 November 1935 and telegram from OAG, Hong Kong to Secretary of State, dated 4 November 1935.
31 Ibid., minute from Caine dated 7 November 1935 and minute from Vernon dated 8 November 1935.
32 Ibid., telegram from OAG, Hong Kong to Secretary of State, dated 7 November 1935 and 8 November 1935.
33 *South China Morning Post*, 11 November 1935.
34 CO 323/1312/11, letter from Chancellor of the Exchequer Neville Chamberlain, dated 15 November 1935.
35 T 160/1069/7, telegram from Secretary of State to OAG, Hong Kong, dated 18 November 1935.
36 Latter, op. cit, p. 15.
37 Hong Kong Hansard, 5 December 1935, pp. 249–52 and T 160/1069/8, note for Governor Caldecott prepared by Young in December 1935, attached to letter to Leith-Ross from Young dated 17 December 1935.
38 *South China Morning Post*, editorial, 7 December 1935.
39 CO 323/1249/9, letter from Ezechiel, Crown Agents to Clauson, Colonial Office dated 4 September 1934.
40 Hansard, House of Commons, speech by Dr Shiels, 11 May 1931.
41 Extract from *Hong Kong Weekly Press*, 2 May 1930 in CO 129/522/6.
42 CO 129/522/6, *Report by the Governor of Hong Kong on the Mui Tsai Question*, dated 25 June 1930.
43 *South China Morning Post*, 22 October 1930, Report of Annual General Meeting of the Anti Mui Tsai Society held on 20 October 1930.
44 CO 129/532/4, letter from Anti-Slavery Society to Secretary of State, dated 12 January 1931.
45 CO 129/522/6, private letter from Peel to Secretary of State, dated 2 July 1930.
46 CO 129/532/3, report of answer given by Lord Passfield to the Archbishop of Canterbury in the House of Lords on 22 July 1931.
47 Ibid., examined in minute dated 15 June 1932.
48 Miners, op. cit, pp. 178–79.
49 CO 129/546/9, letter from Governor Hong Kong to Secretary of State dated 15 October 1934 and Hong Kong Legislative Council Sessional Papers, 1935, p. 200.
50 CO 129/522/6, extract from the *Hong Kong Daily Press* dated 2 May 1930.

51 Hong Kong Legislative Council Sessional Papers, 1935, pp. 215–18.
52 CO 825/20/9, letter from the Anti-Slavery Society to the Secretary of State dated 11 February 1936.
53 Ibid., minute dated 12 February 1936.
54 CO 825/20/12, Despatch from Governor Hong Kong to Secretary of State dated 18 March 1936.
55 Hong Kong Hansard, 27 May 1936, pp. 117–31.
56 Sudan was under the Foreign Office and not the Colonial Office.
57 Edith Picton-Turbervill, OBE, was born in 1872. She served as a YWCA mission worker in India and was a member of the Church League for Women's Suffrage. She stood unsuccessfully as a Labour Party candidate in 1924 for Stroud. She was elected Labour MP for The Wrekin in 1929 and served until 1931. She was described as "robust, deeply religious and determinedly single, she epitomised the world of reformist feminism" (see Pedersen, op. cit., p. 192). She died in 1960.
58 Miners, op. cit., p. 181. For an analysis of the impact of women's reformist groups on the Colonial Office's handling of the *mui tsai* issue, see Pedersen, op. cit., pp. 161–202.
59 CO 825/21/2, evidence before the Commission dated 27 March 1936.
60 The British Commonwealth League was founded in 1925 to secure equality of liberties, status, and opportunities between men and women in the British Commonwealth of Nations. See Susan Pedersen, "The Maternalist Moment in British Colonial Policy: The Controversy over 'Child Slavery' in Hong Kong 1917–1941", *Past & Present*, No. 171 (May 2001), p. 179.
61 Norman Lockhart Smith, CMG, born 1887, BA (Oxon). He was appointed a Hong Kong cadet in 1910 and became a "Passed Cadet" in 1912. He served in postings to the District Office, Colonial Secretariat, the Secretariat for Chinese Affairs and as Postmaster General. He saw military service from 1916 to 1919 and returned to the Hong Kong government. He served as Superintendent, Imports and Exports, from 1921 to 1923, District Officer South 1923, Head, Sanitary Department 1924 to 1927, Postmaster General 1928 to 1929, Colonial Secretariat, 1929 to 1932, Director of Education 1933 to 1934, Secretary of Chinese Affairs 1934 to 1935, Colonial Secretary 1936 to 1941. He was also Officer Administering the Government for periods during 1935, 1937 and 1940. He retired from the Hong Kong government on the day before the Japanese invasion and had an eventful return trip to Britain. He became the first Head of the Hong Kong Planning Unit in London from 1943 to 1944 (see Chapter 3). He died in 1968.
62 CO 825/22/8, minute from Cowell dated 17 March 1937. Sir George Maxwell was a continuous thorn in the side of the Colonial Office. Cowell was aware that, "it was a trait of his [Maxwell's] character that he does not readily forgive any contravention of his own opinions" and that "from experience of Sir George Maxwell's methods, I should advocate the greatest caution in dealing with him".
63 CO 825/21/5, *Summary of the Report on Mui Tsai*, undated, pp. 1–7.
64 CO 825/22/8, minute dated 15 March 1937 and CO 825/21/5, minutes dated 1 and 2 December 1936.

65 Ibid., letter from Secretary of State to Governors of Hong Kong and Straits Settlements dated 24 March 1937 and despatch from Secretary of State to Governors of Hong Kong and Straits Settlement dated 25 March 1937.
66 CO 825/22/9, despatch from OAG, Hong Kong to Secretary of State dated 14 July 1937, OAG, to Secretary of State dated 30 September 1937 and minute by Gent dated 9 September 1937.
67 CO 882/16 dated 2 June 1937. These were the types of cases that had figured in a letter sent to the Colonial Office by a Mrs G. H. Forster that summer setting out, with great pathos, the plight of young girls forced into prostitution in Hong Kong whom she had met in the early 1930s.
68 Roland Arthur Charles North, CMG, BA (Oxon), born in 1889 and appointed cadet, Hong Kong in 1912. He served his entire career as a Hong Kong cadet although during his early career he had a nine-month secondment to the Hongkong and Shanghai Bank in 1918–19, a one-year secondment to Western Samoa in 1921–22 and in 1922–23 spent four months in Japan learning Japanese. He was promoted to Cadet Officer Class I only in 1935. In 1936 he became Secretary for Chinese Affairs and acted during other people's absences as Colonial Secretary and, for a brief period, as Officer Administering the Government. He remained as Secretary for Chinese Affairs until 1941. He was interned during the Japanese occupation and retired in 1946.
69 CO 825/22/10, letter from Northcote to Gent dated 26 November 1937 and letter from Gent to Northcote dated 26 January 1938.
70 CO 825/24/9, minute from Cowell dated 20 April 1938 and minute from Gent dated 20 April 1938.
71 CO 882/16, Northcote to Secretary of State dated 4 July 1938.
72 Sir M. K. Lo, CBE, known as M. K., was born in Hong Kong in 1893. In 1915, he qualified as a solicitor in England and returned to Hong Kong to practise. He became an unofficial JP in 1921 and a member of the District Watch Committee in 1932. He was a member of the Sanitary Board and Urban Council from 1932 to 1936, an unofficial Legislative Council Member from 1935 to 1941 and from 1946 to 1950 and an unofficial Executive Council Member from 1946 to 1958. He died suddenly in 1959.
73 Hong Kong Hansard, Legislative Council, 12 May 1938, p. 32.
74 CO 825/25/4 despatch from Governor, Hong Kong to Secretary of State dated 25 February 1939 and CO 825/30/4, despatch from Governor, Hong Kong to Secretary of State dated 31 May 1941.
75 There is some evidence that the practice continued in parts of the New Territories into the 1950s. See James L. Watson, "Transactions in People: The Chinese Labour Market in Slaves", in James L. Watson, *Asian and African Systems of Slavery* (Oxford: Blackwell, 1980), pp. 242 and 246.
76 Hong Kong Hansard, 3 December 1969, p. 177.
77 Hong Kong Hansard, address by the Colonial Treasurer, 25 May 1917, pp. 41–42.
78 Report of the Inter-Departmental Committee on Income Tax in the Colonies not possessing Responsible Government, Cmd 1788, 1922, para. 7, p. 5.

79. HKRS 41-1-2769 (1), undated minute from Eric Pudney reporting on his visit to the Colonial Office in December 1946 and January 1947. There appears to be no contemporary record of the Committee's suggestions being sent to Hong Kong, or of Hong Kong's response.
80. Miners, op. cit., p. 113.
81. HKRS 41-1-2769 (1), op. cit.
82. Hong Kong Hansard, address by Governor Northcote, 13 October 1938, p. 116.
83. Hong Kong Legislative Council Sessional Papers 1939, Report of Taxation Committee chaired by Financial Secretary Sidney Caine, 5 April 1939.
84. A full or normal income tax meant a tax assessed on an individual's whole income from all sources.
85. Taxation Committee Report, 1940 in Legislative Council Sessional Papers, 1940, p. 100.
86. Michael Littlewood, *Taxation Without Representation* (Hong Kong: Hong Kong University Press, 2010), pp. 33–36; Hong Kong Hansard, 9 and 16 November 1939.
87. Hong Kong Hansard, 9 and 16 November 1939 with the unofficials' views, in pp. 163–80 and 200–3; and address by the Governor at p. 228.
88. Hong Kong Legislative Council Sessional Papers 1940, Report of War Revenue Committee chaired by Attorney-General C. G. Alabaster, 14 February 1940; Hong Kong Hansard, 14 March 1940, pp. 22–31; 25 April 1940, p. 66; 19 June 1941, pp. 140–44 and 26 June 1941, pp. 152–60.
89. Littlewood, op. cit., p. 26.
90. CO 859/112/5, address to Social Service Centre of the Churches on 28 March 1940; CO 967/70, letter from Northcote to Lord Moyne dated 9 June 1940 and *South China Morning Post*, 2 and 5 September 1941.
91. HKRS 41 1/802, letter from John Fleming to Pudney, 21 October 1946.
92. CO 129/536/1, minute from Caine dated 7 November 1931.
93. CO 129/574/11, extract from letter from Caine to Clauson, Colonial Office, dated 21 September 1938 and CO 129/576/6, letter from Governor, Hong Kong to Secretary of State for the Colonies dated 2 February 1939.
94. Hong Kong Hansard, debate on the War Revenue Bill, address by M. K. Lo, 14 March 1940, p. 29 and CO 129/582/7, minute from Caine dated 30 January 1940.
95. CO 129/582/7, minute by Gent dated 2 November 1939.
96. Hong Kong Hansard, proceedings of the Finance Committee, 25 July 1940, pp. 112–20. M. K. Lo pointed out (p. 113) that "the tax-payers of this Colony are being made to pay for the evacuation of a very small and selected section of the community ... leaving some 99.9% of the population uncared for and unprotected when an emergency does come". See also Endacott, *Hong Kong Eclipse*, p. 15.
97. HKRS 170 1/472 (I), despatch from Governor, Hong Kong, to Secretary of State dated 12 November 1946.

Chapter 5 Autonomy and the Threat to Sovereignty

1. CO 825/42/15, minute by Sidney Caine dated 13 February 1942.
2. Steve Tsang, *A Modern History of Hong Kong*, p. 124; Andrew Whitfield, *Hong Kong, Empire and the Anglo-American Alliance at War, 1941–1945* (Basingstoke and New York: Palgrave, 2001), p. 63; Parkinson, op. cit., p. 87.
3. Ronald Owen, (R.O.), Hall, MC and Bar, Anglican Bishop of Hong Kong, was born in England in 1895 and educated at Bromsgrove School. He was commissioned into the army in the First World War, saw much active service as a staff officer and was twice decorated for gallantry. He attended Brasenose College, Oxford and afterwards worked in China and Newcastle, England as a priest. He was ordained Bishop of Hong Kong in 1932 and served until retirement in 1966. He was an active and energetic churchman and widely respected for his social service activities. He died in England in 1975. See David M. Paton, *R.O.: The Life and Times of Bishop Ronald Hall, The Bishop of Hong Kong* (Hong Kong: Diocese of Hong Kong and Macau, 1985); Philip Snow, *The Fall of Hong Kong* (New Haven and London: Yale University Press, 2005), pp. 19–20; Grantham, op. cit., p. 100.
4. Cadets on recruitment in Britain spent a year on a Colonial Administrative Service course at Oxford or Cambridge before they were posted to a colony. See Charles Jeffries, *The Colonial Empire and Its Civil Service* (Cambridge: Cambridge University Press, 1938), p. 135.
5. CO 825/42/15, note left by Bishop Hall dated 16 January 1942. He also saw the Secretary of State.
6. CO 825/42/15, undated typewritten memo by Sidney Caine, January–February 1942 and minute by Sidney Caine dated 13 February 1942; CO 825/35/4, minutes of meeting held on 21 April 1942.
7. CO 967/80, memo dated 1 September 1942.
8. Sir William Battershill, KCMG, CMG, born 1896, educated King's School, Worcester, military service, 1914–19, cadet, Ceylon 1920, Assistant Colonial Secretary, 1925; Jamaica, 1928; Colonial Secretary, Cyprus, 1935; Chief Secretary, Palestine, 1937; Governor, Cyprus, 1939; Assistant Under-Secretary of State for the Colonies, 1941, Deputy Undersecretary of State for the Colonies, 1942; Governor, Trinidad and Tobago, 1945–49.
9. Colonel W. L. Rolleston, CMG, OBE, born 1905, educated Winchester and Royal Military Academy Woolwich. He saw military service in the King's African Rifles from 1930 to 1936 and then served in the Colonial Office from 1940 and in Malaya from 1946 and in Tanganyika from 1950 to 1959.
10. CO 967/80, Battershill Report, para. 41, 44, 48–49 and 50–51 and minute from Sir Ralph Furse dated 15 December 1942. Some of the reporting requirements under Colonial Regulations were relaxed during the war to ease the workloads of colonial governments and to give colonial Governors greater scope for taking action on their own without prior reference to the Secretary of State. See Parkinson, op. cit., p. 86.
11. David Mercer MacDougall, CMG, born 1904, educated St Andrews' University, appointed, Hong Kong cadet in 1928, seconded to the Colonial Office, 1937–39; Secretary, Hong Kong Department of Information and

Secretary, Far Eastern Bureau, British Ministry of Information, 1939, escaped Hong Kong, December 1941, seconded British Embassy, Washington, DC 1942–44, Head Hong Kong Planning Unit September 1944, Chief Civilian Affairs Officer, British Military Administration, September 1945, Colonial Secretary, Hong Kong, 1946–49, retired 1949. He died in 1991.

12 *The Times*, 31 July and 1 August 1942, copies contained in CO 825/42/15 and CO 825/42/15, minute on file dated 26 August 1942. Snow claims MacDougall was the author. See Snow, op. cit., p. 406, n216.

13 CO 825/35/4, note from MacDougall dated March 1942 and minute by Gent dated 1 July 1942; minutes by Gent dated 1 July 1942 and 29 June 1942; and minute from Lord Cranbourne dated 14 July 1942.

14 Quotation from Cranbourne's statement at the meeting contained in Whitfield, op. cit., p. 81.

15 Quoted in Lee and Petter, op. cit., p. 135. The Atlantic Charter is discussed in detail in pp. 117–43.

16 Whitfield, op. cit., pp. 88–99. See also Chan Lau Kit-ching, The Hong Kong Question during the Pacific War (1941–45), *The Journal of Imperial and Commonwealth History* Vol. II (October 1973), No. 1.

17 Rt Hon Oliver Frederick George Stanley, MC, was born in 1896 and educated at Eton and Oxford. He was Parliamentary Under-Secretary of State for the Home Office, 1931–32, Ministry of Transport, 1933–34, Ministry of Labour 1934–35, President of Board of Education, 1935–37; President of the Board of Trade, 1937–40, Secretary of State for War, 1940, Secretary of State for the Colonies, 1942–45.

18 CO 825/42/15, letter from Paskin to Ashley Clarke, Foreign Office dated 27 August 1943 and Whitfield, op. cit., pp. 73 and 106.

19 F. S. V. Donnisson, *British Military Administration in the Far East* (London: Her Majesty's Stationery Office, 1956), pp. 139 and 145.

20 CO 825/35/26, minute from Gent dated 11 June 1943 and memo dated 19 June 1943; letter from Col French, War Office to Paskin, Colonial Office dated 10 August 1943; and minute from Gent dated 15 September 1943.

21 Donnisson, op. cit., pp. 135 and 144.

22 CO 825/35/26, from Gent, Colonial Office to French, War Office dated 25 June 1943; letter from Paskin, Colonial Office to Wilcox, Treasury dated 16 July 1943; Wilcox's reply dated 21 July 1943.

23 Ibid., letter from Ward, Foreign Office to Paskin dated 4 August 1943.

24 Donnisson, op. cit., p. 146. See also Chan Lau, op. cit.

25 CO 825/35/26, letter from J. G. Ward, Foreign Office to Paskin, Colonial Office dated 4 August 1943; letter from William Hayter in Washington to J. G. Ward of the Foreign Office dated 10 September 1943; and minute from Paskin dated 10 August 1943.

26 CO 825/35/26, paper by Gent, *Future Status of Hong Kong*, dated 21 July 1943; letter from Paskin to Ashley Clarke, Foreign Office dated 27 August 1943; letter from Young, Foreign Office to Paskin dated 5 September 1943 and minute from Monson dated 10 September 1943. For a full account of the Colonial Office's inability to call this meeting see Whitfield, op. cit., pp. 111–13.

27 Donnisson, op. cit., p. 146.
28 CO 865/13, minutes from Gent dated 3 December 1943 and 29 September 1943.
29 Smith had left Hong Kong on 7 December 1941, the eve of the Japanese attack. He had an eventful journey home. His ship was bombed to no ill effect en route to Singapore. At the end of December he left Singapore for Australia where he was delayed for many weeks. His ship was then torpedoed, possibly when off Hawaii, and he ended up in the US where he was stranded in New York for two weeks. He eventually arrived home via Halifax in Canada and related his story to Caine when he visited him in the Colonial Office in June 1942. See Caine's diary housed in the London School of Economics library.
30 CO 865/13, letter from Colonial Office to Foreign Office of August 1943.
31 Joseph Patrick Fehily, OBE, MB, BCH, BAO, FACS, DPH, born 1892, Medical Officer, Medical Department, Hong Kong 1924, worked in Port Health, interned 1941, released January 1942, left Hong Kong October 1942, Malayan Planning Unit 1943, HKPU 1944, Deputy Director of Medical Services, Hong Kong, September 1945–46, Chairman Urban Council 1946, Legislative Council Member. Retired 1951. He had been recruited initially into the Malayan Planning Unit but was later transferred to the HKPU (CO 865/13, minute from Wodeman to Paskin dated 23 September 1943).
32 Harold Stuart Rouse, Engineer, born 1888, appointed Land Surveyor Hong Kong government 1912, Assistant Engineer Drainage Office 1913, General Works Office 1915 Engineer-in-Charge, 1921–31, Roads Office, 1931–34, Head Drainage Office 1934–37, Executive Engineer i/c Drainage Office 1937–38, retired December 1939.
33 CO 865/13, minute from Smith dated 14 October 1943.
34 Dr Thomas Walter Ware, MD, ChB, DPH, born 1890, appointed Medical Officer in the Hong Kong government 1927.
35 Walter Morris Thomson, born 1905, appointed Hong Kong cadet 1929, Secretariat of Chinese Affairs, Colonial Secretariat, Import and Export Department, 1935–41, departed on leave on 10 September 1941.
36 Patrick Cardinall Mason Sedgwick, CMG, born England 1911, educated at Brasenose College, Oxford and Queen's College, Cambridge. Appointed Hong Kong cadet in 1935, from 1941 to 1946 he served in Malaya, Chungking, the Hong Kong Planning Unit and the British Military Administration. He was latterly Commissioner of Labour and Hong Kong Commissioner in London before retiring in 1970. He died in 1985.
37 Tsang, *Democracy Shelved*, pp. 191–92.
38 CO 825/39, minute from Sedgwick, HKPU, to Miss Alice Marjorie Rushton, Colonial Office, dated 9 March 1945. The former and serving Hong Kong government officers were MacDougall, W. M. Thomson, Sedgwick, Davies, Rouse, Forbes, Morris, Symons, Hazelrigg, Stokes, Fehily, Ware, Brewer and Goldsmith.
39 CO 825/35/27, minute from Paskin dated November 1943 and CO 129/591/8, minute from Wodeman dated 17 March 1944.

40 All draft directives from which quotations are taken are to be found in CO 129/591/8.
41 CO 865/12, minute from Secretary of State dated 8 October 1945; minute from Miss Rushton dated 10 April 1946; letter to Sir Mark Young dated 13 April 1946 and his reply dated 14 April 1946; and minute from Wodeman dated 21 September 1945.
42 CO 129/594/6, letter from MacDougall to Gater dated 5 December 1945.
43 If Hong Kong had been liberated as the result not of an operation but, for example, because of a general Japanese surrender, then the US would not have been responsible for Hong Kong's administration and Britain would not have been able, as Snow (op. cit., p. 237) described it, to "piggy back" back to Hong Kong under the Americans. They would have had to make other arrangements. See Endacott, *Eclipse*, pp. 154–56.
44 Sir Arthur Morse, KBE, born Ireland 1892, educated Foyle College, Londonderry, joined London Office, Hongkong and Shanghai Bank 1912, posted Hong Kong 1915 and served also in Tientsin and Shanghai. Served in Head Office, Hong Kong from 1929 under the tutelage of Chief Manager Sir Vandeleur Grayburn. Sent to London Office 1940 and, through circumstances, became manager of London Office and Chairman, London Consultative Committee. He kept the Hongkong and Shanghai Bank going during the war years and provided financial support to Hong Kong for reconstruction and became Chief Manager. It was reckoned that he "knew little about technical banking, but banking is both an art and a science, and in the former he excelled". Also involved in various charitable and philanthropic causes. He retired to London in 1953 and died in 1967 (source: *Oxford Dictionary of National Biography* [Oxford: Oxford University Press, 2004]).
45 George Warren Swire, born London 1883, educated Eton and Weimar, became a partner in the family firm of John Swire & Sons 1904. Saw military service in the First World War and served in control of shipping. Assumed full management responsibility for London HQ in 1918 and was chairman of John Swire & Sons 1927–46. He held the firm together during turbulent times in China in the 1920s and 1930s and saw the role of the firm was to serve China's national interests as well as Britain's. He was "an active member of the China Association, a frequent contributor to China discussions at the Royal Institute of International Affairs, and a compulsive writer of strong letters to prime ministers and lesser men". Despite having a difficult manner, he was widely respected (source: *Oxford Dictionary of National Biography* [Oxford: Oxford University Press, 2004]).
46 The China Association was a long-established London-based organisation of British businessmen with links to Hong Kong. It had very close links with the Hong Kong General Chamber of Commerce. During the war, the views it expressed were similar to the views that British unofficials in Hong Kong might have voiced. In promoting the type of constitutional reform that they did they could be said to have been acting as a proxy for the British unofficials.

47 CO 129/592/8, letter from China Association to Colonial Office dated 22 January 1945 and minute from Miss Rushton dated 27 February 1945.
48 Thomas Maynard Hazelrigg, CBE, MC, was born in 1882. He served as a Captain in the Royal Army Service Corps during the First World War and was awarded the Military Cross. He came to Hong Kong in 1920 as Assistant Crown Solicitor and subsequently served as Land Officer, Treasury Solicitor, Registrar of the Supreme Court, Police Magistrate and Crown Solicitor. He was also Honorary Secretary and then a Director of the Society for the Protection of Children. He retired from Hong Kong government service in 1937. He joined the Hong Kong Planning Unit in 1944 or 1945 and came back to Hong Kong after the Liberation and continued in government service until finally retiring again in 1947. He died in 1961.
49 CO 537/1650, minutes of meeting held on 1 May 1945; HKPU paper dated 26 June 1945; notes of meeting dated 1 August 1945; and note from J. R. Jones. He was a former secretary of the Shanghai Municipal Council and an adviser to the China Association. He later became the Hongkong and Shanghai Bank's legal officer.
50 Steve Tsang, *Democracy Shelved* (Hong Kong, Hong: Oxford University Press, 1988), p. 17. Tsang argues that, by dropping the proposals for reform of the Legislative and Executive Councils, the HKPU had, "virtually proposed to change the character of reform". This was so, but it is argued here that the differences in the franchise proposed, as well as the functions to be devolved to the proposed municipal council, represented proposed reforms of two very different natures.
51 CO 537/1650, note from Smith dated 11 May 1945; Part I of paper by Hazelrigg dated 26 June 1945; and handwritten note from Gent on file, dated 10 July 1945 where he recorded that he "mentioned this to the S of S yesterday and he agreed to Messrs Morse & Swire participating as confidential consultants in these discussions".
52 CO 537/1650 minute from Gent to Gater dated 21 September 1945; minute from Gater to Caine dated 24 September 1945; and minute from Caine to Gater dated 27 September 1945.
53 The Colonial Office had been insistent that Young should continue his appointment as Governor of Hong Kong. It was thought "particularly important, as a point of prestige and as a move which would have a striking effect on local opinion that, if at all possible, [he] should personally take back the government of the Colony from the Service authorities" (see CO 537/1667, letter from Lloyd dated 12 January 1946, quoted in Tsang *Modern History*, p. 141). The Foreign Office, on the other hand, was resistant to the notion, considering him to be "yesterday's man" (see Snow, op. cit., p. 289). Young was allowed to continue in post for twelve months from May 1946 to May 1947.
54 CO 537/1650, minute from Miss Rushton on meeting with Young dated 18 January 1946; minute from Mayle to Lloyd dated 4 February 1946; and minute from Miss Rushton to Lloyd dated 8 April 1946. As this must have been apparent to her seniors, it may reflect that she had not been privy to earlier confidential discussions within the Colonial Office.

55 CO 129/595/4, Governor's address on restoration of civil government. Quoted in Tsang, op. cit., p. 32.
56 CO 825/42/15, undated minute from Gent but probably written in late January or February 1942.
57 G. B. Endacott, *Hong Kong Eclipse* (Hong Kong: Oxford University Press, 1978), pp. 262–63.
58 CO 129/594/6, letter from MacDougall to Gater dated 5 December 1945.
59 Endacott, op. cit., p. 267; Donnisson, op. cit., p. 249.
60 CO 129/594/6, letter from MacDougall to Gent dated 19 October 1945 and MacDougall's private papers, Rhodes House Library, Oxford.
61 Interview of David MacDougall by Professor Steve Tsang, housed in Rhodes House library, Oxford.
62 CO 129/594/6, letter from MacDougall to Gater dated 5 December 1945.
63 B. C. K. Hawkins joined the BMA as Secretary for Chinese Affairs and Labour Officer with J. C. McDougall as his assistant, both joining from internment on 1 September 1945. C. B. Burgess arrived in Hong Kong on 7 September 1945.
64 HKRS 211/2/10, as reported by Hazelrigg at a meeting on transition from BMA to civil administration held in the Colonial Office on 2 January 1946.
65 For an exhaustive review of post-war education policy see Anthony Sweeting, *A Phoenix Transformed* (Hong Kong: Oxford University Press, 1993).

Chapter 6 Income Tax and Treasury Control

1 See Chapter 1 and the discussions on Colonial Regulations.
2 HKRS 170/1/182, telegram from Commander-in-Chief, Hong Kong to War Office dated 4 April 1946.
3 Hong Kong Hansard, address by the Governor, 16 May 1946, p. 19.
4 CO 129/606/4, letter from Treasury to Colonial Office dated 13 May 1947 in which reference is made to original War Office document, 16/Abd/1693 dated 23 February 1945. "This said ... that the Treasury, having regard to the Colony's remaining balances and its subsisting liabilities would determine, in agreement with the Colonial Office, the extent, if any, to which the government should be called upon to contribute to the net cost of the military administration." Such determination was not made until April 1948.
5 Sir Sik-nin Chau, CBE, the cousin of Chau Tsun-nin, was born in Hong Kong in 1903 and was educated at St Stephen's College and the University of Hong Kong and graduated in medicine in 1924. He then studied further at the University of London and in Vienna and obtained diplomas in Ophthalmic Medicine and Surgery. He returned to Hong Kong and taught at the University of Hong Kong before turning to private practice. He also became a very successful businessman. He also served on the Urban Council before 1941. He was an unofficial Legislative Council member from 1946 to 1959 and an Executive Council member from 1948 to 1962. He was Chairman of the Hong Kong Trade Development Council from 1966 to 1970. He died in 1982.

6   Hong Kong Hansard, speech by the Financial Secretary, 25 July 1946, pp. 76–77 and speeches of unofficials during the budget debate and Governor's closing address, 5 September 1946, pp. 109–22 and 129.
7   See HKRS 41/1/802 for appointment of committee and minutes of meetings and HKRS 41/1/2772 for copy of final report. The Committee's other members were Lawrence Kadoorie, J. J. Ruttonjee, Kwok Chan, Richard Lee and Dr Y. S. Wan.
8   Charles Geoffrey Shield Follows, CMG, was born on 4 July 1896. He was appointed to the Seychelles, 1920–25; Gibraltar 1925–27; and Northern Rhodesia 1935–45. He was appointed Acting Financial Secretary, Hong Kong, in September 1945 and Financial Secretary on 1 May 1946. He left Hong Kong on pre-retirement leave in May 1951.
9   Ronald Dare Gillespie, was born in Canada in 1890 and was educated at Loretto School, Edinburgh. He served as a Captain in the Gordon Highlanders during the Great War and became a POW. He then joined ICI and served in several cities in China, including Hong Kong. He was interned in Hong Kong by the Japanese and released in exchange for Japanese held by Canada in 1943. He served in the British Raw Materials Mission in Washington until August 1945. He returned to Hong Kong in October 1945 and became Chairman of the General Chamber of Commerce. In April 1946 he was nominated as the Chamber of Commerce's Legislative Council member and served until April 1948.
10 Eric Pudney, ACA, born 1903 and educated Dover County Grammar School. Assistant Accountant, Gold Coast 1930; Assistant Treasurer, Mauritius, 1936; Treasury Accountant, Hong Kong, 1939, Commissioner of Inland Revenue 1947. He left Hong Kong in 1951 and died in 1971.
11 HKRS 41/1/802, minutes of First Meeting of the Taxation Committee, 18 September 1946.
12 HKRS 41/1/2772, Final Report of Taxation Committee.
13 Littlewood, op. cit., p. 76.
14 HKRS 41/1/802, minutes of Sixth Meeting of the Taxation Committee, 5 November 1946.
15 Hong Kong Hansard, moving of the First Reading of the Inland Revenue Bill, 1947 by the Financial Secretary, 24 April 1947, p. 120.
16 HKRS 41/1/2769 (1), Despatch from Governor, Hong Kong to Secretary of State dated 17 May 1947.
17 *South China Morning Post*, 25, 26, 27 and 29 April and 1, 2 and 5 May 1947.
18 Hong Kong Hansard, address by the Governor, 24 April 1947, pp. 125–26.
19 Duncan John Sloss was Vice-Chancellor of the University of Hong Kong from 1937 to 1949. He was interred in Stanley during the Japanese occupation.
20 *South China Morning Post*, 27 March and 29 April 1947.
21 See HKRS 41/1/2766/2 and HKRS 41/1/2776/1.
22 Sir Tsun-nin Chau, CBE, the cousin of Chau Sik-nin, was born in Hong Kong in 1893. He was educated at St Stephen's College, Hong Kong and Queen's College, Oxford from where he graduated in 1915. He returned to Hong Kong and practised as a barrister as well as having wide business

interests. He became a JP in 1923 and also served on the Sanitary Board. He was an unofficial Legislative Councillor from 1931 to 1939 and from 1946 to 1953 and an unofficial Executive Councillor from 1946 to 1959. He died in 1971.

23 Leo d'Almada e Castro, CBE, KC, was born in 1904 and was educated as St Joseph's College and the University of Hong Kong and Exeter College, Oxford where he graduated in jurisprudence in 1926. He returned to Hong Kong where he briefly taught commercial law at the University of Hong Kong before starting to practise law. He was an unofficial Legislative Council member from 1937 to 1941 and from 1946 to 1953. He assisted the Hong Kong Planning Unit in London in the latter part of the Second World War and in 1945 served as President of the General Military Court of Hong Kong during the British Military Administration. He was also a member of the court of the University of Hong Kong from 1937 and President of the Hong Kong Bar Association five times from 1951 to 1962. He died in 1996.

24 Hong Kong Hansard, debate on the Inland Revenue Bill 1947, 1 May 1947, p. 134.

25 Ibid., pp. 139–42.

26 HKRS 41 1/2769(1), despatch from Governor, Hong Kong to Secretary of State dated 17 May 1947 and telegram from Governor, Hong Kong to Secretary of State dated 30 April 1947.

27 CO 129/615/2, minute from Galsworthy dated 11 June 1947.

28 *Hong Kong Telegraph*, editorial, 15 May 1947.

29 D. J. Morgan, *The Official History of Colonial Development, Volume 1, The Origins of British Aid Policy, 1924–1945* (London: 1971).

30 CO 129/617/6, Circular despatch from Secretary of State to all colonies dated 12 November 1945.

31 HKRS 41 1/1233, telegram from the Secretary of State to all colonies dated 19 July 1946.

32 CO 129/591/7, minute from Caine dated 8 May 1946.

33 Ibid., minute from Caine dated 8 May 1946 and HKRS 41 1/2769 (1), undated report from Pudney on his visit to Britain, December 1946 to January 1947.

34 CO 129/591/7, letter from B. W. Gilbert, Permanent Under-secretary, Treasury to Gater, PUS, Colonial Office dated 23 July 1946; telegram from the Secretary of State to Governor, Hong Kong dated 29 July 1946; minute from Caine dated 8 May 1946; and despatch from Governor, Hong Kong to the Secretary of State dated 24 July 1946.

35 HKRS 41 1/1233, note on file dated 20 March 1947.

36 Leo Goodstadt, "The Rise and Fall of Social, Economic and Political Reforms in Hong Kong, 1935–1955", *Journal of the Royal Asiatic Society*, Hong Kong Branch, Vol. 44 (2004), pp. 73–74.

37 Greenwood, op. cit., p. 71.

38 Sikko Visscher, *The Business of Politics and Ethnicity: A History of the Singapore Chinese Chamber of Commerce and Industry* (Singapore: National University of Singapore Press, 2007), pp. 46–53.

39 CO 129/606/4, confidential despatch from Governor, Hong Kong to Secretary of State, 12 December 1947, para. 3.

40 Hong Kong Hansard, 13 March 1947, address by the Financial Secretary, p. 54; 27 March 1947, speeches by D. F. Landale, pp. 68–69, by M. K. Lo, p. 76 and address by the Governor, Young, p. 95.
41 Ibid., question asked by M. K. Lo, 16 October 1947, p. 291 and reply from the Acting Colonial Secretary (Megarry), pp. 291–92; question asked by M. K. Lo, pp. 312–13 and reply by the Financial Secretary, pp. 313–46.
42 CO 129/606/4, despatch from Governor, Hong Kong to Secretary of State dated 12 December 1947.
43 CO 825/69/1, minute from Lloyd to Gater dated 2 August 1946.
44 CO 129/591/7, despatch from Governor, Hong Kong to the Secretary of State dated 24 July 1946, para 16.
45 CO 825/69/1, minute by Mayle dated 15 August 1946 and minute from Paskin dated 23 August 1946.
46 HKRS 41/1/1238, telegram from Secretary of State to Governor, Hong Kong dated 21 March 1947 and telegram from Governor, Hong Kong to Secretary of State dated 26 March 1947.
47 CO 129/606/4, letter from Colonial Office to Treasury dated 23 April 1947 and Treasury's reply dated 13 May 1947.
48 Ibid., letters from Mayle, Colonial Office to Pitbaldo, Treasury dated 29 January 1948 and 16 February 1948; and minute from Caine dated 9 February 1948.
49 CO 129/606/5, notes of a meeting held at the Treasury with Colonial Office staff on 10 April 1948. It is not clear whether either Treasury officials or cabinet ministers disagreed with the Colonial Office's proposed free £5 million grant. Documentary evidence is lacking.
50 CO 129/606/2, telegram from Secretary of State to Governor, Hong Kong dated 16 April 1948; and CO 129/606/4, telegram from Governor, Hong Kong to Secretary of State dated 21 April 1948.
51 Hong Kong Hansard, speech by M. K. Lo during the debate on the Appropriations for 1948–49 Bill, 1948, 30 March 1948, pp. 84–85 and CO 129/606/4, telegram from Governor, Hong Kong to Secretary of State dated 21 April 1948, para. 2.
52 CO 129/606/4, telegram from Governor, Hong Kong to Secretary of State para. 4, dated 21 April 1948.
53 T 220/82. Note by Bancroft dated 22 April 1948 and minute to Pitblado dated 23 April 1948, para. 6(i) and (ii). There was thought to be little practical difference between the financial implications of a £1 million grant and a £1 million 25-year, interest-free loan.
54 CO 129/606/5, telegram from Secretary of State to Governor, Hong Kong dated 23 April 1948 and Grantham's telegram in reply dated 24 April 1948. Grantham had asked that the British government take responsibility for all "denial claims". This was the subject of further discussions between Britain and Hong Kong during 1948.
55 HKRS 163/1/452, telegram from Governor, Hong Kong to Secretary of State dated 22 April 1948, Caine's telegram in reply dated 26 April 1948

and Secretary of State's telegram in reply dated 27 April 1948. See also Chapter 10.
56 Hong Kong Hansard, question by Leo d'Almada e Castro, 26 May 1948, p. 138 and reply by the Acting Financial Secretary, 26 May 1948, pp. 138–39.
57 CO 129/606/5, letter from Landale to Governor, Hong Kong dated 27 May 1948 and CO 537/3702, letter from Grantham to Sidebotham, Colonial Office dated 19 May 1948, para. 2.
58 Hong Kong Hansard, speech by M. K. Lo during motion debate, 2 June 1948, pp. 164–65, speech by D. F. Landale during motion debate, 2 June 1948, p. 164 and speech by Colonial Secretary, p. 166.
59 Record of interview of MacDougall by Dr Norman Miners, 2 August 1979.
60 CO 129/606/1, letter from H. Palmer, Colonial Office to D. R. Serpell, Treasury dated 8 October 1946 and Serpell's reply to Palmer dated 12 December 1946; and CO 129/606/2, minute Palmer to Sidebotham dated 12 May 1948.
61 CO 129/597/1, letter from Mayle to MacDougall dated 12 July 1947; and CO 129/606/1, confidential circular from Secretary of State dated 26 September 1944, referring to Miscellaneous Instruction 460B. Also, minute from Palmer dated 20 April 1947.
62 HKRS 41/1/2769(I), report by Eric Pudney, Hong Kong's Commissioner for Inland Revenue, on his visit to London, December 1946–January 1947 to consult on the form of legislation required.
63 HKRS 41/1/2810, letter from M. K. Lo dated 30 September 1947 and Hong Kong Hansard, debate on the Appropriations 1948–49 Bill, 1948, 30 March 1948.
64 CO 323/1895/2 contains records of the discussions between the Colonial Office and Governors of African colonies about the need to revise Colonial Regulations and give more financial discretion to the colonies themselves. Also, T 220/1086, paper entitled "Treasury Control in the Colonies" dated 14 July 1948, paras 6 and 13.
65 Hong Kong Hansard, address by the Governor, 20 October 1948, p. 280.
66 As early as 1868, the Parliamentary Under-Secretary of State for the Colonies, Sir Charles Adderley, observed that a Crown Colony Governor "may not initiate essential changes without consulting them (the Home Government) and obtaining their sanction, but he may have to guide and influence local opinion and test and even agitate local feeling on questions of reform". CO 273/18 dated 21 May 1868, quoted in Hall, op. cit., pp. 113–14.
67 Martin Wight, *Development of the Legislative Council* (London: Faber and Faber, 1946), p. 161.

Chapter 7 Constitutional Reform and Its Demise

1 CO 882/31, No. 1, Announcement which Sir Mark Young made on 1 May 1946 in reply to a speech of welcome by the Commander-in-Chief.
2 Tsang, *Democracy Shelved*, p. 165.
3 CO 882/31, announcement by Sir Mark Young on 1 May 1946, para. 2.
4 CO 537/1650, confidential despatch from the Secretary of State to Governor, Hong Kong dated 4 May 1946.

5   Hong Kong Hansard, Young's address to the Legislative Council, 16 May 1946, p. 19.
6   CO 537/1651, Despatch from Governor, Hong Kong to Secretary of State dated 22 October 1946, para. 8 and questionnaire organised by the *China Mail* with results published on 26 June 1946.
7   CO 537/4806, secret despatch from Governor, Hong Kong (Grantham) to Secretary of State dated 25 August 1949, para. 7.
8   CO 537/1651, open and confidential despatches from Governor, Hong Kong to Secretary of State dated 22 October 1946; minutes of a meeting of the Far Eastern Committee discussing a joint Colonial Office and Foreign Office paper on the future of Hong Kong, 11 December 1946; minute from Lloyd to Gater quoting MacDougall's views, dated 12 December 1946 and paper by Young in response to a Foreign Office paper on the future of Hong Kong, dated 7 June 1946.
9   Ibid., minute from Caine dated 16 December 1946, minute from Mayle dated 28 December 1946 and minute from Lloyd to Gater dated 31 December 1946; and minute from the Secretary of State dated 18 January 1947, para. 1 and 5 and secret telegram from the Secretary of State to Governor, Hong Kong dated 24 January 1947.
10 C. M. Turnbull, *A History of Singapore, 1819–1975* (Singapore: Oxford University Press, 1989), pp. 234–37.
11 CO 537/4806, secret despatch from Governor, Hong Kong (Grantham) to Secretary of State dated 25 August 1949. Grantham referred to this in para. 8.
12 CO 537/2188, telegram from Governor, Hong Kong to Secretary of State dated 7 February 1947.
13 Tsang, *Democracy Shelved*, p. 43.
14 CO 537/2188, letters from the China Association to the Secretary of State dated 28 April and 10 July 1947 and letter from Creech-Jones to the China Association dated 21 July 1947.
15 CO 882/31, Despatch from Secretary of State to Governor, Hong Kong dated 3 July 1947.
16 William Roger Louis, "Hong Kong: The Critical Phase, 1945–1949", *The American Historical Review*, Vol. 102, No. 4 (October 1997), p. 1058.
17 *South China Morning Post*, Governor's arrival speech, 26 July 1947, quoted in Tsang, *Democracy Shelved*, p. 63.
18 CO 882/31, despatch from the Secretary of State to Governor, Hong Kong dated 3 July 1947, para. 6.
19 CO 537/2188, telegram from Governor, Hong Kong to Secretary of State, dated 15 August 1947.
20 CO 129/609, minute from Galsworthy dated 1 August 1947 and CO 882/31, despatch from the Secretary of State to Governor, Hong Kong dated 3 July 1947, para. 3(o) and telegram from Governor, Hong Kong to Secretary of State, dated 8 October 1947.
21 CO 537/2189, letter from Governor, Hong Kong to Mayle, Colonial Office, dated 17 November 1947.
22 John Henry Burkill Lee, born 1905, appointed Hong Kong cadet in December 1928 and passed exams in Cantonese and Mandarin. He served

in various postings until made a POW in 1941. He stayed with the British Military Administration until going on leave in May 1946 and returned to Hong Kong the following year. He was appointed Assistant Colonial Secretary (Special Duties) on 6 October 1947 and relinquished this post on 23 February 1948 to become Acting Postmaster General. He remained there until he went on leave prior to early retirement in 1950 at the age of 45.

23 CO 537/4806, secret despatch from Governor, Hong Kong to Secretary of State dated 25 August 1949, para. 7.
24 CO 537/3703, despatch from Secretary of State to Governor, Hong Kong dated 27 March 1948.
25 CO 537/2188, minute from Galsworthy to Roberts-Wray dated 12 September 1947.
26 Hong Kong Hansard, Governor's address, 19 March 1948, p. 58.
27 CO 537/3703, telegram from Secretary of State to Governor, Hong Kong dated 5 June 1948; and telegram from Governor, Hong Kong to Secretary of State dated 18 June 1948.
28 Ibid., minute from J. B. Sidebotham to Paskin dated 10 November 1948; minute from Lord Listowel dated 15 November 1948; and telegram from the Secretary of State to Governor, Hong Kong dated 18 November 1948.
29 CO 537/3703, secret despatch from the Secretary of State to Governor, Hong Kong dated 27 March 1948; CO 537/4806, secret despatch from Governor, Hong Kong to Secretary of State dated 25 August 1949, para. 15; telegram from Governor, Hong Kong to Secretary of State dated 1 December 1948; and minute from Sidebotham to Roberts-Wray dated 17 December 1948.
30 Ibid., account by Paskin of his meeting with the unofficials in Hong Kong dated 19 January 1949.
31 Ibid., letter from Wallace, Colonial Office to Col W. Russell Edmonds, Treasury dated 9 March 1949. He remarked to the Treasury rather forlornly "this means, I suppose, that the proposals will in due course go into the melting pot again".
32 Hong Kong Hansard, debate on second reading of the Appropriations for 1949–1950, Bill 1949, 30 March 1949, p. 91.
33 Ibid., address by the Governor in closing the debate on the second reading of the Appropriations for 1949–50, Bill 1949, 31 March 1949, p. 137.
34 Hong Kong Civil Service List, 1935, pp. 278–79.
35 Grantham, op. cit., p. 16 and Louis, op. cit., p. 1069.
36 Interview of David MacDougall by Dr Norman Miners, 2 August 1979.
37 Grantham, *Via Ports*, p. 19. Although becoming Bermuda's Colonial Secretary meant a substantial drop in salary, Grantham noted that none of Bermuda's previous colonial secretaries "had remained there for more than three years before being promoted to a higher post elsewhere". See also pp. 29, 43 and 94.
38 Interview of David MacDougall by Dr Norman Miners, 2 August 1979.
39 CO 537/1662, aide-memoire for Secretary of State to meet representatives from the China Association dated 11 December 1946 and minute from Lloyd to Gater dated 31 December 1946.

40 Grantham, *Via Ports*, p. 94.
41 CO 537/4806, telegram from Governor, Hong Kong to the Secretary of State dated 23 April 1949.
42 Ibid., secret despatch from Governor, Hong Kong to Secretary of State, paragraph 17, dated 25 August 1949; Hong Kong Hansard, 27 April 1949, p. 150.
43 Hong Kong Hansard, motion tabled by D. F. Landale, 27 April 1949, pp. 150–51.
44 CO 537/4806, secret despatch from Governor, Hong Kong to Secretary of State, dated 25 August 1949, para. 17. This was slightly disingenuous. Landale was absent from May until December or January 1950. He attended his last Legislative Council meeting on 4 January 1950.
45 Ibid., telegram from Governor, Hong Kong to Secretary of State dated 3 June 1949 and weekly press summaries for week ending 10 June 1949.
46 Hong Kong Hansard, motion debate, 22 June 1949, pp. 188–205.
47 Sir John Fearns Nicoll, KCMG, born 1899, appointed administrative officer in British North Borneo in 1921 and transferred as a cadet to Trinidad and Tobago in 1925 and became Deputy Colonial Secretary in 1937. He transferred to Fiji as Colonial Secretary under Grantham in 1944 and came to Hong Kong as Colonial Secretary on 16 May 1949. He subsequently became Governor of Singapore and was knighted. He died in 1981.
48 Hong Kong Hansard, motion debate, 22 June 1949, pp. 195–96.
49 Maurice Murray Watson, CBE, JP, was articled in London before the First World War in which he saw active service in France. He came to Hong Kong in 1921 to practise as a solicitor and became managing clerk with Johnston Stokes and Masters. He was made a partner in 1934 and senior partner in 1941. He was interned in Stanley during the Japanese occupation. He was elected to represent the JPs in the Legislative Council in 1946 and gave up his seat on his departure from Hong Kong in 1953.
50 Ibid., speech by M. M. Watson, p. 197.
51 Ibid., pp. 199–203.
52 Hong Kong Hansard, closing address by the Governor 22 June 1949, pp. 204–5.
53 CO 537/4806, secret despatch from Governor, Hong Kong to Secretary of State, dated 25 August 1949, para. 8.
54 MacDougall was Officer Administering the Government from May to July 1947, between Young's departure and Grantham's arrival.
55 CO 882/31, despatch from the Secretary of State to Governor, Hong Kong dated 3 July 1947, para. 3(e).
56 CO 537/4806, secret despatch from Governor, Hong Kong to Secretary of State, dated 25 August 1949.
57 Sir Charles Joseph Jeffries, KCMG, OBE, was born in 1896. He served in the Colonial Office and retired as Deputy Permanent Under-Secretary. He died in 1972.
58 Ibid., minute from Secretary of State (Creech-Jones) dated 7 January 1950.
59 CO 537/6046, secret telegram from Paskin to Grantham dated 15 January 1950; telegram from Grantham to Paskin dated 17 January 1950 and tele-

gram from Grantham to Paskin dated 15 March 1950; minute from Jeffries dated 19 May 1950; Tsang, op. cit., pp. 103–10.
60   Ibid., notes of meeting in the Colonial Office on 21 June 1950; note from Grantham dated 16 June 1950; and Tsang, *Democracy Shelved*, p. 110.
61   Ibid., minute from Paskin dated 24 June 1950; minute from Paskin to Lloyd dated 2 August 1950; letter from Nicoll, OAG, Hong Kong, dated 6 September 1950; minute dated 9 August 1950; and Tsang, op. cit., pp. 112–16.
62   CO 1023/41, copy of letter from Foreign Office to British Consul in Peking dated 7 April 1952 and draft Cabinet paper dated 16 May 1952.
63   Ibid., minute from Hall to Sidebotham re Grantham's letter of 8 January 1952 (see below) dated 24 January 1952; statement attributed to the Secretary of State in minutes dated 2 March 1951 and 6 March 1951 in 54145/4/51 and referred to in a minute from Hall to Sidebotham dated 24 January 1952. This file is not kept by the National Archives and is not part of their CO file series. A record of what happened in 1951 has been reconstituted from enclosures dating from 1952 in CO 882/31 and from comments made on the 1952 file, CO 1023/41.
64   Lyttelton claimed in his autobiography, *The Memoirs of Lord Chandos* (London: The Bodley Head, 1962, p. 374) that he was the first Secretary of State to visit for over 50 years. Tsang, op. cit., p. 151, claims it was the first ever such visit. Tsang is probably correct as there is no record of a previous visit.
65   CO 1023/41, minute from Sidebotham to Paskin dated 25 January 1952.
66   Chandos, op. cit., p. 376.
67   CO 1023/41, minute from Hall to Sidebotham dated 24 January 1952.
68   Ibid., minute from Hall to Sidebotham dated 24 January 1952. Of all the organisations he met, only two raised the issue. These were the Reform Association and "an involved petition from the Chinese Chamber of Commerce".
69   Ibid., minute from Paskin dated 10 March 1952.
70   Lyttelton, op. cit., p. 375.
71   CO 1023/41, secret letter from Grantham to Paskin dated 8 January 1952; and notes of meeting in the Colonial Office attended by Paskin, Sidebotham, Hall and Nicoll on 14 February 1952.
72   Ibid., letter from Sidebotham to C. H. Johnston, Foreign Office dated 19 March 1952. Similar letters dated 19 March 1952 were sent seeking support from the Commonwealth Relations Office, the Treasury and the Ministry of Defence although copies are no longer on file.
73   Ibid., letter from Cabinet Office to A. MacKintosh, Private Secretary to Secretary of State dated 12 May 1952; and brief for the Secretary of State.
74   Ibid., No. 10, secret letter from Paskin to Grantham dated 3 June 1952; and No 13, draft despatch from the Secretary of State to Governor, Hong Kong, para. 3, sent under cover of a secret letter from Sidebotham to Grantham dated 23 June 1952.
75   Ibid., telegram from Governor Hong Kong to Secretary of State dated 26 June 1952.

Notes to pages 131–139   261

76 Tsang, op. cit., pp. 161–62.
77 CO 1023/41, minute from Jeffries dated 12 July 1952.
78 Tsang, op. cit., pp. 164–65.
79 CO 1023/41, telegram from Grantham to Secretary of State dated 12 November 1952; and notes of meeting held in the Colonial Office on 10 July 1951.
80 Brook Antony Bernacchi, OBE, QC, JP was born in 1922 and educated at Westminster School and Cambridge University. He served in the Royal Marines during the Second World War and came to Hong Kong in 1945 with the British forces. He remained in Hong Kong and started to practise as a barrister. He joined the Bar Association in 1946 and became its Chairman in 1963. He helped found the Reform Club and was a member of the Urban Council from 1952 to 1981. He helped found the Hong Kong Sea School at Stanley. He died in 1996.
81 Martin Wight, *Development of the Legislative Council* (London: Faber and Faber, 1946), p. 161.
82 Transcript of interview of David MacDougall 17 February 1983, by Dr Steve Tsang, boxed with other MacDougall papers in the Rhodes House Library, Oxford. He described Grantham as "departmentally, bureaucratically efficient, very efficient".
83 Tsang, *Democracy Shelved*, p. 72; Lee, op. cit., p. 59 who commented that "the Palestine question absorbed too many of the Secretary of State's working hours".
84 Tsang, op. cit., p. 211.
85 Carpenter, op. cit., p. 14.

Chapter 8   Post-war Housing Policy and the British Government

1 CO 129/629/8, minute from Secretary of State Creech-Jones dated December 1949; minute from H. P. Hall to Secretary of State's Private Secretary dated 21 December 1949; and notes of a meeting held on 30 June 1950 chaired by Secretary of State Griffiths attended by Grantham, Jeffries, Sidebotham, Chinn and Hall.
2 HKRS 156 3/4, despatch from the Secretary of State to Governor, Hong Kong dated 28 December 1950.
3 CO 129/629/8, minute from Paskin dated 3 January 1950.
4 CO 537/4802, secret telegram from Governor, Hong Kong to Secretary of State dated 27 May 1949; and telegrams from Governor, Hong Kong to Secretary of State dated 14 and 25 June 1949.
5 CO 129/629/8, note by J. B. Sidebotham dated 28 December 1949; minute by Paskin dated 3 January 1950; and Sidebotham's note on Hong Kong's financial situation dated 30 December 1949.
6 Ibid., minute from Rees-Williams dated 5 January 1950; minute by Secretary of State Creech-Jones dated 5 January 1950; minutes by Paskin and Sidebotham dated 17 January 1950; and minute by Jeffries dated 4 January 1950.
7 Ibid., draft despatch from Secretary of State to Governor, Hong Kong (not sent); notes of meeting with Jeffries, Nicoll, Sidebotham and Dorman, 26

January 1950; minute from the Secretary of State dated 3 February 1950; and minute from Sidebotham to Paskin dated 1 March 1950.
8   Report of the Hong Kong Housing Commission, 1935 in *Hong Kong Legislative Council Sessional Papers*, 1938; Hong Kong Hansard, dated 13 October 1938, pp. 120–22; CO 129/576/1 despatch from Caine dated 2 February 1939; and E. G. Pryor, "A Historical Review of Housing Conditions in Hong Kong", *Journal of the Royal Asiatic Society Hong Kong Branch* Volume 12, 1972, pp. 89–129.
9   CO 129/595/9, *Report of the British Military Administration*.
10 *Report of the Building Reconstruction Advisory Committee*, 9 April 1946, Hong Kong Legislative Council Sessional Papers 1946.
11 *South China Morning Post* editorial, 30 April 1946.
12 Hong Kong Hansard, Governor's address to the Legislative Council, 16 May 1946, pp. 19–23.
13 CO 129/595/6, statement of government's housing policy issued on 10 July 1946 as Enclosure 1 of despatch from Governor, Hong Kong to Secretary of State dated 18 August 1946.
14 Roger Bristow, *Land-use Planning in Hong Kong* (Hong Kong: Oxford University Press, 1984), p. 67.
15 Hong Kong Hansard, address by the Governor, 16 May 1946, p. 22; CO 129/595/6, despatch from Governor, Hong Kong to Secretary of State dated 26 June 1946; CO 129/604/1, despatch from Governor, Hong Kong to the Secretary of State dated 13 June 1946; and Bristow, op. cit., p. 67.
16 CO 129/595/6, minute from Mayle dated 19 August 1946; and minutes from Caine dated 21 August 1946 and 24 August 1946.
17 CO 129/615/7, telegram from Governor, Hong Kong to Secretary of State dated 7 July 1946; and despatches from Secretary of State to Governor Hong Kong dated 14 August 1946 and 24 September 1946.
18 HKRS 156 1/577, minute from Young dated 26 August 1946.
19 Hong Kong Hansard, 16 May 1946, p. 23.
20 Ronald Ruskin Todd, born 1902, educated Cambridge University, appointed Hong Kong cadet 1924 and served in the Import and Export Department, as Secretary for Chinese Affairs, Chairman of the Urban Council and Assistant Financial Secretary. He was interned from 1942 to 1945 and in 1946 became Secretary for Chinese Affairs. He acted as Colonial Secretary several times and retired in 1955. He died in 1980.
21 Hong Kong Hansard, reply by the Acting Colonial Secretary, 21 November 1946, p. 210.
22 Ibid., reply by the Acting Colonial Secretary, 19 June 1947, pp. 183–84.
23 Ibid., speeches by unofficial members, pp. 190–204.
24 HKRS 156/1/364, minute from Acting Colonial Secretary Todd to Attorney-General.
25 Hong Kong Hansard, motion debate, pp. 246–47.
26 Interview of MacDougall by Dr Steve Tsang. Rhodes House Library, Oxford. MSS Ind Ocn s 300.
27 HKRS 163/1/335, minute from MacDougall (Officer Administering the Government) to acting Colonial Secretary dated 17 July 1947.

28 HKRS 163/1/336, despatch from Officer Administering the Government, Hong Kong to Secretary of State dated 24 July 1947.
29 Ibid., telegram from Secretary of State to Governor, Hong Kong dated 28 August 1947; telegram from OAG, Hong Kong to Secretary of State dated 24 July 1947; and telegram from Governor, Hong Kong to Secretary of State dated 18 September 1947.
30 Ibid., telegram from the Secretary of State to Governor, Hong Kong dated 4 October 1947; and minute from MacDougall to Grantham dated 29 January 1948.
31 HKRS 896 1/21, telegram from Governor to Secretary of State dated 1 August 1947 and Secretary of State's reply dated 25 September 1947 and telegram from Governor, Hong Kong to Secretary of State dated 1 August 1947.
32 Hong Kong Hansard, speech by Director of Public Works, V. Kennif, 1 April 1948, p. 102; and speech by M. K. Lo during budget debate 30 March 1948, p. 81.
33 HKRS 835 1/25, despatch from Governor, Hong Kong to Secretary of State dated 18 June 1948; and HKRS 156 1/3500, Hong Kong government press release dated 10 October 1948.
34 HKRS 156 1/808, minute from Acting Financial Secretary to Governor dated 20 November 1947; and minute from Governor dated 22 November 1947.
35 Hong Kong Hansard, speech by the Hon Sir M. K. Lo, 30 March 1949, p. 100.
36 HKRS 163 1/688, letter from Chairman, Requisitioned Properties and Allocation Committee to Colonial Secretary dated 4 December 1948, para 11; and minute from Financial Secretary to Colonial Secretary dated 20 December 1948.
37 HKRS 156 1/1899, minute from the Chairman of the Urban Council (Fehily) to the Colonial Secretary dated 26 January 1949; minute from Public Works Department to Deputy Colonial Secretary dated 26 February 1949; minute from Deputy Financial Secretary (Clarke) dated 7 March 1947; minute from Deputy Colonial Secretary dated 5 March 1949; and minute from Colonial Secretary (MacDougall) to Chairman of the Urban Council dated 23 March 1949.
38 Andrew Nicol, born 1898, appointed Assistant Engineer, Public Works Department, 1921, and spent most of his career in port development.
39 HKRS 156 1/1899, letter from Andrew Nicol, Acting Director of Public Works to Chairman of the Urban Council dated 12 May 1949, commenting on a proposal made by Dr Willis; minute from Andrew Nicol for Director of Public Works to Colonial Secretary dated 20 December 1949; and HKRS 163 1/1153, comment by Commissioner for Labour dated 13 June 1950.
40 MacDougall had instituted a new policy to allow civil servants to retire early at age 45. This was to allow underperforming officers a channel to leave. Ironically, MacDougall was the first officer to retire under this system for reasons which remain unclear.
41 HKRS 156 1/1899, minute from Governor Grantham to Colonial Secretary Nicoll dated 13 June 1949; comment made by Fehily in memo to Colonial Secretary dated 25 June 1949; and minute from Nicoll dated 15 June 1949.

42 Hong Kong Housing Society, *Hong Kong Housing Society Forty-Five Years in Housing* (Hong Kong: Hong Kong Housing Society, 1994), copy of minutes of first meeting, p. 3. The Rev T. F. Ryan was also present.
43 HKRS 156 3/1, note of meeting between the Trustees, Dr S. N. Chau and J. H. Ruttonjee with the Colonial Secretary on 19 September 1949; and minute from Colonial Secretary recording meeting between Morse, Grantham and himself on 27 September 1949.
44 HKRS 156 3/1, minute from Deputy Financial Secretary dated 23 November 1949; and minute from Melmoth dated 11 February 1950; Executive Council Memorandum dated 27 January 1950.
45 Ibid., Part II, telegram from Governor, Hong Kong to Secretary of State dated 22 June 1951 and Secretary of State's reply dated 5 July 1951; minute from Registrar General (Land Officer) dated 30 November 1950; and minute from Assistant Secretary 1 to Deputy Colonial Secretary dated 20 June 1951.
46 Ibid., minute from Melmoth dated 10 January 1950; see below for Grantham's 1950 meetings with the Colonial Office; Grantham, *Via Ports*, pp. 100 and 115.
47 HKRS 337 4/148/1, minute from Melmoth dated 13 October 1949; HKRS 156 3/1, minute from Melmoth dated 10 January 1950; and HKRS 156 3/1 Pt II undated memorandum from the Hong Kong Housing Society to the Hong Kong government.
48 David Drakakis-Smith, *High Society: Housing Provision in Metropolitan Hong Kong 1954 to 1979* (Hong Kong: Centre for Asian Studies, 1979), p. 47.
49 C. J. Mackay, "Housing Management and the Comprehensive Housing Model in Hong Kong: A Case Study of Colonial Influence", *Journal of Contemporary China* Vol. 9, No. 25 (2000), pp. 453–55.
50 HKRS 156/1/1899, minute from Colonial Secretary MacDougall to Chairman of the Urban Council dated 23 March 1949.
51 HKRS 41 1/796, minute from Governor to Colonial Secretary dated 4 June 1946.
52 CO 129/617/6, Colonial Office circular dated 12 November 1945.
53 HKRS 41 1/796, referred to by Carrie in minute to the Colonial Secretary dated 24 April 1950; HKRS 156 1/1899, minute from Assistant Secretary 1 to Special Adviser (Carrie) dated 4 January 1950; and HKRS 156 1/3425, circulation approval record, May 1950.
54 William James Carrie, born 1891, educated Edinburgh University, appointed Hong Kong cadet 1914, military service May 1918 to August 1919. Had an extensive range of postings in the Colonial Secretariat and departments until interned from 1941 to 1945. He retired in 1947 but was retained on temporary employment from 1948 until 1950 or later. Served as Custodian of Enemy Property, Chairman of the Colonial Development and Welfare Committee and then Chairman of the Housing Committee.
55 HKRS 156 1/3425, various minutes from 25 May to 16 June 1950.
56 HKRS 156/1/2528, minutes of meetings of the Housing Committee held on 7 July 1950, 21 July 1950, 8 August 1950, 8 September 1950 and 12 December 1950.

Notes to pages 153–163   265

57 CO 537/6070, notes of meetings held in Colonial Office at 12.45 pm on 21 June 1950; and CO 129/629/8, minute from Paskin dated 24 June 1950 and record of meeting held in the Colonial Office on 30 June 1950.
58 HKRS 156 3/4, minute from Governor to Colonial Secretary and Financial Secretary dated 21 November 1950 and undated paper on housing, likely to dated around December 1950.
59 HKRS 156 3/4, notes of meeting held at Government House on 20 December 1950.
60 HKRS 156 31/3500, despatch from Secretary of State to Governor, Hong Kong dated 28 December 1950.
61 Ibid., despatch from Governor, Hong Kong to Secretary of State dated 10 February 1951.
62 HKRS 156 3/4, Executive Council Memorandum dated 26 June 1951.
63 HKRS 156 1/11127, Executive Council Memorandum XCS 48 dated 7 May 1952, para. 4.
64 See Chapter 9 for a discussion on the development of the government's squatter resettlement policy.
65 HKRS 156 3/5 Enclosure 1, Report of Ad Hoc Committee on Housing, attached to Executive Council Memorandum entitled Housing dated 20 April 1953.
66 HKRS 523 2/1, Minutes of Executive Council meeting held on 19 August 1952.
67 Arthur Grenfell Clarke, CMG was born in 1906 in Athlone, Ireland, and educated at Mountjoy School, Dublin and Trinity College, Dublin. He was appointed a Hong Kong cadet in 1929 and held various posts in the Secretariat for Chinese Affairs, Colonial Secretariat and District Office prior to 1941. He was also Assistant Commissioner and later Commissioner of War Taxation from July 1940 to August 1941. He was interned during the Japanese occupation and went on leave from October 1945 to September 1946. On his return, he became Director of Commerce and Industry, Deputy Financial Secretary and Financial Secretary from 1952 until his retirement in 1961.
68 HKRS 156 3/5, Executive Council Memorandum dated 10 April 1953; and minutes of Executive Council meeting held on 28 April 1953.
69 HKRS 156 3/5 para. 14 (b), Enclosure 1, Report of Ad Hoc Committee on Housing, attached to Executive Council Memorandum entitled Housing dated 20 April 1953; Hong Kong Hansard, meeting of the Legislative Council 7 April 1954, p. 155.
70 Hong Kong Hansard, speech by M. W. Lo, 28 April 1954, pp. 189–93.

Chapter 9 Squatter Resettlement

1 Denis Bray, *Hong Kong Metamorphosis* (Hong Kong: Hong Kong University Press, 2001), p. 52.
2 Denis Campbell Bray, CBE, CVO, born 1926, educated Cambridge, and then served in the Royal Navy. Appointed a Hong Kong cadet in 1950 and posted as Assistant Secretary for Chinese Affairs; Assistant Secretary, Colonial Secretariat 1953; District Officer, Tai Po 1954; Assistant Director of Urban

Services 1956; Assistant District Commissioner New Territories 1958; District Officer Sai Kung 1960; Colonial Secretariat 1962–64; Deputy Secretary for Chinese Affairs then Deputy Secretary of Home Affairs 1968–73; Secretary of Home Affairs 1973; Commissioner, London 1977–80; Secretary of Home Affairs; Colonial Secretary 1984. He retired in 1985 and died in 2005.

3   Mills, op. cit., p. 388; Annual Report of Commissioner of Labour and Mines, 1957–58, pp. 60–61 and Grantham, "Housing Hong Kong's 600,000 homeless", *Geographical Magazine* Volume 31 (1959), p. 575.
4   Endacott, *Eclipse*, pp. 11–12 and Sir Selwyn Selwyn-Clarke, *Footprints, The Memoirs of Sir Selwyn Selwyn-Clarke* (Hong Kong: Sino-American Publishing Company, 1975).
5   Endacott, *Eclipse*, p. 303 and pp. 309–10. This figure can only be taken as approximate as there were several different estimates of population at that time. The government adopted an estimate of 1,750,000 in May 1948. See Smart, *The Shek Kip Mei Myth*, p. 43.
6   HKRS 156 3/3 Report of "Interdepartmental Committee on the Squatter Problem", under covering memo from the Committee's Chairman, also the Chairman of the Urban Council, to Colonial Secretary dated 30 June 1948.
7   Ibid., letter from General Officer Commanding Land Forces to the Colonial Secretary dated 20 January 1948.
8   HKRS 156 1/602, minute from Grantham to the Colonial Secretary dated 23 December 1947.
9   Tsang, *Democracy Shelved*, p. 83.
10 Tsang, *A Modern History of Hong Kong*, p. 40; Tsang, *Democracy Shelved*, pp. 81–84; Wesley-Smith, op. cit., pp. 77–79; and Grantham, *Via Ports*, p. 132.
11 Snow, op. cit., p. 150 in which he claims that "twenty thousand Chinese villagers were cleared out of their homes in the neighbourhood to enable the work [expansion of Kai Tak airfield] to take place".
12 HKRS 156 1/3900, minute from Colonial Secretary (MacDougall) to the Governor, dated 4 February 1948; minute from Secretary for Chinese Affairs to the Colonial Secretary dated 30 January 1948; and minute from the Principal Assistant Colonial Secretary to the Colonial Secretary dated 30 January 1948.
13 Ibid., minutes from the Secretary for Chinese Affairs (Todd) and the Deputy Colonial Secretary (Barnett) both dated 30 January 1948; and minutes of Executive Council meeting, 9 March 1948.
14 HKRS 156 3/3, letter from the General Officer Commanding to Colonial Secretary dated 20 January 1948; minute to Assistant Colonial Secretary dated 21 January 1948; and memo from the Chairman of the Urban Council (Fehily) to Colonial Secretary (MacDougall) dated 2 February 1948.
15 Ibid., letter from the Colonial Secretary to the General Officer Commanding dated 14 February 1948; confidential minute from Colonial Secretary to the Acting Chairman of the Urban Council (Sedgwick); and minute from Colonial Secretary to Governor dated 3 June 1948.
16 Ibid., minute from the Chairman of the Urban Council to Colonial Secretary dated 6 April 1948.
17 Ibid., Report of Interdepartmental Committee on the Squatter Problem.

Notes to pages 168–171   267

18 Ibid., minute from Colonial Secretary (MacDougall) to Governor (Grantham) and minute from Governor to Colonial Secretary both dated 5 July 1948.
19 HKRS 163/1/780, Executive Council Memorandum XCS 2/52 discussed on 15 January 1952, para. 1. Finance Committee approved the expenditure in principle on 12 July 1951.
20 HKRS 156 3/3, minutes of Executive Council meeting on 5 January 1949.
21 Ibid., meeting in Urban Council Chambers on 28 October 1948 and minute from the Chairman of the Urban Council (Fehily) to Deputy Colonial Secretary dated 14 December 1948.
22 Ibid., minute from the Chairman of the Urban Council (Fehily) to Deputy Colonial Secretary dated 14 December 1948.
23 HKRS 156/1/1899, minute from Acting DPW to Colonial Secretary dated 20 December 1949.
24 Ibid., report from the Chairman of the Urban Council to Deputy Colonial Secretary dated 20 December 1949; report from the Senior Health Officer dated 19 December 1949; note from Social Welfare Officer dated 30 July 1949; and memo from the Chairman of the Urban Council to Deputy Colonial Secretary dated 24 August 1949.
25 HKRS 156 3/3, memo from Chief Fire Officer, Kowloon to the Colonial Secretary dated 23 August 1949; and memo from the Chairman of the Urban Council to Deputy Colonial Secretary dated 26 September 1949.
26 Smart, *The Shek Kip Mei Myth*, pp. 59 and 67.
27 John Crichton McDouall, CMG, JP, born 1912 at Tientsin, educated Jesus College, Cambridge. He was appointed a Hong Kong cadet in July 1934 and posted as Assistant Secretary for Chinese Affairs in August 1939 and as Assistant Defence Secretary in April 1941. Served in the Hong Kong Royal Naval Volunteer Reserve and was a POW from 1941 to 1945. He became Assistant Secretary for Chinese Affairs and Assistant Labour Officer from September 1945 to 3 April 1946 in the British Military Administration before proceeding on leave. He was Social Welfare Officer from August 1947 and posted to Malaya as Chief Social Welfare Officer from 1952 to 1957 when he returned to Hong Kong as Secretary for Chinese Affairs. He retired in 1966.
28 HKRS 163/1/779, Report on Squatters by the Social Welfare Officer dated 8 November 1950.
29 Ibid., minute from Deputy Colonial Secretary dated 16 November 1950.
30 CO 1023/164, Annex A to Executive Council Memorandum XCS 42/51 dated 29 June 1951, para. (i), Annex A being the detailed minutes of the Executive Council meeting held on 5 December 1950.
31 James Tinker "Jimmy" Wakefield, born 1915, served in the British Military Administration from 1 September 1945 and appointed Cadet Officer Class II in March 1947. He served as District Officer South, Assistant Social Welfare Officer and Assistant Secretary for Chinese Affairs before visiting Singapore to study the Singapore Improvement Trust in 1950. He was Chief Resettlement Officer from December 1951 until April 1954 and then served as Registrar of Co-operatives, Labour Officer, District Commissioner of the

New Territories and, in 1965, became Commissioner for Resettlement. He retired in 1967. He died in 2011.
32 CO 1023/164, Executive Council Memorandum dated 29 June 1951 and Executive Council Memorandum discussed on 3 July 1951; HKRS 163/1 780, Executive Council Memorandum discussed on 15 January 1952.
33 HKRS 163/1/781, memo from the Chairman of the Urban Council to Colonial Secretary dated 19 November 1952; and HKRS 163/1/780, Executive Council Memorandum XCS 2/52 dated 3 January 1952 and discussed on 15 January, Appendix F.
34 Ibid., memo from the Chairman of the Urban Council to Colonial Secretary dated 20 December 1952; memo from Commissioner of Police to Colonial Secretary dated 31 December 1952; and memo from Secretary for Chinese Affairs to Colonial Secretary dated 8 January 1953.
35 Smart, *The Shek Kip Mei Myth*, p. 89.
36 HKRS 163/1/781, notes of a meeting held on 12 January 1953.
37 Ibid., note on file dated 15 January 1953.
38 *South China Morning Post* dated 17 December 1952 with account of the Urban Council meeting of 16 December 1952; and editorial dated 17 December 1952.
39 Ibid., dated 11 February 1953 with account of the Urban Council meeting of 10 February 1953.
40 HKRS 163/1/781, addendum dated 12 February 1953 attached to a memo from the Chairman of the Urban Council to Colonial Secretary dated 5 February 1953, pp. 7–8; and note of a meeting at Government House held on 19 February 1953.
41 CO 1023/164, minute to Mr Harris dated around 28 January 1953 and letter from Sidebotham to Grantham dated 4 February 1953.
42 Ibid., letter from Grantham to Sidebotham dated March 1953.
43 Hong Kong Hansard, address by the Governor dated 4 March 1953, p. 25.
44 *South China Morning Post* dated 11 March 1953 with account of Urban Council meeting of 10 March 1953.
45 CO 1023/164, Reports from the Chairman of the Urban Council dated 1 May 1953 and 22 December 1953.
46 HKRS 163 3/64, minute from Colonial Secretary to Deputy Colonial Secretary dated 11 November 1953 and minute from Deputy Colonial Secretary (Burgess) to Colonial Secretary dated 26 November 1953.
47 HKRS 163/1/781, letter from Colonial Secretary to the Director of Public Works dated 26 November 1953 and record of a meeting in the Governor's Deputy's office held on 1 December 1953.
48 Bray, op. cit., p. 51.
49 HKRS 163 1 1578, savingram from Governor, Hong Kong to Secretary of State dated 26 January 1954, para. 2–4.
50 Bray, op. cit., p. 52.
51 HKRS 163 1/1578, para. 9, 11 and 12.
52 Bray, op. cit., p. 52 and HKRS 163 1/1578, Record of meeting held at Government House at 10.30 am on Saturday 26 December 1953. Bray seemed to give the impression that the meeting took place at 6 am but the

record of the meeting clearly states it was held at 10.30 am. It is possible that the decision to hold the meeting was made at 6 am and then passed to those required to attend. This is corroborated by Grantham's own later account of having returned to the Governor's yacht "early on the morning of Boxing Day 1953" after a walk in the hills on an outlying island, when a police launch approached with a message from the Colonial Secretary about the fire. Grantham sent a reply that he was returning immediately and asked him to summon the Executive Council and others concerned to a meeting at Government House. This, therefore, could not have taken place at 6 am. See Grantham, *Housing Hong Kong's 600,000 Homeless*, p. 573.
53 Smart, *The Shek Kip Mei Myth*, p. 101.
54 HKRS 163 1/1578, Record of meeting held at Government House at 10.30 am on Saturday 26 December 1953 and *aide memoire* for Executive Council meeting on 29 December 1953, para. 23. It is not apparent from the remaining records why there was such a sudden change in government's stance.
55 CO 1023/164, telegram from Governor, Hong Kong to Secretary of State dated 29 December 1953, para. 4; minutes of Executive Council meeting held on 29 December 1953; and telegram from Governor, Hong Kong to Secretary of State and telegram from Secretary of State to Governor, Hong Kong both dated 26 December 1953.
56 Ibid., telegram from Governor, Hong Kong to Secretary of State dated 29 December 1953, paragraph 12 and telegram from Secretary of State to Governor, Hong Kong dated 30 December 1953. This was subject to parliamentary approval which was forthcoming. Grantham later claimed that nothing was received from the British government. See Rhodes House library archives, interview with Crozier 21 August 1968.
57 Ibid., minute from Harris to Sidebotham dated 29 December 1953.
58 Sir John Douglas Clague, CBE, MC, QPM, CPM, TD, JP, born 1917 in Southern Rhodesia and educated at King William's College, Isle of Man. He saw military service in Hong Kong and China during the Second World War. He became a prominent Hong Kong businessman as Chairman of John D. Hutchison & Co. Ltd. and also held other directorships. He was Chairman of the Hong Kong General Chamber of Commerce 1957–59 and was active in voluntary service, including as a Legislative Council and Urban Council member, as Chairman of the Hong Kong Housing Society and others. He was also Commandant of the Hong Kong Auxiliary Police from 1962 to 1980. He died in 1980.
59 HKRS 163/1/1578, letter from J. D. Clague to the Chairman of the Urban Council (Barnett) dated 30 December 1953, pp. 2–3.
60 HKRS 438/1/1, minutes of meeting of the Committee of the Whole Council held on 5 January 1954.
61 HKRS 163/3/20, Report of Emergency Resettlement Sub-Committee.
62 Grantham, *Housing Hong Kong's 600,000 Homeless*, p. 577.
63 Claude Bramall Burgess, CMG, OBE, born 1910 and educated at Oxford University. He was appointed a Hong Kong cadet in 1932. He was a POW from 1941 to 1945 and, on liberation, he became a Staff Officer Grade I in the British Military Administration on 7 September 1945. He was seconded

to the Colonial Office in 1946 and promoted to Cadet Officer Class I on 14 October 1948. He became Deputy Colonial Secretary on 8 March 1949 and attended the Imperial Defence College from January to December 1951. Thereafter he served in the Colonial Secretariat and became Colonial Secretary in 1958. He retired in 1963 and died in 1998.

64 HKRS 163 3/20, paper by the Deputy Colonial Secretary dated 29 January 1954 and notes of a Meeting held at Government House on Clearance and Resettlement Policy on 8 February 1954.
65 Ibid., Interim Report of the Emergency Resettlement Areas Sub-Committee dated 10 February 1954.
66 Ibid., Report of Emergency Resettlement Committee.
67 Sir David Ronald Holmes, CMG, CBE, MC, ED. Born 1913 and educated at Cambridge University. Appointed Hong Kong cadet 1938 and mobilised with the Hong Kong Volunteer Defence Corps in 1941. He left Hong Kong in January 1941 and served in the British Army and then in the British Military Administration from September 1945. After leave, he attended the Imperial Defence College and then had subsequent postings in the Defence Branch and the Secretariat for Chinese Affairs. He became Commissioner for Resettlement in 1954 and then Chairman of the Urban Council and Chairman of the Housing Authority, 1955–57. He was District Commissioner, New Territories 1958–62 and Director of Commerce & Industry Department from 1962 to 1966. He became Secretary for Chinese Affairs in 1966 and retired as Director of Home Affairs in 1971. He died in 1981.
68 HKRS 163 3/20, paper from Commissioner for Resettlement Holmes, dated 11 March 1954.
69 Ibid., minute from Deputy Colonial Secretary (Burgess) to Colonial Secretary dated 15 March 1954 and minute from D. R. Holmes to Deputy Colonial Secretary (Burgess) dated 15 March 1954.
70 Ibid., meeting between Colonial Secretary, Deputy Colonial Secretary and Holmes on his paper held on 16 March 1954 and minute from Holmes to Deputy Colonial Secretary dated 18 March 1954.
71 Ibid., minute from Governor to Colonial Secretary dated 1 April 1954.
72 HKRS 896 1/74, memo from Colonial Secretariat to the Director of Urban Services (also Chairman of the Urban Council) dated 25 March 1954.
73 Ibid., memo from Colonial Secretariat to Director of Public Works dated 9 April 1954 and Minutes of Executive Council meeting, 6 April 1954.
74 Hong Kong Hansard, address by the Colonial Secretary, 14 April 1954, pp. 178–9.
75 CO 1030/390, telegram from Governor, Hong Kong to Secretary of State dated 23 July 1954.
76 Smart, *The Shek Kip Mei Myth*, p. 131.
77 HKRS 163 3/20, Executive Council memorandum discussed on 5 October 1954.
78 HKRS 156 1/4430, letter from Social Welfare Administration, Republic of the Philippines dated 2 November 1954 and letter from the US Consul-General dated 15 November 1954.

79 HKRS 163 3/20, Executive Council memorandum discussed on 9 November 1954.
80 Luke S. K. Wong, *Housing in Hong Kong* (Hong Kong: Heinemann Educational Books (Asia) Ltd., 1978), p. 27.
81 HKRS 163 3/20, note on file dated 17 November 1954.
82 Smart, *The Shek Kip Mei Myth*, pp. 147–48.
83 HKRS 163 3/20, Commissioner for Resettlement to Colonial Secretary dated 23 November 1955 and minute from Commissioner for Resettlement to Assistant Secretary 1 dated 24 April 1954.
84 Keith Hopkins, "Housing the Poor", Keith Hopkins, ed., *Hong Kong: the Industrial Colony* (Hong Kong: Oxford University Press, 1971), Chapter 7, pp. 283 and 296. Although this referred to a survey conducted in 1968, the fear of fire and typhoons is likely to have been a perennial fear of squatter area residents.
85 HKRS 163 3/20, note from Commissioner for Resettlement dated 3 June 1955. Unfortunately, no record of the proceedings of most of these committees' meetings is available.
86 Manuel Castells, *The Shek Kip Mei Syndrome* (Hong Kong: Centre of Urban Studies and Urban Planning, 1986), p. 332.
87 David Drakakis-Smith, *High Society: Housing Provision in Metropolitan Hong Kong 1954 to 1979*, p. 155.
88 Hansard, address by Hon M. W. Lo, 28 April 1954, p. 190.
89 Smart, *The Shek Kip Mei Myth*, p. 122.

Chapter 10 Financial Autonomy

1 Hong Kong Hansard, address by the Governor, Sir R. B. Black, 6 March 1958, p. 46.
2 CO 1030/392, minute from J. T. A. Howard-Drake to Mr Macintosh dated 5 October 1955, para. 11.
3 See Chapter 4.
4 HKRS 163 1/1003, confidential telegram from Governor, Hong Kong to the Secretary of State dated 22 February 1949 and HKRS 163 1/1367, confidential telegram from Governor, Hong Kong to the Secretary of State dated 22 February 1951. A similar one was probably also sent in 1950 but does not appear to have survived in the archives.
5 HKRS 163 1/1507, confidential telegram from Governor, Hong Kong to Secretary of State dated 25 February 1952 and minute from Financial Secretary (Clarke) to Governor dated 23 February 1952. A savingram was a less formal and less abbreviated means of communication between the Colonial Office and colonies. It was introduced in 1931 to save money and to avoid bringing low priority material to the personal attention of the Governor. See the National Archives available at http://yourarchives.nationalarchives.gov.uk/index.php?title=Savingrams_and_Saving_Telegrams [accessed 25 November 2011].
6 CO 129/606/2, despatch from Secretary of State to Governor, Hong Kong dated 24 September 1948, para. 4.
7 HKRS 163 1/1507, minute from Assistant Secretary 7 to the Confidential Registry dated 29 February 1952 and reply dated 1 March 1952. See also

comments by Colonial Office officials, for example, CO 1030/393, minute by Howard-Drake to Mackintosh dated 5 October 1955.
8 HKRS 229 2/1, minute from Assistant Secretary 6 to Financial Secretary dated 12 January 1951.
9 CO 129/606/2, despatch from the Secretary of State to Governor, Hong Kong dated 24 September 1948.
10 HKRS 229 2/1, minute, possibly from Deputy Financial Secretary to the Clerk of Councils dated 24 March 1953; memorandum from Director of Audit to Financial Secretary dated 20 July 1955; savingram from Governor, Hong Kong to Secretary of State dated 10 August 1955; and telegram in reply dated 12 September 1955.
11 Ibid., minute from Assistant Secretary 6 dated 12 January 1951 and minute from Financial Secretary to Assistant Secretary 6 dated 15 January 1951.
12 CO 1030/392, minute from Wheatley to Gibbins dated 4 August 1955, para. 2.
13 HKRS 170 1/181, minute from Director of Public Works to Colonial Secretary dated 3 June 1946 and HKRS 70 1/245(1), Note entitled "New Territories Construction at Tai Lam Chung" dated 28 August 1951.
14 HKRS 156 1/3370/1, letter from Binnie, Dean and Gourlay setting out their proposals for a phased construction of the Tai Lam Chung Reservoir, dated 31 July 1951; minute file dated 15 August 1951; and extract from the minutes of the Finance Committee dated 22 August 1951.
15 CO 1023/199, references in a minute from Harris dated 6 December 1953 and in a minute from Littler dated 6 December 1953, para. 1. The original Colonial Office file, original reference 53687/51 is unavailable in the National Archives.
16 HKRS 156 1/3370/1, memoranda from the Director of Public of Public Works to the Colonial Secretary dated 13 and 18 April 1953 and extract from minutes of Finance Committee meeting held on 7 October 1953.
17 CO 1023/199, savingram from Governor, Hong Kong to the Secretary of State dated 27 November 1953.
18 CO 1023/199, various minutes written during December 1953.
19 HKRS 156 1/3370/1, memorandum from the Director of Public Works to the Financial Secretary dated 7 January 1954; minute from Deputy Financial Secretary to the Financial Secretary dated 14 January 1954 and from the Financial Secretary to the Governor dated 15 January 1954 and Grantham's approval dated 18 January 1954.
20 HKRS 163 1/1368, minute from Financial Secretary to Governor dated 25 January 1951 and despatch from Governor, Hong Kong to Secretary of State dated 27 January 1951.
21 CO 1030/905, minutes on file from 3 February to 20 February 1954.
22 CO 537/5020, undated *Note by the War Office on the Garrison of Hong Kong*. It probably dates from about October 1949.
23 CAB 21/2428, top secret telegram from General Headquarters, Far Eastern Land Forces to Ministry of Defence, London dated 15 December 1948 and extract from conclusions of a meeting of the Cabinet held at 10 Downing Street on 28 April 1949.

24 Tsang, *A Modern History of Hong Kong*, pp. 154–57.
25 CO 537/5008, minutes of Chiefs of Staff meeting held on 18 May 1949 and extract of minutes of Chiefs of Staff meeting, referring to this Cabinet decision, held on 27 May 1949.
26 *South China Morning Post* article, 15 June 1949, p. 1.
27 CO 537/5020, undated *Note by the War Office on the Garrison of Hong Kong*. It probably dates from about October 1949.
28 Correlli Barnett, *The Lost Victory* (London: Macmillan, 1995), pp. 92–102.
29 T 225/772, minute dated 26 August 1949; minutes of inter-departmental meeting with Colonial Office and service departments held on 6 September 1949; and minute to Sir Bernard Gilbert dated 12 May 1948.
30 For a summary of the payment of defence costs before 1941 see Miners, *Hong Kong under Imperial Rule, 1912–1941*, pp. 103–6.
31 CO 537/5028, paper entitled *Note by the Colonial Office on the Defence Commitments and Financial Situation of Hong Kong*; secret telegram from Governor, Hong Kong to Secretary of State dated 29 October 1948.
32 Ibid., confidential despatch from Governor, Hong Kong to Secretary of State dated 12 May 1949; letter from Treasury to the Air Ministry dated 21 June 1949; and letter from the War Office to the Colonial Office dated 7 July 1949.
33 Ibid., minutes of inter-departmental meeting with Colonial Office and service departments held on 6 September 1949 and minutes of meeting held on 5 July 1949.
34 Ibid, minute from Paskin dated 5 October 1949.
35 Ibid., minutes of inter-departmental meeting with Colonial Office and service departments held on 6 September 1949; secret letter from Paskin, Colonial Office to Grantham, Governor, Hong Kong dated 19 September 1949; minute from Wallace dated 26 September 1949; minute from Paskin dated 5 October 1949; and secret telegram from Secretary of State to Governor, Hong Kong dated 11 October 1949.
36 Ibid., secret telegram from Governor, Hong Kong to Secretary of State dated 21 October 1949.
37 CO 537/5028, memorandum on background to Hong Kong's post-war finances dated 22 October 1949 and secret telegram from Secretary of State to Governor, Hong Kong dated 27 October 1949.
38 T 225/772, letter from War Office to Treasury dated 20 January 1950; letter from J. R. MacGregor, War Office to Humphreys-Davies, Treasury dated 24 January 1950; and minute from Hudspith to Humphreys-Davies dated 26 January 1950.
39 CO 537 6315, minute to Morgan dated 8 February 1950.
40 T 225/772, minute from Hudspith to Humphreys-Davies dated 31 March 1950 and minute to Clough dated 8 February 1950.
41 CO 537 6315, minute to Morgan dated 8 February 1950 and minute dated 6 December 1950.
42 T 225/773, minutes of meeting held on 29 April 1950; telegram from Governor. Hong Kong to Follows in London dated 3 May 1950; minute

dated 15 May 1950; and minute from Hudspith to Humphrey-Davies dated 8 May 1950.
43 Hong Kong Hansard, 24 May 1950, pp. 173–80.
44 T 225/774, letter from Sidebotham, Colonial Office to Grantham in Hong Kong dated 26 February 1951 and T 225/775, copy of letter from Grantham to Sidebotham dated 20 June 1951.
45 HKRS 41/1/5599, minute from Financial Secretary to Assistant Secretary 6 dated 11 January 1951.
46 T 225/775, letter from Dodd, Colonial Office to Harvey, Air Ministry and copied to Treasury dated 24 July 1951.
47 Ibid., minute to Hudspith dated 25 August 1951; minute from Hudspith to Russell-Edmonds dated 24 August 1951; minute from Bancroft dated 29 November 1951; and minute from D. A. Lovelock to Shaw dated 30 November 1951.
48 Ibid., letter from Jeffries, Colonial Office to Crombie, Treasury dated 6 December 1951. For an account of his visit to Hong Kong, the first by a Secretary of State for the Colonies, see Chandos, op. cit., pp. 374–77 and Grantham, *Via Ports,* p. 174.
49 Ibid., letter from Crombie, Treasury to Jeffries, Colonial Office dated 10 December 1951 and telegram from Paskin in Hong Kong to Jeffries dated 14 December 1951.
50 Ibid., minute to Bancroft, Shaw and Crombie dated 4 January 1952 and letter from Crombie, Treasury to Jeffries, Colonial Office dated 7 January 1952.
51 Ibid., copy of telegram from Secretary of State to Governor, Hong Kong dated 15 January 1952 and letter from Armitage-Smith, Colonial Office to Bancroft, Treasury dated 18 February 1952.
52 Hong Kong Hansard, address by unofficial members 19 March 1952, pp. 98–128.
53 T 225/775, minute from Colonel Russell-Edmonds to Bancroft dated 20 August 1952 in which he described the waivers claimed by the Hong Kong government as "pettifogging".
54 Ibid, letter from Bancroft, Treasury to Trafford-Smith, Colonial Office dated 16 September 1952.
55 Hong Kong Hansard, address by the Financial Secretary and reply by Chau Tsun-nin on behalf of all unofficial members, 31 December 1952, pp. 298–300.
56 T 225/775, letter from Trafford-Smith, Colonial Office to Bancroft, Treasury dated 18 August 1952 and minute from Bancroft dated 30 July 1953.
57 Ibid., internal Treasury minute dated 8 July 1953.
58 Ibid., internal Treasury minute dated 8 July 1953; letter from Bancroft, Treasury to Armitage-Smith, Colonial Office dated 16 July 1953; and letter from Armitage-Smith, Colonial Office to Thompson, Treasury dated 18 September 1953.
59 Ibid., draft d/o letter from Secretary of State to Governor, Hong Kong dated December 1953. A copy of the original sent is not on file.
60 CO 968/456, letter from Grantham to Paskin, Colonial Office dated 29 January 1954; T 225/775, letter from Armitage-Smith, Colonial Office to

Treasury dated 5 March 1954; telegram from Secretary of State to Governor, Hong Kong dated 8 March 1954; and telegrams from Governor, Hong Kong to Secretary of State dated 11 and 18 March 1954.

61 CO 968/456, telegram from Governor, Hong Kong to Secretary of State dated 8 April 1954 and T 225/776, note from Barraclough to Russell-Edmonds dated 28 April 1954.

62 WO 32/15525, draft paper for the Executive Council of the Army Council entitled "The Future Garrison of Hong Kong". Likely prepared in early 1954.

63 T 225/776, note from Allen to Humphreys Davies dated 9 April 1954 in which he referred to the Defence Committee's decision; letter from War Office to Colonial Office dated 23 April 1954; minute from Allen to Macpherson dated 5 May 1954; and handwritten note from Macpherson to Allen dated 7 May 1954.

64 CO 968/456, minute from Harris dated 24 November 1954.

65 T 225/776, letter from Carstairs, Colonial Office to Serpell, Treasury dated 7 December 1954 and extract from Cabinet proceedings on 5 November 1954.

66 Ibid., top-secret telegram from Governor, Hong Kong to Secretary of State dated 20 December 1954; minutes from Harris, Sidebotham and Bennet all dated 22 December 1954 and minute to Sir John Martin dated 4 January 1955.

67 Ibid., minute from Sir J. Martin to Carstairs dated 7 January 1955. See CO 968/456, note on the background and present position of the negotiations over Murray Barracks dated 23 February 1954.

68 T 225/776, note by Allen dated 13 December 1954 and another dated before 7 January 1955; letter from Hobbs, War Office to Serpell, Treasury dated 4 January 1955; telegram from Governor, Hong Kong to Secretary of State dated 25 February 1955; minute from Allen dated 2 March 1955; letter from Radice, Treasury to Carstairs, Colonial Office dated 13 June 1955; letter from Radice, Treasury to MacKintosh, Colonial Office dated 19 July 1955; and letter from MacKintosh, Colonial Office to Allen, Treasury dated 26 November 1955.

69 CO 129/606/5, letter from Landale to Governor, Hong Kong dated 27 May 1948.

70 CO 1030/392, arguments contained in minute from Wheatley to Gibbins dated 4 August 1955. In it, Wheatley referred to a minute from Sidebotham in original Colonial Office file no 15517/49 dated 25 January 1949. The file seems to be unavailable in the National Archives.

71 Ibid, minute from Gibbins to Scarlett dated 9 August 1955 and minute from Howard-Drake to Mackintosh dated 5 October 1955.

72 CO 1030/392, minute from Howard-Drake to Mackintosh dated 5 October 1955, para. 10 and minute from Hulland to Ashton dated 29 May 1956.

73 CO 968/456, minute from Bennett dated 4 March 1954 who commented that he had "never been able to discover by what principle, if any, this question of Colonial contributions to Imperial Defence is held to be governed".

74 CO 1030/392, minute from Hulland to Ashton dated 29 May 1956 and minute from Wheatley dated 4 August 1955.

75 See, for example, T 225/775, letter from Bancroft, Treasury to Trafford-Smith, Colonial Office dated 16 September 1952 in which Bancroft considered the surplus Hong Kong was due to make was "extremely comfortable". See also note dated 8 July 1953 on Hong Kong's forecast surplus of HK$20.4 million on total estimated revenue of HK$176.9 million.
76 CO 1030/392, minute from Howard-Drake to Mackintosh dated 5 October 1955, para. 11.
77 Ibid., series of minutes starting from Howard-Drake to Macintosh dated 5 October 1955, and including minutes from Hulland to Ashton dated 29 May 1956, from Ashton to Hulland and Johnston dated 10 July 1956, from Johnston to Melville dated 14 July 1956 and from Vile dated 27 August 1956; and minute from Howard-Drake to Mackintosh dated 5 October 1955.
78 Ibid, minute from Ashton to Hulland and Johnston dated 10 July 1956, para 8 (a).
79 Ibid., minutes from Ashton dated 10 and 24 July 1956; minute from Melville dated 16 July 1956; letter from Hulland, Colonial Office to Russell-Edmunds, Treasury dated 7 September 1956 and letter from Russell-Edmunds, Treasury to Hulland, Colonial Office dated 2 November 1956.
80 Hong Kong Hansard, address by the Governor, Sir R. B. Black, 6 March 1958, p. 46.
81 HKRS 229/2/1, dispatch from Secretary of State to Governor, Hong Kong dated 14 January 1958.
82 CO 1030/392, minute from Vile dated 27 August 1956.
83 HKRS 229/2/1, minute from the Acting Financial Secretary to the Governor dated 30 April 1957.
84 CO 854/84, circular dispatch to colonial Governors dated 10 June 1932; Miners *Hong Kong Under Imperial Rule,* pp. 122–24; and CO 854/104, circular dispatch from the Secretary of State dated January 1937. Also reproduced in Jeffries *The Colonial Empire and its Civil Service,* pp. 243–47.

Chapter 11 Conclusions

1 Miners, op. cit., pp. 40, 278 and 284.
2 Carpenter, op. cit., pp. 5 and 14.
3 Scott, op. cit., p. 163 claims "the strengthening of the state machinery at the centre ... gave the state civil capabilities which it had never before possessed". Grantham's, Nicoll's and Black's seeming inability to co-ordinate policy formulation and implementation effectively was an example of what could happen if the centre was unable to exercise such control.
4 Carpenter, op. cit., p. 14.
5 Hong Kong Hansard, address by the Governor, Stubbs, on a motion by Colonial Secretary dated 29 January 1920, pp. 3–4.
6 Ibid., proceedings of the Finance Committee, pp. 111–18, dated 25 July 1940.
7 CO 537/3702, letter from Grantham to Sidebotham dated 19 May 48.
8 Whitfield, op. cit., p. 99.

9   Hong Kong Hansard, speech made by the Hon Leo d'Almada e Castro during motion debate 10 July 1947, p. 242.
10 HKRS 41/1/2768, telegram from Secretary of State to Governor, Hong Kong dated 15 March 1948.
11 For example, M. K. Lo trained as a solicitor in England; S. W. T'so was educated in England; Shouson Chow was educated in the US and Chau Tsun-nin was educated at Oxford University.
12 Smith, op. cit., pp. 96 and 98.
13 See, for example, Correlli Barnett, *The Lost Victory* (London: Macmillan, 1995), pp. 152–55 and David Kynaston, *Austerity Britain 1948–51: A World to Build* (London: Bloomsbury, 2007) pp. 101–2 and *Smoke in the Valley* (London: Bloomsbury, 2007), pp. 42–43 and pp. 318–26.
14 Carpenter, op. cit., p. 4.
15 CO 825/42/15, undated typewritten memo by Sidney Caine, c. Jan–Feb 1942 and the two articles in *The Times* of 31 July and 1 August 1942 by MacDougall.
16 Sir Henry Taylor, a noted mid-nineteenth-century senior Colonial Office official, referring to a colonial Governor's role stated "I think ... that the essential object was and is to uphold authority". From Sir Henry Taylor, *Autobiography 1800–1875*, 2 Vols., 1885, quoted in Hall, op. cit., p. 106.

Bibliography

Primary sources

Hong Kong government official files

Files from the following series containing general correspondence held at the Hong Kong Public Records Office, Kwun Tong were consulted.

HKRS 41	HKRS 170	HKRS 523
HKRS 46	HKRS 211	HKRS 835
HKRS 156	HKRS 310	HKRS 896
HKRS 163	HKRS 337	

British government official files

Files from the following series held at The National Archives, London, were consulted.

Cabinet files

CAB 96 War Cabinet and Cabinet: Committees on the Far East: Minutes and Papers.

Colonial Office files

CO 129 Colonial Office: Hong Kong, Original Correspondence (to 1951).
CO 131 Colonial Office: Hong Kong Sessional Papers.
CO 323 Colonies, General: Original Correspondence.
CO 537 Colonial Office and predecessors: Confidential General and Confidential Original Correspondence.
CO 825 Colonial Office: Eastern Original Correspondence.
CO 852 Colonial Office: Economic General Department and predecessors: Registered Files.

CO 859   Colonial Office: Social Services Department and successors: Registered Files.
CO 865   Colonial Office: Far Eastern Reconstruction Original Correspondence.
CO 882   Colonial Office: Confidential Print Eastern.
CO 967   Colonial Office: Private Office Papers.
CO 968   Colonial Office: Defence Department: Original Correspondence.
CO 1023 Colonial Office: Hong Kong and Pacific Department: Original Correspondence (from 1951).
CO 1030 Colonial Office and Commonwealth Office: Far Eastern Department and successors: Registered Files.

Treasury files

T 160   Treasury: Finance Files.
T 220   Treasury: Imperial and Foreign Division: Registered Files.
T 225   Treasury: Defence Policy.

War Office files

WO 32   War Office.
WO 106   War Office: Directorate of Military Operations and Military Intelligence, and predecessors: Correspondence and Papers.
WO 203   War Office: South East Asia Command: Military Headquarters Papers, Second World War.

Hong Kong government publications

Hong Kong Civil Service List, 1935.

Hong Kong Hansard, 29 January 1920, 18 July 1921, 28 September 1922, 28 December 1922, 18 October 1934, 5 December 1935, 27 May 1936, 12 May 1938, 9 November 1939, 16 November 1939, 14 March 1940, 25 July 1940, 2 and 5 September 1941, 16 May 1946, 25 July 1946, 25 July 1946, 5 September 1946, 12 November 1946, 21 November 1946, 13 March 1947, 27 March 1947, 24 April 1947, 24 April 1947, 1 May 1947, 19 June 1947, 10 July 1947, 16 October 1947, 6 November 1947, 19 March 1948, 30 March 1948, 1 April 1948, 26 May 1948, 2 June 1948, 20 October 1948, 31 March 1949, 27 April 1949, 22 June 1949, 24 May 1950, 19 March 1952, 22 October 1952, 31 December 1952, 7 April 1954, 14 April 1954, 28 April 1954, 6 March 1958, 3 December 1969.

Hong Kong Legislative Council Sessional Papers 1929.
Hong Kong Legislative Council Sessional Papers 1930.
Hong Kong Legislative Council Sessional Papers 1935.
Hong Kong Legislative Council Sessional Papers 1940.
Hong Kong Legislative Council Sessional Papers 1946.
Hong Kong Government Administration Reports, 1920, 1922.
Hong Kong Government Gazette, 10 March 1922.

Other publications

Basic Law of the Hong Kong Special Administrative Region of the People's Republic of China. Hong Kong: Joint Publishing (Hong Kong) Co. Ltd, 1991.
Colonial Regulations. 1935, amended 1945. London: His Majesty's Stationery Office, 1945.

Newspapers

Hong Kong Telegraph, 15 May 1947.
Hong Kong Weekly Press, 2 May 1930.
Manchester Guardian, 16 January 1929.
South China Morning Post, 28 May 1919. 29 May 1919, 20 January 1922, 22 October 1928, 22 October 1930, 24 October 1934, 17 and 26 April 1935, 11 November 1935, 7 December 1935, 30 April 1946, 27 March 1947, 25, 26, 27 and 29 April 1947, 1 May 1947, 26 July 1947, 15 June 1949, 17 December 1952, 5 March 1953, 11 February 1953, 11 March 1953.

Interviews

Interview of Sir Alexander Grantham by Douglas J. S. Crozier, former Director of Education in Hong Kong, 21 August 1968. The transcript is housed in the Rhodes House Library, Oxford.

Interview of D. M. MacDougall by Dr Norman Miners, 2 August 1979.

Interview of D. M. MacDougall by Dr Steve Tsang, 17 February 1983. The transcript if housed in the Rhodes House Library, Oxford in MSS Ind Ocn s 300.

Secondary sources

Airlie, Shona, 1989. *Thistle and Bamboo*. Hong Kong: Oxford University Press.
Bard, Solomon. 2002. *Voices from the Past*. Hong Kong: Hong Kong University Press.
Barnett, Correlli. 1995. *The Lost Victory*. London: Macmillan.
Boyne, G. A. 1993. Central Policies and Local Autonomy: The Case of Wales. *Urban Studies* 30(1): 87–101.
Bray, Denis. 2001. *Hong Kong Metamorphosis*. Hong Kong: Hong Kong University Press.
Bristow, Roger. 1984. *Land Use Planning in Hong Kong: History, Policies and Procedures*. Hong Kong: Oxford University Press.
Burton, Ann M. 1966. Treasury Control and Colonial Policy in the Late Nineteenth Century. *Public Administration* 44: 169–94.
Carpenter, Daniel P. 2001. *The Forging of Bureaucratic Autonomy*. Princeton and Oxford: Princeton University Press.
Castells, Manuel. 1986. *The Shek Kip Mei Syndrome*. Hong Kong: Centre of Urban Studies and Urban Planning, the University of Hong Kong.

Chan Lau Kit-ching. 1973. The Hong Kong Question during the Pacific War (1941–45). *The Journal of Imperial and Commonwealth History* II (10), No. 1: 56–78.

———. 1990. *China, Britain and Hong Kong, 1895–1945.* Hong Kong: The Chinese University Press.

Chan Wai-kwan. 1991. *The Making of Hong Kong Society.* Oxford: Clarendon Press.

Cheek-Milby, Kathleen. 1995. *A Legislature Comes of Age.* Hong Kong: Oxford University Press.

Cheng, T. C. 1969. Chinese Unofficial Members of the Legislative and Executive Councils in Hong Kong up to 1941. *Journal of the Royal Asiatic Society Hong Kong Branch* 9: 7–30.

Clark, Gordon. 1984. A Theory of Local Autonomy. *Annals of the Association of American Geographers*: 195–208.

Clark, Gordon L., and Dear, Michael. 1984. *State Apparatus.* Boston: Allen & Unwin.

Clark, Peter B., and Wilson, James Q. 1961. Incentive Systems: A Theory of Organisations. *Administrative Science Quarterly* 6, No. 1(6): 129–66.

Clayton, David. 1997. *Imperialism Revisited.* New York: St Martin's Press.

Coates, Austin A. 1977. *Mountain of Light: The Story of the Hongkong Electric Company.* London: Heinneman.

Crisswell, Colin, and Watson, Michael. 1982. *The Royal Hong Kong Police (1841–1945).* Hong Kong: MacMillan.

Donnisson, F. S. V. 1956. *British Military Administration in the Far East.* London: Her Majesty's Stationery Office.

Downs, Anthony. 1966. *Inside Bureaucracy.* Boston: Little, Brown and Company.

Drakakis-Smith, David. 1966. *Housing Provision in Metropolitan Hong Kong.* Hong Kong: Centre of Asian Studies, University of Hong Kong.

———. 1979. *High Society: Housing Provision in Metropolitan Hong Kong 1954 to 1979.* Hong Kong: Centre for Asian Studies.

Endacott, G. B. 1964a. *A History of Hong Kong.* Hong Kong: Oxford University Press.

———. 1964b. *Government and People in Hong Kong, 1841–1962: A Constitutional History.* Hong Kong: Hong Kong University Press.

———. 1978. *Hong Kong Eclipse.* Hong Kong: Oxford University Press.

Faure, David, ed. 1997. *A Documentary History of Hong Kong: Society.* Hong Kong: Hong Kong University Press.

———. 2003a. *Colonialism and the Hong Kong Mentality.* Hong Kong: Centre of Asian Studies, The University of Hong Kong.

———. 2003b. *Hong Kong: A Reader in Social History.* Hong Kong: Oxford University Press.

Ferguson, Niall. 2003. *Empire.* London: Penguin Books.

Fernando, P. T. M. 1969. The British Raj and the 1915 Communal Riots in Ceylon. *Modern Asia Studies* 3(3): 245–55.

Furse, Sir Ralph. 1962. *Aucupararius.* London: Oxford University Press.

Geiger, Theodore, and Geiger, Frances M. 1975. *The Development Progress of Hong Kong and Singapore.* London: The MacMillan Press.

Gill, Graeme J. 2003. *The Nature and Development of the Modern State*. Basingstoke: Palgrave MacMillan.
Goodstadt, Leo F. 2004a. Social, Economic and Political Reforms in Hong Kong, 1930–1955. *Journal of the Royal Asiatic Society Hong Kong Branch* 44: 57–81.
———. 2004b. The Rise and Fall of Social, Economic and Political Reforms in Hong Kong, 1935–1955. *Journal of the Royal Asiatic Society, Hong Kong Branch* 44: 73–74.
———. 2005. *Uneasy Partners: The Conflict between Public Interest and Private Profit in Hong Kong*. Hong Kong: Hong Kong University Press.
———. 2007. *Profits, Politics and Panics: Hong Kong's Banks and the Making of a Miracle Economy, 1935–1985*. Hong Kong: Hong Kong University Press.
Grantham, Alexander. 1959a. Hong Kong. *Journal of the Royal Central Asian Society* 46(4): 119–29.
———. 1959b. Housing Hong Kong's 600,000 Homeless. *Geographical Magazine* 31: 573–86.
———. 1965. *Via Ports: From Hong Kong to Hong Kong*. Hong Kong: Hong Kong University Press.
Hall, Henry L. 1937. *The Colonial Office*. London: Longmans.
Hannum, Hurst, and Lillich, Richard B. 1980. The Concept of Autonomy in International Law. *The American Journal of International Law* 74 (4): 858–89.
Harris, Peter. 1978. *Hong Kong: A Study in Bureaucratic Politics*. Hong Kong: Heinneman.
Haslewood, Lieutenant Commander Hugh Lyttleton, and Haslewood, Mrs H. L. 1930. *Child Slavery in Hong Kong: The Mui Tsai System*. London: Sheldon Press.
Ho, Eric Peter. 2005. *Times of Change: A Memoir of Hong Kong's Governance, 1950–1991*. Hong Kong: Hong Kong University Press.
Ho Pui-yin. 2004. *The Administrative History of the Hong Kong Government Agencies: 1841–2002*. Hong Kong: Hong Kong University Press.
Hoe, Susanna. 1991. *The Private Life of Old Hong Kong*. Hong Kong: Oxford University Press.
Hong Kong Housing Society. 1994. *Hong Kong Housing Society Forty-Five Years in Housing*. Hong Kong: Hong Kong Housing Society.
Hopkins, Keith. 1971. Housing the Poor. *Hong Kong: The Industrial Colony*, edited by Keith Hopkins, pp. 271–339. Hong Kong: Oxford University Press.
Jeffries, Charles. 1938. *The Colonial Empire and Its Civil Service*. Cambridge: Cambridge University Press.
Kannangara, A. P. 1984. The Riots of 1915 in Sri Lanka: A Study in the Roots of Communal Violence. *Past and Present* 102(1): 130–64.
Kaufman, Herbert. 1981. *The Administrative Behavior of Federal Bureau Chiefs*. Washington, DC: The Brookings Institution.
King, Frank H. H. 1988. *The Hongkong Bank between the Wars and the Bank Interned, 1919–1945*. Cambridge: Cambridge University Press.
Kirk-Greene, Anthony. 1967. *A Biographical Dictionary of the British Colonial Service 1939–1966*. London: H Zill.
———. 1999. *On Crown Service*. London: I. B. Tauris.

Kynaston, David. 2007a. *Austerity Britain 1945–48: A World to Build*. London: Bloomsbury.
———. 2007b. *Austerity Britain 1948–51: Smoke in the Valley*. London: Bloomsbury.
Latter, Tony. 2004. Hong Kong's Exchange Rate Regimes in the Twentieth Century: The Story of Three Regime Changes. HKMIR Working Paper No. 17/2004, September.
———. 2007. *Hong Kong's Money: The History, Logic and Operation of the Currency Peg*. Hong Kong: Hong Kong University Press.
Lee, J. M. H. 1967. *Colonial Development and Good Government*. Oxford: Clarendon Press.
Lee, J. M., and Petter, Martin. 1982. *The Colonial Office, War and Development Policy*. London: University of London, for the Institute of Commonwealth Studies.
Lee, Pui-tak. 2005. *Colonial Hong Kong and Modern China: Interaction and Reintegration*. Hong Kong: Hong Kong University Press.
Lethbridge, H. J. 1978. *Hong Kong: Stability and Change*. Hong Kong: Oxford University Press.
Littlewood, Michael. 2010. *Taxation Without Representation: The History of Hong Kong's Troublingly Successful Tax System*. Hong Kong: Hong Kong University Press.
Louis, William Roger. 1997. Hong Kong: The Critical Phase, 1945–1949. *The American Historical Review* 102, No. 4 (10): 1052–84.
Lyttelton, Oliver. 1962. *The Memoirs of Lord Chandos*. London: The Bodley Head.
MacKay, John. 1999. Fashion in Public Administration: The Foundation of the Hong Kong Housing Authority and the Northern Ireland Housing Executive. *International Review of Administrative Science* 65, No. 1 (3): 87–101.
MacKay, John. 2000. Housing Management and the Comprehensive Housing Model: A Case Study of Colonial Influence. *Journal of Contemporary China* 9, No. 25: 449–66.
Mills, Lennox A. 1942. *British Rule in Eastern Asia*. London: Oxford University Press.
Miners, Norman. 1986a. *The Government and Politics of Hong Kong*. Hong Kong: Oxford University Press.
———. 1986b. Plans for Constitutional Reform in Hong Kong 1946–52. *China Quarterly*, No. 107(9): 463–82.
———. 1987. *Hong Kong Under Imperial Rule, 1912–1941*. Hong Kong: Oxford University Press.
Moreno, Luis, 1997. Federalisation and Ethnoterritorial Concurrence in Spain. *Publius* 27(4): 65–84.
Morgan, D. J. 1980. *The Official History of Colonial Development Vol. 1, The Origins of British Aid Policy, 1924–1945*. Atlantic Highlands, NJ: Humanities Press.
Oxford Dictionary of National Biography. 2004. Oxford: Oxford University Press.
Parkinson, Sir Cosmo. C. 1946. *The Colonial Office from Within, 1900–1945*. London: Faber & Faber Limited.
Paton, David M. 1985. *R.O.: The Life and Times of Bishop Ronald Hall, The Bishop of Hong Kong*. Hong Kong: Diocese of Hong Kong and Macau.
Pedersen, Susan. 2001. The Maternalist Moment in British Colonial Policy: The Controversy over 'Child Slavery' in Hong Kong 1917–1941. *Past & Present* 171(5): 161–202.

Pryor, E. G. 1972. A Historical Review of Housing Conditions in Hong Kong. *Journal of the Royal Asiatic Society Hong Kong Branch* 12: 89–129.

Ramanathan, P. 1916. *Riots and Martial law in Ceylon, 1915.* London: Unknown publisher; New Delhi: Asian Educational Services [republished], 2003.

Richardson, J. Dillon. 2011. Rule Is From Mars, Home Rule Is From Venus: Local Government Autonomy and the Rules of Statutory Construction. *Publius* 41(4): 662–85.

Schenk, Catherine R. 2001. *Hong Kong as an International Financial Centre.* London: Routledge.

Scott, Ian, 1989. *Political Change and the Crisis of Legitimacy in Hong Kong.* London: Hurst.

———. ed. 1998. *Institutional Change and the Political Transition in Hong Kong.* New York: St Martin's Press.

Selwyn-Clarke, Sir Selwyn. 1975. *Footprints: The Memoirs of Sir Selwyn Selwyn-Clarke.* Hong Kong: Sino-American Publishing Company.

Sinn, Elizabeth. 2003. *Power and Charity: A Chinese Merchant Elite in Colonial Hong Kong.* Hong Kong: Hong Kong University Press.

Skocpol, Theda. 1992. *Protecting Soldiers and Mothers.* Cambridge, MA: The Belknap Press of Harvard University Press.

Skowronek, Stephen. 1982. *Building a New American State.* Cambridge: Cambridge University Press.

Smart, Alan. 1992. *Making Room: Squatter Clearance in Hong Kong.* Hong Kong: Centre of Asian Studies.

———. 2004. *From Tung Tau to Shek Kip Mei: Squatter Fires, Geopolitics and Housing Interventions in Hong Kong in the 1950s.* Hong Kong: Centre for China Urban and Regional Studies, Hong Kong Baptist University.

———. 2006. *The Shek Kip Mei Myth: Squatters, Fires and Colonial Rule in Hong Kong, 1950–1963.* Hong Kong: Hong Kong University Press.

Smith, Carl. 1981. The Chinese Church, Labour and Elites and the Mui Tsai Question in the 1920s. *Journal of the Royal Asiatic Society, Hong Kong Branch,* 21: 91–113.

———. 1988. The First Child Labour Law in Hong Kong. *Journal of the Royal Asiatic Society, Hong Kong Branch,* 28: 44–69.

Snow, Philip. 2005. *The Fall of Hong Kong: Britain, China and the Japanese Occupation.* New Haven and London: Yale University Press.

Sweeting, Anthony. 1993. *A Phoenix Transformed: The Reconstruction of Education in Post-War Hong Kong.* Hong Kong: Oxford University Press.

Thornton, A. P. 1959. *The Imperial Idea and Its Enemies: A Study in British Power.* New York: St Martin's Press.

Tsai, Jung-fang. 1993. *Hong Kong in Chinese History: Community and Social Unrest in the British Colony, 1842–1913.* New York: Columbia University Press.

Tsang, Steve. 1988. *Democracy Shelved: Great Britain, China, and Attempts at Constitutional Reform in Hong Kong, 1945–1952.* Hong Kong: Oxford University Press.

———. ed. 1995. *A Documentary History of Hong Kong: Government and Politics.* Hong Kong: Hong Kong University Press.

———. 2004. *A Modern History of Hong Kong.* Hong Kong: Hong Kong University Press.

Turnbull, C. M. 1989. *A History of Singapore, 1819–1975*. Singapore: Oxford University Press.
Visscher, Sikko. 2007. *The Business of Politics and Ethnicity: A History of the Singapore Chinese Chamber of Commerce and Industry*. Singapore: National University of Singapore Press.
Wallerstein, Immanuel. 2004. *World Systems Analysis*. Durham and London: Duke University Press.
Watson, James L. 1980. Transactions in People: The Chinese Labour Market in Slaves. In *Asian and African Systems of Slavery*, edited by James L. Watson, pp. 223–336. Oxford: Blackwell.
Weiss, Carol H. and Barton, Allen H. ed. 1980. *Making Bureaucracies Work*. London: Sage Publications.
Wesley-Smith, Peter. 1973. The Walled City of Kowloon: Historical and Legal Aspects. *The Hong Kong Law Journal* 3: 67–96.
Whitfield, Andrew. 2001. *Hong Kong, Empire and the Anglo-American Alliance at War, 1941–1945*. Basingstoke and New York: Palgrave.
Wight, Martin. 1946. *Development of the Legislative Council*. London: Faber & Faber.
———. 1952. *British Colonial Constitutions 1947*. Oxford: Clarendon Press.
Wilson, James Q. 1989. *Bureaucracy*. New York: Basic Books.
Wong, Luke S. K. 1978. *Housing in Hong Kong*. Hong Kong: Heinemann Educational Books (Asia) Ltd.
Zeng, Huaqun, 2003. Hong Kong's Autonomy: Concept, Development and Characteristics. *China: An International Journal* 1(2): 315.

Index

Adderly, Sir Charles n14:232; 66:258
Admiralty 65
Air Ministry 206
Airport, new at Deep Bay 102; reduction of loan amount for 103
Alabaster, Sir Chaloner 30, 34; n13:237
Anti-*Mui Tsai* Society 38, 56, 57, 59
Anti-Slavery and Aborigines Protection Society 37, 41, 56, 59; n46:240
Archbishop of Canterbury; housing 135, 153, 160; *mui tsai* 38, 59
Archbishop of York; and *mui tsai* 38, 59
Associated Exchange Banks 48
Atlee, Clement 23, 71
Attorney-General 32, 125, 174; 1947 motion debate on housing 144
Au, P. D.; Urban Council Emergency Resettlement Sub-Committee 179
autonomy 1, 26; basis of 3–5; Carpenter's theory 5–6; of Hong Kong government 4–5, 6–8, 8–12, 15, 28, 43, 65, 67, 85, 108–109, 116–117, 134, 136, 159–161, 163–164, 189, 214–215, 217, 227, 228

Bank of China 178
Bank of England 51, 53–54
banking policy directive 76
Barnett, K. M. A. 18; housing 149; squatters 170; Shek Kip Mei fire 178, 179; squatter resettlement and Chairman of the Urban Council 171–172, 173, 175, 182; n34:234
Battershill, Sir William; Battershill Committee 69, 82; n8:247
Basic Law 1
Bermuda 121
Bernacchi, Brook 132, 173; n80:261
Bird, H. W. 35
Bishop of Hong Kong. *See* Hall, Bishop Ronald "R. O.", MC
Black, Sir Robin 16, 188; housing 157; squatter resettlement policy 172, 176; financial autonomy 191, 213; n18:232
Bombay 35, 46
Borneo 74, 83; North Borneo 72
Bowley, F. B. L. 29, 30, 31; n5:236
Boy Scouts 176
boycott, 1925–26 14, 16
Bray, Denis 163, 175, 176; n2:265, 52:270
Brazier, Miss D. 57. *See also* Salvation Army.
Breen, M. J. 47; n4:241
British civil service 21, 22
British Commonwealth League 58; n60:244
British Exchequer. *See* Treasury.
British government 217–218, 221, 226–227; ability to impose policies upon Hong Kong 43, 45, 85, 224; advance of funds 98–99;

constitutional reform 111, 112, 134; defence 208; evacuation of British women and children 64; financial dispute 12, 99; housing 137; Labour government 27, 225; governance of Hong Kong 1–2, 4; relationship with unofficials 87, 108–109, 134, 223; Tai Lam Chung Reservoir 197
British Inland Revenue Department 91
British Military Administration 67, 77, 83–84, 85, 166, 221, 227; authorisation of expenditure 97; Civil Affairs Unit 83; Chief Civil Affairs Officer 83; estimates of revenue and expenditure 88; housing 139–140; rent controls 140
British Trade Dollar 46
British Treasury. *See* Treasury.
Building Reconstruction Advisory Committee 140, 141
bureaucracy 13, 17, 225
bureaucratic entrepreneur 6, 12, 17, 65, 87, 107
Burgess, Claude 175, 179, 182, 183; n63:269
Burma 101

Cabinet 6, 23; Cabinet Minister 3, 6; constitutional reform 131, 132; currency 56; Defence Committee 197–198; evacuation of British women and children 63; reduction in garrison strength 208–209; reinforcement of Hong Kong's garrison 126, 137, 198
cadets 17–18, 20–22, 23, 42, 82, 221, 226; Bishop Hall's and Caine's views 68, 82; language training 17; need to employ 82; role 27–28, 65; Sanitary Board 28; strengths 17, 225
Caine, Sir Sydney; 75-year leases 141; cadets 68, 83; constitutional reform 80, 81, 114; financial dispute 102, 107; Financial Secretary 11, 14, 18, 20, 23, 45, 64, 215; housing and Exchange Fund 62, 139; Hong Kong's future 67; income tax and Taxation Committee 61, 62, 63, 64, 65, 91, 95; n6:231
Caldecott, Sir Andrew 16, 215, 220, 223; and *mui tsai* 58, 59, 219; n22:233
Cambridge University 16, 18
Campbell, Sir John 49, 51; proposed municipal council 80, 81, 82
Canton 16, 165
Cantonese language 18, 21
Cape, T. C., MP 31
Carpenter, Professor Daniel; bureaucratic entrepreneurs 65; theory of autonomy 5–8, 14, 17, 25–26, 87, 191, 217, 219–220, 228
Carrie, W. J. 152, 154; n54:266
Ceylon 16, 18, 97; Stubbs as Colonial Secretary 36
Chadwick Report 28
Chai Wan 180
Chairman of the Urban Council. *See* Urban Council, Chairman.
Chan Kai-ming 29; n12:237
Chancellor of the Exchequer 54, 56, 199
Chartered Bank 46
Chater, Sir Paul 34, 35; n35:239
Chatham, William 30; n14:237
Chau, Sir Sik-nin; Inland Revenue Bill 1947 93; constitutional reform 124; 1947 housing 144; trustee of Housing Society 151; visit to Colonial Office 119; n5:252
Chau, Sir Tsun-nin; 1946 budget debate 89; constitutional reform 124; Inland Revenue Bill 1947 93; n22:253
Chau Siu-kai 38; n50:240
Chief Civil Affairs Officer. *See* British Military Administration and MacDougall, D. M.
Chief of the Imperial General Staff 198

Chief Resettlement Officer 173; Urban Council Emergency Resettlement Sub-Committee 178

Chiefs of Staff 197–198

Children 42; Children's Act 1908 29; Commission on Industrial Employment of children 31; Commission's visits to factories 31–32; Commission's recommendations 32; employment 29; Industrial Employment of Children Bill 32

China 14, 25–26, 27, 45, 108, 187, 189, 211, 221, 222, 227, 228; currency 54; return of Hong Kong 67, 70, 71; HMS *Amethyst* 126; political difficulties 101; silver 49, 50, 51, 53

China Association; constitutional reform 125; Creech-Jones 115; Governor 121–122; municipal council 78, 79, 80, 82, 85, 112; trade embargo 205; n46:250

China Mail 112, 113

Chinese Chamber of Commerce 128, 129

Chinese Communist Party 27, 129, 131, 134

Chinese community leaders 19

Chinese government 25–26, 221, 223, 224; return of Hong Kong 11; Kowloon Walled City 164; Shek Kip Mei fire 178; squatters 169

Chinese guilds 78, 79

Chinese merchants 17, 21

Chongqing. *See* Chungking.

Chow, Sir Shouson; factory legislation 31, 32, 33; *mui tsai* 38, 59; n22:238

Chungking 71

Church of England, Men's Society 29, 31

Churchill, Sir Winston 14, 23, 218; Mansion House speech, November 1942 71; *mui tsai* 38, 39, 41, 135

Civil Affairs Charter 73; Combined Civil Affairs Committee 73; London Sub-Committee 74; US British Embassy's views 74

Civil Affairs Unit. *See* British Military Administration.

Civil Aid Services 176

Clague, Sir Douglas 175, 178, 224; Chairman of the Urban Council Emergency Resettlement Sub-Committee 178, 180–181, 225; Urban Council and squatter resettlement 182, 183, 187; n58:269

Clague's Sub-Committee. *See* Urban Council.

Clarke, Arthur 215; 1948 financial controls 192; housing 157; n67:265

Clementi, Sir Cecil 16, 20, 56, 64, 83, 133, 222, 226–227, 228; currency 47; Tai Lam Chung Reservoir 196; *mui tsai* 41, 42, 135, 218, 220; unofficials 223; n19:233

Colonial Administrative Service 18, 22, 82, 122

Colonial Development & Welfare; 1929 Act 95; 1940 Act 95; 1945 Act 94, 95; funding for housing 154, 155; Hong Kong Colonial Development & Welfare Committee 152; Colonial Development & Welfare Fund 222

Colonial Office 16, 20, 26, 43, 218, 221, 229; advice to colonies 27; Advisory Committees (Labour, Social Welfare and opium) 76; Battershill Committee 69; charter on colonial policy 71; Committee on Post-War Problems re Malaya and Hong Kong 68; directives 75–76, 85; factory legislation 31, 32; Financial Secretary 215; Foreign Office and War Office 72–74; Hong Kong's future 67, 69, 84; MacDougall 75, 83, 84,

227; officials 1, 9, 24; role 11, 22–23
constitutional reform 114, 116, 118–119: abandonment of 131–132; Chau Sik-nin's visit 119; Colonial Office 77–78; Grantham's 126–127, 128; Municipal Council 77–82, 85, 116 currency 51, 52, 53, 54; Currency Committee 49–50; Economic and Financial Adviser 49; export silver tax 53
defence costs contribution 197, 200, 205, 206, 207, 208, 209, 214; local defence costs 199; reduction in garrison strength 208–209
financial autonomy 191–192, 197 211–214, 224; 1948 financial controls 193, 193-194; Tai Lam Chung Reservoir 194–195, 196 financial dispute; denial claims 104, 137, 201–204; Grantham's despatch 99; Hong Kong's post-war finances 100; Malta style grant 101; unofficial support 108–109, 116–117
housing 136, 159, 220; 75-year leases 141; housing schemes 146; June 1950 meetings with Grantham 153–154, 160 income tax: Model Income Tax Ordinance 61; Inland Revenue Bill 1947 94–97; Pudney's visit to London 91; taxation, views on 91, 97, 106–107
mui tsai 37-8, 41, 56, 59–60; District Watch Committee 59 squatter resettlement 174; Shek Kip Mei fire 177–178, 187–188

Colonial Secretariat 121, 148, 181, 182
Colonial Secretary; 16, 25, 75, 121, 143; Ceylon 16, 36; defence contribution and denial claims 203, 210; housing 152, 154, 157, 158; squatter resettlement 169, 172, 173, 175, 176, 183, 184, 188; Treasury control 105
Colonial Treasurer 25, 215; currency 47, 48; Exchange Fund 55; income tax 61; rent controls 34
Colonial Veterinary Surgeon 28
Colonial Welfare and Development Act 1940 14,
Combined Civil Affairs Committee. *See* Civil Affairs Charter.
Commissioner for Resettlement 179, 181, 184; squatter resettlement 185, 186, 221
Commissioner of Inland Revenue. *See* Pudney, E. W.
Commissioner of Police. *See* Hong Kong Police, Commissioner of.
Conservatives 129
constitutional reform 12, 17, 100, 111, 112, 114, 116, 117, 120, 123, 127–129, 131, 132, 133–134, 188, 218, 219, 227–228
Convention of Peking 164
Cranbourne, Lord 70, 71
Creech-Jones, Arthur 14, 23; constitutional reform 114, 125, 126–127, 133, 134; housing 135, 137, 138, 139, 153, 227; policy directives 77; Young 115; n4:231
Crisp, Col G. B. 30
Crombie, Sir James 206
Crown 3, 22, 217
Crown Agents 49, 51
Crown Colony 22
Crown Lands & Survey Office 167
Crown Solicitor 29
Cunliffe-Lister, Philip 23; n55:235
currency, 11, 46; Colonial Office 52; Colonial Office Currency Committee 49–50, 51, 52; Hong Kong visit 50; Currency Bill 55; excess note issue 48; Hong Kong Currency Commission 48–49; premium on banknotes 46–47; silver standard 51–56; silver export tax 52

D'Almada, Leo e Castro; constitutional reform 124; evacuation of British women and children 64; financial settlement 104; housing 145; Inland Revenue Bill 1947 93; n23:254
David, E. B. 212
defence contribution 197–210, 214; background to 199
Defence Secretary. *See* Minister of Defence.
denial claims 98, 100, 104, 137, 201–204
Deputy Colonial Secretary 149, 165, 173, 179, 182
Deputy Director of Public Works 220
Deputy Financial Secretary 149, 193, 196
Development and Housing Corporation 157
Development Fund 155, 194, 195, 196, 197, 222
directives. *See* Hong Kong Planning Unit.
Director of Public Works. *See* Public Works.
Director of Recruiting. *See* Furse, Sir Ralph.
District Office 18
District Watch Committee 19, 25, 57; *mui tsai* 38, 40, 42, 56, 57, 59, 60
Dublin, Trinity College 16
Duke of Devonshire 40

Earnings and Profits Tax. *See* income tax.
Eastern Cadets and Cadetships 16, 18, 22
Eden, Sir Anthony 71, 74
Edinburgh University 16
education 85
Endacott, G.B. 8
English language 132
evacuation of British women and children 45; 63–64, 224
Exchange Fund 55, 65, 98, 99, 100; housing 62, 139

Executive Council 13, 15, 20; 75-year leases 141; advice of 2; Sir Paul Chater 34; Chief Civil Affairs Officer 83; constitutional reform 125, 127, 130–132; Defence contribution 208; factory legislation 30, 31; Hong Kong Housing Society 150, 156; housing 138, 161; Housing Authority 156–158; influence on policy 219; Kowloon Walled City 165; municipal council 118; re-establishment post-War 76; proposed 1945 reform 78; rent controls 34; Secretary of State 129–130; Shek Kip Mei fire 177; squatters 168, 170, 172, 174, 185; Urban Council Emergency Resettlement Sub-Committee report 183–184; Wakefield Report 171

factory legislation 11, 29, 30, 42, 43; Factory and Workshop Act, 1901 30
Fehily, Dr J. P. 75; housing 148, 149; MacDougall 166; squatters 165–166; n31:249
Female Domestic Service Ordinance. See *mui tsai*.
Fiji 121, 122
Finance Committee of the Legislative Council 98, 214, 222, 223, 229; defence costs 206, 208; evacuation of British women and children, 1940 64, 65; reform of 16, 25, 108, 224; Shek Kip Mei resettlement 183; squatter resettlement 168, 185; Tai Lam Chung Reservoir 194, 195
financial autonomy 12, 131, 191–192, 224; defence contribution 210–213
financial dispute with Britain 97–109; advance of funds to Hong Kong 98–99; Colonial Office's offer 102; Treasury 102, 105, 106–107
financial policy directive 76

292   Index

Financial Secretary 25, 65, 221; 1946 budget 88; 1948 financial controls 192; advance of funds 99; denial claims 98, 99, 203–204, 210; financial autonomy 213; Financial Secretary post 215; housing 148, 154, 157, 161; housing for government staff 148; income tax 89; Leo D'Almada e Castro 104; M. K. Lo and housing 142–143; Secretary of State and wartime expenditure 99; squatter resettlement 169
Fire Brigade 176
First World War 35
Fleming, John and Taxation Committee 61
Follows, C. G. S. 215; 1946 Taxation Committee 89, 90; 1948 financial controls 192, 193; denial claims 204; retirement 205; n8:253
Foreign Office 23; charter on colonial policy 71; Civil Affairs Charter 73–74; constitutional reform 129, 130–131; Hong Kong's future 70; recovery of Hong Kong 72–74, 77; payments to refugees in Macau 101
Foreign Secretary 71
France 54
Furse, Sir Ralph 22, 69; n47:235

Garrison; costs of reinforcement of 197; reinforcement of 198
Gater, Sir George 84; proposed municipal council 80, 81
General Chamber of Commerce 3, 24; building materials 140; constitutional reform 118, 125, 129; income tax 93, 97; Legislative Council representation 113, 128
General Office Commanding 165, 166
Geneva 208
Gent, Sir Gerard 14, 23; Battershill Committee 69; Foreign Office 74; Hong Kong Planning Unit 74–75; Hong Kong's recovery 72; income tax 97; Malaya 96; municipal council 77, 80, 82, 85, 134; n5:231
Germany 61
Gibson, Adam 28, 30; n4:236
Gillespie, R. D.; 1946 Taxation Committee 89, 90; 1947 housing 144; income tax 93, 97; Inland Revenue Bill 1947 93; n9:253
Gimson, Sir Franklin 96, 97
Gladstone, Viscountess Dorothy 32
Goodstadt, Leo 9–10
Gorman, W. J. 169
Governor 2, 3, 13, 15, 21–22, 24, 224–225, 226; appointment of 1, 218; Colonial Office and housing 138; constraint on power 77; currency 56; defence costs 205, 206, 212; financial autonomy 69, 106, 213; Financial Secretary post 215; Hong Kong's defence 198; income tax 91; leadership role 60, 63, 65; London 8, 111; municipal council 78, 81; official majority 62, 107; power to influence opinion 108, 111; rent controls 35; role 15–17, 21–22; Sanitary Board 28; Shek Kip Mei fire victims 179; Tai Lam Chung Reservoir 196; unofficals 3, 87, 97, 111, 224
Grantham, Sir Alexander 9, 15, 21, 222, 228, 229; arrival in Hong Kong as Governor 117, 143; autonomy 10, 227; career background 121–122; leadership 225–227; Lyttelton 130; official majority 121; unofficials 109; n:8:231; 9:232
    constitutional reform: 1950 constitutional reform proposals 127–129; 1952 constitutional reform proposals 129–131; abandonment 131–132; Colonial Office 118–119; doubts on

118; position on 132–134, 218; Secretary of State 117, 125
    financial autonomy and defence costs: Clarke 158; Colonial Office 204–205, 214; defence costs 200–201, 204–207, 208, 209, 210; denial claims 201–204; financial autonomy 213, 214; local defence costs 199; reduction in garrison 208–209; Tai Lam Chung Reservoir 195, 196; unofficials 223–224
    financial dispute 108; denial claims 103, 201–204; financial settlement 100; Hong Kong's financial position 99, 100, 101; Secretary of State 102–103; Treasury control 106–107; unofficials' and Britain's commitment to Hong Kong 104, 108
    housing 135–136, 161; 1950 Colonial Office meetings 153–154, 160; Housing Committee under Carrie 152; Housing Authority 156; housing policy 149; housing schemes 146, 147; Morse 150, 221
    squatter resettlement: 166, 168, 174, 180, 183, 186–187, 188; Shek Kip Mei fire 176; Urban Council involvement 173

Grayburn, Sir Vandeleur 48, 51, 53, 64–65; Exchange Fund 55; Taxation Committee 61
Griffiths, James 23, 128, 129, 153; n54:235
Grindle, Sir Arthur 39; n59:241
Guangzhou. *See* Canton.
Guinea 16

Hall, George Henry, 1st Viscount Hall 23; n53:235
Hall, Bishop Ronald "R.O.", MC 81, 83, 219; cadets 68; housing 150, 151, 153, 160, 226; n3:247

Hallifax, E. R.; factory legislation 30; n16:238
Harcourt, Rear-Admiral C. H. J. 83
Haslewoods 58, 219, 226, Clara 37; Lt-Cdr Hugh, RN 37
Hazelrigg, T. M.; municipal council 1945 78, 79, 80; special adviser 112; retirement in 1947 118, 133; n48:251
Health Officers 169
Hickling, Dr Alice 29; n9:237
HK & Kowloon Chinese Anti-Direct Tax Introduction Commission. *See* income tax.
HMS *Amethyst* 126
home civil service. *See* British civil service.
Holmes, Sir Ronald 181, 182, 185, 186, 221; n67:270
Hongay 83
Hongkong and Shanghai Bank 46; 1947 AGM 93; Chief Manager 11, 48, 49, 50, 55; housing 150, 151, 153; note issue 46, 47, 48, 49, 50; storage facilities 50
Hong Kong Club 24
Hong Kong (Coinage) Order 1895 46
Hong Kong Council of Social Service 150
Hong Kong Currency Commission. *See* currency.
Hong Kong, future of 71
Hong Kong Garrison. *See* Garrison.
Hong Kong General Chamber of Commerce. *See* General Chamber of Commerce.
Hong Kong Government 9, 24, 26, 84, 85; accountability 6; autonomy 7, 10, 11, 28, 42–43, 64, 65, 164, 166, 169, 180, 217–228; bureaucracy 6; British government and unofficials 11; Clarke 215; constitutional reform 111, 112, 117, 118, 130, 132, 134; currency 46, 48, 49, 51, 54, 55; defence contribution 209; Grantham 121; financial autonomy 191, 192–193,

194–195, 197, 200, 202, 213; financial dispute with Britain 101, 102, 109; financial policies 106; housing 136, 137, 139, 141, 142, 143–145, 146, 147–148, 150, 151–153, 154, 156–157, 159, 161; income tax 87, 88, 93, 94; *mui tsai* 42–43, 45, 56, 58; opium 77; postwar change 67–70, 84, 85; squatter resettlement 163, 164, 165, 166, 169, 170, 171, 178, 179, 180, 182, 186–189; social services 9
Hong Kong Housing Authority 151, 135, 155, 159, 161, 196, 219; formation of 156–158, 183, 188, 218; Housing Authority Bill 158–159
Hong Kong Housing Society 149, 151–152, 155, 157, 196, 222; formation 150; grant 151; Sheung Li Uk 156, 161
Hong Kong Island 165, 166, 171, 176, 180
Hong Kong Jockey Club 24
Hong Kong Model Housing Society 151, 157, 222
Hong Kong officials 1, 15
Hong Kong Planning Unit 67, 97, 134, 166, 227; Colonial Office 72, 74; costs 73; directives 74, 75–77; government in waiting 85; origins 72–74; municipal council 77–82, 112; recruitment and staffing 74–75
Hong Kong Police 20, 164, 165, 171, 172, 176
Hong Kong Police, Commissioner of 172, 173
Hong Kong population 14, 27, 34, 45, 164
Hong Kong Royal Naval Volunteer Reserve 98
Hong Kong Social Welfare Council. *See* Hong Kong Council of Social Service.
Hong Kong Society for the Protection of Children 57

Hong Kong Special Administrative Region 1
Hong Kong Volunteer Defence Corps 98
House of Commons. *See* Parliament.
housing 12, 14, 33–34, 220, 224; 1940 Housing Commission 139; 1947 motion debate 143–154, 223; ad-hoc committee on housing 157, 158; building of new houses 1911–1921 34; draft Colonial office despatch 138; Commission of Enquiry 27; Exchange Fund 62; Housing and Town Planning Sub-Committee 152; Housing Committee 152, 159; housing schemes 142, 148, 150; Low Cost Housing 183
Housing Authority. *See* Hong Kong Housing Authority.
Housing Trust 149
Howard-Drake, J. T. A. 191
Humphrey's Estate 34

imperial tariff preferences 45
Import and Export Department 28
Improvement Trust. *See* Housing Authority.
income tax 11, 12, 16, 45, 112, 220; 1917 proposal, 61; 1946 Legislative Council budget debate 89; 1947 Taxation Committee 91–92; Caine's views 91, 107; Colonial Office and Treasury 94–97; difficulty of increasing 139; earnings and profits tax 96; Grantham 128; HK & Kowloon Chinese Anti-Direct Tax Introduction Commission 93; Inland Revenue Bill 1947 91–94; Legislative Council debate 61; Model Income Tax Ordinance, 1922 61; Morse's committee 92; Pudney's London visit 91; tax on interest 62; Taxation Committee 61, 89–91; Secretary of State 91; surtax 91; Sir Mark Young 116

Indian Civil Service 18
Industrial Employment of Children Bill. *See* factory legislation.
Inland Revenue Bill 1947. *See* income tax.
International Labour Convention 30, 32, 42
International Labour Organisation 27, 30

Jamaica 121
Japan, 54,164, 165; defeat 14, 79, 83, 84, 227; Japanese forces, 11, 14, 45, 67, 139; Japanese occupation 76, 88, 89, 101, 108, 132, 170; military yen 83
Jardine's Lookout 142
Jardine Matheson and Co. 24, 34; Paterson and Taxation Committee 61
Jeffries, Sir Charles; constitutional reform 126; 127, 129, 131; housing 138, 139; defence costs 206; n58:261
Joint Declaration 1
Jones, J. R. 151
Jury List 38, 78, 125, 132
Justices of the Peace 3, 24, 93; Legislative Council representation 113, 128, 130

Kai Fong 19
Kai Tak 165
Korea 208; Korean War 128
Kotewall, Sir Robert 25, 49; n58:236
Kowloon 166, 171, 180
Kowloon Tong; squatter fire 184
Kowloon Walled City 164, 165, 166, 169, 187; squatter fire 169
Kuala Lumpur 96
Kuomintang 14, 27, 113, 115, 119

labour; policy directive 76, 85
Land and Survey Directive 76
Land Investment Co 34
Landale, David F. 210, 226; constitutional reform 120, 122–124; denial claims 98; financial settlement 105; housing 143; Inland Revenue Bill 1947 93
Lau Chu-pak 35; n 37:239
laws, disallowance of 2
League of Nations 27, 30, 33; Labour Conventions 32; Permanent Advisory Committee on Slavery 57
League of Nations Union 32
leases, 75-year 140–141, 144
Lee Gardens 145
Lee Hysan Estate Company Limited 145–146, 148, 219
Lee, J. H. B. 118 n22:257
Lee, Richard Charles; Urban Council Emergency Resettlement Sub-Committee 179
Legislative Council 1, 2, 13, 15, 20, 24, 25, 187, 223; 1947 motion debate on housing 143–154, 223; approval of estimates 191, 212–213, 214; Chief Civil Affairs Officer 83; Commissioner for Resettlement 184; Currency Bill 55; defence costs 205–207, 208; factory legislation 31, 32, 42; Governor and housing 138; Housing Authority Bill 158–159; influence on policy process 219; local defence costs 199–200; *mui tsai* 39, 40, 41 58, 60; post-War re-establishment 76; proposed 1945 reforms 78; rent control 33–5; Rents Bill 36; Shek Kip Mei fire 163, squatters 164, 174; unofficials 212

constitutional reform, 133–134; abandonment 131–132; Creech-Jones 114, 126–127; Grantham's 1950 reform proposals 127–129; Grantham's 1952 reform proposals 130; Grantham's March 1948 report on constitutional reform 118; Landale's 120; motion debate 122–124; official majority 121,

205; meeting with Secretary of State in Hong Kong 129–130; Young 112–113, 115, 125
  income tax and financial dispute: 1946 budget 88, 89; advance of funds to Hong Kong 98–99; British Treasury control 106–107; budget debate and approval of annual estimates 192, 193, 213, 214; denial claims 98, 203–204; financial dispute with Britain 101, 105; Inland Revenue Bill 1947 92, 93; Taxation Committee 61; War Revenue Bill 1940 62

Leith-Ross, Sir Frederick 53
Letters Patent 1
Li Ping 31, 32
Listowel, William Francis Hare, Lord 103, 119
Lloyd, Sir Thomas 114, 121–122
Lo, Bingham and Mathews 61
Lo, Sir Man-kam; taxation 61, 89, 90; constitutional reform 123; denial claims 98, 99, 103, 204; evacuation of British women and children 1940 64; housing 142–143, 144, 145, 148; financial settlement 105; Inland Revenue Bill 1947 93–94; *mui tsai* 60; Treasury control 106; n72:245
Lo Man-wai 158, 188
Lockhart, Sir James H. S. 18, 19, 21, 22, 27, 40, 116, 226; n33:234
London Missionary Society 29
Lord Mayor of London's Air Raid Distress Fund 150
Loseby, F. H. 57
Louey, William S. T. 132
low-cost housing. *See* housing.
Lugard, Sir Frederick, 1st Baron Lugard 18, 20; n31:234
Lyttelton, Oliver, Viscount Chandos 14, 23, 129, 130, 131, 160, 227; n2:231; 64:260

Macau 101
MacDonald, Malcolm 14, 23, 198; n3:231
MacDougall, David M.; 75-year leases 141; Chief Civil Affairs Officer 83, 84, 221; Colonial Office and Treasury 95; constitutional reform 114, 115, 125, 133; departure 136, 149, 150, 188, 220; Fehily 166; Follows 215; Hong Kong's future 69, 70; Hong Kong Planning Unit 75; housing 139, 140, 144–145, 149, 151, 159; housing schemes 142, 145, 146, 151, 219; leadership 116, 149, 226; municipal council 78, 79, 81; policy directives 77; squatters 165–166, 168, 186–187, 225; n11:247; 40:265
Mainland. *See* China.
Malacca 18
Malaya 16, 18, 57, 58, 82, 122; colonial administration 69; Colonial Office Committee on Post-War Problems re Malay and Hong Kong 68; financial settlement 101, 102, 103; Japanese arms 68; Malayan Planning Unit 72
Malta 100, 101
Manchester Guardian 41
Martin, Sir John 209
May, Sir Francis 16; *mui tsai* 37; n17:232
Mayle, N. L. 114, 118; renewal of 75-year leases 141
Maxwell, Sir George 57, 58, 59
McDouall, J. C. 170; squatter resettlement 169–170; n27:267
McKenny, Dr Charles 31; n20:238
Medical Department 76
Melmoth, C. G. F. F. 149
Mercantile Bank 46
Mexican silver dollar 46
migrants (from the Mainland) 14
Mills, Lennox 8, 87
Milner, Viscount 23
Miners, Norman 8

Minister(s) 23, 127, 202, 203, 214
Minister of Defence 198, 199
Minister of Health 118
Mont Tremblant 75
Morse, Sir Arthur; Hong Kong Housing Society 150, 151; income tax 92, 97; municipal council 78, 79, 81, 82, 85; 1946 Taxation Committee 89; n44:250
Moyne, Lord 62
mui tsai 11, 42, 43, 94, 108, 134, 135, 160, 188, 214, 218, 219, 220, 223, 224, 225, 226; 1878 examination of 37; 1922 Commission 39; Anti-*Mui Tsai* Society 38; Female Domestic Service Ordinance, 1923 40, 60; Loseby Committee 57; Majority Report 58, 59, 60, Minority Report 58–59, 60; nature of 37; registration of 41: Society for the Protection of *Mui Tsai* 38; Stubbs 37; Woods Commission 57–59, 64, n75:247
Mumbai. *See* Bombay.
Municipal Council 78, 218; 1946 announcement 112; autonomy 85; Colonial Office 118; Creech-Jones 114; Executive Council 118; Hong Kong Planning Unit 77–82; Kuomintang 113; Municipal Council Bills 117, 123, 124; Young 112–113
Murray Barracks 209
Myanmar. *See* Burma.

Naval Dockyard 209
New Territories 18, 71, 74, 194
Ngau Tau Kok 171
Nicol, Andrew 149
Nicoll, Sir John F. 188; constitutional reform 123, 128, 129, 130; housing 138, 139, 149; n47:259
Nigeria 121
North Borneo. *See* Borneo.
North Point 150, 151
North, R. A. C. 59, 60; n68:245

Northcote, Sir Geoffry 16, 45, 62, 64–65, 93, 220, 226; housing 139; income tax 61; 63; *mui tsai* 59, 60, 219, 225; unofficials 65, 87, 223; n23:233
Norton, Lieutenant-General E. F. 65

opium; policy directive 76, 85
Oxford University 16, 18
Ozorio, Dr F. M. 30, 31

Palestine 134
Parkinson, Sir Cosmo 8
Parliament 2, 6, 14, 15, 23, 26, 42, 203, 214; constitutional reform 127; *mui tsai* 37, 38, 40, 41
Paskin, Sir John; constitutional reform 120, 127, 128; defence costs 206; housing 136, 153; municipal council 79
Passfield, Sydney James Webb, Lord 14, 23, 218; *mui tsai* 41, 56, 135; n1:230
Paterson, John Johnstone and Taxation Committee 61
Peel, Sir William 16, 20, 56, 58, 64, 83, 214, 222, 228; currency 50, 51, 52, 55; *mui tsai* 57, 160, 220; unofficial support 65, 223; n21:233
Penang 18
Philippines 185
Picton-Turbervill, Miss Edith 58, 59, 60, 219; n57:244
Pitts, Miss Ada 29, 31, 33; n6:236
Po Leung Kuk 19, 25, 39, 57; and *mui tsai* 38
Pollock, Sir Henry; rent controls 35
Portuguese 24, 78, 79
postage rates 76
Prime Minister 131
Privy Council 2
Public Health and Buildings Ordinance 29, 30
Public Health (Sanitary Provisions) Regulations 171, 174
public schools 16, 21

Public Works, Director of 25, 145, 149; housing schemes 147; substandard housing 168; Shek Kip Mei fire 179, 180, 181; squatter resettlement 168, 172, 173, 174, 175, 176, 185; Tai Lam Chung Reservoir 194–196; Urban Council Emergency Resettlement Sub-Committee 178
Public Works Department 137, 145, 148, 157; Shek Kip Mei fire 177; squatter resettlement 172, 188
Pudney, E. W.; London visit 91; Taxation Committee 89, 90; n10:253

Quebec 75

Rees-Williams, David R. 137
Reform Club of Hong Kong 130, 132
refugees, from China 27, 136, 139, 164
Registrar General's Office 18, 20, 21
Rehabilitation Loan 192
rent controls 27; causes of 34; nature of 33; Rent Bill 36; British Military Administration 140
Resettlement Office 172
Retrenchment Commission 45
Robinson, Sir Hercules 17; n29:233
Rolleston, Colonel 69; n9:247
Ross, S. B. C. 31: n19:238
Rouse, H. S. 75; n32:249
Royal Instructions 1, 121, 133
Royal Marine Commando 198
Rushton, Miss Alice 81
Ruttonjee, J. H.; Housing Society 151; squatter resettlement 173

Salvation Army 57. *See also* Brazier.
Sanitary Board 28; factory legislation 31, 42; Sub-Committee 29
Sanitary Department 28, 29
Sarawak 72
Scott, Ian 9
seaman's strike 40

Secretariat for Chinese Affairs 18; and *mui tsai* 59
Secretary for Chinese Affairs 30; *mui tsai* 58; re-establishment post-War 76; rent control 33; squatters 165, 172
Secretary of State for the Colonies 1, 13, 14, 15, 218, 219, 221, 224–225; advice to colonies 27, 108; China Association 80; Colonial Regulations 2; currency 47, 49, 54, 56; defence contribution 201, 205; direct taxation 95–96; expenditure during Second World War 99; financial autonomy 191, 213, 215; financial controls 106–107, 192, 193–194, 214; financial dispute 102; Governor, appointment of 218; laws, disallowance of 2, 15; disregard of local views 86; limits of power 137; Lord Moyne 62; *mui tsai* 41, 42, 56, 60; officials 2, 22; policy directives 77; revenue and expenditure 2; role of 23, 107; squatter resettlement 188; Treasury control 105, 106–107; visit to Hong Kong 129, 206; Woods Commission 57, 59; Young 113
    constitutional reform 111, 119, 130, 133–134; Creech-Jones 114; Grantham 125; municipal council 80, 112; Municipal Council Bill 117
    housing 135–136, 154–155, 159, 161, 220, 224; 75 year leases 141; housing schemes (estates) 141, 146, 147, 148, 150; meetings with Grantham 153–154, 160

Sedgwick, P. C. M. 75; n36:249
Severn, Sir Claud 33; *mui tsai* 37; n25:239
Sham Shui Po 177
Shanghai 83, 147, 165; dollar 52, 55; Shanghai Municipal Council 115

Shek Kip Mei; fire 163, 164, 176–178, 182, 187, 225; squatter resettlement 179, 183, 185–186
Sheung Li Uk. *See* Hong Kong Housing Society.
Shiels, Dr Drummond 41, 56; n68:241
Shing Mun Reservoir 194
Sidebotham, J. B. 119, 139, 174
silver standard, Hong Kong 14
Sing Tao Jih Pao 132
Singapore 18, 68, 70; income tax 96, 97; Legislative Council elections 114, 115; visit to Singapore by Hong Kong official 156; Singapore Improvement Trust 156
Sino-British Joint Declaration. *See* Joint Declaration.
Slim, Field Marshall William 198
Sloss, Duncan; income tax in 1947 93, 97; Taxation Committee 61; n19:253
Smith, Norman Lockhart; evacuation of British women and children 64, 65; Hong Kong's future 70; Hong Kong Planning Unit 75; *mui tsai* 58, 59; n61:244; 29:249
Social Service Centre of the Churches 62
Social Welfare; direct taxation 95; policy directive 76, 85; Social Welfare Advisory Committee 76; Social Welfare Officer 76
Social Welfare Office 167; emergency relief 193; Shek Kip Mei fire 176; squatters 169, 172
Social Welfare Officer 167, 168, 170, 171, 172, 173
South China Morning Post; constitutional reform 131; Exchange Fund 55
Southorn, Sir Thomas; currency 52, 53, 54, 55, 64
Soviet Union 198
squatter resettlement 12, 157, 164, 188, 219, 221, 224; 1948 policy 166–169; Barnett 171–172; McDouall 169–170; Fehily 166–168; "tolerated" and "approved" resite areas 171; Urban Council 173, 188; Wakefield 171
St John's Ambulance 176
Stanley, Colonel Oliver 71; n17:248
Straits Settlements 18, 35, 58, 59, 122
Stubbs, Sir Reginald 15–16, 20, 41, 133, 134, 222, 226–227, 228; Ceylon 36; Finance Committee 16, 25, 108, 224; housing 34; *mui tsai* 36, 37, 39, 40, 135, 218, 220; rent controls 34; views on opposition 35; views of unofficials 223; n16:232
Sun Yat-sen 40
Swire, G. W.; proposed municipal council 78, 79, 81, 82, 85; n45:250

Ta Kung Pao 123
Tai Lam Chung Reservoir 191, 214; proposed construction of 193–197
Tang Shiu-kin 57
Taylor, Sir Henry n16:279
Taxation Committee. *See* income tax.
The Times 69
Thomson, W. M. 75; n35:251
Todd, R. R. 143, 144, 172; n20:264
Town Clerk, proposal by Bishop Hall 68
Town Planning Unit 152
Tratman, D. W. 28
Treasury 11, 22, 23; 1948 financial controls 194; advance to Hong Kong 99; airport 103; Colonial Office 95; currency 49, 50, 51, 53, 55; defence contribution 197, 199, 200, 205, 206, 207, 208, 209, 210, 214–215; denial claims 202, 210; direct taxation 95; financial autonomy 211–212, 213, 214; first financial settlement offer 102, 103; Grantham 99; Hong Kong Planning Unit 73, 75; Hong Kong's post-War finances 100;

housing schemes 142, 146, 150; Inland Revenue Bill 1947 94–97; Malta style grant to Hong Kong 101; municipal council 118; Treasury control of Hong Kong's finances 87, 98, 105, 106–107, 109
Tsang, Steve 8–9
Tso, Dr Seen-wan 29; and *mui tsai* 38, 57; n11:237
Tung Wah Hospital 19, 25; and *mui tsai* 38

United States 71, 217, 221, 227; Civil Affairs Charter 73–74; Congress 5; Drug Administration 5; Federal Agencies 5, 6, 7, 14; Hong Kong's return to China 11, 67, 70, 71; Post Office 5; post-War area of responsibility 72; silver 45, 50, 52, 53, 54, 56; squatter resettlement 185; US military commander 77, 84
unofficals, 1, 13, 14, 24–25, 26, 219, 220, 222, 225, 227, 228, 229; 1946 Taxation Committee 90; appointment of 2–3, 218; Britain's commitment to Hong Kong 104, 108, 113, 114; constitutional reforms 133; defence costs 206–207; denial claims 203; evacuation of British women and children 63; financial settlement 103–104; Governor 107, 111, 223; housing 142–143, 143–154; importance of 107, 108, 109, 111, 223–224; income tax 89; official majority 121, 205; Rees-Williams 137; role of 65, 86, 212; War Revenue Ordinance 1940 63
universities, British 21, 225: Scottish and Irish 18. *See also* Cambridge, Edinburgh, and Oxford Universities.
University of Hong Kong 61, 93, 100, 102

Urban Council 76, 218, 224; elections 132; housing 148; Housing Authority 156, 157, 158; influence on policy 219; reform of 123, 124, 128, 129, 131; role of 78; Urban Council Chairman 148, 168
squatter resettlement: 172–175, 181–182, 183, 186–187, 225; 1948 review of policy 169–170; Commissioner for Resettlement 184; Emergency Resettlement Sub-Committee 178, 180–181, 182, 183–184, 208; policy co-ordination 172; Select Committee on Resettlement 173, 174, 175; Shek Kip Mei fire 163, 178, 180, 225; squatters 165, 166, 167

Urban Services Department 157, 168, 188

Victorian values 21

Wa Kiu Yat Po 123
Wakefield, James; review of squatter policy 171; n31:267
War Office; Colonial Office 72–73; directives 75; defence contribution 197, 200, 202, 205, 206, 209, 210, 214; Hong Kong Planning Unit 77; US 74
War Revenue Ordinance, 1940 61–63, 65, 89, 90, 91; 1946–47 estimated receipts from 88; Colonial Office 63; Legislative Council 62; 63; War Revenue Committee 62
War Taxation Department 96
Ware, Dr T. W. 75; n34:249
Washington, DC 73, 74, 75
Watson, M. M.; Inland Revenue Bill 1947 93; constitutional reform 123–124; n49:259
Webb, Sidney. *See* Passfield, Lord.

Wedgewood, Josiah; and *mui tsai* 38; n54:240
Wells, Rev H. R.; factory legislation 31, 32, 33; n21:238
Willis, C. A. 58
Willis, Dr J. S. 149; housing scheme for workers 167
Wong, J. M. 57
Woods Commission 57–59, 65, 219
Woods, Sir Wilfred 58

Yangtze River 126
YMCA; and *mui tsai* 38
Young, Sir Mark 9, 16; 75-year leases 141; 1947 Inland Revenue Bill 92, 94, 107; departure from Hong Kong 115, 143; financial situation 88; housing 140, 141, 142; income tax 89, 96, 97, 220, 225; leadership 96, 107, 108, 112, 116, 132–133, 222, 224, 226–227; Malta style grant 101; policy directives 77; rent control 141; Secretary of State 91; unofficials 87, 116, 223; Young's replacement 121–122; n24:233; 53:251
　　constitutional reform 111, 218; municipal council and Legislative Council reforms 80–81, 112–113, 116, 114; 112, 115, 118, 124, 125, 132, 133, 134, 218; General Chamber of Commerce 112, 125; "Young Plan" 116, 119; external and financial control of proposed Municipal Council 117
　"Young Plan" 116, 119, 125, 126, 128, 218

Young, Norman 51, 54; arrival in Hong Kong 52; Exchange Fund 55
YWCA; and *mui tsai* 38